THE FIGHTING CHEYENNES

THE
FIGHTING CHEYENNES

BY

GEORGE BIRD GRINNELL

Published in the USA 1995 by JG Press
Distributed by World Publications, Inc.

The JG Press imprint is a trademark of JG Press, Inc.,
455 Somerset Avenue, North Dighton, Mass. 02764.

This edition published by special arrangement with
W.S. Konecky Associates.

ISBN: 1-57215-123-4

Printed and bound in the USA

PREFACE

THIS book deals with the wars of the Cheyennes. A fighting and a fearless people, the tribe was almost constantly at war with its neighbors, but until 1856 was friendly to the whites.

The Cheyennes fought well, but they will fight no more. Their wars have long been over. Their tribal wanderings ceased before 1880. Since then they have been confined on two reservations, one in Oklahoma, the other in Montana.

When their struggles with the white men began, some of their older and wiser men strove earnestly to preserve peace, but their efforts failed. In an Indian camp individual liberty is the law, and the Cheyennes were a proud, headstrong, and obstinate people.

During these first wars between the whites and the Cheyennes, the United States Government was struggling for its very life. Its attention was concentrated on the war between the North and the South, and the movements of a few Indians on the thinly settled frontier attracted little notice. The so-called Sand Creek Massacre took place toward the close of the Civil War, and the ensuing interference with trans-Missouri travel led to an inquiry by Congress. The published results of this inquiry first made this tribe known to the general public. As more and more people pushed into the West, there was more and more fighting with Indians, until in 1878-9 it ceased—so far as the Cheyennes were concerned.

For many years the government of the Indians by the United States was carried on in haphazard and often dishonest fashion by officials alike ignorant and careless of the customs and ways of thought of the savages with whom they were dealing. The killing of a large number of men, women, and children at Fort Robinson in January, 1879, was the direct result of such unfortunate ignorance.

Since the Indians could not write, the history of their wars has been set down by their enemies, and the story has been told always from the hostile point of view. White writers have lauded white courage and claimed white successes. If it has been necessary to confess defeat, they have abused those who overcame them, as the defeated always abuse the victors.

Evidently there is another side to this history, and this other side is one which should be recorded; and, since the wars are now distant in time, the Indians' own descriptions of these battles may be read without much prejudice. I have tried to present the accounts by whites and Indians, without comment.

I acknowledge with cordial thanks help received from friends who took part in the later Cheyenne wars, and who have commented on and criticised the chapters dealing with the battles in which they fought. These accounts are thus in fact narratives by eye-witnesses. Such assistance has been given me by Major-General E. S. Godfrey, by Major-General W. S. Schuyler, by Colonel Homer W. Wheeler, by Colonel D. L. Brainard, by Colonel E. P. Andrus, by Captain L. H. North, by George Bent, and by many Cheyenne friends whose names are mentioned in the text.

Besides this, Mr. Charles B. Reynolds has kindly read the manuscript, and Mr. George E. Hyde has verified most of the references and has given me the benefit of his careful study of the history of early travel on the plains. To all these friends I return hearty thanks.

A long association with the Cheyennes has given me a special interest in them, and a special wish that they should be allowed to speak for themselves. What the Indians saw in the battles here described—and in many others—I have learned during years of intimate acquaintance with those who took part in them.

The old time Cheyennes possessed in high degree the savage virtues of honesty, trustworthiness, and bravery in the men, and of courage, devotion, and chastity in the women. Of the older people who took part in the fighting with the white troops some are still living and to-day are the only sources of original information concerning the former ways of the wild Cheyennes, the old free life of the Western plains.

G. B. G.

August 10, 1915.

CONTENTS

		PAGE
	PREFACE	v
CHAPTER		
I.	THE CHEYENNES	1
II.	THE WAYS OF WARRIORS	9
III.	A CROW BATTLE	22
IV.	WARS WITH THE KIOWAS AND COMANCHES	32
V.	THE BATTLE ON WOLF CREEK, 1838	42
VI.	THE PEACE WITH THE KIOWAS, 1840	60
VII.	WARS WITH THE PAWNEES	67
VIII.	WHEN THE POTAWATOMI HELPED THE KIT KA HAH KI, 1853	80
IX.	BEFORE WARS BROKE OUT	93
X.	THE SUMNER CAMPAIGN, 1857	107
XI.	GOLD IN COLORADO, 1858–1863	118
XII.	HARRYING THE INDIANS, 1864	131
XIII.	BEFORE SAND CREEK, 1864	143
XIV.	THE SAND CREEK MASSACRE, 1864	159
XV.	RAIDING ALONG THE PLATTE, 1865	174
XVI.	THE POWDER RIVER EXPEDITION, 1865	195
XVII.	PLATTE BRIDGE FIGHT, 1865	207
XVIII.	FORT PHIL KEARNY, 1866	221
XIX.	HANCOCK CAMPAIGN, 1867	236
XX.	MEDICINE LODGE TREATY, 1867	254

viii CONTENTS

CHAPTER   PAGE

XXI.   BEECHER ISLAND FIGHT, 1868. THE CARPENTER FIGHT . 267

XXII.   THE BATTLE OF THE WASHITA, 1868 287

XXIII. BATTLE OF SUMMIT SPRINGS, 1869 299

XXIV.   FIGHT AT ADOBE WALLS, 1874 308

XXV.   CROOK'S FIGHT ON THE ROSEBUD, 1876 316

XXVI.   THE CUSTER BATTLE, 1876 333

XXVII. CAPTURE OF DULL KNIFE'S VILLAGE, 1876 . . . 346

XXVIII. SURRENDER OF TWO MOON'S BAND AND LAME DEER FIGHT,
        1877 369

XXIX.   LITTLE WOLF AND DULL KNIFE, 1876–1879 383

XXX.   THE FORT ROBINSON OUTBREAK, 1879 399

XXXI.   SCOUTING FOR THE SOLDIERS, 1878–1890 412

        INDEX 419

MAPS

[These rough-sketch maps indicate the relations of localities referred to in the text, and, in certain cases, the movements of the Indians over a country the early history of which is now well-nigh forgotten.]

PAGE

Situations of camps and route of attacking Cheyennes and Arapahoes 51

The plains in 1864-1865 113

Blunt's fight 156

Plan of Cheyenne camp at Sand Creek 165

Country raided December, 1864, to February, 1865, showing stage
and telegraph lines and ranches 190

Scene of the Fort Phil Kearny fight, 1866 231

Western Kansas in 1867 246

Indian country west of Indian Territory, 1868-1874 295

THE FIGHTING CHEYENNES

I

THE CHEYENNES

THE Cheyennes are one of three groups of Indians of the Western plains belonging to the Algonquian family. They are recent immigrants to the region. According to the statement of Black Moccasin,[1] who was long regarded as their most reliable historian—the man with the best memory—some of them reached the Missouri River about 1676, two hundred and four winters before 1880, when the statement was made. Before this they had lived for a time on the river bearing their name, which runs into the Red River of the North from the west, and on which one of their old village sites still exists. Earlier still they were in Minnesota. They have traditions of long journeyings before they reached there.

For a number of years after coming to the Missouri the Cheyennes lived on its banks, cultivating the ground, and occupying earth lodges not unlike those used up to recent times by the Rees and the Mandans. Gradually they drifted out on the plains, gave up their sedentary habits and began to move about over the prairie, dwelling in skin lodges and following the buffalo. As recently as 1850 they tilled the soil to some extent, and men have described to me their mothers' corn patches on the Little Missouri at about that date.

The people whom we know as Cheyennes are made up of two related tribes, Tsĭs tsĭs'tăs and Sūh'tāī. The latter have been absorbed by the former, and have left hardly any trace. They were the tribe known to early writers as Stā ĭ tăn', i. e., Sūh'tāī hē' tan ē—a man of the Suhtai.

[1] Măhk stă'vo yăn'st st.

1

I have known many Cheyennes who remembered old people who were Suhtai—born in the separate Suhtai camp. They agree that the Suhtai language differed somewhat from the Cheyenne, "it sounded funny to them," and that the Suhtai had many customs of their own which later were laughed at, because unusual. In 1831, at the time when Bent's Fort was completed, the Suhtai still camped apart by themselves—were still a separate tribe.

The name Cheyenne is not in use by the tribe. They call themselves Tsĭs tsĭs′ tăs, a word variously translated which Rev. R. Pettér our authority on the Cheyenne language believes to mean "similarly bred." If this is its meaning, it resembles so many other Indian tribal names which are explained to mean variously, "the people," "the real people," etc., and perhaps actually mean "*the* people," *i. e.*, "the folks," "our folks," "us." Tsĭs tsĭs′tăs might also mean the cut or gashed people, and the tribal sign signifies cut or gashed, though often explained as referring to striped feathers sometimes, but by no means always, used in feathering the arrows. The word Cheyenne is frequently explained as coming from the French *chien* in allusion to the Dog Soldiers, but it is, in fact, a Sioux term Shā hĭ′ē la, or Sha hĭ′e na, people speaking language not understood.

The Sioux speak of those who talk intelligibly to them as "white talkers," and call those who speak a language not understood "red talkers." I′ā or ĭ′ē is to talk intelligibly. I ē′skā used as a verb means to speak fluently and intelligently. As a substantive the word means an interpreter. In speaking of one who talks their language the Dakotas use the verb Skā ē′ā, to talk white. Of one whose language they cannot understand and who cannot understand them they say Shā ē′ā, to talk red; that is, unintelligibly. The name given by the Sioux to the Cheyennes, Shā hĭ′ē la, means red words, or red speech—speaking a foreign tongue.

Partly as a result of long association with the village tribes of the Missouri—Rees, Mandans, and Hidatsa—the Cheyennes have among them a strong infusion of foreign blood. A still greater mingling of alien blood comes from their warlike character, so pronounced during many years of the last century, which resulted in the capture from their enemies of great numbers of children of both sexes who in due course were adopted into the tribe, grew up as Cheyennes, and married and reared children. Old Cheyennes have told me that it is difficult to find any Cheyennes without a strain of foreign blood, and as I think over my acquaintances I can recall hardly any whose ancestry can be traced far back wholly in the Cheyenne tribe. In another book I have given a list of twenty-eight tribes from which captives had been taken by the Cheyennes.[1]

When the Cheyennes first met the white people they were shy and timid, and endeavored to avoid the newcomers. Lewis and Clark speak of this, and old men among the Cheyennes say that they have always been told that in former times the chiefs advised that the white strangers be avoided. This may have some reference to the speech attributed to the Cheyenne Culture Hero, in which he prophesied a meeting with a people whose skins were white and whose ways were different, and predicted that misfortune to his people would follow their knowledge of these strangers.[2]

The late Ben Clark, in the manuscript prepared at the request of General Sheridan, declared that the Cheyennes were called the Kite Indians, because perpetually on the move—always seen at a distance and fleeing.

Among the tribes of the plains the Cheyennes have had one ally on whose fidelity they could always depend. These were the Arapahoes, who for many generations have been associated with the Cheyennes on terms of the closest friendship, camping with them for long periods, uniting with them in their wars, or at other times being the medium through whom have come proposals for peace from hostile tribes.

The tradition as to when the Arapahoes joined the Cheyennes is vague enough, and we know little about it, though much has been written on the subject. A milder and more easy-going people than the Cheyennes, they yet fought side by side with them in many a stubborn battle. There is a large infusion of Arapaho blood in the Cheyenne tribe, for many Cheyenne men married Arapaho women. On the other hand, it is my impression that comparatively few Cheyenne women have married Arapaho men.

Historical knowledge of the Cheyennes begins with the accounts of Lewis and Clark, though many years earlier the French

[1] *Indians of To-day*, p. 72. (Chicago, 1900.)   [2] *Ibid.*, p. 174.

trappers and traders had penetrated their country, which was on
the plains near the Black Hills, and especially on the upper
courses of certain streams which flow out of those hills. I think
it very possible that long before this the Cheyennes had been
met by the Verendryes, and that they may have been the tribe
which the *Verendrye Journal* terms *Gens de l'arc*. Perhaps this
can never be shown, but the name *Gens du serpent*, given to their
enemies by the people of the Bow, suggests the Cheyenne term
Shĭ shĭ' nĭ wī hē tăn ĭŭ, snake men, the name given by the Cheyennes to the Comanches, who, the Cheyennes declare, occupied
that country at the time when they reached the neighborhood
of the Black Hills. The Cheyenne name for the tribes called
Snakes by the whites is Sŭs'sŏn ĭ.

Although the books constantly speak of the Cheyennes as at
war with the Sioux, I do not find among them any tradition that
they ever had serious quarrels with the plains people whom we
know and speak of as Sioux. On the other hand, they were at
bitter enmity with the northern Dakota or Assiniboines, and
traditions of their wars with them run back a long way. Later
enemies were the Kiowas, the Comanches, and the Crows, all of
whom they gradually expelled from the country that they had
invaded. The Cheyennes were long at war with the Pawnees and
with the Shoshoni, and these hostilities endured up to the time
when intertribal wars ceased.

Early in the nineteenth century they were at peace with the
Kiowas and Comanches, and in the *Journal of Jacob Fowler* for
November, 1821, are found references to Kiowa Comanches,
Kiowa Apaches, Cheyennes and "Snakes" (Comanches?) travelling together in more or less amity. Cheyenne tradition speaks of
the Kiowas as peacable co-occupants with them of the Little Missouri country long after the Spaniards had come up there from the
southwest to trade and before the Cheyennes had ever seen the
French or English whites. The last great battle with the Kiowas,
Comanches, and Apaches took place in 1838. Two years later a
peace was made which has not since been broken.

The Cheyennes were long at war with the Utes. At the time
of the first settlement of western Colorado, after gold had been
discovered, miners had come into the country, and villages and
towns had been established on the flanks of the mountains in

that territory, war journeys by Cheyennes and Utes against each other were constantly taking place. The reports from officials of the Indian Service during the years 1862 to 1865 frequently complain of the trouble given to the settlers by the Cheyennes and Arapahoes in their war journeys against the Utes and by the Utes when they went against the Cheyennes.

Farther to the northward the Cheyennes had other enemies in the Crows, on whose territory they had begun to encroach after they had crossed the Missouri River and moved westward toward the mountains. Their battles with the Crows lasted at least seventy years, and perhaps longer, but were interrupted by a truce which perhaps endured from 1851 to 1854 or thereabouts.

With the Blackfeet, still farther to the north, the Cheyennes did not often come in contact, though occasionally they met, and when they met they fought.

The village tribes of the Missouri—Mandan, Arikara, and Hidatsa—were commonly on good terms with the Cheyennes. This is what we should expect from the fact that these were the first tribes that they met in friendship on the plains and since they lived with or near them for a long time. Still there were occasional quarrels even with these people. Maximilian tells of stories of battles with the Cheyennes that he heard from the Mandans, while the Cheyennes give accounts of fights that they had with the Arikaras.

On their way west, perhaps long before they reached the country of the Red River, the Cheyennes met the Assiniboines —the Ho hé. It is related that the two tribes came together when each was trying to surround a herd of buffalo. They quarrelled over this and came to blows. Old Assiniboines have told me that at this time the Cheyennes were armed only with clubs and with sharpened sticks, and this is precisely what the Cheyennes themselves say. The Assiniboines, however, had guns and killed a number of the Cheyennes and scalped them.

The sound of the guns and their dreadful power terrified the Cheyennes and they fled. As they had never before been attacked by enemies, the Cheyennes did not know what to make of the situation, but after a time one of them stood up and harangued the people and said: "Now we have fought with these people; they attacked us and have killed some of us. After this let us fight with all people we meet, and we shall become great men." So they began to fight all tribes wherever they met them and it did make great men of them. They came to be great warriors and took many prisoners.

However, there is a tradition of a time when the Cheyennes and their kindred, the Sūh'tāī, lived in the far northeast—long before the battles with the Ho hé—when those two tribes fought with one another. During their last great fight they discovered that they spoke a similar language and that they were related, and then made a peace which was never broken.

Not a few traditions are handed down of the battles of the Cheyennes and the Ho hé, in which the Cheyennes were always defeated. Some Cheyenne authorities include the Ojibwa among the Ho hé. It was the practise of the Ho hé to come at night to attack the Cheyenne camps. They carried horns made of the hollow stems of some plant, with which they signalled to each other, making a call like that of the buffalo in spring, so that, if the Cheyennes heard them approaching, they might suppose buffalo were coming and thus not be on the lookout for the enemy. They slew many Cheyennes.

An oft-told story explains how a dog saved a family from death by the Ho hé.

In those days a man, his wife, and well-grown son were camped apart from the tribe. They had a dog, whose puppies were in the lodge. One night the mother dog went out to look for food for the puppies, and returning to them after a time began to cry over them and lick them. The man saw what she was doing and wondered. He spoke to the dog and said: "Why do you do this? If you know that something bad is going to happen, tell me what it is. We do not wish to die. If we are in danger, help us, and we will save your puppies. Try in some way to help us."

After he had spoken thus to the dog, she went out of the lodge and was gone for some time, and then came back and stood in the lodge looking toward the door. The man's wife told him to take up the puppies. He put them in his robe on his back, and they all made ready to go out, but first the man made up a large fire in the lodge, so that any one who saw it would suppose the people were still there.

The dog left the lodge and they followed her, and she led them down to the river and straight across. After a time they heard guns sounding all around their camp, and they knew that the Ho hé were attacking the lodge with the fire burning in it. They went on to another camp where Cheyennes were living and told them that the Ho hé had attacked their lodge, so the Cheyennes moved away and all escaped. The story of how the dog saved her master has been told in the camp since that time.

For a long time the Cheyennes possessed no arms that they could use in fighting the Ho hé. They talk much about those dreadful days, and tell of the terror that they felt of these enemies, of the triumph when on rare occasions and through some accident they succeeded in killing one, of the care with which their camping-places were chosen to avoid attack, and of how finally, through the ready wit of an old woman, they succeeded in obtaining a few guns.

In those days, long before they had horses, they travelled from place to place, packing some of their property on dogs and carrying the rest on their backs. Once the people were camped in their earth lodges and were chasing buffalo on foot. They had hunted for three or four days and now had abundant meat. They left this camp and moved a short distance down the stream. One old woman, however, who was busy making grease, remained at the old camp. She said: "I shall stay here for a time, because I wish to finish pounding up my bones, and boiling them, and skimming off the grease."

The night was dark and the old woman was alone in the camp. She was still boiling her bones and skimming the grease from the pot. She had made a torch and tied it to a stick and thrust the stick down her back, between her dress and her body, so that the torch stood above her head, and threw light on the pot. She was blowing the grease off the water when a person entered the lodge and sat down by the head of her bed. She did not look up, but kept blowing the grease from the water. Then, one after another, walked into the lodge about fifty great, tall Assiniboines.

There was plenty of food hanging in the lodge, and at one side was some pounded meat. The Assiniboines said to each other: "We will get something to eat first, and then we will kill her." They made signs to her that they were hungry, and to each one she gave some pounded meat, and then began to roast some fresh meat.

The old woman was badly frightened. She kept saying to herself: "They will surely kill me. What can I do to save myself?" Hanging up in the lodge was a great sheet of back fat—tallow—and the old woman took it down to roast it so that the visitors might eat it with their meat. She put it on a stick and hung it over the fire until it had begun to cook and the hot grease was dropping from it. Then, lifting it as if to turn it, she took it from the stick and gave it a mighty swing around her head, throwing the hot fat in the faces of the Assiniboines sitting around the circle, and all jumped back burned. Then she rushed out of the lodge.

Not far in front of the lodge was a high cut bank above the river, with rocks below. The Assiniboines, furious with their burns, rushed after the old woman, following the torch that she carried over her head. She ran fast toward the bank and when close to it threw her torch ahead of her and turned sharp to one side, running along the edge of the bank. The Assiniboines followed the blazing light, and all ran over the bank and, falling on the rocks below, were hurt or killed. The old woman hurried away after the Cheyenne camp and overtook it. She told of the Assiniboines who had come to her lodge, and of what she had done, saying: "I could hear them fall over the cliff; I think all fell over." The next morning the men returned to the old camp, and here under the bank they found the fifty Ho hé, some of them dead, some with broken backs, some with broken legs, and some with broken arms, creeping about. They killed them all and secured their guns.

The Cheyennes were driven by the Assiniboines in a southwesterly direction until they reached the Missouri River, not far from where Fort Pierre now is. Here for a long time they remained, living with the Mandans and the Arikaras in earth lodges, raising their crops, and making journeys away from the village to secure game or to catch fish; to gather the eggs and young of water-birds in summer, or to collect skunks in the autumn when they were fat.

Later they wandered out on the plains after buffalo.

II

THE WAYS OF WARRIORS

AFTER the question of providing subsistence for himself and his family, the main thing that occupied the mind of the Cheyenne was the protection of his people from the attacks of enemies and the effort to reduce the power of those enemies by attacks on them.

The fighting spirit was encouraged. In no way could a young man gain so much credit as by the exhibition of courage. Boys and youths were trained to feel that the most important thing in life was to be brave; that death was not a thing to be avoided; that, in fact, it was better for a man to be killed while in his full vigor rather than to wait until his prime was past, his powers were failing, and he could no longer achieve those feats which to all seemed so desirable. When a man was old he could no longer get about easily; the labors of the hunt and of the war-path were too much for him; he was pushed aside by the more active and vigorous. He lost his teeth; he could not enjoy his food; he sat on the cold side of the lodge; life seemed to hold for him nothing good. How much better, therefore, to struggle and fight, to be brave and accomplish great things, to receive the respect and applause of everyone in the camp, and finally to die gloriously at the hands of the enemy!

Among the Cheyennes, as among other plains tribes, this feeling was very strong. They fought not only to gain the approval of their tribesfellows but for pure enjoyment of the struggle—real *gaudium certaminis*. The spirit of the camp was such that young men going into battle thought of it as the beginning of a good time that they were to have. To them fighting was a real joy. Perhaps they regarded their fights somewhat as the big game hunter of modern times regards his pursuit of dangerous game. The personal risk must have added enormously to the excitement and enjoyment of the contest.

9

The chapters in this book are devoted chiefly to conflicts between considerable bodies of men, but it must be remembered that the war-paths of the plains Indians were carried on in a great variety of ways. Men might go off with a special purpose, one, two or three together, or a great war party of hundreds might go; they journeyed on foot or on horseback, according to circumstances.

It will be readily conceived that among people who possessed ideals such as these there would be many exciting adventures. From a mass of individual stories and accounts of small war parties I have chosen three which will perhaps give some notion of the ways of warriors.

THE DEATH OF MOUSE'S ROAD

In 1837, the year before the great fight with the Kiowas and Comanches, the Cheyennes were camped on the South Platte River. A war party of fourteen started south on foot to take horses from the Kiowas and Comanches. Stone Forehead and Pushing Ahead were the two who carried the pipes [1]—the leaders.

They found the camp of the enemy at the head of what the Cheyennes called Big Sand Creek, which runs into the Red River (of Texas). That night the Cheyennes went into the camp in couples. Stone Forehead was with a man named Angry. It was very dark. Close behind a lodge which they passed stood a pole with a shield hanging to it. Angry untied the shield from the pole and put it on his back, and they went on, looking for horses. They came to a bunch of fifty or sixty, and went around them and drove them a little way, and each caught a gentle horse, mounted it, and drove off the herd.

When they reached the place where it had been agreed that they should meet, they found the others of the party already there, excepting only six men. Stone Forehead said: "We cannot wait here; we must start." They did so. Stone Forehead and Pushing Ahead went behind, where it is the custom for the leaders to travel, while the others went ahead. They drove their bunches along side by side, but two or three hundred yards apart. When day came they looked carefully at their horses so that they should know them again, and then they bunched the horses into a single

---

[1] Carrying the pipe. The leader or leaders of a war party carried each a pipe, which on certain occasions was ceremonially smoked.

herd. The way was so rough that they drove very slowly, and Pushing Ahead, who knew the country, kept saying: "We are going so slowly that they will surely overtake us."

It was a little past the middle of the day when they saw the Kiowas and Comanches coming. There were only a few of them —not over thirty. Then the Cheyennes began to catch the swiftest horses, so that they could get about quickly. Pushing Ahead was a brave man. He said: "We must not let them take our horses. I do not think there are many of them." The Cheyennes mounted the fast horses and bunched up the herd, and, sending two young men ahead to ride one on each side so as to hold the horses together, they stopped. One of the Cheyennes got off his horse and fired at a Comanche, and shot his horse through the body. The Comanche rode back, and soon his horse began to stagger, and the Comanche left it and mounted behind one of his fellows. Then the Cheyennes made a charge on the Kiowas and Comanches, and they turned about and went back.

Of the other six men two, Little Wolf and his partner, Walking Coyote, were alone. They were on the head of the Washita, in level country. They had taken only a few horses. They saw a big party of Kiowas and Comanches coming in two bands. There was a ravine near them, and Little Wolf said: "These horses are tired out. We cannot drive them much farther; the enemy will soon overtake us. Let us dismount and hide in this ravine." They ran down the ravine and hid in a little hollow, and lay there. If the Kiowas had looked for them they would have found them, but just then they saw the four other Cheyennes far off, and turned to rush to them. Little Wolf and Walking Coyote stayed there till night, and then set off for home on foot.

When the Kiowas and Comanches charged Mouse's Road and his three companions, the Cheyennes did not run; they rode up on a little hill and got off their horses and began to kill them. They had already left behind the horses they had taken and had only those that they were riding. Now, as the Kiowas and Comanches came up, the Cheyennes were seen to be taking off their leggings so that they could run fast and easily. The enemy charged them, and the Cheyennes fought bravely, though they had but few arrows, for they had been out a long time. In a little while the enemy had killed three of the Cheyennes.

Early in the fight Mouse's Road's bow was broken in two by a ball, and he threw it away. A Comanche chief, seeing him thus disarmed, charged up to kill him with his lance, but Mouse's Road avoided the blow, caught hold of the Comanche, pulled him from his horse, and killed him with his knife. Mouse's Road was still unwounded. He let the Comanche's horse go, and signed to the Kiowas: "Come on."

There was a man named Lone Wolf, a chief, and a brave man, who had been behind the other Kiowas. He called out: "I have just come and I wish you all to look at me. I intend to kill that man." He said to a Mexican captive: "Do you ride close behind me." The two charged upon Mouse's Road, and the Mexican rode straight at him, but Mouse's Road, though on foot, did not run away; he ran to meet the Mexican and, springing at him, seized him, pulled him from his horse, and plunged his knife into him several times. While he was doing this Lone Wolf dismounted and rushed up to help the Mexican. Mouse's Road dropped the dead Mexican and rushed at Lone Wolf, who ran at him with his lance held in both hands above his head, so as to deal a blow of great force. As he thrust with the lance Mouse's Road stooped and ran under the lance, caught Lone Wolf by the left shoulder, and struck him a terrible blow with his knife in the hip. Lone Wolf turned to run and Mouse's Road caught him by his hair ornament and with all his force thrust at his back. The knife struck one of the silver hair plates and broke in two, leaving about four inches of the blade on the handle. Lone Wolf screamed for help to his people, but no one came, and Mouse's Road continued to stab and hack and cut him with the stump of the knife until Lone Wolf fell to the ground, pretending to be dead.

Now came a Comanche chief riding a fine horse, and armed with a lance and bow and arrows. Mouse's Road took up the lance Lone Wolf had dropped, and ran to meet the Comanche. He parried the Comanche's lance thrust and drove his own lance into the Comanche and lifted him high out of the saddle, and the Comanche died.

Now the Kiowas and Comanches saw something that they never had seen before—a man who seemed swifter than a horse, more active than a panther, as strong as a bear, and one against whom weapons seemed useless. There were more than a hundred of the Kiowas and Comanches, and only one Cheyenne on foot, without arms, but the Kiowas and Comanches began to run away. Others, braver, made signs to Mouse's Road, who had now mounted the Comanche's horse: "Hold on! wait, wait. Take that horse that you have. We will give you a saddle. Go on home to your village and tell your people what has happened."

"No," signed Mouse's Road, "I will not go home; my brothers have all been killed and if I were to go home I should be crying all the time—mourning for these men. You must kill me."

When he said this all the Kiowas started to run, and Mouse's Road charged them. Behind the main body of the enemy were two Kiowas who had just come up. Both had guns, and when they saw Mouse's Road coming they got off their horses and sat down and waited until he was close to them, and then both fired. One of the balls broke his thigh, and he fell from his horse. Yet still he sat up to defend himself with his lance, and the Kiowas and Comanches, though they surrounded him, dared not go near him. One crept up from behind and shot him in the back, and he fell over. Then all the Kiowas and Comanches rushed on him and cut off his head, and when they had done that Mouse's Road raised himself and sat upright.

The Kiowas and Comanches jumped on their horses in fright, and fled to their village and told the people they had killed a medicine man and he had come to life again, and was coming to attack them. And, the women swiftly packing up a few of their things, the whole camp moved away, leaving many of their lodges standing.

This is the story told by the Kiowas. The Cheyennes have no account of it, for all the Cheyennes were killed. Lone Wolf lived for a long time, scarred and crippled from the cutting he had received. He died not long ago. The Kiowas and Comanches said that Mouse's Road was the bravest man they ever saw or heard of.

LONG CHIN'S STRATEGY

In 1855 runners were sent out from Bent's New Fort on the Arkansas River to call in the different tribes to receive their annuity goods there. The issue was to be made in the late summer, for the goods were transported by wagon, and it took ox-trains sixty or seventy days to make the journey from Kansas City landing to Bent's New Fort. At this time, the Cheyennes, Arapahoes, Kiowas, Comanches, and Apaches were all under one Indian agent.

When these different tribes got together, camping near the fort, it was a happy and social time. In all the villages drumming, singing, dancing, visiting, and the giving of presents among the people went on night and day. Among the Cheyennes the soldier societies—Elk Horn Scrapers, Bow Strings, Kit Foxes, Red Shields, and Dog Soldiers—took turns having dances in the fort, and the soldier societies of the other tribes did the same. At the fort it was the custom on these occasions to cook food and feast the Indians. They also gave them presents of paints, knives, shirts, looking-glasses, and handkerchiefs.

The tribes were camped about the fort for some time, and after the goods had been issued the Arapahoes moved down the river, the Comanches, with half the Kiowas and the Apaches, moved south to their country, and the remainder of the Kiowas moved north to the Smoky Hill River. Before this about thirty young men of the Elk Horn Scrapers soldier band had set out on the war-path to look for Pawnees, who would be found, they were told, somewhere on the Smoky Hill River, whither the whole Cheyenne tribe was going to renew the medicine arrows.

The Cheyennes and Kiowas moved north slowly, and at length camped on the Smoky Hill River, where Black Butte Creek runs into it. The Cheyennes were camped on the north side of the river, in a great circle which opened to the east, while the Kiowas camped by themselves on the south side of the river. After reaching this place the two tribes held a council, and agreed that after the arrows had been renewed they would start north on the war-path to look for the Pawnees.

About the second night after they had reached this camp a war party of Pawnees came into it and took all the horses that were on Black Butte Creek. From there the trails led north. The Cheyennes at once sent word to the Kiowas that their horses had been taken. Sitting Bear, Light Hair, and Eagle Tail were then the Kiowa war chiefs. They sent a message to the Cheyennes asking them to get together on the trail, and to wait there for them, and not to permit anyone to go ahead of the main party. The Cheyennes waited for the Kiowas where the trail was plainest, and when the Kiowa chiefs rode up, Eagle Tail said to the Cheyennes: "Leave this matter of trailing to us. As you people know, we have had more horses taken from us than any other tribe. We are accustomed to following these trails, and are far better able to do it than any other people." The Cheyennes replied that they were glad to have the Kiowas feel interested in the matter, and they would leave everything to them. The day was clear and bright. The Kiowa chiefs took the trail and followed it fast. Toward sundown it began to get cloudy, and as the sun set it began to rain and grow foggy. The trail seemed to go in the direction of Beaver Creek.

At dark the Kiowas said to the Cheyennes: "Now we should all stop here for the night on this trail, and in the morning we will take it up again." The Kiowas thrust into the ground a stick pointing in the direction the trail was going. The Dog Soldiers got off their horses a little to one side of where the main party of the pursuers had stopped.

When Long Chin and Tall Bull were talking over this among themselves, they said that they did not like the way in which the Kiowas were following the trail. The Dog Soldiers all came together in a little group, and had a council among themselves. It was still raining and very foggy.

Long Chin was an old warrior. He had been in many fights and had had much experience. He said to the Dog Soldiers: "Saddle up now, and during the night we will go on to Beaver Creek, and will follow that stream down, and if the Pawnees went that way we shall certainly strike their trail." They followed his advice and about sixty Cheyennes started on. Long Chin, Tall Bull, and Good Bear took the lead to go toward Beaver Creek. These men knew the country well, and even though it was dark and raining they had no trouble in going to the stream, which they reached very early in the morning. After the sun had risen the weather grew clear, and following down the stream they soon struck the trail of the Pawnees. The Kiowas and the Cheyennes who had been left behind did not start until morning, and then followed the trail, but when they reached Beaver Creek and saw that Long Chin and his party were before them they went on slowly, for it was useless to try to overtake those who were in advance.

The first discovery made by Long Chin was a buffalo carcass which the Pawnees had killed not long before, and from which they had taken the best parts of the meat.

"Ha ha," said Long Chin, "now we shall catch them. Somewhere on this creek they will stop to cook food and eat, and we shall overtake them." The Dog Soldiers began to go faster. Old Whirlwind was with this party. All his horses had been taken by the Pawnees, but from a Kiowa friend he had borrowed a good horse, which his friend had told him was fast.

Long Chin was really the head of this party, most of whom, but not all, were Dog Soldiers. He was a half-brother of Tall Bull. Long Chin now rode some distance ahead of the party to look about and try to discover the Pawnees. At length he rode up on a hill, and as he peeped over it he saw a smoke, and he made signs to his party that they should get ready. They got off their ponies and began to put bridles on the war horses that they were leading; to uncover their shields, and such of the Dog Soldiers as had dog ropes began to prepare them.

Presently Long Chin rode back and told the young men that the Pawnees were a long way off, and that it was too far to charge on them from that place. They must remember that the Pawnees had a number of fast horses, and if they were given time to get ready they would mount and escape. "The horses," he went on, "are all about where the smoke rises from, and as I looked I saw one or two men walking about among the herds. These people are at the mouth of Cherry Brush Creek, and the best thing for us to do is to ride close together, and to go down into the bed of Beaver Creek and get as close as we can before we make a charge. If we can take the Pawnees by surprise, they will not have time to get on their fast horses. One thing you may remember, my young men: if a Pawnee is armed only with a bow and arrows, do not fear him. Last night their bows and arrows got wet and the bowstrings will stretch and break when they pull on them. Now let us go."

They went down into the stream bed, as Long Chin had ordered, and when they had come close enough Long Chin crept up and looked again. The Pawnees were roasting meat all around the fire. Some were eating and some were lying down. Long Chin motioned for his young men to charge. The Pawnees were taken completely by surprise. Some of them jumped up and started to run without their bows, but one Pawnee cried out something, and then they all came to their senses, and ran back for their bows and quivers. One Pawnee was on foot, herding the horses. He started to run back to his party, but was cut off. Old Whirlwind, on the Kiowa horse, found that his friend had told him true. The horse proved to be fast and ran ahead of all the others, and Whirlwind counted the first coup.[1] When he had done this, he ran on toward the horses, so that the Pawnees could not mount any of them. The Pawnees ran down into the creek bottom. One Pawnee fought bravely. He remained behind the others, trying to hold back the Cheyennes, so that his young men might get away, and he wounded Good Bear and Picket with arrows. The Pawnees did not have a single gun among them. All carried bows and arrows. Before sundown all had been killed.

When the Cheyennes went back to the Pawnee camp-fire and looked about it they found there eleven buffalo robes which the Pawnees had spread out on the ground to dry, but when they counted the Pawnees that had been killed there were only ten, so they were sure that one of them had hidden in the brush and had escaped.

A few years ago there was living in the Pawnee tribe a man who said that his father was the only one who escaped in this fight. The father was in the bushes when the Cheyennes made their charge, and he hid there. After it grew dark he went down the way the Pawnees had retreated and found a blanket that some one had lost, and this he wore back to his home.

The Cheyennes used to call this fight "Long Chin's victory on Cherry Brush Creek," for Long Chin had planned everything that was done.

That night as they were returning Long Chin's party met the Kiowas and the main part of the Cheyennes. Long Chin

---

[1] To count a coup was to "touch the enemy with something held in the hand, with the bare hand, or with any part of the body." "Coup and Scalp Among the Plains Indians," *American Anthropologist*, New Series, vol. XII, p. 297, April–June, 1910.

presented the Pawnee scalps to the Kiowas, so that they might dance over them.

It was said that Eagle Tail and the other Kiowa chiefs felt ashamed of themselves, because, after they had boasted to the Cheyennes that they would overtake the Pawnees, Long Chin had outgeneralled them.

When this party returned to the village something took place that is known to have happened only once before. The thirty Elk Horn Scrapers who had started out from Bent's Fort to look for Pawnees had killed two Pawnees on the Solomon River, and were coming back to the village on the Smoky Hill River. Early in the morning the leader of this party with the two Pawnee scalps sat on his horse ready to run into the circle of the village from the southeast side, and Long Chin's party, which had just arrived with their many scalps, sat on their horses ready to run into the village from the northeast side, and to go about the circle. Neither of the two parties knew that the other was there, and the two ran into the circle at the same time, shooting off their guns. Some of Long Chin's party mistook some of the Elk Horn Scrapers for members of their own party, and mingled with them before they found out their mistake. This did no harm as both parties had scalps, and both marched into the centre of the village.

The scalp dance that they had after these victories was one of the biggest ever known. After it was over the Kiowas moved away to their country south of the Arkansas River, and the Cheyennes moved away in bands to good hunting grounds, as it was now near the fall of the year.

How Six Feathers Was Named

Once, long ago, a big village of Arapahoes and a few Cheyennes were camped on Cherry Creek, in Colorado. A large war party, most of them Arapahoes with some Cheyennes, left the camp to go against the Utes to take horses from them. When they had come near the Ute camp, they left their robes and other things in a place nearby and then the men entered the camp and began to take horses. The Utes discovered them, and they were obliged to run.

When the Utes chased them the Arapahoes and Cheyennes scattered on the way back to where they had left their things.

A few shots were fired. The Utes still followed them. When they had come to the place where they had left their things, the Arapahoes and the Cheyennes stopped and they had a fight. Then the Utes left them and went back to their camp, and the Arapahoes and Cheyennes went on toward home.

An Arapaho named Crane had taken a few horses and had mounted a big black one, but the Utes had followed him so closely that he was forced to abandon all the horses except the one he was riding. He was separated from the rest and driven off to one side. When the Arapahoes and Cheyennes started back Crane was not with them; he had not appeared.

That night, after Crane had ridden away from the Utes who had followed him, while he was still riding fast, his horse ran over a smooth rock and fell with him and broke his leg. He bound up his leg and mounted his horse again, and travelled all that night and all the next day until toward evening. Now his leg began to swell and became so painful that he could no longer ride. He looked up and down the stream for a good hiding-place, and at last he found one where the rocks projected over the bank to form a sort of cave, and a pine tree had fallen over against the mouth of it so as partly to hide it. He rode up to the mouth of the cave, and almost fell off his horse, for he was nearly helpless. But he held the animal by the bridle, and raising himself to his knees he shot it in the head. It was late in the fall, after the leaves had fallen, and the weather had begun to get cool. He cut the flesh of his horse into flakes and hung them upon the limbs of the tree to dry.

After he had been there one moon and a half, one day as he sat looking over the valley a speckled eagle came and alighted in the pine tree just above him. Crane thought to himself: "This is a pretty bird; I believe I will shoot it." He reached out his hand for his gun, but as he did so he began to think, and presently he said to himself: "No, I will not shoot it. This may be some medicine bird." He sat there, and the eagle sat on the limb turning its head, looking this way and that and sometimes looking down at him, and at last the eagle bent down its head and spoke and said to him: "You shall get back safely to your home, and when you get there your name shall be Six Feathers." After it had said that the eagle flew away.

It was not long after this that the eagle came again and alighted on the pine tree, and after a little time it again spoke to him and said: "Friend, your name is now Eagle Head." Then after a little while the eagle said: "Cover your head now with your robe and I will doctor your leg." Crane covered his head as he had been told, and presently he could feel the eagle's wings touching his leg, but he could not see what the eagle did.

Crane remained in this place five months. He had plenty of clothing and could keep warm. He was very careful of his food, and each day ate only a little bit. In the fifth month he could hop down to the creek. Before that he had got his water from the snow. When he got down to the stream he cut himself two crutches, and winding the heads with horse-hide that he had dressed, he practised until he could walk well with the crutches. He could now bear a little weight on his leg, but feared to rest too much on it lest he should break it again.

He now started out to find the camp of his people. Three times on his way he killed a buffalo. The first time he killed he stopped and rested three nights. When he killed the second buffalo he stopped two nights and rested. The next one was killed close to the South Platte River, near its head. He lay there ten days.

It was now spring and the trees were beginning to bud. Crane cut out the meat of the buffalo and dried it, and he stretched the hide over a great stump and made a bull-boat. He waited here until the hide had dried. By this time all his people in the camp were mourning for him, and had cut off their hair, for they thought him dead.

After the boat was dried and stretched over the willows Crane put his meat in the boat and got in himself, and with a stick for a paddle he started to float down the stream. Whenever he wished to stop for the night or rest he dragged his boat out on the shore.

At this time the people were camped on the Cache la Poudre River. One morning, very early, the young men were all out for their horses, when one of them heard some one singing. He looked up the stream and saw Six Feathers come floating down, singing as he came along. When he had reached the camp an old man went about through the village, calling out that they must put up a separate lodge, for Six Feathers had returned. The eagle had told Six Feathers to announce his name as soon as he reached the camp, and he did so. A lodge was put up as directed, and when Six Feathers's boat had come opposite to it he landed and hobbled up to it, and there he told his story. He told it all and then said to his young brother: "An eagle took pity on me and helped me, and after you have counted your first coup your name shall be Eagle Head."

Six Feathers lived to be a great man among his people, and at last he became a great chief. He always used to say that if he had become frightened and lost his senses he never could have saved himself, but he kept his wits about him all the time.

Six Feathers lived for a long time with the tribe, but at last a horse fell with him and killed him.

III

A CROW BATTLE

With the Crows the Cheyennes were at war for many years. How many it is impossible to say, but traditions tell us of fights which took place in the very first years of the last century.

As nearly as may be gathered from the stories, the Cheyennes in the year 1801 attacked and captured a Crow village of thirty lodges. Lewis and Clark in 1804 saw at the Arikara village some Cheyennes who had with them Crow prisoners.[1] They record that the Cheyennes were then at war with the Crows.

About 1820 an important battle took place between the Cheyennes and Crows of which vivid tradition still remains. It was the greatest of many encounters, and was the second remembered move of the medicine arrows against a hostile tribe.

The year before this event—probably in 1819—another, quite as well remembered, took place. A party of thirty-two Cheyennes, most of them Crooked Lance soldiers, were travelling on the war-path through the northern country. While moving among the mountains they met a Crow scout who was in advance of the Crow camp. The Cheyennes overtook the scout and killed him, but had hardly done so when a great force of Crows appeared and charged them. The Cheyennes retreated to the top of a hill, where, surrounded, they fought for a long time. Not far off were three different camps of Crows. These were sent for and camped all about the hill, so that the Cheyennes could not get away.

The story of what followed comes from the Crows, since none of the Cheyennes with the party survived. The Crows declare that one of their men had crept close to the Cheyennes and was

[1] *Lewis and Clark*, vol. I, p. 189. (New York, 1904.)

shooting at them through a cleft in the rock and had killed several. One of the Cheyennes had a gun and the others pointed out to him the situation of the Crow. The Cheyenne lay down and aimed at the cleft and when the Crow raised his head to shoot the Cheyenne fired, hitting him in the forehead and killing him. The Crow sprang forward and his body lay head downward, half over the rock. Then the Cheyenne sang a song and held up his gun toward the sun, and struck the butt on the ground, and fired and killed a Crow. Four times he did this and killed four Crows. These were his last shots. The Crows wished to know who this man was, and afterward asked the Cheyennes, and sang for them the Cheyenne's song. When they heard the song his people knew who the man was, for the song belonged to One-Eyed Antelope.

The Cheyennes fought the first day and night and the next day, but by the evening of the second day they had run out of ammunition and arrows. When they had nothing more to shoot with—soon after One-Eyed Antelope had fired his last shot—they threw away their bows, drew their knives, and made a charge on the Crows, and in hand-to-hand fighting all were killed. The Crows say that the Cheyennes killed twenty-five of their people, but some Crows say that many more than that were killed. The only Cheyennes who escaped were two scouts who had been sent out before the Crows were encountered, and who watched the entire fight from a distance. They brought to the Cheyenne camps the news of what had happened.

The stream near which this fight occurred is commonly called Crow Standing Creek by the Crows, because, it is said, a Cheyenne during the fight acted like a crow (bird), cawing and walking about outside of the breastworks. On the other hand, some of the Cheyennes of the present day say that the stream is called Crow Standing Off Creek, i. e., Where They Stood Off the Crows (Indians). The map name to-day is Prairie Dog Creek, and the scene of the killing could not have been very distant from where the Fetterman command was annihilated nearly fifty years later.

To revenge this injury the Cheyennes the following year moved toward the Crow country and camped on Powder River. They attacked the Crow camp and won a great victory. The story is told in two ways. In one version Cheyennes and Sioux were together,[1] the Cheyenne camp being on one side of Powder River and the Sioux camp on the other side, about a mile away. The Crows had sent out scouts to locate the camp of the enemy, and these scouts finding the camps near sundown rode into the river-bed to hide. After dark they left their hiding-place and rode in between the two camps, where they came upon a Cheyenne passing from one camp to the other and shot him. At the news of the attack men rushed out to their horses, the best of which were tied close to the lodges, and rode out to look for the Crows. It was dark and nothing could be seen, but the Cheyennes and Sioux heard the Crows whipping their horses as they hurried to escape, and following the sounds overtook and killed two Crows, the others getting away in safety.

A very large war party now left the Crow camp to attack the Cheyennes and Sioux, while at the same time the Cheyennes and Sioux left their camp to attack that of the Crows. Thus the camps were left almost unprotected. The two hostile war parties passed each other, the Crows going on toward the Cheyenne and Sioux camps while the men from those camps pushed forward toward that of the Crows. For some unexplained reason the Crow party missed their way and failed to find the Cheyenne and Sioux camps, but the Cheyennes and Sioux were more successful.

In the other version nothing is said about the presence of the Sioux, but it is declared that the Cheyennes had moved with the medicine arrows against the Crows. This version relates that the whole Cheyenne camp was present at the Crow fight, as was always the case when the arrows were moved.

The Crows knew that the Cheyenne camp was near and sent out a large war party to attack it. A Crow who was late in starting was following up the trail of his war party, trying to overtake them. As he was moving along he was seen by a Cheyenne scout, Whistling Elk, who lay in wait for him and struck

---

[1] The Sioux were probably present, for the winter-counts in the *Fourth Annual Report Bureau of Ethnology* mention the affair, under date "Winter of 1820–1," which probably means late summer or fall, 1820. The account says a village of one hundred lodges of Crows was captured. Larocque, in 1805, says the Crows were divided into three bands and had three hundred lodges all told. The winter-count thus suggests the capture by the Cheyennes and Sioux of one-third of the whole Crow tribe. *Larocque's Journal,* 1805.

him twice on the head with a hatchet and knocked him down. Supposing his enemy dead, Whistling Elk left him and returned to his party.[1]

The Crow was only stunned, and when he recovered his senses started to return to his own camp. As he was going on he heard the sound of the main party of enemies coming—the trampling of the feet of many horses, which sounded like buffalo moving. As swiftly as possible he hurried to his village, reached there in the night, and at once seeking out the chiefs said: "While I was following our party to war I met a small number of enemies and escaped from them, and as I was returning here I heard the sound of a great war party coming. We ought to go away from here to-night."

A little while before this man had stolen the wife of another Crow, and after the Crow chiefs had listened to what he had to say they did not believe his story. They said to one another: "He must have overtaken our people and the man whose wife he stole has beaten him with a quirt. No Cheyenne did that. If a Cheyenne had attacked him he would have killed him. There are no Cheyennes near here. If there had been, our war party would have killed them."

"Very well," said the man. "You must do what you think is right. I have told you what is true."

He left the chiefs and went to the lodges of all his relations and told them what had befallen him, and said: "We must go away from here to-night. Pack your things quickly. Let us go and try to save ourselves. Many of the enemy are coming. We shall surely be attacked."

His relations believed him, packed their possessions, mounted and left the camp, but before they had gone far they stopped, for they felt uncertain what they ought to do. Some of them said: "Let us go back. It is too cold out here, and that man may be lying." So some of them set out to return to their camp.

It was still night when the Cheyennes came to the camp and surrounded it, and just at daylight they made the attack. It was a camp of about one hundred lodges, and in it there were no fighting men, only middle-aged and old men, so there was not

---

[1] Whistling Elk was the father of Spotted Wolf, who died in 1896, aged seventy-six years.

much fighting, but everyone in the camp was killed or captured. Much property was taken and many women and children. The Cheyennes did not want the old women, but instead of killing them they told them to go away and join their own people. With the Cheyennes were many women, who took part in the fight and afterward secured much plunder. An old Crow woman went to a Cheyenne woman[1] who had captured a little Crow girl, a relation of the old woman, and said to the Cheyenne woman: "My eyes are not good and unless I have some one to lead me I am afraid that I cannot find my camp." The Cheyenne woman gave her the child.

A small Crow boy who in some way escaped from the camp followed up the Crow war party and told them that their camp had been captured. The Crows rushed back to the assistance of their people, but on the way their horses became exhausted and they reached the place too late.

The Crow people who during the night had gone off with the man who had been beaten by Whistling Elk finally for the most part turned about and started back to the camp. It was a little after sunrise when they neared the camp. The Cheyennes saw them coming and hid themselves, and just as the Crows reached the border of the camp they rode upon them from all directions and captured them all. A Crow woman then captured used to say that when the Cheyennes swept down upon the returning Crows they drove them to the Cheyenne camp like a herd of horses.

Lieutenant J. H. Bradley [2] has published the Crow tradition concerning the capture of this camp. According to this version the camp was attacked by one thousand Cheyennes and Sioux. The plains were "literally strewn for a considerable distance with the corpses of men, women, and children. . . . At least five thousand of the Crows had fallen, but that was not all. All their lodges—a thousand in number—all the equipage of their camp, and hundreds of horses had passed into the hands of the victors, who also carried away as captives four hundred young women and children."

These statements may be considered wild exaggerations, per-

[1] White Bull's grandmother.
[2] *Montana Hist. Cont.*, II, p. 179.

haps mere literary flourishes to make impressive this defeat which was sufficiently severe without enlargement.

I cannot fix with precision the year in which this battle took place. Bradley gives it as 1822, which is probably near enough. Whistling Elk's son, Spotted Wolf, was presumably born in 1820, but we do not know the age of Whistling Elk at the time of this occurrence. No doubt he was a young man from eighteen to thirty. White Bull was born in 1837. His grandmother was present at the fight, and his grandfather was probably a middle-aged man, between forty and fifty years old. Long Chin, who died in 1887 or 1888 at the age of eighty-two, declared that he was a young man at the time of the fight. It seems probable that the date was not far from 1820, and if this is the fact it was one of the earliest Cheyenne fights of which we have definite knowledge.

It was not very long after this that out on the prairie the Cheyenne camp was moving from place to place. They had many Crow captives. In some lodges there were four or five.[1]

One day they were camped in the circle when on a hill not far off a man was seen riding backward and forward. He was nearest that place in the circle of the camp where the Dog Soldiers' lodges stood—so near, in fact, that some women who had gone out for wood and water heard his voice, but they could not tell what he was saying, nor were they certain what he was doing. Some of them said to each other: "That man is mourning and crying." Others said: "No, he is singing a song." The man looked like a Crow, and some suspected that this might perhaps be some stratagem of the Crows to get revenge, and called to their fellows: "Look out; be careful; perhaps this man has come here to lead us into a trap. Let no one go toward him until we are all ready and can go together."

Notwithstanding this advice, twelve young men—relations of the keeper of the medicine arrows—who were anxious to catch the man, did not listen to what was said but jumped on their horses and started toward him. All the other Cheyennes were getting

[1] George Bent says the old Southern Cheyennes always place this second Crow fight at the mouth of Horse Creek on the North Platte, thirty-seven miles east of where Fort Laramie was later built.

ready, but waited for the last ones, and finally all went out together. They were some way behind the twelve who had started
first. When the man who was riding on the hill saw that he was
being followed he rode away over the hill, and the twelve young
Cheyennes rode after him. The Crow had a long start, but his
horse did not seem fast. He went slowly until the Cheyennes
had come close to him. Then his horse ran a little faster, and the
man was seen to whip it on both sides. All the Cheyennes were
riding hard, each one striving to be the first to get near him.
They were all watching him and not looking at anything else.
The man rode to a little gap between two hills and passed through
not very far ahead of the twelve Cheyennes. Then, as they followed him, they heard the war-cry from both sides, and from each
side saw a great party of Crows charging them. The Cheyennes
turned to ride back, but it was too late. They were surrounded
and eight were killed. From a distance the main body of the
Cheyenne warriors saw rising behind this hill a great dust that
cast a dark shadow over the prairie. They passed through the
gap and met the Crows; turned them back and drove them a long
distance, killing six.

After the Crows had been driven off, the Cheyenne women
went out with their travois and brought to the camp the bodies
of the dead. In the lodge of the keeper of the medicine arrows they
made up eight beds and on them put the bodies of the men.
From some the Crows had cut off the heads and from others the
arms and legs, but they put them together as best they could.
The relations of the killed had some Crow captives, and of these
they killed eight and piled them up against the outside of the
lodge as logs are laid on the border of a lodge covering to keep
out the wind.

At the Fitzpatrick treaty (1851) the chief of the Crows present pointed out to the Cheyennes a certain man and said to them:
"There is the one who led you into a trap that time." The
Cheyennes looked and saw the Crow, an old man painted red all
over, and wearing a necklet of crow feathers, the tips of which
had been cut off, hanging down all about his neck. The Cheyennes said to him: "We have been wanting to see you for a long
time, for some of our people who heard you at that time said
that you cried and some said that you sang." The Crow an-

swered them, saying: "I did both. I cried for those who had been killed, and I sang a war song for revenge."

Much of the story of this capture comes from the descendants of women taken in the battle, of whom there are many in the Cheyenne camp. The grandchildren of those who took part in the fight and the grandchildren or children of those captured are now old people.

Some years after the capture of the Crow village, and after the fight in which the young men, relatives of the medicine arrow keeper, had been drawn into the trap and killed by the Crows, the Crow chief learned that his son, who had been captured in the village, was still alive and was among the Cheyennes. When he heard of this, probably from some Arapahoes, he sent a runner to the Arapaho chief to notify him that he was coming down to the Platte with his band on a friendly visit.

This was soon after the Cheyennes and Arapahoes began to move south of the Platte to live, perhaps 1831, and at this time there was a camp of Cheyennes, Arapahoes, and Atsē'nas on the South Platte, at the mouth of Crow Creek, which heads near Cheyenne Pass, where Cheyenne, Wyoming, now stands, and empties into the Platte east of Greeley, Colorado.

When the Crows arrived they set up their camp at some distance from the Arapahoes and Atsenas and farther away from the Cheyennes, and the Crow chief then prepared a feast and invited the Arapaho and Atsena chiefs to attend. The Cheyennes stayed away. After everyone had eaten, the Crow chief spoke to the Arapaho and Atsena chiefs and told them that he had come to try to induce the Cheyennes to give up his son. When the feast broke up the Arapahoes and Atsenas went to the Cheyenne camp and repeated what the Crow chief had said. The Cheyennes then spoke to the Crow chief's son, who was called Big Prisoner, and asked him what he thought of this matter. Big Prisoner had now been with the Cheyennes for several years and had been treated very well. His adopted parents had given him everything he wanted and he was very fond of the Cheyennes and had recently married a Cheyenne girl; so when the subject of his return to the Crows was spoken of he said that he wished to remain with the Cheyennes. The Cheyennes told the Arapahoes to repeat to the Crows what Big Prisoner had said.

The Crow chief was not satisfied with this answer. He saw that there were only fifty lodges of Cheyennes and he had nearly twice as many lodges with him. He now gave a second feast to the Arapaho and Atsena chiefs, and after they had eaten he said to the Arapahoes that their tribe and his had always been pretty good friends and the Arapahoes had not helped the Cheyennes attack the Crows. He said the Cheyennes were bad people, always attacking their neighbors, and he wished the Arapahoes to show their friendship for him by handing over the Cheyennes to him.

There was a young Atsena present at this feast. He was a very brave man who had recently been made a chief by the Arapahoes. This Atsena, Small Man, now said to the Crow chief that the Cheyennes and Arapahoes had always been friends and had been living together and dying together for many years, and that if the Crows wished to fight these Cheyennes they must count on fighting the Arapahoes and Atsenas also. Several Arapahoes spoke and approved of what this Atsena had said. The Crow chief then said that he had done all he could to recover his son and he now intended to let the matter lie where it was. He said that the next day the Crow warriors would give a big dance in the Arapaho camp in honor of their friends, the Arapahoes and Atsenas, and after that he would return home.

There was a man in the Crow camp who had friends or relations in the Arapaho camp, and that night he slipped over to the Arapaho lodges and told one of his friends that the Crows intended to come to the camp in great force and well armed, and that during the dance they intended to attack the Arapahoes, Atsenas, and Cheyennes by surprise, kill them all, and get back Big Prisoner and all the other Crow captives. He said that two big Crow men had been selected to ride up on each side of the Crow chief's son, pick him up by the arms, and carry him off between their horses at a gallop. The Arapahoes at once notified the Cheyennes of this plot. Councils were hastily held and it was decided to remain on guard all night. All kept their clothes on, and the men lay with their arms beside them. The Cheyennes and Arapahoes kept sending out scouts all through the night, and, seeing these scouts, the Crows knew that their plan had been discovered, so they also were on guard until morning.

The next day the Crows did not come to dance in the Arapaho camp. They kept in their own camp, with scouts out. Toward noon the scouts on either side came into collision and at once all the warriors mounted and formed in two lines, the Crows in front of their camp, the Cheyennes, Arapahoes, and Atsenas in front of theirs. The women and children packed up everything and prepared to run away, leaving the lodges standing. Neither side made a charge, but brave men rode out and met between the lines, and these single combats were going on most of the time for several hours. In these fights, Small Man, the Atsena who had spoken at the feast, was very brave, and the Cheyennes say they saw Little Mountain, the Kiowa chief, fighting on the Crow side. Toward evening the Crow women took down their lodges and moved off up Crow Creek, and soon afterward the warriors followed, guarding the rear. The Cheyennes, Arapahoes, and Atsenas did not pursue them.

Big Prisoner remained with the Cheyennes until his death, some years later.

IV

WARS WITH THE KIOWAS AND COMANCHES

WHEN the Cheyennes began to work west and southwest from the Missouri River they found the country occupied by the Kiowas and the people whom they call—when they are in the mountains —Sŭs'sŏni, and on the plains *Shĭ shĭ' nĭ wo ĭs tăn ĭū:* Snake People—the Comanches. The Cheyennes recognize the extremely close relationship which exists between these two tribes of the mountains and the plains, and say that the Shoshoni ought to be called the Mountain Snakes or Mountain Comanches. The Comanches, they say, ranged from the Yellowstone River south to beyond the Platte.

The wide range of the Shoshoni stock on the plains has perhaps not yet been fully appreciated. I believe that, at the time of the migration southward of the Blackfeet, the Snakes, or Shoshoni, occupied much plains territory from the St. Mary's River, in Montana and British America, southward, perhaps to the Yellowstone. As late as 1840 the Mountain Shoshoni used to make war excursions out on the plains of the north, and a war party of them once came as far south as Bent's Fort, where, during a quarrel arising from their insistence that they should be admitted within the fort at an inopportune time, one of them was killed.

Some of the writers on the plains tribes seem not to have understood the close relationship of Shoshoni and Comanches, and persons who are aware that the Comanches were reported in the eighteenth century as ranging in Texas and Mexico perhaps have not realized that people of the same blood and speaking the same language may have lived at the same time on the northern plains under another name. A realization of that fact may serve to clear up some apparent confusions. I believe that in the matter of the relationships of the tribes who lived about him the Indian was a much better ethnologist than the early trapper, trader, or missionary who wrote books upon the West, which he had just ventured into and whose people and products were absolutely new to him.

The Kiowas were found by the Cheyennes living about the Black Hills and along the Little Missouri, Powder, and Tongue Rivers, and the Cheyennes say that it was from the Kiowas that the Little Missouri River received its name Antelope Pit River,[1] for there the Kiowas used to entrap great numbers of antelope in pits, and it was there and from observing the traps made by their predecessors that the Cheyennes learned to catch antelope in this manner.

The Kiowas had long been dwellers in the northern country. They were near neighbors of the Crows and their close association and friendship with that tribe is historic and was never interrupted. They have a band or division known as the Ree band, descendants of people said to have been especially intimate with the Arikaras. This suggests a range on the plains between the Crows on the west and the Rees on the east. It is certain that in early times there was much friendly intercourse between the Crows and the tribes later known as the Village Indians of the Missouri.

The early meetings of the Cheyennes with the Kiowas and Comanches were friendly. I have heard no tradition of the origin of their first quarrels, but fightings did take place, with the result that Kiowas and Comanches were gradually pushed farther south and finally expelled from their former range, until at the beginning of the historic period the range of the Kiowas was about the North Platte River. From here they kept working farther southward, partly, no doubt, attracted by the horses which were so easily obtained from the Mexicans, and partly perhaps pushed south by their enemies to the north—Cheyennes and Sioux.

The Cheyennes say that when they first secured possession of the Black Hills country, which included the Little Missouri and the Cheyenne Rivers and the country lying toward Powder River, the Yellowstone, and the North Platte, there were no Sioux in that country; that their migration thither came only after the Cheyennes were thoroughly established there. They

[1] Antelope Pit River—Wōkaihē' yūniō' hē.

declare that the first Sioux who came were very poor and had no horses, which the Cheyennes had already obtained either by capture of wild horses or by taking from people to the south or west; that when the Sioux came, carrying their possessions on dog travois, the Cheyennes took pity on them and occasionally gave them a horse; that this generosity resulted in the coming of more and more Sioux to receive like presents, until as time went on still more Sioux crowded into the country and they became very numerous.

This statement is supported by one of the Sioux winter counts[1] which states that the Black Hills were discovered by a Dakota in 1775, at which time the Cheyennes had long occupied them. Mooney believes that the Kiowas were expelled from that region by the Dakotas, but mentions 1770 as the date of a great battle between Kiowas and Dakotas in the Black Hills region. Only four years before that date Carver found the Nadouessi of the plains living at the head of the St. Peter's River, a long way from the Black Hills. The earlier travellers on the Missouri River recognized that the Dakotas had only recently come to that stream, and the Mandans told Verendrye (1738) that to the south of them there were no Sioux; all were to the east. Even in 1804 the Teton Sioux had not all crossed the Missouri River.

Besides crowding out from their early home the Kiowas and Comanches, the Cheyennes, as they moved out over the plains country, in like manner forced the Crows westward toward the mountains. From the old Cheyennes much is heard at the present time about the wars with the Kiowas and Comanches less than a century ago, but all this fighting seems to have taken place in the southern country, where about 1835 the Arkansas River separated the range of the Cheyennes and Arapahoes from that of the allied Kiowas, Comanches, and Prairie Apaches, who roamed in the country south of that river and toward Texas.

Between about 1826 and 1840 a bitter warfare was waged between these two parties of allies. This very likely arose from the need for horses, which they obtained chiefly from the south, and it is likely that the horse was an important cause for the southward movement of all these tribes. The Kiowas and Comanches

[1] Records, painted on skins, of the chief event of each one of a series of years. See *Handbook of American Indians,* "Calendar."

made frequent raids into the country of the Mexicans, in Texas and south of the Rio Grande, and from these forays brought back great herds of horses. These in turn were taken from them by the Cheyennes and Arapahoes, from whom again they were captured by the Pawnees and by other tribes still further to the north. In this way the horses were passed along from tribe to tribe and spread with extraordinary rapidity from the south northward over the whole plains country. That many of these were taken from the Mexicans is shown by the fact that many were branded.[1]

Although, according to tradition, the wars that were waged between the Cheyennes and Arapahoes and the Kiowas, Comanches, and Apaches lasted for many years, it is nevertheless certain that in 1820–21 they, or a part of them, were on perfectly good terms with each other and commonly associated. In 1820 or thereabouts Long found all these tribes moving to the head of the South Platte River, where they were reported recently to have returned from the Arkansas River or further south. He refers to a trading visit reported four years earlier. In November, 1821, Jacob Fowler reported that he had travelled with seven hundred lodges of Indians up the Arkansas River, of whom he mentions: Ietans, Arapahoes, Kiowa Padduce, Cheans, of whom there were two hundred lodges, and Snakes—presumably Comanches. The Kiowa Padduce were very likely the Kiowa Apache.[2]

In 1828, however, the Cheyennes and Comanches were at war, and in this year the well-remembered battle took place between Comanches under Bull Hump and Cheyennes and Arapahoes under Yellow Wolf.

With a large party of Comanche warriors Bull Hump[3] had come to the stockade which William W. Bent had built at the mouth of Huerfano River. While they were there some of the

---

[1] Dutisne (1719) to Bienville, in Margry, vol. VI, p. 313. Umfreville in 1789 says: "I myself have seen horses with Roman capitals burnt in their flanks with a hot iron." *The Present State of Hudson's Bay*, p. 178.

[2] *Journal of Jacob Fowler*, edited by Elliot Coues, pp. 55, 59, 65. (New York, F. P. Harper, 1898.)

[3] Old Bull Hump signed a treaty about 1835. A Bull Hump is mentioned in 1850 in Schoolcraft's *Indian Tribes*. The son or nephew of this man signed the treaty of 1865 as Bull Hump, third chief of the Penetethka band.

young men went out and saw the moccasin tracks and other signs of a war party of Cheyennes which had just left the post. Bull Hump asked Bent if he knew where these Cheyennes came from; where their village was. Bent told him they had come in from the northeast. The Comanches remained there that afternoon and went away that night to begin a search for the village of the Cheyennes. They sent out a small party of scouts who at length returned and reported that the Cheyenne village was a little farther ahead on a stream which the whites now call Bijou Creek. That night a number of Bull Hump's men slipped off from him and went over to the village and ran off all the Cheyenne horses, so that the Cheyennes could not follow them, for they had nothing to ride.

At this time Yellow Wolf and Little Wolf, Cheyennes, with eighteen or twenty men had been out chasing wild horses on the Arkansas River. During the trip Walking Coyote, a Ponca captive, caught a great many wild horses—about thirty-five head.

They were returning up the Arkansas River with their horses, and above where Sand Creek runs into the Arkansas turned off toward their camp on the South Platte, where the main Cheyenne village was. As they were going along in the night, Yellow Wolf and Little Wolf and Big Old Man being in the lead while the others were behind with the horses, the leaders smelled burning buffalo-chips. They stopped and when the others had come up Yellow Wolf said: "Can you smell that?" All said: "Yes." Yellow Wolf directed two of his men to go forward on their fastest horses and see who it was that had made this fire.

It was in the middle of the night. They were making for the Black Lake (Mōhksta'āv ihan'), about forty or forty-five miles due north of old Fort Lyon, where there is a spring. Black Lake was so called from the color of the soil round about. The water was alkali, but horses and buffalo drank it, though people did not. The large fine spring was west of it. This was a great range for wild horses, and horse trails as deep as the old buffalo trails came to it from many directions.

To the scouts starting out Yellow Wolf said: "Go to the spring. That is the only water about here, and if they have camped anywhere they must be there. Find out who they are, but be very careful."

The scouts started, following up the smell of the smoke. When it got strong and they thought they were pretty near to the fire they stopped, and one of them held the two horses while the other crept up very quietly, closer and closer, until he had come near enough to see a number of small fires and to hear people talking. Getting still nearer, he could hear that they were talking Comanche. He saw also that the camp was a large one, and that the place was black with horses.

Yellow Wolf was a great chief, a very wise man. When the scouts returned he said: "We must turn off here and go around and get on the opposite side of them." This would bring the Cheyennes on the side of the Comanches which was toward their own camp, so that if the Comanches pursued them they would be running toward the big Cheyenne camp and not from it. Everyone kept very quiet and they drove along slowly and silently until they had come to the opposite side of the Comanche camp. Here Yellow Wolf left some men with the herd of captured horses and said to them: "Just as soon as daylight comes, so that you can see well, start your horses along. We will go down there and they will charge on us and you will hear firing. When you hear this, do not wait. Hurry the horses along as fast as you can." The other men rode quietly up as close as they dared to the Comanche camp and waited there until just about daylight, till they could begin to see fairly well.

Yellow Wolf told his young men that there were many Comanches and that they would be sure to fight. To Walking Coyote, his adopted son, of whom he thought more than he did of his own sons, he said: "My son, you know what to do? Do your best. You have a fast horse and you must stay behind and try to fight off these Comanches, while we run off the horses. We cannot very well fight and run off their horses, too. Afterward we will divide the horses up in equal shares."

As soon as it was plain daylight they could see horses everywhere. The Comanches had had herders out, but at daylight, thinking that everything was perfectly safe, they went into the camp. The Cheyennes could see that the Comanche horses were still pretty well bunched up together as they had been left by the herders. Many of the Comanches had their finest horses picketed in the camp.

When it had grown light enough Little Wolf said: "Let us go; do not make too much noise at first." They rushed toward the camp, and after they had got around the horses began to whoop and yell, and then to shoot, starting all the loose Comanche horses to running and sweeping them all off. When the Comanches saw the horses running they began to shoot at those who were driving them and to shout directions to each other. One especially fine horse was picketed right in the camp, and Walking Coyote rode down into the camp, jumped off his horse, cut the rope which held the Comanche horse, mounted again and started off with it. Walking Coyote overtook his party and handed the rope of the horse he had cut loose to Yellow Wolf, his father. The Comanches began to jump on their horses and to ride after the Cheyennes. The Cheyennes rushed the horses off, but Walking Coyote and the other men stayed behind to fight the Comanches, to try to keep them back.

Of the Comanches whose fast horses were tied in camp there were not very many, perhaps not more than twenty-five or thirty, but these followed fast. Many of the tied horses, frightened by the charge and the shooting, broke their ropes or pulled up their pins and followed the herd. Every now and then a frightened horse that had pulled up his pin, but had run off in some other direction, would come up from behind and join the herd. The Cheyennes who were driving the herd and were close behind it said that they had to keep dodging to avoid the flying picket-pins at the ends of the ropes pulled up by the Comanche war horses.

As the light grew stronger and the men driving the horses were able to see them better they began to recognize Cheyenne horses in the herd that they were taking off—those that the Comanches had taken from the Cheyenne village only a short time before.

A man who was behind rode up to Yellow Wolf and said: "They are getting close. They will soon overtake us."

Yellow Wolf replied: "Now, all who have guns must turn back and charge on them. That is the only hope we have of getting away from them. We must fight them."

When Yellow Wolf gave the word all the Cheyennes who had guns turned about and charged back among the Comanches.

Yellow Wolf rode up close to a Comanche and poked his gun against his body and fired, and the Comanche dropped from his horse. Walking Coyote counted coup on him. Another man shot a Comanche off his horse; and the Comanches were so surprised and frightened at the suddenness of the attack that they all whirled about and began to run. That ended the pursuit.

When the Comanches left them the Cheyenne party had almost overtaken the young men who were driving the captured wild horses, and they signalled them to stop and wait for them. It was only about this time that they fully recognized the great number of Cheyenne horses in the herd which they had taken from the Comanches.

Yellow Wolf then said: "We have here some Cheyenne horses and these we shall have to give back to the owners, but the Comanche horses we will divide." They did so.

Before they reached the Cheyenne village Little Wolf, who died about 1886, aged ninety-two years, tied one of the Comanche scalps on the ramrod of his Hudson Bay gun, while Yellow Wolf tied the other scalp on a pole, and when they charged down into the village Little Wolf shot his gun off in the air and the two rode about waving the scalps.

When they drove the herds into the camp and the Cheyennes who had lost their horses saw that they had been recaptured, there was great rejoicing. The men who had brought back these horses afterward said that their necks were sore from being hugged by the people whose horses they had returned.

After peace had been made with the Comanches, in 1840, Bull Hump said that the pursuing Comanches, when they saw the herd of loose horses ahead, supposed that they were approaching a large Cheyenne camp, and that it was chiefly for this reason that they gave up the pursuit.

From this time fighting was constantly going on between the Cheyennes and the Kiowas and Comanches, though most of the trips by the Cheyennes against the tribes to the south were made on foot and solely for the purpose of taking horses. On the other hand, when the Cheyennes went to war against the Pawnees to try to kill Pawnees and take scalps, they usually went on horseback. Nevertheless, if a convenient opportunity offered to attack the Kiowas it was not neglected. Such opportunities occurred more or less frequently, since for very many years after they had moved south the Kiowas were accustomed to make frequent trips north to visit the Crows and renew old friendships. In making these journeys they usually kept in close to the flanks of the mountains to avoid the Cheyennes and Arapahoes, who commonly camped well down on the plains. Nevertheless, sometimes such a travelling Kiowa camp was seen and attacked.

On one such occasion—about 1833—some Cheyenne hunters discovered in the sand hills, east of where Denver now stands, a camp of about a hundred lodges of Kiowas travelling northward. They had with them many ponies which they expected to trade to the Crows for elk teeth and ermine skins. When the young men who had discovered the Kiowa village reported at the Cheyenne camp, it was determined to start during the night so as to reach the Kiowa camp in time to attack it early in the morning. By an error the Cheyennes were led to the wrong place, and when daylight came saw that the Kiowa camp was a long way from them, and that the Kiowas had already packed up and were about to move. The Cheyennes charged toward them and the Kiowas fled, but as the Cheyennes followed they overtook a Kiowa woman who had fallen from her horse carrying a little child. A Cheyenne rode up and counted coup on the woman, touching her with his lance but inflicting only a flesh-wound. The child which the woman carried on her back was but two or three years old, a little white girl captured by the Kiowas a short time before. She was taken to the Cheyenne camp and reared there, and in 1912 was still alive and known as the Kiowa Woman.[1] Her Cheyenne name is White Cow Woman. She can speak only Cheyenne, but is apparently of Irish parentage, having blue eyes, brown hair, and an Irish countenance.

Another story, told by Snake Woman, who said that as a young girl she was present at this fight, declares that Yellow Wolf's band of Hair Rope people and Black Shin's Suhtai were moving south, looking for buffalo, when they discovered the Kiowas on the march going north. The Kiowas fled to the timber on Scout Creek, afterward called Kiowa Creek, where the Kiowa

---

[1] The Cheyennes do not speak of her as Wĭt'ă păt e (=a Kiowa woman), but call her Ĕ nū tah″, meaning a woman who is a member of some other tribe, a foreigner to their own blood.

women and children took shelter while the men held back the Cheyennes. A very brave Kiowa, on a fine white horse and armed with a lance, charged the Cheyennes alone again and again. On one of these charges he lanced Man Above and knocked him off his horse. Finally, charging right through the Cheyennes, he was shot with three arrows, and turned and rode back toward his own people but fell before he reached them. The Kiowa women had dug pits in the timber and tied the horses among the trees. The Cheyennes charged up to them many times, but could not get the horses and finally left them. Snake Woman said that after the fight was over she saw the captured Kiowa woman wounded by the lance sitting in front of Black Shin's lodge.

Bent says that in 1857 his father built a temporary trading-house on Scout Creek, and that the Bent boys used to go out and play in the pits that the Kiowa women had dug.

When the great peace was made, in 1840, the Kiowas bought back from the Cheyennes the captured Kiowa woman, but did not wish the little white girl, who remained with the Cheyennes.

V

THE BATTLE ON WOLF CREEK

1838

THE medicine arrows were the most sacred possession of the Cheyennes, and in the whole camp there was no one to whom greater reverence was shown than the keeper of the medicine arrows; but even his sacred character did not always protect him from the younger men.

Some years after the capture of the arrows by the Pawnees in 1830, a Cheyenne was killed by a fellow tribesman, and it became necessary to hold the ceremony of renewing the arrows. Until this had been done, no war party could set out with any hope of success.

It happened at this time that the Bow String soldiers (Hĭm ă tăn ō'hĭs) were anxious to go to war. They wished the arrows to be renewed so that they might set out at once, but when they spoke to Gray (Painted) Thunder, the arrow keeper, about it he told them that the time and place were not propitious and advised them not to go. There was much dispute about this, but at length the Bow String soldiers told Gray Thunder that he must renew the arrows. He refused; whereupon, the soldiers attacked and beat him with their quirts and quirt-handles until he promised to renew the arrows for them. Gray Thunder was then an old man, over seventy. He renewed the arrows as ordered, but before the ceremony he warned the Bow String men that the first time they went to war they would have bad fortune.

At this time the Southern Arapahoes,[1] who were camped with the Cheyennes, were holding a medicine-lodge. The man who had vowed the ceremony lay on his belly on the ground and had a vision and prophesied. He said: "When we finish this medicine-lodge dance we will make up a big party and go to war."

[1] Nūm o sĭn'hă nhĭ' ā, Build the Fire in the South.

He referred not only to the Arapahoes but to the Cheyennes as well. While the ceremonies were still being performed and they were dancing another man called out: "Wait, wait, let everyone stop and keep quiet. You people who are talking about going to war and you Bow String soldiers, do not go. I have seen heads (scalps) coming into the camp from all directions, but I do not think they are the heads of enemies; I think they belong to our own people. There was no place in this medicine-lodge from which blood did not flow.'

Most of the people listened to what this man said, but, nevertheless, small parties of young men began to steal away from camp, for the Cheyennes were a headstrong, obstinate people, and when they had made up their minds that they wanted to do a thing they were likely to undertake it even though they disregarded the ceremonies and violated the oldest laws.

After the ceremonies the big camp began to split up quietly, but a man named Hollow Hip[1] kept talking of going to war. He said: "Why should we not go to war? It is a bad thing to live to be an old man. A man can die but once." Bear Above[2] also urged this, and at last they made up a small party of Bow String soldiers in which were four Contraries,[3] and three servants went along to roast the meat. After this party had gone some distance on their way they began to see the trails of small parties which had stolen away from camp before them, and some time later they overtook them. The parties that had now come together numbered forty-two men, all belonging to the Bow String soldiers, and their intention was to go south in search of a Kiowa or Comanche camp from which they could take horses and perhaps a few scalps. They were on foot.

At first they found little game and were obliged to eat the food they had carried with them. Soon after that was exhausted they found game, but in killing it shot away most of their arrows. They travelled many days and at last they found the Kiowas, Comanches, and Apaches encamped in the valley of Washita

---

[1] Hollow Hip (Tsōhp tsĭ'ŏn a).

[2] Bear Above (Hē ămmă nāh'ku).

[3] Contraries, men possessing special powers and living according to special rules. One of these was that their speech or acts reversed what they wished or were asked to do. Hence the term contrary.

River. Here the party hid in a ravine and two scouts went to
the top of the bluffs, where they lay and watched the camps in
the valley below.

Early the next morning a Kiowa started out to hunt before
any of the rest, and as he passed over the bluffs he saw the heads
of the two Cheyenne scouts as they peered over the hill-top. The
hunter rode nearer to get a better view of these people, and they
fired at him. They missed him, but one of the bullets struck his
horse and crippled it for a moment; the scouts rushed forward
to kill their enemy, but before they reached him the horse recovered
and carried its rider safely off. The Kiowa returned to camp and,
pointing to his horse, said that he had been fired at by two enemies.

The Kiowas and Comanches seized their arms and rode swiftly
to the place where the hunter had been attacked. They found
there a few tracks on the ground, but the grass was starting
strongly and in the grass it was impossible to trail men on foot.
The Kiowas spread out and began running over the hills, looking
everywhere for the enemy. Sa tank' led a large party to the northwest, but no trace of the Cheyennes could be found. When they
had searched the whole country without success, the Kiowas
turned back toward their camp, but on the way back a Mexican
captive discovered a breastwork of stones thrown up at the head
of a ravine, and at once signalled his find. Other Kiowa nar-
rators, however, say that a signal was flashed with a mirror and
that when they looked in the direction of the flash they saw a
Cheyenne standing on the hill, signalling with his blanket for them
to come to him. What probably happened is this: The Mexican
found the Cheyennes, and the Cheyennes, seeing that they had
been discovered and wishing to show their bravery, called the attention of other returning parties of Kiowas by flashing the mirror at them and then signalling with the blanket for them to
come and fight.

The Kiowas surrounded the Cheyenne position, and they
fought there for some time. At length, however, according to
the Kiowas, the Cheyenne ammunition gave out, and when this
happened they charged upon the party and killed them all.
They scalped them, but did not strip the bodies of their arms and
clothing. James Mooney[1] says that there were forty-eight men

[1] *Seventeenth Annual Report Bureau American Ethnology,* p. 271.

in the Cheyenne party and that one of them strangled himself with a rope to avoid capture. The Cheyenne account says nothing about this. Only six Kiowas were killed, a fact perhaps due to lack of ammunition among the Bow String men. This happened in 1837. Mooney says that this fight took place on a small tributary of Scott Creek, an upper branch of the North Fork of Red River, in the Panhandle of Texas.

The Cheyennes did not know the fate of the Bow String soldiers, for not one escaped to take home the news. Some time after the fight a party of Southern Arapahoes went somewhere to make a trade—probably to Fort Adobe, and not to Bent's Fort, for, as the Cheyennes and Arapahoes were constantly at Bent's in those days, the Kiowas and Comanches would not have gone to trade at a point where they would have been almost certain to meet enemies. As the Arapahoes approached this trading-store they saw that many Comanches, Kiowas, and Apaches were camped there and were holding war dances. The Arapahoes went over to look at them, and among the scalps that were being danced about they recognized the hair of Red Tracks and that of Coyote Ear, by the length and fineness and the way the hair was braided and tied up and the ornaments attached, but they said nothing.

With the Arapahoes was a Sioux named Smoky Lodge. After he had seen the war dance he left the Arapahoes and started to the Cheyenne camp to tell the news. At last he reached the camp and told all that he had seen and heard; that the enemies had killed and scalped the Bow Strings but had not robbed the bodies. After he had told the news at the first camp, runners were sent out to take the news to all the camps. When they had heard it all the people were anxious to revenge these injuries. The most distant Cheyenne camp was that of the O mĭs′sĭs, who sent word that they would come as soon as possible. They were then chasing wild horses, and would soon be at Horse Butte and would follow down the stream. Horse Butte[1] is a square butte near the forks of the Platte.

Early in the winter Porcupine Bear, the chief of the Dog Soldiers, set out to go about from camp to camp arranging to get

[1] Possibly the square butte known as the Court House Rock. There are but three or four notable buttes near the forks of the Platte, and the Court House is the only square one.

the people together for the journey to war. With him he carried whiskey to give to the chiefs of the camps he came to, and at a big camp on the South Platte many of the Indians got drunk on the whiskey. In a drunken brawl with men of the camp the cousin of Porcupine Bear and Little Creek came to blows. The two were rolling on the ground, fighting, and Porcupine Bear's cousin kept calling on him for help; Porcupine Bear, also drunk, was sitting quietly by singing his songs, but at last, roused by his cousin's repeated calls, he drew his knife and stabbed Little Creek, who was holding down and beating his cousin. Porcupine Bear then called to all his relations and asked them to do as he had done. All drew their knives and cut Little Creek so badly that he died. In this way Porcupine Bear and those who had taken part in the fight became outlaws; Porcupine Bear lost his position as chief of the Dog Soldiers and was expelled from the band, and, with his relations who had taken part in the killing of Little Creek, from the main camp. They and their families, however, camped near the village—a mile or two from it.

Little Wolf, chief of the Bow String soldiers, now took up the work of inciting the different soldier bands to avenge the killing of the forty-two Bow Strings, and soon the different camps began to come together.

When the O mĭs′sĭs[1] came in sight of the big camp where the Cheyennes had assembled everyone was mourning; never were seen so many people mourning. All the women had gashed their legs, and blood was everywhere. When the O mĭs′sĭs were seen from the camp a crier was sent to meet them to tell them to stop; not to advance farther. Some people came to them from the ·main camp, wailing and mourning, and all the women of the O mĭs′sĭs camp began to feel badly and wailed and cried with them. They told the women of the O mĭs′sĭs to move into that place in the camp circle left for the O mĭs′sĭs, but all the men of the division remained behind. The young men all put on their war costumes and rode to the top of a hill as if about to charge an enemy's camp. When their women had made camp and turned loose the horses, the O mĭs′sĭs charged, shooting. They did not charge through the camp, but near to it and then rode up on a hill and the men of the soldier bands formed by fours, and

---

[1] O mĭs′sĭs, one of the clans or divisions of the Cheyennes.

thus entered the circle of the village and rode around it to the opening and then out and, turning to the left and riding round the other way on the outside, entered the circle again, dismounted and dispersed. A short time after this ceremony was ended two men rode in and said: "In a little while a camp will move in; wait for them." Two days later in the afternoon the men of this newly arrived camp charged on the main camp and turned off before reaching it. After that the camp moved in and took its place in the circle. This band was Mā sĭhk'kōta.

Now that the whole Cheyenne tribe had come together they put up in the middle of the camp circle a large shade for the use of the different bands of soldiers. After all the soldiers had collected there, those who had lost children or relatives in the Bow String party came with horses and other presents and passed their hands over the faces of the soldiers, asking them to take pity on and help them. Blood was running down the arms and legs of the women, and when they passed their hands over the soldiers' faces they left blood on them. An old man, Hole in the Back (Wōhkō wĭ'păh), mounted a horse and rode slowly around the camp, calling out the names of all the soldier bands four times and of those young men who had not joined the soldier bands, and said: "All these presents are brought to you soldiers and to you young men, to induce you to take pity on these people."

It was left to the chiefs to decide what action should be taken, but they would not decide. Then it was left to the Red Shield soldiers to say what should be done, and the Red Shields ordered all the soldiers to fix their war bonnets and their shields and medicine head ornaments—to prepare for war. They said: "Look at the people who have given you all these things and take pity on them." So all was done as the Red Shields ordered.

After this decision they remained for some time at this place. One band had all their horses stolen; one of these, the Chubby Roan Horse, is talked about to this day. Now, it began to snow and the snow got deep. When they moved they had to step in the footprints of those who went before them. Some horses got very thin, and some even starved to death; the camp was so large that they could not get game enough to support them and the people came near starving. The snow was too deep for them to move about. As the season wore toward spring the big snow went off, but snow still lay on the ground. Through the winter they had seen no buffalo, but now some began to appear, and soon they were plenty. By this time in their search for food the big camp had been somewhat split up and scattered, but now messengers were sent out to ask all to come together.

They thought that someone must be disturbing the buffalo and driving them toward their camp, so young men were sent out to see whether they could find the enemy. A man whose son had been killed said: "I am beginning to think about my son. I should like to go and look for him."

When all had come together they moved south by way of Bent's Fort, and there obtained supplies of arms and ammunition—Hudson Bay guns, flints, powder, and balls. From there they kept moving down the Arkansas River. The Arapahoes were encamped six or seven miles above Chouteau's Island on the Arkansas, and the Cheyennes moved down and camped just above them. In the Arapaho village was a certain Arapaho who possessed a medicine war club and who from this club was named Ē kŭ kŏ nŏ hohwi′, Flat War Club. After the Cheyennes had made camp they put up in the centre of the village a large lodge in which to hold a council, and sent runners to ask all the Arapaho chiefs to come and eat with them. When this word was taken to Flat War Club he sent a message to the Cheyennes saying that he wanted his Cheyenne friends to come and carry him over to the Cheyenne camp and to the centre lodge where they were going to have the feast. This was a request that the Cheyennes should pay him a very high honor.

When this word was brought to the Cheyenne chiefs, they designated certain soldiers who took a strouding blanket and went to Flat War Club's lodge and put it on the ground. He sat down on it and the young men took hold of the edges and carried him over to the big centre lodge. Several times on the way they put him down on the ground and rested, for he was a large, heavy man, but at last they carried him into the lodge and put him down on the ground at the back, in the place of honor. After they had eaten Flat War Club rose to his feet and said: "My friends, I have asked you something pretty strong—that you Cheyenne chiefs should carry me over here to your camp—but I had a reason for doing this. From this war-path on which we are going I

shall not come back. I am giving my body to you. I want to
have the privilege of talking to your wives, because after this I
shall never again be able to talk to anyone." Yellow Wolf and
some other Cheyennes called out in response: "That is good.
You shall do so. We will have the old crier call that out through
the camp." Big Breast,[1] a Cheyenne, also declared that he would
not come back from this war-path. When the crier called out
this news Big Breast walked ahead of him about the circle, carrying his lance and singing his death song. Big Breast had a wife
and two little children, but he took no pity on them. Ponca
Woman, then a girl of twenty, remembers Flat War Club's song
and sang it to me in 1908.

At this council Yellow Wolf and other chiefs said to the
Arapahoes: "Friends, we have made this road—come to this
decision—that no prisoners shall be taken. These people have
killed many of our young men, Bow String soldiers, and that is
the road that we have made—to take no one alive."

From the Arkansas River they began to send out scouts to
look for the enemy. Pushing Ahead[2] and Crooked Neck[3] were
the first two sent. These men went south looking for the enemy,
but kept too far to the westward; nevertheless, one day while
they were lying on a hill overlooking the valley of Wolf Creek
they saw a small war party—only two or three men—coming down
the stream, leading their horses and carrying shields and lances.
"There," said Pushing Ahead, "there is a war party returning
to the main camp."

When the scouts had seen the Kiowas disappear they returned
to the Cheyenne camp, which they found on Crooked Creek,
which runs into the Cimarron from the north, and when they had
made their report the chiefs called to the centre of the village a
number of young men, Gentle Horse and some others, and sent
them south to Wolf Creek to try to find the hostile camp. Meantime the main Cheyenne camp moved on farther south, the
scouts, of course, having been told at what points the different
camps would be made.

Gentle Horse had asked Pushing Ahead's opinion as to where
the enemy's camp would probably be, but he and his party still

[1] Mŏ′mā kĭ tăn hāh′, Big Breast.   [2] Mā ĭt′ sĭsh ŏ mĭ′ŏ, Pushing Ahead.
[3] Nĭm′ĭ ŏ tāh″, Crooked Neck.

struck too far to the west. Nevertheless, one day as they were
going up a ravine to cross the divide between Beaver and Wolf
Creeks they unexpectedly saw some Kiowa and Comanche buffalo hunters ride over the hills in front of them. The scouts
dropped in the grass of the ravine, and presently, as the Kiowas
and Comanches scattered out more, they crept down into the very
bed of the creek, so that they were lying in the water among the
rushes. In the chase a man, riding a bay mule, passed close by
them; it was a good mule, very fast, and at once ran up close to
a buffalo, which the Kiowa shot. The buffalo and hunter passed
within a few yards of the Cheyenne scouts, but the man was
watching his game and did not look about him. If he had turned
his eyes toward them he must certainly have seen them.

The Cheyennes waited, hidden, until the Kiowas had finished
killing their meat and had begun to pack it into camp, and then
carefully creeping through the grass and keeping in the ravine,
they at last got out of sight, so that they were able to run away.
Even now they did not know just where the Kiowa camp was;
they knew only that it must be somewhere close at hand.

The Cheyenne camp had just been pitched upon the Beaver
when the scouts returned. When they came in Wolf Road was
ahead, for he was the leader. As a sign that he had seen something, Wolf Road carried in his hand the wolfskin which he always
had with him. The approach of the scouts had been observed,
and the chiefs had already gathered in the centre of the camp to
receive the report. They were singing and some men were piling
up a heap of buffalo-chips, behind which the chiefs stood. The
scouts came toward the village running swiftly, and just as they
reached the entrance of the circle they began to howl like wolves,
and to turn their heads from one side to the other, like wolves
looking.

They entered the circle in single file. The men of the camp,
who from these signs knew what the scouts were about to report,
were putting on their war clothing, getting out their shields, and
jumping on their war horses, for they knew that good news was
coming—that the camp of the enemy had been found. The
scouts ran around in front of the chiefs and stopped. Wolf
Road told what he had seen, then Gentle Horse, then each of the
others. They passed on around behind the chiefs, and then from

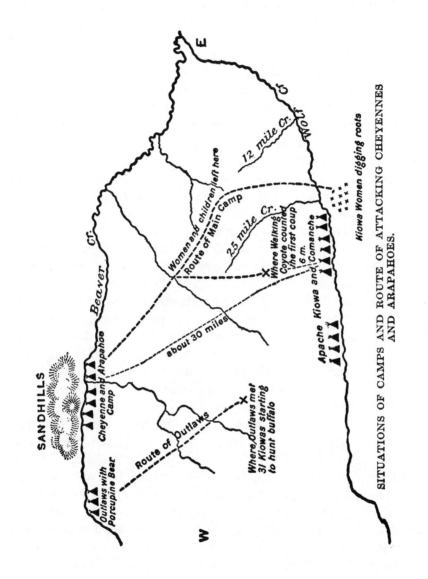

SANDHILLS

Outlaws with
Porcupine Bear

Cheyenne and Arapahos
Camp

Beaver Cr.

Women and children left here

Route of Main Camp

25 mile Cr.

12 mile Cr.

Wolf Cr.

E

about 30 miles

Where Walking
Coyote counted
the first coup

6 m.

Kiowa Women digging roots

Apache Kiowa and Comanche

Route of Outlaws

Where Outlaws met
31 Kiowas starting
to hunt buffalo

W

SITUATIONS OF CAMPS AND ROUTE OF ATTACKING CHEYENNES
AND ARAPAHOES.

all sides of the camp the young men on their horses charged toward the centre, each trying to be first to reach the pile of buffalo-
chips and to strike it, for it represented an enemy. Three men
might count coup on it.

Then all the mounted young men rode around the chiefs while
they were singing, and afterward they dispersed.

All were now preparing for the attack on the camp of the
enemy. The Cheyennes and Arapahoes were camped together
in one big circle, the Arapahoes at the northeast end.

Now a crier mounted his horse and went to the south end of
the circle, and from there rode about it, telling what these scouts
had seen. He cried out that the village would move against the
enemy that night. It was a time of great confusion—men singing their war songs, painting themselves and their horses, fixing
up their things and preparing to start. The lodges were left
standing. The women built platforms on which to put some of
their things, so that they should be above the ground and the
wolves and coyotes should not gnaw and destroy them. During
the night they set out for the camp of the enemy.

Some time during that same afternoon—according to the story
told years afterward by the Kiowas—some Kiowas who were out
on the divide between Beaver and Wolf Creeks looked over toward Beaver Creek, eight or nine miles distant, and one of them
saw something white. He pointed it out to his companion and
said: "What is it that shines white there? It looks like a number
of lodges, and are not those horses about them?" The others
looked, and then one of them said: "No, those things that you
see are the white sand hills on the other side of the Beaver, and
on this side of the next hill there are a lot of buffalo. That is
what you see." Then the first Kiowa said: "But are there not
white horses there?" "No," said the others, "that is the white
of the sand hills, which you see beyond the buffalo when they
move apart." They talked about this for a time, and then went
back to their camp. It is probable that they saw the Cheyenne
camp, which had just been pitched there and the horses feeding
about.

All night the Cheyennes marched south, still ignorant of the
precise location of the enemy's camp. Extremely anxious to
make the attack a surprise and fearing that parties of young men

might steal away to strike a blow in advance, they surrounded the marching column with guards from the different soldier societies to prevent anyone from leaving it. All night long they went on, stopping occasionally to rest. The men were on horseback, while the women walked, leading the pack-horses, which hauled the travois on which the children slept. When daylight came they found themselves still upon the high prairie and not yet within sight of the stream on which the Kiowa and Comanche camp was. As it proved, they were too far east and so down-stream from the Kiowa camp.

In this journey toward Wolf Creek the Cheyennes and Arapahoes had started together, but in the darkness and the uncertainty as to the precise position of the enemy's camp they had split up into at least two main parties and marched independently.

Meantime the outlaws—whose camp was not far west of the large camp and who were aware of all that was happening—had gone forward at the same time with the main body, and from their position to the westward had approached Wolf Creek directly opposite the Kiowa camp. Just after the dusk of the morning Porcupine Bear, later called the Lame Shawnee, saw people ride over a hill before him—men and women going out to hunt buffalo. He was a little ahead of his party when, looking from a crest of a hill, he saw them coming. He called to his men to keep out of sight, saying: "Keep down, keep down out of sight. I will deceive them." His men remained hidden and he threw down his lance and began to ride backward and forward, making the sign that buffalo had been seen. When the Kiowas saw him they supposed that it was someone from their camp who had gone out before them and had found buffalo. They began to move toward him faster, still riding their common horses and leading the running horses. Porcupine Bear did not turn his face toward the enemy, but kept gazing off over the prairie, as if watching distant buffalo. He continued to do this until the Kiowas were so close that he could hear them talking.

Down in the ravine behind him were the other Cheyennes, lying down on their horses, some fixing their shields, or putting arrows on the strings, and some already prepared for the charge. Presently Porcupine Bear said to them: "Be ready, now; they are getting close. We must not give them time to prepare for us."

At last, when he could hear them talking plainly, he reached down to the ground, caught up his lance and, turning his horse, charged the Kiowas, and all the other Cheyennes followed him. The Kiowas were so close that the Cheyennes were on them before they had time to act or time to think. They had no time to change horses, no time even to get their bows out of their cases. The Cheyennes lanced them and shot them down one after another until they had killed them all. They captured all their horses. The last Kiowa of all, with his wife, was so far behind that he had time to jump on his running horse and turned to flee, but his wife called to him: "Do not leave me," and he turned and rode back to help her and was killed. Porcupine Bear killed twelve, Crooked Neck killed eight. There were seven Cheyennes and thirty Kiowas, men and women.

Thus these Cheyennes gained the glory of counting the first coups of this great fight, but because they were outlaws, the honor of it was not allowed to them, but to another man who counted the first coup in the general battle an hour or two later. Still, everyone knew what Porcupine Bear's young men had done.

At this time the chief men of the Crooked Lance Society, or Hĭm'ŏ wĕ yŭhk ĭs, were Medicine Water,[1] Little Old Man,[2] and White Antelope.[3] The Red Shields were with the main party to the north and east of where later Walking Coyote killed a woman.

Though the medicine arrows and the buffalo hat were with the tribe, an attack on the enemy was made before the ceremony of the arrows had taken place, and so the supernatural power of the arrows against the enemy was nullified. This is the reason universally given by the Cheyennes for the loss of so many brave men in the fight.

It was well on in the morning, perhaps ten o'clock, when the soldiers who were scattered out on the south side of the western-most column of Cheyennes saw a man and woman ride up in sight, and they immediately charged on them. Walking Coyote, who was on a black horse given to him by his adopted father, Yellow Wolf, was in the lead. The Kiowa man and woman turned to ride away, and the man who was on a fast horse got away ahead

[1] Mā ĭ yūn'ĭ măp ĭ, Medicine Water.
[2] Mă ăhk'sĭ hĭs, Little Old Man.
[3] Wōkaĭ hwō'kō măs, White Antelope.

of his wife; she called to him to wait, but he was cowardly and rode on; so Walking Coyote overtook her, counted coup on her and then killed her.   The man also was overtaken and killed.

After the Kiowa man and woman had been killed, the main column went down a tributary of Wolf Creek far below the Kiowa camp, and from here, at last, they saw the camp above them on Wolf Creek.   They turned and charged toward the lower end of the Kiowa village, and, seeing a number of people scattered about on the opposite side of the stream, not a few men crossed it. Here, on the south bank, almost opposite the lower end of the village, some Kiowa women were digging roots, and they killed twelve of them.

Before they crossed the stream they overtook two men who were riding a single horse.   A Cheyenne counted coup on the two men with a single blow, and called to the next Cheyenne behind him to ride up and hit the two men sideways, and count coup on them.   His friend tried to do this, but struck only one of them; then the first Cheyenne shot the two Kiowas through with a gun. One fell from the horse at once; the other hung on a little longer and then fell.   These two Cheyennes were of the same family.[1]

Those who did not cross the stream charged up toward the Kiowa village.   Among these was Gentle Horse, who was seen to ride through the upper part of the Kiowa village and round up a large herd of horses and drive them off into the hills.   He wore his hair tied up in a knot over his forehead and an eagle feather stuck through it, which was an ancient method of dressing the hair for war.

After they had killed the women on the south side of the stream, Little Wolf, Medicine Water, and those who were with them charged up toward the Kiowa village and tried to cross the stream.   It was deep and muddy, and on the side where the vil-lage stood the bank was high; their horses went slowly through the stream and could not get up the bank.   Medicine Water had ridden close to the bank, which his horse could not climb, and above him on the bank stood a Kiowa in a yellow shirt.   Medicine Water reached out with his lance to count coup on the Kiowa but the Kiowa seized the lance and dragged it out of his hand.   Then

---

[1] One was called Mō ē′yu, the other Frog Lying on the Hillside (Ōhn ā hku′hā mĭsh).

he looked carefully at Medicine Water, who was wearing the iron shirt, to find some place where he might wound him, and finally wounded him in the neck close to the collar-bone. Little Wolf and another man counted coup on the Kiowa; then a great number of Kiowas, Comanches, and Apaches rode down to where Yellow Shirt[1] was standing, and Medicine Water, Little Wolf, and the other Cheyennes were obliged to turn about and retreat through the stream to the south bank. The Kiowas followed them over, and there for a while was hot fighting and six Cheyennes and Arapahoes were killed. The Comanches made a charge and the Cheyennes retreated. One was behind, going slowly, and his companions called to him to hurry. He turned his head to look behind him and a Comanche shot him in the face with an arrow. The Comanche tried to knock him off his horse, but he whipped up and escaped. His first name was Medicine Bear.[2] The enemy were now pushing back the Cheyennes, crowding them back. Howling Wolf was shot in the breast. The Cheyennes and Arapahoes on the south side when driven back crossed the stream to the main party.

Gray Thunder was killed soon after Walking Coyote had counted his coup. He had said: "I will now give the people a chance to get a smarter man to guide them. They have been calling me a fool." A large party of Kiowas and Comanches rushed on them and rode right over them, killing Gray Thunder and Big Breast. Later Gentle Horse was wounded in the jaw, a Kiowa riding up behind him and putting the muzzle of his gun close to Gentle Horse's head. Gray Thunder was the first of the chiefs to be killed; next was Gray Hair;[3] then an older man, named Deaf Man,[4] was killed. He belonged to the Red Shields. He was their servant, an important man, for the servant's advice is almost always followed by the members of the soldier band to which he belongs. As Rising Sun[5] was crossing the river he was wounded and fell off his horse. He rose to his feet and waded across, and as he reached the bank fell dead. Several other brave men, fighters, were killed in this battle.

On the north side the Cheyennes and Arapahoes followed the

---

[1] Sleeping Bear was one of his Kiowa names; Wolf Lying Down another.
[2] Nāh'kū măĭ yūn, Medicine Bear.   [3] Wōhk'pa ĕh", Gray Hair.
[4] Hōn yă tăn mā hăn, Deaf Man.   [5] Ĭ'shĭ o mĭ ĭsts', Rising Sun.

Kiowas right up to their camp, and there they fought behind the lodges. While the fight was going on some of the Kiowa women were digging rifle-pits in the sand-hills, breastworks to fight behind in case the Cheyennes absolutely got into the camp. Some of the women were putting saddles on their fastest horses and putting in the saddle-bags their most prized possessions, in case they should be obliged to run away. The Kiowas hid behind their breastworks.

Porcupine, the son of the outlaw, Porcupine Bear, jumped into the Kiowa breastworks and was killed there after doing great things and killing several of the enemy. During a charge by the Kiowas, Two Crows jumped off his horse and said: "I shall ask none of you to take me on behind you. While I am fighting here you can get away." He was surrounded and killed. He was an important man.

About the middle of the fight the Cheyenne and Arapaho women and children were moving up to the top of the hill to look over toward the battle-field and see what was taking place. As they were doing this some of the dogs began to bark in a ravine, and when the women ran over there a great tall Kiowa woman, wearing a blanket, jumped up. The widow of Medicine Snake rushed up to her and caught the Kiowa woman in her arms, calling out: "Come and help me; she is very strong." The Cheyenne women ran up and killed the Kiowa woman with their knives.

When the people in the Kiowa and Comanche camp saw these women and children appear on the hill they were still more frightened, for they thought that it was another detachment of Cheyennes coming to attack them. The old Kiowa crier called out through the camp, telling the women to get their horses ready and to take the way up the creek, if they were forced to run. There was another camp of Comanches on the South Canadian, and the Comanches who were here with the Kiowas expected to run to that camp on the Canadian.

Yellow Shirt, on whom coup had already been counted three times, now started out to fight on horseback. He was very brave, and in the fighting coup was again counted on him three times; then he returned, got another horse, and again came out to fight. Before he had been fighting long, someone shot him and broke his thigh, and he fell off his horse, but sat up with his bow and arrows to fight on. Here coup was counted on him three times more and he was killed.

A Comanche chief, who early in the morning had gone out to hunt buffalo, heard of the fighting and returned to the camp as fast as he could. He mounted his war horse and charged, and many Comanches followed him. During the fight his horse was killed, but he returned to the Comanche village and got another and came out again. The Kiowas and Comanches were fighting behind their lodges, and behind breastworks that they had thrown up, but when the Comanches charged, the Kiowas followed them. Crooked Neck called out to his men: "Come, let us run and draw them away from the village." The Cheyennes all turned and ran and the enemy followed, riding hard, this Comanche chief in the lead. When they had gone far enough, Crooked Neck called out to his people: "This is far enough, now turn." The Cheyennes turned and charged, and the Comanches and Kiowas then turned and ran. Sun Maker, who was on a fast horse, almost overtook them, and shot an arrow into the back of the Comanche chief.

Sun Maker watched the chief, and, as he drew close to the village, saw him begin to sway, and then saw him throw out his arms to catch his horse's neck, and saw him fall to the ground and women run toward him from all directions. After the peace was made, the Comanches learned who it was that had killed this chief.

There was fighting about the village until the sun was low in the west, but at last the older people began to call out that they should stop fighting; that the Southern Arapahoes were going to make peace. As the Cheyennes were drawing off and crossing the river they found a woman hidden in some driftwood; she supposed she had been seen and crept out and they shot her. They took pity on no one.

The Cheyennes and Arapahoes went back to where the women were and prepared to go away. Then they set out to return to the camp on the Beaver. As they began to move, the Kiowas all mounted and rode up on a ridge and watched them from a distance. A Cheyenne said: "We must look out for them; they may charge down and try to split the camp."

Two days afterward a camp of Osages, who were then at peace with the Kiowas and Comanches, came up Wolf Creek to the camp. They tried to persuade their allies to follow the Cheyennes and attack them, but the Kiowas, Comanches, and Apaches said: "No, they are gone; let them go."

Lightning Woman said that after Gray Thunder was killed his wife took charge of the medicine arrows and carried them back to the Arkansas, where the tribe encamped near Bent's Fort. Here Lame Medicine Man of the Ridge Men band was given temporary charge of the arrows, but later Rock Forehead was selected as arrow keeper. Gray Thunder and Rock Forehead were both Aorta[1] men.

[1] The clan or division known as Ĭ vĭs tsĭ nĭh″ pāh′.

VI

THE PEACE WITH THE KIOWAS

1840

In the summer of 1840 peace was made between the Kiowas, Comanches, and Apaches and the Cheyennes and Arapahoes—at the "Treaty Ground." The Cheyennes call this place "Giving presents to one another across the river." It is a wide bottom on both sides of the Arkansas River, about three miles below Bent's Fort. The site of Bent's Fort is on the north side of the Arkansas River, about six miles east of La Junta.

Some time before this a kinsman of Little Raven, an Arapaho, had married an Apache woman, and for this reason the Apaches had some friendly intercourse with the Arapahoes, but as these camped and lived with the Cheyennes, who were at war with the Kiowas, Comanches, and Apaches, the Arapahoes were often obliged to fight the Apaches. On one occasion some Apaches came to the Arapaho camp and told them that the Kiowas and Comanches were camped on the Beaver River—the north fork of the North Canadian—and wished to make peace with the Cheyennes and Arapahoes. The visiting Apaches were staying in the lodge of Bull, a noted Arapaho chief.

At this time a war party of eight Cheyennes, under the leadership of Seven Bulls, was in the Arapaho camp, having stopped there on their way south to take horses from the Kiowas, Comanches, and Apaches.

When Bull learned of the wishes of these tribes he invited the Cheyenne young men to meet the Apaches. They went to his lodge, and after they were seated, Bull filled the pipe and offered it to the Cheyennes. Seven Bulls declined to smoke, saying to the host: "Friend, you know that we are not chiefs; we cannot smoke with these men nor make peace with them. We have no authority; we can only carry a message."

Bull said to the eight Cheyennes: "The Kiowas and Comanches wish to make peace with you people, and if you will make peace they will bring back to you the heads (scalps) of those Bow String soldiers, wrapped up in a cloth. They will also give you many horses—horses to the men, and also to the women and children."

Seven Bulls said to his host: "I have listened to what you say and to-morrow with my party I will start back to the Cheyenne village, and will carry this word to the chiefs. They must decide what shall be done. We are young men; we cannot say anything; but we will take your message back to the chiefs."

When Seven Bulls got back to the camp on Shawnee Creek, a tributary of the Republican from the north, he told what had been said by Bull. The second morning the chiefs caused a big lodge, made of two lodge coverings, to be pitched in the centre of the circle, and all assembled there. They sent for Seven Bulls and the others of his party. The chiefs sat in a circle about the big lodge, and the young men sat near the door. After they had delivered their message, the chiefs discussed the matter, and it was finally agreed that a decision should be left to the Dog Soldiers, as they were the strongest and bravest of the soldier bands. High Backed Wolf sent one of the two doorkeepers to call Little Old Man to the council and the other to bring White Antelope. These were two of the bravest of the Dog Soldiers.

When they had come in and sat down, High Backed Wolf told them the message that had been brought, and said: "Now, my friends, do you two men go and call together your Dog Soldiers and talk this matter over, and let us know what you think of it; what is best to be done."

The two left the lodge and called together their soldiers. There were many of them—all brave men. White Antelope told them what the chief had said. Then he went on: "The chiefs are leaving this matter to us, as being the strongest band of soldiers. It is my opinion that our chiefs are in favor of making peace with the Kiowas, Comanches, and Apaches. Now we are all here, what do you all think about it?"

Beard, a head man among the Dog Soldiers, rose in his place and said: "I think it will be best that we leave the decision to you two men, White Antelope and Little Old Man. Whatever you

say will please us all." And all the soldiers sitting about agreed
that this should be done. Then these two chiefs said: "Very
well, let it be so. We will make a peace with these tribes. Now,
we will go back and tell our chiefs that we have decided; that we
have determined to make a peace. We will tell them that we
will meet these people at the mouth of the Two Butte Creek,
at the south side of the Arkansas River, where the dead timber
lies so thick. Those tribes can meet us there, and we can then
make arrangements about what we shall do afterward." The
mouth of the Two Butte Creek is about fifty miles below Bent's
Fort.

Little Old Man and White Antelope went back to the council
of the chiefs, and when they had entered the lodge told High
Backed Wolf and the other chiefs that they would make a peace
with the Kiowas, Comanches, and Apaches. The chiefs all
stood up and said: "*Ha ho'ha ho', Hōtăm'i tăn iu*" (Thank you,
thank you, Dog Soldiers). They were glad to have the peace
made.

After that High Backed Wolf rode about the camp telling what
had been done; that the chiefs and Dog Soldiers had agreed to
make a peace with the Kiowas, Comanches, and Apaches, and
that no more war parties should start out against them. Then
the whole camp moved toward the Fort, for they were anxious to
trade for many things in order to make presents to the Kiowas,
Comanches, and Apaches.

Meantime they sent runners to the Arapaho camp and noti-
fied the Apaches of what had been done. The runners went to
Bull's camp, and told him what the Cheyennes had agreed to.
The visiting Apaches at once started south to notify the Kiowas,
Comanches, and Apaches.

Two days after the Cheyennes and Arapahoes had gone into
camp at the mouth of the Two Butte Creek[1] they saw four Kiowas and a boy, two Comanches and an Apache come over the
hill south of the camp and ride down toward them. The prin-

---

[1] The Cheyennes called this place "Piles of Driftwood" (Māhks'ĭ tsĭ kā'ŏ
ĭhka). Apparently at some time there was a tremendous cloudburst and
flood somewhere on Two Butte Creek and great quantities of driftwood,
large and small trees, were swept down to the mouth of the stream, where the
wood still lies heaped up in great piles.

cipal Kiowa was named *To'hau sĕn,* which is commonly translated Little Mountain. The others were Sā tănk', or Sitting Bear, Yellow Hair, and Eagle Feather. The boy, who was a son of Yellow Hair, was called Yellow Boy. The Comanches were Bull Hump and Shavehead, and the Apache was Leading Bear. They rode into the circle, and in the midst of it dismounted and sat down in a row, and put the boy in front. After they were seated all the chiefs of the Cheyennes, carrying their pipes, went to where the strangers were sitting and sat down beside them, making a long row. Eagle Feather was carrying a pipe already filled. As soon as the Cheyennes had seated themselves Eagle Feather lit his pipe and stood up and passed along before the row of men, offering the pipe to each one, and each one took a puff. Thus the peace was declared.

The strangers had brought with them the forty-two scalps wrapped up in a big bundle in a fancy Navajo blanket. Eagle Feather said to the chiefs: "Now, my friends, we have brought these heads, and they are here." But High Backed Wolf said to him: "Friend, these things if shown and talked about will only make bad feeling. The peace is made now; take the heads away with you and use them as you think best; do not let us see them or hear of them."

Then High Backed Wolf stood up and called out to his people: "Now we have smoked and made peace with these tribes; if any of you have any presents that you wish to give these men, bring them here." Then Mountain stood up and said: "We all of us have many horses; as many as we need; we do not wish to accept any horses as presents, but we shall be glad to receive any other gifts. We, the Kiowas, Comanches, and Apaches, have made a road to give many horses to you when we all come here."

Now the Cheyennes began to come forward, bringing their presents and throwing them on the ground before the strangers, and pretty soon all that could be seen of the boy was his head over the pile of blankets that surrounded him. After the presents had been given, the strangers were taken to a big lodge and feasted there. The Comanches and Apaches did not have much to say—they let the Kiowas do the talking.

After they had eaten, Mountain said to the Cheyenne chiefs: "Now, friends, choose the place where we shall come to meet you; it must be a wide place, for we have large camps and many horses."

The Cheyenne chiefs answered, saying: "Just below the Fort is a big place on both sides of the river. We will camp on the north side and you people on the south side. Let us meet there."

"It is good," said Mountain; "there we will make a strong friendship which shall last forever. We will give you horses, and you shall give us presents. Now, in the morning we will go back, and when we get to our camp we will send you a runner and let you know when we shall be there." The next day the strangers went away.

Soon after that the Cheyennes moved up to the appointed place, and they had been there only three days when the Kiowa runners began to arrive. When at last the villages came, big dusts could be seen rising off to the south where the camps were marching and the many horses were being driven. When at last the camps were made they filled up the whole bottom on the south side of the river.

Except when making a sun-dance the Kiowas do not camp in a circle, but in a body up and down the stream; and on this occasion it was so that they camped. When all had moved in, and the lodges had been pitched, High Backed Wolf mounted his horse and crossed the stream, and invited all the Kiowa and Comanche chiefs to come across to his camp to feast. He put up a special lodge in the centre of the circle and High Backed Wolf told all the Cheyenne chiefs to send kettles of food to the lodge. All the visitors entered the lodge and ate there.

After they had finished eating, Mountain, the Kiowa, said: "Now, my friends, to-morrow morning I want you all, even the women and the children, to cross over to our camp and sit in a long row. Let all come on foot; they will all return on horseback."

The next day they all waded across the river, women and all, and sat in rows, the men in front and the women and children behind them. The first Kiowa to come up was Sa tank'. He had a bundle of sticks too big to hold in the hand, so he carried them in the hollow of his left arm. He began at one end of the row of men and went along, giving a stick to each. At length when all the sticks had been given away he went to some brush and broke off a good many more. Mountain said: "Do not lose those sticks. We do not know your names, but as soon as we get through you must come up and get your horses." All the other Kiowas gave many horses, but Sa tank' gave the most; they say that he gave away two hundred and fifty horses.

Some unimportant men and women received four, five, or six horses, but the chiefs received the most. The Cheyennes did not have enough ropes to lead back their horses; they were obliged to drive them across in bunches. The Kiowas, Comanches, and Apaches had sent their Mexican captives and their young men to bring in their horses from the hills and hold them close to the lodges, and they would walk along with the Cheyennes and point to one after another, saying: "I give you that one; I give *you* that one."

After these presents had been given, High Backed Wolf invited the Kiowas, Comanches, and Apaches to come over the next day, asking them to bring their horses so that they could carry back the presents that would be given them. He told them that when they came they should go to the centre of the circle and sit in rows across it. After he returned to the Cheyenne village he rode through it, and told everyone to cook food for the visitors.

The next day the people of the three tribes crossed the river, and entered the circle of the Cheyenne camp, where they sat down in rows. The chiefs of the three tribes sat in front. Then the Cheyenne women brought out the food in kettles and everybody ate. At that time, of civilized foods the Cheyennes had only rice, dried apples, and corn-meal, and to sweeten their food they had New Orleans molasses. They had no coffee and no sugar. But this food that the Cheyennes had was strange to the people from the south, and they liked it.

After all had eaten, High Backed Wolf called out to his people that now their guests were through eating and they should bring their presents. "Those of you who are bringing guns must fire them in front of the lodges; not here close to these people." He spoke to the chief guests, saying: "Do not be frightened if you hear shots; it is our custom when we are going to give a gun to anyone to fire it in the air." Then for a little while it sounded like a battle in the Cheyenne camp—a great firing of guns. The

Cheyennes brought guns, blankets, calico, beads, brass kettles—many presents.

After all these had been presented, High Backed Wolf said to the guests: "Now, we have made peace, and we have finished making presents to one another; to-morrow we will begin to trade with each other. Your people can come here and try to trade for the things that you like, and my people will go to your camp to trade." It was so done, and this was the beginning of a great trade.

The peace then made has never been broken.

VII

WARS WITH THE PAWNEES

THE Cheyennes possessed two great medicines or protective charms—the medicine arrows and the buffalo cap or sacred hat. These were the most sacred objects owned by the tribe. They were deeply reverenced by all, and about them clustered some of the tribe's most important ceremonial. They have already been described in some detail,[1] but something must be said about them here.

The arrows—believed to have been given to the Tsĭs tsĭs′tăs by their Culture Hero—are four stone-headed arrows of very fine workmanship. Their power is for the men. The women of the tribe have nothing to do with them and may not look upon them, but all males of the tribe should do so, and whenever they are exposed to view even little baby boys are brought up to them so that they may see them. The arrows—ma hūts′—are in charge of a keeper who holds the office through life, or until he voluntarily gives it up, usually being succeeded by a son or a nephew. They are kept in the arrow keeper's lodge, wrapped up in a piece of fur cut from the back of a coyote and are exposed to view only on special occasions, which come at irregular intervals, when some man pledges himself to renew the arrows. This act is a sacrifice, or offering, made for the purpose of obtaining some favor or of avoiding some misfortune. On such an occasion large gifts must be made to the arrow keeper and to those who are to assist him in the work of renewing them. This commonly consists in rewrapping the arrows with fresh sinew and sometimes putting on new feathers. The ceremony lasts four days, and at the end of the fourth day the arrows are tied to a forked stick set up in the middle of the camp circle and—the women all withdrawing—the men pass by the arrows and pray to them.

[1] *American Anthropologist*, New Series, vol. XII, No. 4, October to December, 1910, p. 542.

The sacred hat is called buffalo—Ĭs′sĭ wŭn—and seems to typify the buffalo and food. I believe also that it pertains chiefly to the women. It is a head covering made of the skin of the head of a buffalo cow, to which, when it came to the Sūh′tāī from their Culture Hero, were attached two carved and painted buffalo horns. The hat is also in charge of a chosen man who, like the arrow keeper, is a chief priest and one of the most important men in the tribe.

A multitude of beliefs, ceremonies, and taboos belong to these two sacred objects. They are prayed to, sacrificed to, sworn by. Both are potent to bring good fortune and to heal the sick. Both are strong war medicines, and have often been carried to war—not always with success, because sometimes the people of the tribe have failed to observe the laws which govern them. It must be understood, however, that the hat and the arrows might not be carried on small or individual war parties, nor might they be separated. When they were taken to war the whole tribe—men, women, and children—was obliged to make the war journey. The men walked first and the women followed, carrying their babies or leading the horses that hauled the travois on which the children slept.

When the hat or arrows were taken to war it was required that before the battle began certain ceremonies be performed, and if the enemy was attacked before these ceremonies were completed this act nullified the ceremonies and for the time being destroyed the protective power of the arrows and of the hat. Since absolute liberty prevailed in an Indian camp and such a thing as discipline was practically unknown, and since each young man was eager to distinguish himself in the eyes of all the people by the performance of some brave deed, it often happened that when the enemy had been discovered and an attack was about to be made, some young men would steal away from the main body and, getting as close to the enemy as possible, would take a scalp or make a charge before the arrow ceremonies were completed. Such acts, in Cheyenne belief, accounted for some of their defeats or for other great misfortunes.

The occasions when the whole tribe moved to war against any enemy and the medicine arrows and the sacred hat were carried along came but seldom, and usually followed some great provocation. So far as I can learn there are but six recorded movements of the arrows. The first of these took place, probably in 1817, against the Shoshoni, at which time the enemy were not met. The second time was in 1820 or about that year against the Crows. The Crow camp was captured and many prisoners, women and children, were taken. The third move was against the Pawnees, in the year 1830, at which time the medicine arrows were captured by the Pawnees. The fourth move was in 1838 against the Kiowas, Comanches, and Apaches; the fifth against the Shoshoni in 1843, and the last against the Pawnees in 1853.

In three of these cases some of the Cheyennes, by their impetuosity, neutralized the protective power of the arrows. One of the moves was fruitless, and only two were successful.

I am unable to find among the Cheyennes or Pawnees any tradition which tells of a permanent peace between these two tribes. Temporary cessations of fighting there were after the capture of the medicine arrows, in 1830, and after the Fitzpatrick treaty—also called the Horse Creek treaty and the Big Treaty— in 1851, but there was no permanence whatever to these truces. The Cheyennes regarded the Pawnees as brave people, and said that the Pawnees and the Crows were the two enemies against whom they had to fight the hardest. They used to say that when they met either of these tribes in battle the fight was like that of two buffalo bulls, both pushing hard; first one would push back the other, until he got tired, and then the other would push harder and drive back his opponent, and so the battle would swing back and forth.

The Cheyennes were always anxious to exterminate the Pawnees, and their attacks against them were continual. Perhaps the most important battle that ever took place—to the Cheyennes —was in 1830, when, carrying their two great medicines, they set out to destroy the Pawnees. The accounts of this fight, which I have had from a number of men who took part in it, are given in detail in the article already referred to. Briefly it was as follows:

The Cheyennes set out to the northeast to look for the Pawnees, and, after crossing the Platte River and following up Birdwood Creek, found the Skidi Pawnees on the head of the South Loup, in what is now Nebraska. It was a great ceremonial gather-

ing of the whole Skidi tribe, for they were about to sacrifice a
captive to the Morning Star. The Cheyennes attacked a party
who were out buffalo hunting, beginning the fight before the
ceremonies connected with the medicine arrows had been performed.

At the beginning of the fight, when the two tribes were drawn
up in line of battle, a Pawnee, who had long been ill and was
discouraged and no longer cared to live, went out in front of the
Pawnee line and sat down on the ground so that he might be
killed at once. He was touched but not killed in the first charge
the Cheyennes made. After that Bull, the Cheyenne who was
carrying into the fight the medicine arrows, tied as usual near
the head of a lance, rode up to the Pawnee and thrust at him with
the lance. The Pawnee avoided the stroke, grasped the lance,
and pulled it out of the hands of Bull, who rode away lamenting.
The Pawnee, discovering the bundle tied to the lance, called to
his tribesmen, who rushed up and took the arrows, though the
Cheyennes made a brave charge to try to recover them. The
Cheyennes gave up and went away.

The Pawnees kept the arrows. Subsequently two of the four
were recovered by the Cheyennes—one by a trick, the other by
purchase from some band of the Brulé Sioux. Meantime, however, the Cheyennes had made four new medicine arrows, but
when they recovered two of the old ones they offered two of the
new ones in sacrifice. The Cheyennes believe that the tribe's
misfortunes—and they have been many—began when these arrows were captured.

Fighting between the Cheyennes and the Pawnees continued
up to the early seventies. By that time the Pawnees had become
greatly reduced in numbers and efforts were being made to remove them from their old home on the Loup Fork, in Nebraska,
to the Indian Territory. This was done in 1874. A short time
before they were moved, one or two brave Pawnees went down
south to the Indian Territory and endeavored to make peace
with a number of their ancient enemies, among them the Cheyennes, Kiowas, Comanches, and Wichitas. The difficult task
was finally accomplished, and since that time there have been no
wars between these two tribes.

At the treaty of 1851 no Pawnees seem to have been present.

All the Cheyennes were there and Alights on the Cloud,[1] often written Touching Cloud, or He Who Mounts the Clouds, was one of their most important men. Later a chief of the Pawnee Loups declared himself eager to make peace with all the enemies of the Pawnees, but Alights on the Cloud declined to accept the pipe offered to him.

At the close of the treaty Alights on the Cloud, with two other men, White Antelope, who was killed at Sand Creek, and Little Chief, called by Father De Smet Red Skin, who died about 1858, went to Washington. The following year, after his return, Alights on the Cloud was killed in a battle with the Pawnees.

Among certain plains Indian tribes the personal name Iron Shirt often occurs. This name refers to coats of mail brought to the southern United States by the Spaniards in very early days and which passed into the hands of the Indians and were worn by them. There are traditions of several cases of this kind.

Armor of a certain sort was used by Indians of the Pacific Slope, but no armor of metal was ever known to the aborigines except as it came through the white men. Most of the traditions of these coats of mail are vague, yet of some we have definite knowledge. Fragments of metal shirts have been found in Kansas. Andreas Martinez, a trustworthy man, who has spent his life with the Kiowas, tells that they had two coats of mail, one of which, worn by a Kiowa in the fight with Kit Carson in 1864 at Adobe Walls, was captured by the Ute scouts who were with Carson, the wearer having been killed. The other was buried with its owner.

The Comanches seem to have had such coats of mail,[2] for in

---

[1] Wō ĭv'stō'ĭs—Alights on the Cloud.

[2] Iron Jacket, the Comanche chief who owned the armor, wore it with a fine buckskin war shirt over it, and gained a great reputation among the Comanches and Kiowas. He was finally killed in a fight with the Texas Rangers at Antelope Hills on the Canadian, May 12, 1858. Captains Ford and Ross had about one hundred rangers and old Placido had about the same number of Tonkawas, Anadakos, Caddos, and Wacos. The fight was at Iron Jacket's village. He lined his men up in front of the lodges, facing the enemy, and then rode out and rode up and down the line shooting arrows at Ford, Ross, and Placido. Everyone fired at him, but he seemed to have a charmed life. At length Jim Pock-mark, the Anadako chief, succeeded in shooting Iron Jacket and the Comanches at once turned and fled, the troops pursuing them into the sand hills. This account does not say what became of the armor. *Comprehensive History of Texas*, p. 735.

the year 1858 the Caddos killed a Comanche who wore one. Mr. J. H. East, now or lately of Douglas, Arizona, while engaged with a party of cowboys in the year 1880 in clearing out a spring in Oldham County, Texas, found a coat of mail so badly rusted that it fell to pieces as it was taken from the water. Long before this La Salle reported having found a shirt of mail in the hands of Indians occupying villages on the Mississippi River in latitude twenty-eight or thirty degrees.[1]

In the year 1838, and perhaps much earlier, the Cheyennes possessed a suit of Spanish armor which appears to have been in the possession of the tribe, or of their allies, the Arapahoes, for thirty or more years before that. In 1838 it was owned by Medicine Water, of the Cheyennes, who wore it in the great fight with the Kiowas and Comanches. At the time of the Fitzpatrick treaty of 1851 it was worn by Alights on the Cloud. Clad in this iron shirt Alights on the Cloud had performed many marvellous feats. It is possible that the first time he wore it may have been in the year 1844 in a fight with Eastern Indian trappers. This took place on a stream known to the Cheyennes as Săv ăn i'yō hē, or Shawnee Creek, a tributary of the Arickaree Fork of the Republican.

At this time a large village of Sioux and Cheyennes was camped here, and their lodges pitched in the narrow stream bottom were more or less hidden from anyone who was approaching by high bluffs which rose on either side.

One day in the spring a Cheyenne named Plover had been out hunting, and on his way back, and when he had almost reached the village, he saw some coyote puppies run into a hole. When he reached his lodge he said to his wife, Tall Woman: "To-morrow get your little brother and we will go out and catch some young coyotes. I have just seen several run into a hole. The boy is small and he can creep in with a rope and we can drag them out one by one, and will have some good food." The next day his wife called her little brother, and the three went out to the coyote den. The boy was just creeping into the hole when Plover, looking up, saw people coming over the hill toward them, carrying guns across their saddles. He saw that these were strangers— enemies—and dragged the boy out of the hole, and said to his

[1] *Margry,* II, p. 198.

wife and her brother: "You run to the village as fast as you can, and I will stay behind and fight off the strangers." Tall Woman and the little boy, afterward called Widower, reached the village and a little later Plover also came in, unhurt. The enemies could not see the village until they were almost immediately above it. The strangers were now recognized by the Cheyennes and Sioux as Shawnees or Delawares, tribes well known and friendly to the Cheyennes, who called both by the same name, Săvănē'—Shawnee.[1] The Cheyennes and Sioux were at peace with them and no one understood why they pursued the man, woman, and boy into the village and shot at them.

When the leading Delawares saw the village they turned and rode back to the others. They were quite a company, and had many loaded pack-animals. They were a party of trappers returning from the mountains with their season's catch of fur.

The Cheyennes all mounted their horses and rode out toward the Delawares, but Yellow Wolf, a Cheyenne chief, said to his people: "Wait; go slowly now; we are not at war with these people; let us try to make peace with them."

"But," said one of the others, "they have just been shooting at this man. Why should we make peace?"

"Well," said the chief, "wait. We will try to have the meeting peaceful."

The Delawares drew back to a little ravine and drove their horses down into it, out of sight, and then came up on the prairie to fight on foot, and whenever the Cheyennes rode toward them, making peace signs, the Delawares shot at them.

Still the Cheyennes kept trying to talk to the Delawares. They even took a little boy whose father was a Delaware and held him up, calling out his name to the Delawares, but these kept shooting. Four times the Cheyenne chiefs rode out toward them and tried to talk, but the Delawares would not let them come near them.

At last old Medicine Water made up his mind that the Delawares wished to fight, and that it was useless to try to make

[1] These are commonly spoken of as Shawnees or Delawares; no doubt they were the latter. The Shawnees seem to have been farming people who usually remained near home, while the Delawares were adventurers, trappers, travellers, and scouts.

peace. He said to his son (nephew), Alights on the Cloud: "Now, my son, these people insist on fighting. Here is the shirt." And he handed it forth from where he held it, on the front of his saddle, and said: "Put it on and wrap that red cloth about you so as to hide the shirt, and then ride up close to them." Alights on the Cloud put on the shirt and wrapped a red strouding blanket about him.

Meantime they had notified the Sioux to prepare to fight, and one brave Sioux, who had armed himself with two short guns and a hatchet in his belt, started on foot for one end of the Delaware line, running up the ravine in which the Delaware horses were and so keeping out of sight.

One of the Cheyenne chiefs called out to his people: "These people want to fight; now let us get ready and kill them." And Medicine Water answered, saying: "My son, Alights on the Cloud, will empty their guns."

Then, when everything was ready, Alights on the Cloud rode twice around the Delawares and close to them, and they all shot at him, emptying their guns as they tried to kill him, but the shots did not harm him. While they were shooting at him the brave Sioux on foot almost reached the end of the Delaware line. Now the Cheyennes all made a charge and the Delawares, having nothing in their guns, ran back and down into the ravine, where their horses were, but before they had time to load again the Cheyennes were upon them and killed them all. Some of them had the ramrods in their guns, the balls only half-way down the barrels. The Cheyennes took much plunder—bear, panther, beaver, and otter skins, and quantities of dried beaver tails.

In this fight Porcupine Bear received the name Lame Shawnee. He had jumped in among the Delawares and was striking them right and left with his hatchet when a Delaware who was lying down shot him in the thigh. The Cheyennes were afterward more or less alarmed by what they had done, fearing lest the act might be revenged. That summer they spoke of the matter to Fremont, who mentions the occurrence.[1]

[1] *Fremont Exploring Expedition*, p. 288. (Washington, 1845.) A talk was held at Bent's Fort, August 9, 1845, between the Cheyennes and the Delawares who were with Fremont. See Lieutenant J. W. Abert, *Senate Document* 438, 29th Congress, 1st Session, p. 4.

Alights on the Cloud was wearing the iron shirt when, in 1852, he was killed by the Pawnees, and the account of the battle and of his death has been given me by several men who took part in the fight.

The expedition against the Pawnees was a very large one, made up of representatives of five tribes, there being two hundred and thirty Cheyennes, besides Arapahoes, Sioux, Apaches, and Kiowas. It was the practise of the Pawnees to make each year two great hunts on which they secured enough buffalo meat to last them for six months. One hunt was made in the winter, when the robes were good and the buffalo fat, and the other in summer. This battle took place during the summer hunt.

This account is made up from statements by Bald-Faced Bull, Iron Shirt, and Kiowa Woman, all of whom were present:

The Pawnee camp was big. All of them were there. The day before the fight they had seen a great dust rising and buffalo running, and knew that people were chasing them, but as yet had seen no one. They learned afterward that on this day some of the Kiowas had been fighting the Pawnees. All night long buffalo were heard running, and late that night three or four parties of young men went out and then scouts were sent directly ahead to look for the enemy. The Pawnee camp was found in the morning, but they had moved away, and when the main body of the Cheyennes came up and passed the camp they found in it dead people, and also some scalps tied to sticks standing in the ground.

The morning of the fight a heavy mist lay over all the prairie. One could see only a short distance, but when the mist rose the scouts who had been sent on saw all about them small parties of Pawnees killing buffalo. The scouts sent word back that all should mount their horses and come on, and all did so. When the Cheyennes attacked and chased them the Pawnees ran. Alights on the Cloud overtook a Pawnee and touched him. White Horse and Big Hawk also struck enemies with their lances. They followed them almost into the camp, but when the Pawnees in camp saw the enemy coming they jumped on their horses and ran to meet them, and the Cheyennes turned and ran. Alights on the Cloud was behind. He was dressed in iron clothing.

The Pawnees shot him with arrows, but they did not pierce the coat he wore.

At last the Cheyennes turned to fight. Alights on the Cloud was rushing up behind a Pawnee to strike him, and rode up on his right side, thinking that in this way the Pawnee could not shoot with the bow, but the Pawnee must have been left-handed, for he turned on his horse and shot Alights on the Cloud, and the arrow entered his right eye. When Ear Ring learned that his brother, Alights on the Cloud, had been killed he turned his horse and charged back among the Pawnees; jumped from his horse and took his brother in his arms and hugged and kissed him, saying: "My brother is dead; I, too, will die." He stayed there, rushing about, charging on the Pawnees, and shooting at them until he was killed. After killing Alights on the Cloud the Pawnees killed White Horse and then Big Hawk. Red Bird was killed and Black Wolf and Medicine Standing Up.

Where these men were killed the Cheyennes made a stand and fought for a long time, for by this time a second party of Cheyennes had come up. Then another party of Cheyennes came and charged the Pawnees on the flank, and they began to yield and to run back to their camp, and those whose horses were wounded or were tired out fell behind and were killed—eight in all. The Pawnees had cut up all the Cheyennes that they had killed and taken the iron shirt, and now the Cheyennes got the bodies of the Pawnees and cut them up in the same way, unjointing their bones. The battleground was a wonderful sight—buffalo and horses and Pawnees and Cheyennes all scattered about. If the second party of Cheyennes had been a little later the Pawnees would have killed all the first party. The Pawnees were too strong for the second party also, but when the third party of Cheyennes came up they held the Pawnees, and at length began to drive them to their camp.

After the Pawnees had retreated the Cheyennes gathered together the fragments of the men they had lost and put the bodies together and placed them in a nearby ravine and left them there. Then they went back home, having lost the best men they had. It was a sad time. They all cried, and cut themselves with knives, and cut off their hair and the tails of their horses. It took the party five days to reach their home, travelling day and night.

Alights on the Cloud was as handsome a man as you would ever see—a good man, kind-hearted, and very brave.

The story that Alights on the Cloud, in pursuit of a mounted Pawnee, rode up on his right hand so that the Pawnee could not use his bow sounds well and one would like to believe it, but it is not true. Pawnees who were in the fight state that Alights on the Cloud, whom they know as Iron Shirt, was killed by a certain Pĭtă hāu ĭ'răt, who was the possessor of four sacred arrows, the history of which is as yet unknown. These arrows belonged in the Pĭtă hāu ĭ'răt tribe of the Pawnees, and their ownership was handed down from father to son. They were not kept purely for ceremony, but were for use on certain special occasions, and it was the law handed down from one generation to another that when the arrows received or made by one man had been lost or shot away he might make a new set, but this new set he could not himself use but must pass on to his son, who might use them. If the man who had owned the four arrows did not make a new set to be used by his son it was his duty to teach the son how to make these, and they would belong to the son, who might use them during his life, but when the four had been used his power, so far as these sacred arrows was concerned, was ended. It was by such a sacred arrow that Iron Shirt was killed.

Eagle Chief, born in 1833, told me the story of the killing of Alights on the Cloud which was witnessed, of course, by many Pawnees:

At that time the Pawnees were living at Pahŭk' [1] and in the spring started to hunt buffalo. They went a few days' journey up the Platte and then turned south to the Republican River, where they camped for only one night. The following day they were attacked by enemies and had a big fight. A Skidi named Kō'kā'kā was killed here, and his wife and child. The next day the Skidi went south along Beaver Creek, and here they met the other three tribes, the Tsau ĭ' and Kĭt'kă hāh kĭ, and Pĭtă hāu ĭ'răt. Next morning all the men started out to hunt. Someone had seen buffalo and they went out to look for them.

The next day about noon more enemies came down and attacked the Pawnees. They began fighting at noon and fought all the afternoon until about four o'clock. A man named Lā'hĭ kă—Wearing Horns—was killed here. In the same fight Crooked Hand had his leg broken.

---

[1] Near Fremont, Nebraska.

They camped here four days, and on the fifth moved, and started southeast and camped for the night. The next morning Sioux came down; they
could recognize them by their talk. The next day they had another fight,
which lasted all the afternoon. A Skidi chief was killed here—Lē sā tā
lĭt′ka—Dusty Chief.

The next morning they moved camp again, and about sunrise the day
after some Pawnees began to call out, saying: "The Sioux are coming down
again." There was a big crowd of enemies. They rode off toward the east
end of the camp, to try to drive off and capture the Pawnee horses, but the
horses were frightened and ran back into the camp and the Pawnees got them.
The fight began, and it must have been about noon when they killed a Kaw.
Afterward they learned that it was the Comanche Indians they were fighting,
and that with them there were some Kaws who had their heads shaved like
the Osages.

Very likely these may not have been Kaws, but Osages, for
the Osages were allies of the Comanches.

The camp moved again next morning, and went on southeast and made
a long march, for they had been much alarmed by the successive attacks of
all these different tribes. The next morning it was raining a little, and a
party of Cheyennes, Arapahoes, Comanches, and Kiowas came down. They
began fighting at eight o'clock and the fighting continued all through the
forenoon. At this time the Pawnees were very many, but the four different
tribes made a great war party. Their line of battle must have been a mile
and a half long. They fought all through the forenoon and at noon stopped
fighting for a time, but began again in the afternoon and presently someone
came down the line who was a stranger of some sort. It was Iron Shirt.

He rode one of the largest horses they had ever seen, a roan horse, and
in his hand he held a sabre. I myself, was standing near the west end of
the line and looking over saw the man coming from the east end, holding up
the sabre in his hand, riding down the front of the line going toward the
west. He rode close to where the Pawnees were, and as he passed them they
gave back a little. When he reached the end of the Pawnee line this man
did not go back the way he had come, but went around on the other side,
where his own people were and went along in front of that line very slowly,
and when he came to the other end of it he turned and made another charge
in front of the Pawnee line, just as he had done before. He had nothing
wrapped about him. He could not bend over, but sat straight up on his
horse. His head was round and partly covered up with this iron, so that his
hair could not be seen. [In other words, his long hair was under the iron shirt
and not outside of it.]

When he made the first charge down the line he did not try to run over
people. The second time he started to make a charge as he had done before.
As he was coming down the line the second time all the Pawnees on the east
end made a backward movement, because this terrible man was coming.

There was one man, however, a warrior named Carrying the Shield in Front, Ta wĭ ta da hĭ′ la sa, who did not move back. He stood there in the same place. Iron Shirt came toward him, thinking that he was going to kill Carrying the Shield in Front. Just as he came quite close to him Iron Shirt raised the hand in which he held the sabre, but just as he reached down to hit the Pawnee, Carrying the Shield in Front shot him with an arrow, and it struck Iron Shirt in the eye, and he fell off his horse in front of the Pawnee. After he was killed all the Pawnees rushed forward to where Carrying the Shield in Front was and cut Iron Shirt open. The Cheyennes made a fierce charge, trying to get their man, but they could do nothing. The Pawnees cut the shirt in small pieces and carried them away and scalped the man. The iron shirt reached to his knees and to his elbows, and covered him in front and around his neck.

Carrying the Shield in Front has long been dead, but his son, known to the Pawnees as Tom Morgan, has told me the story of his father's deed:

When Carrying the Shield in Front went out to the battle he took with him one of the sacred arrows—the white arrow. When he reached the battle-field men told him that this was the hardest day they had ever come to, and that among those who were attacking them was a man of wonderful power, whom the Pawnees could not shoot.

Carrying the Shield in Front rode out in front of the line, dismounted, and let his horse go free. After a little Alights on the Cloud came toward him, and the Pawnees called out a warning to Carrying the Shield in Front, but he said: "Let him come on, and do you move away from me so that he may come close to me. If he possesses great power I shall not kill him. If he does not possess this great power perhaps I shall kill him."

He took out his arrow and made ready to shoot, and began to pull his bow. He said to himself: "I shall let him come near to me." When Alights on the Cloud had come close, Carrying the Shield in Front was ready. He took no aim but loosed the arrow and it struck Alights on the Cloud in the right eye, and he fell from his horse.

VIII

WHEN THE POTAWATOMI HELPED THE
KIT KA HAH KI

1853

THE death of Alights on the Cloud, and of other brave and prominent men in the fight with the Pawnees, in 1852, was a great misfortune to the Cheyennes. Alights on the Cloud was kindly, generous, brave, and good-hearted—a man of great popularity. Moreover, his feats of daring, while protected by the iron shirt, had given to the people generally an impression that he possessed spiritual power—was invulnerable. His death deeply stirred the whole tribe, and at once there was talk of trying to avenge him. This was discussed in every camp, yet not until the end of the winter were efforts made to bring together the tribe for an expedition against the Pawnees.

In the spring of 1853 Little Robe,[1] according to the Northern Cheyennes, or Yellow Nose or Crow Indian,[2] according to the Southern Cheyennes, carried the pipe about to the various camps of the Cheyennes. He found the main village at the mouth of Beaver Creek on the South Platte. There a large lodge was set up as a meeting-place for each of the soldier bands. To each such place came the relations of those killed the year before to implore the soldier bands to take pity on them and to help to revenge their injuries. These mourners brought many presents to the Dog Soldiers, and it is said that each Dog Soldier received seven horses.

The messenger went also to the Burnt Thigh Sioux, Arapahoes, Kiowas, and Apaches, and offered them the pipe trying to persuade these tribes to unite with the Cheyennes against the Pawnees and destroy them. The Crows also were invited to join them,

---

[1] Skī′ ō māh″, Little Robe.　　　　　　[2] Ō′ Ĭ tăn, Crow Indian.

and some Crows accepted.[1] A Cheyenne presented a fine horse to the Crow chief, who mounted it and rode about the camp singing a song in praise of the generosity of the donor. However, a little later the Crows and some of the Sioux turned back and left them.

The different tribes assembled on the headwaters of the Republican River and there the Cheyennes held their medicine-lodge. The Kit Fox Soldiers had charge of the ceremonies and were obliged to suffer as the dancers were suffering, for it is the law that the soldier society which is in charge of this ceremony must endure as the dancers endure—must go without food and drink during the period of the ceremony.

On the last day of the ceremony Wood[2] and Two Thighs,[3] chiefs of the Fox Soldier band, talked with one another about finding out where the Pawnees were.

Wood said: "Now, this is the last day of the dance; we are not far from the country of the Pawnees, and it is time for us to choose scouts and send them out to find the Pawnee camp."

Two Thighs agreed and they consulted as to whom they should choose. One of them said: "There is Mad Wolf[4] over there. He is pretty cunning; let us choose him for one."

The Fox Soldiers were sitting in a row under their shade as was the custom, and in front of the row they spread down a blanket and then Wood and Two Thighs set out to look for Mad Wolf.

It was etiquette that a man should not appear anxious to receive the honor of being chosen to go as a scout, but that when called he should hang back, declare that he did not want to go, and even resist and try to escape from those who were bringing him to the place where he was to be told of the service he must perform.

The two men found Mad Wolf and, grasping his arms, they hurried him up to the shade where the Fox Soldiers were sitting and told him to be seated on the blanket, facing the row of Fox Soldiers. They said to him: "Sit here now for a time, until we bring up those who are to sit by you."

---

[1] The treaty of 1851 was still respected, therefore, by the Crows and the Cheyennes.

[2] Ka mahk', Wood. [3] Nĭsh' i no māh'', Two Thighs.

[4] Hăhk' ŏ nĭ' or Mĭv'a wŏ nĭh'', Mad Wolf, born 1825, died 1905.

They next went after War Bonnet[1] and, finding him in his lodge, brought him up to the Fox Soldiers and made him sit down on the blanket by Mad Wolf. Then they brought Tall Bull,[2] then Starving Elk,[3] a Northern Cheyenne, and Little Wolf.[4]

Then Wood and Two Thighs consulted and said: "Now let us get Yellow Bear, of the Arapahoes, and bring him up. They did so and afterward they chose Dirt on the Nose from among the Kiowas. These seven men were sitting in a row in front of the Fox Soldiers.

When Wood had taken his place among the Fox Soldiers, he spoke to these men and said: "Now, my friends, you know what the feeling is in this camp; that we want to find the enemy. You men have been chosen for this purpose because we think that you are good men, and we want you to go ahead and to do your best. You must remember that you are not going out to count coups, nor to take scalps nor horses, but are going out to find where the enemy is, and then to bring back the news to the camp. I intend to go along with you to see that you do what you are told. You can go now and get your horses and start on down the river. I will go ahead and will stop at a certain place, where we will all meet late this afternoon."

Thus dismissed, the scouts went off to get their horses, and Wood saddled his horse and set out down the river. He travelled almost all day, but late in the afternoon went up on a hill and sat there, and as the scouts came along one by one they joined him.

Following along with the scouts were two or three young men who had not been ordered out. When they appeared Wood said: "Well, we cannot send them back; let them go along. Let us now go down to the river and take a bath and start in the cool of the evening and travel at night."

They went down to the river and all went in swimming. At this place there were great multitudes of buffalo. It was the month of June, and the bulls were fighting and grunting and running about, and many that had been in the timber and thick brush

[1] Kӑ kō yūʹĭ sĭ nĭh', War Bonnet.
[2] Hōtūʹӑ ĕ hkāʹash tӑĭt, Tall Bull.
[3] Mŏhkʹstāʹwo ūmsʹts, Starving Elk.
[4] Ohʹkŭm hkāʹkĭt, Little Wolf.

had grape-vines and branches twisted about their horns, where they had been shaking their heads in the thick brush. Tall Bull used to tell of one big bull that came out of the brush, his head all wrapped in grape-vines and dragging long strings of them behind him. He charged the Cheyennes and scattered them.

After the Cheyennes had finished their bath, Tall Bull mounted his horse and rode out a little way into the timber to a herd of buffalo coming down to water and killed a fat cow. They cut out the choice pieces and tied them on their horses, and Wood said: "We will travel along and stop a little further down the stream and roast the meat." Not long afterward they stopped and ate and then travelled on through most of the night, and then stopped again and lay down to rest for a while, but before morning went on again and travelled through the day until afternoon. Then as they were going along some one saw wolves running away from a place on the prairie and riding up there they found the freshly killed carcass of a buffalo and in it an arrow which they recognized as Pawnee. Then as they looked about under the hill and down the valley they could see, scattered here and there, carcasses and skeletons where many buffalo had been killed.

Presently, Tall Bull and War Bonnet rode up to the top of the hill and peered over, and when they returned to those who were gathered about the buffalo carcass, looking at it and at the arrow, they said: "We saw two or three persons going over that hill over there; probably the camp is down in the valley below it."

"Very well," said Wood, "we have done what we came to do; it is not necessary to go farther. Look at these fresh carcasses all about us. Let us now return to the village and report."

They rode off a little way out of sight of the place and stopped by a hill to rest. When they stopped, Yellow Bear, the Arapaho, who was a Dog Soldier of the Arapahoes, got on his horse and began to ride around in a circle, singing his war songs and saying that they ought not now to go back to the village without taking a scalp to show, but Wood went up to him and caught hold of his horse and stopped it and said: "My friend, we came out to find the enemy and then to go back and report to the village. We did not come out to take scalps nor to count coups. Let us do what we came to do and nothing else." They set out for the camp and rode all night, stopping just before daylight to lie down and take a little rest, but not unsaddling their horses. Then they went on again.

About noon Yellow Bear asked them if they were hungry, and when they said they were, he replied: "I will go down then and kill a cow." He did so, and they went to the stream and there ate.

Along about the middle of the afternoon, as they were riding fast toward the village, a young man who had been out hunting met them, and they sent him ahead as a messenger to notify the Cheyenne camp that they were coming. He went ahead and when he reached the camp the scouts from their position on the prairie saw people running about, gathering up their horses; a big dust was rising.

Wood said to War Bonnet: "You go on now and notify the camp and let the others follow you. I will come last and give them the news." So the seven scouts rode on in single file, War Bonnet in the lead and Wood far behind. As they rode, they howled now and then like wolves, and then stopped and turned their heads from side to side.

Meantime in the camp there was great bustle and preparation. Men were throwing the saddles on their horses; getting out their shields; painting their faces; arranging their war medicines; and in the middle of the camp circle heaping up the great pile of buffalo-chips on which coup was to be counted. By the time the scouts had come near to the camp many of the young men had mounted their horses and were riding about singing their war songs, tossing up their shields in the air, and preparing to count coup on the pile of buffalo-chips, while the women and children stood at one side looking on.

When War Bonnet reached the camp, the chiefs asked him what news he brought, and he replied: "My friend, who is coming behind, will tell you that;" and he and the other scouts rode around behind the chiefs and formed in line. Then Wood came in and reported just what they had seen and done.

Soon after this the crier went about the camp calling on all the soldier societies to get together, and have a ceremonial march about the village. They must first paint their horses and array themselves as if for war, and then come together on a hill just south of the opening of the camp circle. After a time they gathered there the Crooked Lances, the Bow Strings, the Dog Soldiers, the Fox Soldiers, and the other societies.

The chief had told them which society was to lead off, and the chief of this society called out the names of two brave men, and said: "These two men are to lead." Then he called out the names of two other brave men, and said: "You two are to bring up the rear." So it was done with each society, and then the first one started off, the two men leading and the others in single file and two men bringing up the rear. A hundred yards behind them followed another society, and behind that another, and so on until all were marching. The leading society marched to the opening of the circle, then turned to the left, entered, marched around the circle behind the lodge where the arrows were kept, and the lodge where the hat was kept, keeping on until they reached the opening of the circle. They passed through that opening and, turning to the left, marched back outside of the circle. All the societies followed. All were singing their war songs and their different society songs. The women were shouting the war cry.

After they had passed around outside the circle to the point from which they started they dismounted, took off their shields and war bonnets and put them back in their cases and put the covers on their lances and, carrying these things in their arms, returned to their lodges. Before they could go into the lodges it was necessary that the sacred paint should be washed off the horses, and some old man or boy was asked to take each animal down to the stream and wash off the paint before turning him loose. It was against the custom for a horse to be turned loose while still painted with this spiritual paint. In returning to their lodges the young men did not go around and enter the opening of the circle, but passed directly through the circle of the lodges.

The next day the camp moved on down the stream, and that afternoon after camp had been made the chiefs gathered in the centre of the circle and told the crier to call out the names of certain men who that night should go out and look for the Pawnee camp. They directed him to call Tall Bull and War Bonnet, because these two had seen the enemy on the previous scout. Then they called the names of four other men, one of whom was Wolf Face. On this occasion there was no ceremony of bringing the young men up before the soldiers. Their names were called and they were ordered to go. Tall Bull and Wolf Face started in the afternoon and told the others to look for them at a certain place farther down the stream. Late in the afternoon they were joined by the others. They rode on down the stream and travelled most of the night, sleeping a little toward morning, and then starting on and travelling until the heat of the day, when they stopped.

In the afternoon they went on again and before very long came to the hill from which Tall Bull had seen the Pawnees. He took his men up there, and pointed over to where he had seen them pass out of sight. They all rode over to that hill and when they looked over it could see down below in the creek valley where a big camp had been, but now there was no camp there. They went down to the place and looked it over. It was a big camp; there were many fires. It seemed as if the Pawnees had been camped there killing buffalo for a long time. There were still many dogs in the camp. On one side was a well-beaten trail which led to another camp two hundred yards off where a number of people had been camped, not in lodges but in shelters made of willows bent over, after the fashion of a sweat-house.

To the southwest a broad trail led off over a hill to the valley of another stream beyond, and the scouts followed this trail for some distance and then stopped to rest. After a time, when the sun got low, Tall Bull said to them: "Well, come on; let us saddle up and go." They did so and followed the trail, going very slowly and cautiously. They were constantly looking and listening, always expecting to see something ahead of them. Whenever they came near the top of a hill they turned off to one side away from the trail, and lifted their heads and peeped over the hill with great care. After a time it grew dark, and they went a little faster, but still very carefully, stopping every few minutes to look and to listen, and sometimes getting off and putting their heads close to the ground to see if they could hear anything.

During one of these stops dogs were heard barking, and some one said, "Ah, there is the village," but the sound was a long way off. They went on farther, and at length heard the beating of drums. Presently they came upon a pony feeding by the trail, but they passed it by and went on, and at last saw and heard the Pawnee village which was situated between the forks of a creek.

Before they reached the stream Tall Bull said: "Let us stop here and tie our horses close together in this brush so we shall know where they are, and they will not be calling to each other. Then we will separate and go close to the camp and look into it."

They did this.   Tall Bull and Wolf Face left the others and, getting into the stream bed above the village, crept down to the camp and then raising their heads above the bank looked into it. There they saw a great fire blazing in the middle of a circle and all about the fire Pawnee men, women, and children were dancing, and off to one side they could see men standing who they knew, by the arms they carried and by their hats with feathers tied in them, were Shawnees or Delawares.   The two Cheyennes were so close to the Pawnees that they could plainly recognize their features.   After they had watched them for a little while Tall Bull and Wolf Face went back to the horses, and then the other men went down and watched the dancers.

After these men had come back Tall Bull proposed that the Cheyennes, one at a time, should put their blankets about them and enter the camp and mingle with the Pawnees.   His idea was to go into the camp and jostle and touch some of the Pawnees, and in that way to count coups, but one of the others who was with them said: "No, we had better not do that.   We were not sent here to count coups or to mingle with these people, but to find the camp.   Let us go back."

They did so, mounting their horses and striking off northwest across the country to get to the Republican River, near where the village was, for before leaving they had been told where the people would camp.   They travelled all night, and about noon next day reached the camp.

The next day the Cheyenne village moved on down the stream to another camp.   Here the women put up their lodges and erected platforms on which to keep their goods out of reach of the wolves and coyotes; and that night the whole village started for the Pawnee camp.   The men were riding ahead and the women followed, while the children were carried in travois.   That night they stopped on the divide, only a short distance from where the Pawnee camp had been seen by Tall Bull and Wolf Face.

Next morning they started and, when they had come within four or five miles of where the camp had been seen, the women and children all stopped behind a big hill, and the men rode off a little in front and began to unwrap their medicines. Then the ceremonies were gone through with. The sacred hat (ĭs′sĭ wŭn) was placed on the ground on a bed of stems of the sage, and an arrow was taken out from the arrow bundle and given to Wooden Leg, who, standing in front of the line, pointed it toward the enemy, singing the arrow song and dancing in time to the singing, and, as he sang and danced, thrusting the point of the arrow toward the enemy. As he sang and danced all the men in the lines stamped their feet in time to the song and made motions with their weapons or shields toward the enemy, in time to the motions which Wooden Leg was making with the arrow, and when Wooden Leg had finished the fourth song all the young men whooped. Then Wooden Leg walked back to the keeper of the arrows, who was Rock Forehead,[1] and passed him the arrow, feather toward him, to put back into the bundle.

Meantime Long Chin had ridden up to the keeper of the hat, and told him that he would wear it into the battle. The hat keeper gave it to him, but as Long Chin was tying the string which passed under his chin the string broke. Then Long Chin publicly pledged himself to give a woman to be passed on the prairie, and he tied the string to the hat and under his chin. Black Kettle[2] carried the arrows into the fight tied to his lance.

While these ceremonies were going on Big Head and his party, eight in all, had slipped off to one side and ridden away toward the Pawnees, intending to be the first to count a coup and take a scalp. This action, of course, was against the law and broke the medicine of the arrows and the hat, because until the ceremonies in connection with these mysteries had been completed, it was not permitted for any one to pass beyond the hat or the arrows toward the enemy.

Now the whole tribe, men first and women following, charged toward the camp which Tall Bull and Wolf Face had seen, but when they reached the place there was no camp there. The Pawnees had moved, and there was nothing to see except the ashes of their fires.

---

[1] Rock Forehead, Hō hō nāi′vĭ uhk′tăn ūhk″.
[2] Some informants contend that White Powder and not Black Kettle carried the arrows on this occasion.

The Cheyennes charged up the stream and turned about and charged back, looking everywhere for the enemy, but not finding them.

Presently men on horseback were seen coming and the Cheyennes all charged toward them, thinking that they were Pawnees, but when they got closer they saw Big Head waving a scalp, and he said to them: "The camp is right over the hill. Go slowly, for there are many of them."

The Cheyennes charged over the hill and there down in the valley saw a big camp of Pawnees. They had had warning of the coming of this great party, and all their women and children and horses were down in the stream protected by its banks, while the men were ranged along the edge of the bank to do the fighting. Some of the Pawnees had gone out early and from a high hill had seen the allied tribes coming a long way off. They had brought the news back to the camp, and the Pawnees had made ready to fight behind the breastworks formed by the bank of the stream.

The Cheyennes charged down again and again toward the Pawnees, but the Pawnees would not come out and show themselves. They fought cautiously. So the fight went on almost all day with little result, but about the middle of the afternoon the Cheyennes saw a number of men coming over the hill. The Cheyennes were getting tired now and were about ready to leave the Pawnees, when they saw these men who carried long guns, which glistened in the sun. They knew that these must be the Shawnees that had been seen in the camp by Tall Bull.

When they saw the Săvănē' coming the Kiowa said to the Cheyennes: "We know those people; wait, we will talk to them." But the Săvănē' did not wait for any talk and the first man killed was a Kiowa. The Cheyennes and their allies ran, and the Săvănē' followed them for quite a long distance. Then the Cheyennes and the others charged back and chased the Săvănē' back a little, and the Săvănē' charged and chased the Cheyennes back. The Săvănē' followed them, and at last the Cheyennes stopped and the Săvănē' stopped and two of the Săvănē' dismounted. The Cheyennes charged back and killed these two. Satanta, the Kiowa, lanced one from his horse and Good Bear, Cheyenne, shot another. Here there were killed seventeen Cheyennes and four Arapahoes, and how many of other tribes they do not know. After this the Cheyennes, who by this time were tired of fighting, drew away and left the Pawnees.

The Cheyennes do not know how the Potawatomies learned that a fight was in progress. Some think that early in the fight a Pawnee carried word to the Shawnees, who had left the Pawnee camp only that morning, that his people were surrounded. At all events, the arrival of the eastern Indians ended the battle.

While the Cheyennes believe that this camp was that of the whole Pawnee nation, as a matter of fact it was that of only one tribe, the Kĭt'kā hāhkĭ. In those days the Pawnee tribes were much larger than in later times.

Some time before this, on their way to the buffalo country, the Kĭt'kā hāhkĭ had encountered a company of hunters from the Potawatomi mission, chiefly Potawatomi but with some Sac and Foxes. These Indians, whose intercourse with the whites had been considerable, had adopted many white customs, wore civilized clothing to some extent, and were for the most part armed with excellent rifles, just those in fact which the white hunters of the prairie carried.

The plains tribes of that day did not differentiate between the various eastern tribes that had recently moved out onto the border of the prairie, but called them all by a single name, including under the common name Săvănē'[1] Delawares, Shawnees, Potawatomi, Sac and Foxes, and Iroquois.

The Potawatomi and the Pawnee camps travelled and hunted together for a long time, and had only just separated on the day when the allied tribes attacked the Kĭt'kā hāhkĭ village. The Pawnee account of the end of this battle is as follows:

The Kĭt'kā hāhkĭ, under Sky Chief, were moving up the Republican River,[2] and the Potawatomi were camped with them. All the women and children were along. The two camps had been together for some time, but one day they talked about separating and going in different directions. The Potawatomi

---

[1] Presumably an attempt to reproduce the English word Shawnee.

[2] Republican River, Cheyenne, Mā hō hē va'o he', Red Shield (Society) River; Pawnee, Kī'rā rū tāh, Manure River (kīts'ū and ŭt'ăt ū, dung; or perhaps rā'rū tah, it is filthy). So called because of the enormous numbers of buffalo which resorted to it, polluting the waters.

moved off to another stream and the Pawnees started up the river. Just as the Pawnees got to the hills they saw the enemy coming, and in a short time the enemy surrounded them.

Sky Chief owned a mule which one of the Potawatomi wanted and for which he had offered Sky Chief a horse, but at the time Sky Chief did not wish to trade. Nevertheless, after the camps had separated, Sky Chief determined that he would let the Potawatomi have his mule, and, mounting the animal, set out to overtake the Potawatomi and make the trade. He had gone some little distance when, looking back, he saw the enemy coming to attack the Kĭt'kā hāhkĭ camp. He was tempted to go back and fight for his people, but he knew he ought to keep on and go to the Potawatomi to bring aid. When he reached the Potawatomi village he said to them: "I want you to come and help my people; the enemy are killing them."

The chief of the Potawatomi chose twenty of his men who had good rifles and said: "Now, do you men come with me; we must go over there where they are fighting."

When they reached the battle-ground, he directed his men to get ready to fight, saying to them: "I want half of you to fire and then to fall back and load and let the others fire. When you shoot, shoot to kill."

The Potawatomi were accustomed to shooting from horse-back. Their horses were trained to stand still when they were shooting, and each Potawatomi carried two long sticks, the ends of which he rested on the ground, crossing the two at the top and resting his rifle in the fork thus formed. This enabled them to shoot with great accuracy, and these Săvănē' had the reputation among the whites and Indians alike of being excellent rifle-shots.

When the Cheyennes saw these other people coming they made a charge, but instead of running, ten of the Potawatomi stopped their horses and fired and each shot counted, and when the first ten men fell back the other ten came forward ready to shoot, and then the Cheyennes fell back. The Potawatomi went forward and when they reached the place where the men lay whom they had killed they opened their breasts, took out their hearts and put them in their bullet-pouches and then, thrusting their hands into the breasts of these enemies, smeared the blood across their faces.   These human hearts were to be used to make a strong medicine to be put on their bullets, so that when shooting they should not miss.   When the Cheyennes saw what they were doing they all turned and ran away.

IX

BEFORE WARS BROKE OUT

To the plains Indians of early days the terms "stranger" and "enemy" were almost synonymous. A man or a small party not recognized was likely to be attacked without warning, and cases have occurred where a war party has been attacked by another party of its own tribe and men killed and wounded before the fighters recognized each other. With the trappers, fur traders, and occasional explorers or travellers whom the Indians met in early days they were usually on friendly terms, yet sometimes collisions took place. Between 1840 and 1850 many small fights occurred. The Frapp battle,[1] about which little is known, in which the Cheyennes and Sioux were supposed to be the aggressors was one of these. Ruxton speaks of the hostility of the Arapahoes in 1846–7, and during the summer of 1847 the Kiowas, Apaches, Pawnees, and Comanches were reported to have been at war with the whites, and to have done much injury.[2] Yet there was no general movement against the invaders, and the occasional killing of white men or the running off of live stock was not the act of the tribes but of small parties of young men who, when opportunity offered, were unable to resist the temptation to capture a few animals or to count a coup.

In the winter of 1847 the Kiowas, Apaches, and Comanches endeavored to induce the Cheyennes and Arapahoes to join in a general movement against the whites, but Lieutenant-Colonel Gilpin—afterward governor of Colorado—marched two companies of cavalry into the middle of the Cheyenne and Arapaho villages and camped there.[3] They did not join the alliance.

If the tribes were not generally hostile to the white men it was not because they lacked cause of complaint against them.

---

[1] *Fremont Memoirs*, p. 113. *Stansbury*, pp. 239, 240.
[2] *Massacres of the Mountains*, p. 231.
[3] Bancroft, *History of Colorado*, p. 414.

93

Lawless white men roved over the plains, killing the game, often treating the Indians with the utmost arrogance, and bringing disease and liquor among them. It was the trader Gantt who brought their first whiskey to the Cheyennes. As they disliked its taste, he is said to have mixed sugar with it, and in this manner to have induced them to drink. In 1832 he built a post on the Arkansas,[1] possibly the one near the mouth of Fountain Creek mentioned by Dodge in 1835 as then abandoned, and traded whiskey to the Cheyennes and Arapahoes. Less than five years later the tribe was reported "a nation of drunkards,"[2] and, whether this was true or not, it is certain that the habit had taken strong hold on them.

In 1835 Colonel Dodge came to Bent's Fort and found some Mexicans camped on the south bank of the river—in Mexican territory and therefore out of reach of the United States authorities—who were trading whiskey to the Cheyennes.

It has already been said that a year or two later when the news of the killing of the company of Bow String soldiers by the Kiowas was received by the Cheyennes, Porcupine Bear, the Dog Soldier chief, while drunk stabbed Little Creek, for which deed he and his relatives were outlawed. Such tragedies were of daily occurrence during the trading season on the Platte; brothers killed their brothers in drunken rage; men mounted and raced their horses wildly over the plains, often falling and breaking their necks; the people traded everything they had—horses, weapons, clothing—for drink. Similar conditions prevailed among the Indians wherever the white trader with his alcohol had penetrated.[3]

The year 1841 was a turning-point in the history of the plains tribes, for that season the first emigrant train passed up the Platte on its way to Oregon. Hitherto the fur men had been almost the only ones who crossed the northern plains, and they were few in number; but from this year on an annually increasing swarm of emigrants poured up the Platte. The Indians, at first

[1] Sage, *Rocky Mountain Life*, 1846, pp. 247, 248.

[2] Merrill, *Nebraska Historical Society Publications*, vol. IV, p. 181. (The date is April 14, 1837.)

[3] *New Light on the Northwest, Journals of Alexander Henry and David Thompson*, by Elliot Coues. (New York, 1897.) Larpenteur, *Forty Years a Fur Trader*.

astonished, soon became alarmed and with good reason. The emigrants cut down and wasted the scant supply of wood along the road; their herds of oxen, horses, and mules gnawed the bottoms bare of grass; the buffalo were shot down and left to rot on the ground and, worse still, the herds were frightened from the country. In 1835 the Ogallala were hunting at the forks of the Platte. Ten years later, to get meat they were obliged to go to the Laramie plains and among the mountains in hostile Snake country. They went with no good will toward the emigrants who had driven away the buffalo. The Indians were in a bad temper and many of the emigrant trains that passed up the Platte met with small misadventures. Those who did not were always fearing trouble of this kind.

No sooner had they reached Oregon than they began to write home to the States. Their complaints about the Indians were printed in the newspapers; they petitioned Congress for the protection of the "emigrant road," and as early as 1845 had given all the plains tribes a thoroughly bad reputation in the East. In that year Colonel Kearny, guided by Fitzpatrick, marched up the Platte to hold talks with the Indians, and to open the road and try to make the Indians treat the white men with more consideration. He held councils with the Sioux, Cheyennes, and Arapahoes and for a time things seemed to improve. Following Kearny's trip, two posts, Fort Laramie and Fort Kearny, were established in 1849.[1] In that year along the Platte cholera carried off many Indians.

[1] Fort Kearny was on the Platte just at the upper end of Grand Island, 191 miles from Omaha and 253 miles from Atchison, Kansas; Fort Laramie on the North Platte at the mouth of Laramie River, 573 miles from Omaha and 635 miles from Atchison, Kansas. For some years before 1846 the government had been urged to establish posts to protect the Oregon trail and settlers in Oregon, and this was about to be done when the Mexican War came on. Congress was asked for permission to raise a mounted rifle regiment to do this work, and such a force was authorized, but as soon as recruited the War Department sent it to Mexico. In the meantime, in 1847 or 1848, a small company of soldiers was sent up the Missouri River and built a small post, "old Fort Kearny," on the site of the present Nebraska City. This post was abandoned late in 1848, and a new one begun by the same small body of troops at Grand Island. This new post was named Fort Kearny in the last days of 1848, and was put in actual use in the spring of 1849. It was not really garrisoned until the spring of that year. Watkins, *History of Fort Kearny*, Nebraska State Historical Society, vol. XVI, p. 227.

Meantime the condition of the tribes was constantly becoming worse. Food was harder to procure; they were often hungry, and no amount of advice makes much impression on an empty stomach. Every year the Indians' complaints against the emigrants grew more bitter, and each year the emigrants complained more loudly against the Indians.

The hostility that was thus growing up between Indians and white men was racial. To the white man an Indian was an Indian, and the white man who had been robbed or threatened by an Indian felt himself justified in taking vengeance on the next Indian that he saw, without regard to whether he had been injured by that man or by men of that tribe. In the same way if an Indian had been killed by a white man the members of his tribe were ready to revenge the injury on the next white man that came along. Thus it came about that persons innocent of any fault were constantly punished for the harm done by one of their race. The guilty never suffered. As a result of this feeling neither Indians nor white men felt that they could trust one of the opposite race, and each held the other always in suspicion.

TREATY OF 1851

In the summer of 1851 a famous council was held on Horse Creek, thirty-five miles east of Fort Laramie, with a number of plains Indian tribes to promote peace between the tribes and between Indians and white people.

This treaty, commonly called the Big treaty, is known also as the Fort Laramie treaty, the Horse Creek treaty, or the Fitzpatrick treaty.[1] It is still remembered by old Indians. There were present Sioux, Assiniboines, Gros Ventres, Crows, Shoshoni, Arikaras, Cheyennes, and Arapahoes, and perhaps some Mandans. The total number camped in the various villages was estimated at from eight to twelve thousand. Many of the tribes had never before met except in battle.

Father De Smet[2] gives a long description of the meeting and

[1] *Report Commissioner Indian Affairs*, 1851, pp. 60, 70. D. D. Mitchell, Superintendent of Indian Affairs in the north, and Thomas Fitzpatrick—of the broken hand—then Indian Agent for the Upper Platte Agency, report on the matter with extreme brevity.

[2] *History of Western Missions and Missionaries*, by Rev. P. J. De Smet, S. J., p. 101 *et seq.* (New York, P. J. Kennedy.)

emphasizes its harmony, and the union and amity that appeared to exist among tribes that had long been hostile. He speaks with enthusiasm of the politeness and evidences of kindly feeling to each other shown by the Indians during their stay in the camp, and closes with bright anticipations of an era of peace on the plains.[1]

FIGHT WITH THE SAC AND FOX, 1854

In the battle with the Pawnees in the summer of 1853 a number of Cheyennes, Kiowas, and Comanches were killed. This led to a war journey by the allied tribes in 1854, directed against the eastern or immigrant Indians who had been moved west by the government.

According to Kiowa accounts the expedition was undertaken at the request of a Kiowa to seek revenge for a brother killed by the Pawnees the year before. The Cheyennes had injuries of their own to revenge, and so had the Comanches, for the battle of 1853 had inflicted severe losses on all three of the allied tribes. Cheyenne accounts indicate that the expedition was directed chiefly against the eastern Indians, no doubt in revenge for the assistance which they had given the Pawnees in the battle of 1853.

The Cheyennes say that in that fight two important men, a Kiowa and a Comanche, had fallen, and their tribesmen felt that these deaths must be avenged. Soon after the Pawnee fight, therefore, the Kiowa and Comanche chiefs, carrying the pipe, set out to ask the assistance of their friends in avenging their dead. They came to the Cheyenne camp and rode into it, wailing and mourning, and sat down in the centre of the camp circle. A large council lodge was erected, in which the visiting chiefs were received and a feast was set before them. The Cheyenne chiefs and head men sat around the inside of the lodge in a circle, and the Comanches and Kiowas passed around the circle and offered the pipe to the lips of each Cheyenne. If the man to whom the pipe was offered accepted it and drew four whiffs he promised by this act to aid the visitors in their expedition. Old Whirlwind smoked the pipe, as did also his father-in-law, Bad Face,[2] and a

---

[1] *Indian Land Cessions in the United States*, Royce, B. A. Eth., 18th Ann., p. 786. The treaties were not ratified by Congress.

[2] Ugly Face, also known as Old Bark. His real name was Feathered Bear.

number of others. After the pipe had been offered the feast was eaten. Many men among the Cheyennes declined to smoke, and the number who joined the war party was not large. The Kiowas and Comanches went about from camp to camp of the tribes with which they were on friendly terms offering the pipe and asking for help. Of the Arapahoes, Little Raven, Bull, and Storm smoked. Sioux, Apaches, and Osages also smoked, and the next summer (1854) all these people came together in one big village and set out to avenge the losses of the year before.

Agent Whitfield[1] reported:

> The Indians were encamped on Pawnee Fork, at the crossing of the Santa Fe Road, where they were collected in larger numbers than have ever been known to assemble on the Arkansas River before. Old traders estimate the number at from twelve to fifteen hundred lodges, and the horses and mules at from forty to fifty thousand head. The entire Kiowa and Prairie Comanche were there; several hundred of Texas or Woods Comanche had come over; the Prairie Apache, one band of Arrapahoe, and two bands of Cheyenne, and the Osages composed the grand council. They had met for the purpose of forming their war-party in order, as they in their strong language said, to *"wipe out"* all frontier Indians they could find on the plains.

At some place near the Kansas River they met about one hundred Sac and Fox Indians, and the fight commenced, but the combined forces were compelled to retreat, leaving their dead on the field. They reported their loss at about sixteen killed and one hundred wounded. The prairie Indians were armed with the bow and arrow, formidable at close quarters but useless at long range. The others had fine rifles. The rifle told almost every shot, either on rider or horse.

Seven tribes were engaged in this alliance—Kiowas, Comanches, Apaches, Arapahoes, Cheyennes, Osages, and Sioux. There were said to have been with them also a few Crows. If these last were present it shows that the peace of 1851—the Horse Creek treaty—was still in force between the Crows and the prairie tribes.

The allies started north, but before they had reached the Republican River, when they were not far from the place where the summer before they had fought the Pawnees, a scouting party of Prairie Apaches, led by the chief Plenty of Old Camps, one

---

[1] *Report Commissioner Indian Affairs*, 1854, p. 89.

morning came on a hunting party of less than one hundred Sac
and Fox who were proceeding to the plains in search of buffalo.
In the little skirmish which ensued Plenty of Old Camps was
shot at and his people retreated to the main body. When they
came to the other warriors and told the news the allies prepared
for battle and rode out to meet the Sac and Fox, with whom were
a few Potawatomi.

It is uncertain how large the party of Sacs was. Hewitt says
they numbered fifty. Others say not over two hundred. The
usual estimate is one hundred. The number of the prairie Indians
is no doubt much exaggerated in the printed reports, but it must
have been large.

About the year 1897 George Bent talked with an old Sac who
had been with the party of hunters. This man said that when
they saw the great force of prairie Indians coming toward them
they were much alarmed. The Sac chief ordered his men to retreat to a ridge nearby, and this move, the old man said, saved the
party from annihilation. They were hardly in position when the
mounted men charged them from every direction. The Sac
and Fox were all armed with good guns, and fought on foot, but—
except the Osages—the prairie Indians had few firearms. The
attacking party charged again and again, but were unable to get
near enough to their enemies to use effectively either their bows
or their old smooth-bore trade guns. The Sac and Fox soon saw
the advantage the superiority of their arms gave them and that,
notwithstanding the numbers of the enemy, they could keep them
at a distance. Having some idea of discipline and order, they so
handled their rifles that all the guns were never empty at the same
time. They fought much as did the Potawatomi who had come
to the assistance of the Kĭt′kā hāhkĭ the year before; they fired by
relays, and thus were able always to repel the charges made on
them.[1]

By his bravery in this fight Old Whirlwind[2] added greatly to

---

[1] The Sacs lost five men killed and four wounded, and this loss was inflicted by the Osages, who had good guns. The Sacs knew this and later
declared war on the Osages. A Sac who had lost a brother in the fight approached the Osage camp, and met two Osages, one of whom he killed and
scalped, allowing the other to return to take the news to camp.

[2] Hē vō vĭ tăs′tămi ŭtsts′, Moving Whirlwind.

his reputation. He wore a war bonnet from which nearly all the feathers were shot away, but the little stuffed hawk tied on the left front of the headpiece was untouched, and Whirlwind believed that this charm saved his life. He has more than once told me of the circumstances. "The balls," he said, "were flying thick all about me. The feathers were cut from my war bonnet, yet the hawk that was on it in front was not hit, and I was not hit. The Sacs were fighting on foot in a little hollow—a place like a buffalo wallow—and I was riding a horse and kept trying to charge up close. Afterward I wondered that I had not been killed. Hĕ′ămmă vī′hĭo and the hawk protected me."

The prairie Indians at length retreated, having lost several Kiowas and Comanches, one Apache, and two Osages. Only a few Cheyennes were engaged in the fight, and the number of Arapahoes was still smaller; in fact, it is said that the Arapahoes stood off and looked on, taking little or no part in the battle.

GRATTAN AND ASH HOLLOW, 1854–5

Fort Laramie was an important station on the Platte, and near it were various trading-posts. Near the trading-posts were usually camps of Indians—Sioux, Cheyennes, and Arapahoes.

An event in which the Sioux were chiefly concerned, yet which the Cheyennes witnessed, and which had a bearing on the whole Indian situation, was the killing of Lieutenant Grattan and his command near Bordeaux's trading-post, nine miles east of Laramie. This was followed a year later by Harney's battle north of Ash Hollow.

In 1852 things were quiet enough along the Platte, but about this time Major Hoffman, of the Sixth Infantry, wrote to headquarters remonstrating against the policy of placing a handful of troops under inexperienced officers in the heart of the Indian country. No attention was paid to this protest, and in the following year trouble occurred.

In the summer of 1853 a Minneconjou Sioux, a visitor recently from the Missouri, had fired across the river at a soldier who was in a boat. The local Indians were in no sense responsible for this. Lieutenant Fleming was sent across the river to the Indian camp to arrest this man, or others, to be held as hostages, and found nearly all the men absent. The Indians, alarmed at the invasion of the troops, fled, firing as they ran, and the troops in turn fired at them and killed three or four. The Indians were not unfriendly but simply frightened, as testified by Captain Edward Johnson, who pointed out that there were at that time out and at a distance from the fort the herd guard, a hay party, and a party at the post farm, all of whom the Indians might easily have killed. Instead of opening hostilities, however, the Indians came into the fort next day and told the commanding officer that perhaps the soldiers had done right according to their way of thinking. Nothing more was done in the matter, but the Indians felt badly about it, and complained that the white soldiers, who had been brought among them to keep the peace, had been the first to make the ground bloody.

The following year the first real fighting with the plains Indians was brought on by the inexperience and hot-headedness of a young army officer, Lieutenant Grattan, stationed at Fort Laramie. The matter is fully discussed in official papers, but the account has been given me also by William Rowland, who had married into the Cheyenne tribe and was living with them, and who then was in the Sioux camp.

Grattan, a young Irish officer, was boastful, hot-headed, and rough. As he went about the post he often abused and threatened the Indians, shaking his fist close to their faces and telling them what he would do if ever he had a chance to get at them. Grattan seemed to think that Lieutenant Fleming had greatly distinguished himself the year before, when he had led a party against the Sioux and had killed some of them, but declared that the Indians should have been punished more severely.

It happened at one time some young Cheyennes ran off a part of the horses belonging to the post interpreter, who was very unpopular with the Indians, and a party of citizens from the post pursued them, but when the Cheyennes halted and showed fight the citizens also stopped and finally returned to the fort, where they were much ridiculed by Grattan. He declared that all Indians were cowards, and that with ten soldiers he could whip the entire Cheyenne nation, while with thirty he would make all the tribes of the plains run. He was eager to show himself an Indian fighter, and persuaded the commanding officer at the post to promise that the next time there was any trouble he should be sent out to deal with the Indians.

Shortly after this a foot-sore, worn-out cow, abandoned by an emigrant, was found by a Sioux Indian, who, seeing the beast's condition and needing a piece of hide, killed the cow and skinned off so much of the hide as he required. Somewhat later the emigrant, having learned that his cow had been killed, went to the post and complained against the Indian, no doubt thinking here was a chance to make a little money or to get another animal in place of the one abandoned.[1] About the same time the Brulé chief, Bear that Scatters (apparently Bear that Scatters his Enemies) appeared at the post to report the killing of the animal. The Mormon was offered by the Indians ten dollars as pay for his worn-out beast, but demanded twenty-five dollars, and this was refused. The Indian who had shot the animal was not a Brulé but a Minneconjou. Bear that Scatters requested Lieutenant Fleming, who was in temporary command at the fort, to send some soldiers after this Indian, for he felt sure that he could persuade the man to surrender, or could induce his people to give the man up. Fleming seems to have considered the matter of no importance and refused to send for the Indian, saying that he would wait until the Indian agent arrived and would lay the complaint before him.

The testimony of the post surgeon indicates that the killing of the cow would have been overlooked but for the importunities of Grattan, who begged so hard to be allowed to go and get the Indian that Fleming yielded and sent Grattan with a detachment to make the arrest. Fleming limited Grattan's orders, directing that the Indian was to be taken only "if practicable and without unnecessary risks."

When Grattan received the orders he became violently excited, so much so that some spectators thought him drunk. He was ordered to take twenty men, but instead of taking the detail he called for volunteers "for dangerous service" and took thirty men, with a sergeant and corporal, and two howitzers. Declaring his purpose to "conquer or die," he left the post about three

---

[1] *Senate Documents*, 34th Congress, 1st and 2d Sessions, vol. XIV, p. 1 of Document 91; see also *House Executive Document*, No. 63, 33d Congress, 2d Session.

o'clock in the afternoon and marched down the valley toward the Indian village.

The troops moved on to the Sioux camps, about nine miles east of Fort Laramie. One of these, west of Bordeaux's buildings, was of Ogallalas, and the other, between Bordeaux's and the river, was of about one hundred lodges of Brulés, among which were twenty lodges of Minneconjous. In one of these last was the man who had killed the cow. Grattan marched his men into the open space in the camp, and to within about sixty yards of the Minneconjou lodges.

When the troops halted, they formed in line—the two howitzers in the centre and the soldiers on either side. The men, wholly unconcerned, threw themselves on the ground and sat there while for the better part of an hour Grattan talked with the chiefs. Of what passed between them only the Indian version can be had. Both the Brulé chief and Man Afraid of his Horses[1] are said to have urged Grattan to return to the post and leave the matter until the coming of the agent. The Brulé chief even offered to give a mule if the lieutenant would postpone the matter until the agent's arrival. Grattan refused these requests. Man Afraid of his Horses made great efforts for peace.

At length the men who were looking on from the trader's house saw the soldiers rise to their feet and bring their guns down as if to fire; then a shot sounded, and the fight began. At the first volley Bear that Scatters was wounded in three places. The soldiers fired first.

The soldiers were at once fired on by the Indians, and began to retreat, but almost immediately met the Ogallalas coming from the other camp, and all fell before the arrows. As soon as they had killed the soldiers, the Indians made a rush for the trading-houses, no doubt intending to plunder them, but the chief stopped them and protected the white people there. The wounded chief came to the trader's store and there placed a guard of Indian soldiers, but all night long Indians were coming and demanding goods from Bordeaux, who feared to refuse them anything. Mean-

---

[1] The proper interpretation of this name is "they fear his horses," meaning that his enemies are frightened when they see even his horses, with the implication that if they saw the man himself they would be still more frightened. This man was the real chief of the Ogallalas as late as 1873.

time the women had taken down the lodges and moved across the river.

Bordeaux, who for years had been a trader at Laramie,[1] was thus robbed by wholesale. In the East he was also called liar and renegade, because he expressed the opinion that the Indians had been forced to fight by Grattan's conduct. Bear that Scatters, who among the white men bore the reputation of a good old man, was abused as being the chief figure in this "massacre." He had always acted in the most friendly way toward the whites; had returned property taken from them, to the indignation of some of his own people, and on two or three occasions had killed men of his own band as punishment for injury to the whites. Now, however, the newspapers in the East declared that he had led Grattan into an ambuscade, and that the whole affair was a plot to entrap and kill the soldiers. Not long after this the chief died of his wounds.

The War Department declined to accept the testimony of the officers of the post that Grattan was responsible for the fight, and the Eastern public refused to believe that the Indians had been attacked. People in the East insisted that the Indians had treacherously massacred a gallant young officer and his men, and that the murderers must be severely punished.

Colonel William S. Harney was chosen to lead a punitive expedition against the supposedly hostile Indians, and marched from Fort Leavenworth up the Platte in the late summer of 1855. Near the forks of the Platte, September 2, he learned that a part of the Brulés, under Little Thunder, were camping on the Blue River just north of the North Platte. On September 3 Colonel Harney sent his cavalry to take a position in the rear of the Indian camp to cut off their retreat, and shortly after, with the infantry, he marched up the valley of the Blue. Colonel Cooke was in command of the cavalry and was guided by Tesson,[2] an old trapper. Marching on the high prairie, he several times started to go down into the valley, but on each occasion saw that the camp extended farther up the creek, and it was not until about sunrise that he

[1] Parkman mentions him as the chief trader in 1846.

[2] Very likely the same Tesson who in 1844 was sent away from Bent's Fort by Colonel St. Vrain because he had shot at a negro blacksmith who had been one of a party that had shivareed Tesson the night before. (Boggs's manuscript, Colorado State Historical Association, Denver, Colorado.)

reached the upper end of the camp, estimated to be four miles long, and hid his forces in a dry gully, from which point he afterward made his charge.

When the infantry marching up the valley came in sight of the Sioux camp the Indians had already taken the alarm, had pulled down their lodges, and were moving off up the valley. They were persuaded to stop, and Little Thunder came down to talk with Harney. He threatened the Brulé chief and demanded that the slayers of Grattan be given up. The chief, unable to comply with the demand, went back to his people and told them that the troops were about to attack them. About this time a movement among the Indians indicated that the cavalry had been discovered, and Harney moved forward to the attack. The Indians were on a bluff at the right of the valley, and when charged by the troops they were driven beyond it, while the cavalry charged on them from up the stream. The Indians fled without resistance. They received the fire of the infantry at long range from the right, while the cavalry charged them on the left and rear. The chase was kept up for five or six miles. Numbers of the Indians were killed, and the rest were scattered. Colonel Harney reported eighty-six Indians killed, five wounded, and about seventy women and children captured. Some horses and mules and a great amount of Indian property were taken.

This fight near Ash Hollow is a good example of the way in which Indians have often been treated by the troops, acting, of course, under orders from Washington. The individuals or groups of Indians who have committed depredations run away, while the friendly camps, easily found, are attacked by troops, and their inhabitants slaughtered. Several considerable killings of Indians, where this precise thing has taken place, readily suggest themselves. Such are Ash Hollow, 1855; Sand Creek, 1864; Battle of the Washita, 1868; and the Baker fight on the Marias River in 1870. In all these attacks on friendly villages the women and children, least able to get away, have been the chief sufferers. In the reports of Indians killed they are usually counted full-fledged warriors.

Harney's fight was very popular in the East, and General Scott approved his first report. Dunn says, however,[1] that Gen-

[1] *Massacres of the Mountains*, p. 236.

eral Scott "objected seriously to the killing of women and children that had occurred at Ash Hollow."

The blow struck terror to the Sioux, and when after the fight Harney moved to Laramie and again demanded the "murderers" of Grattan, five Indians dressed in their war clothes rode up to the post singing their death songs. These were Red Leaf and Long Chin, two brothers of the dead Bear that Scatters, and Spotted Tail, together with Red Plume and Spotted Elk, the last two coming in as hostages for two of the "murderers," one of whom was too ill to come, while the other had fled. These seven men who had surrendered, with their women, were sent to Fort Leavenworth.

In March, 1856, Harney held a council with the Sioux at Fort Pierre. They were very humble and agreed to give up the man who had killed the cow, and to make reparation for the destruction of property. The Cheyennes, however, were not humble. They had committed some trifling depredations, and Harney seemed to feel that they should be punished as well as the Sioux and recommended that an expedition be sent against them in the spring. Before anything was done the border ruffian troubles in Kansas gave the troops something else to think of for the time, and the Cheyennes escaped.

X

THE SUMNER CAMPAIGN

1857

WHAT was really the first collision between the Cheyenne tribe and United States troops took place the year following General Harney's attack on the Sioux camp at Ash Hollow.

In the spring of 1856 a camp of Cheyennes near the Upper Platte Bridge was reported to have four horses said to belong to white men. They were strays picked up on the prairie. The commanding officer of the post sent word to the Cheyennes that these horses should be brought in, and three or four of the Indians went to the fort to talk about this. They were told that the horses must be given up, but that their white owners would pay the Indians a reward for finding and caring for the stock. It was understood that the Indians agreed to return the horses, but only three of them were brought in, for it was declared that the fourth had not been found at the place nor at the time described by the owner, and that it had been a long time in the Indian camp. The man who had it refused to give it up. This was Two Tails, afterward and at the time of his death known as Little Wolf,[1] who in the Dull Knife outbreak, in 1878, led the party of Cheyennes north to the Powder River country. The Cheyennes to-day say that the people generally wished Little Wolf to bring in this horse, and even talked about seizing Little Wolf and giving him up to the soldiers because they feared that his obstinacy would bring about war. Little Wolf, however, was firm in his refusal to give up the horse, and even as early as this he was a man of so much influence that the Indians could do nothing.

When the Indians refused to give up the fourth horse the commanding officer ordered certain Cheyennes to be arrested. One was caught by the guard and the others broke away and fled.

[1] Coyote—Oh′kŏm.

The printed reports say that the soldiers firing upon them killed one.[1] The man arrested was Wolf Fire. He was held in custody for a long time, and finally died in the guard-house, although it was perfectly well understood by soldiers and Indians alike that he had committed no offense whatever. On his arrest Wolf Fire's relations, men, women and children, fled to the Black Hills, leaving their lodges standing, and the troops confiscated all the possessions they had left behind. The following night an old trapper, named Ganier, who was returning to the fort, met the Cheyennes, who killed him. The remaining Cheyennes fled southward and joined the Southern Cheyennes, on the Arkansas. They moved up to its head, and then over to the Smoky Hill River,[2] and then to the Solomon River.[3]

Toward the end of August, 1856, a considerable war party of Cheyennes who had started north against the Pawnees camped in the bottom of the Platte River, on Grand Island, just below Fort Kearny, not far from the wagon-road. As they were resting there during the day, some of the young men saw approaching the mail wagon coming up the river on its way to Fort Kearny. Among the Indians was a young half-breed to whom some of his companions said: "You are a white man; go out and speak to the driver and ask him to give you a piece of tobacco. We have nothing to smoke, and perhaps he will give you something." With a companion the young half-breed walked out to the road and when the wagon drew near made signs to the driver, asking him to stop. The driver, however, was frightened by the appearance of the Indians and whipped up his animals and, drawing a pistol, fired at the Indians. They jumped to one side and, angered by the demonstration, shot arrows at the driver and wounded him in the arm. Meantime the leaders of the Cheyenne party, hearing the shot, jumped on their horses and rode out to see what the matter was and, finding that the young men had shot at the driver, rode after them, quirted them severely, and drove them back to the camp. The day was rainy and cold, and the Indians did not continue their journey but sat about, huddled up in their buffalo robes.

[1] *Report Commissioner Indian Affairs for* 1856, pp. 87 and 100.
[2] Grove of Timber Creek, Mănō′iyō′hē′.
[3] Turkey Creek, Măhkī′nē ōhē.

The next morning they saw troops coming toward them and wondered where they were going, but the troops charged straight at them, and the Indians, seeing that they were coming with hostile intent, dropped their bows, arrows, and robes and ran away on foot, leaving their horses. Six of the Indians were killed. This is the story told me by William Rowland, who was in the Cheyenne camp at the time and heard of the matter at first hand immediately after it happened.

The report of Captain G. H. Stewart, of the First Cavalry, who commanded the troops, forty-one in number, states that ten Indians were left dead on the field, and that eight or ten were badly wounded; that twenty-two horses and two mules were captured, and a number of saddles, shields, lances, buffalo robes, etc., were found.

He adds significantly:

I lost no men, and not a wound was received.[1]

The Indians thus attacked, driven from their camp, and robbed, crossed the river and, falling in with a small wagon-train, killed two white men and a child and took some property, thus avenging the attack made on them. This occurred on Cottonwood Fork, about thirty-three miles northeast of Fort Kearny.

On September 6 a small Mormon train was attacked and two men and a woman and child were killed, and a second woman was carried off. These acts were all the direct consequences of the blunder made by Captain Stewart in attacking the war party. Captain Stewart was quick-tempered and impetuous. His action led the Indians to believe that the government wished to fight them, and encouraged the young men to go to war and attack the defenseless trains, and finally brought about the Sumner campaign.

During this summer other Cheyenne war parties had been out searching for Pawnees, and some of them, when they failed to find the enemy, turned about, went up the Platte River, and stopped at Fort Kearny. They were invited in to see the commanding officer, who told them nothing about the killing of the six Cheyennes but said that there had been fighting up above, and then

[1] *Kansas Historical Collections*, vol. IV, p. 491.

brought out two arrows and put them on the table and asked them to what tribe these arrows belonged. The Cheyennes at once identified them as Sioux arrows. The commanding officer then asked: "Are there any Sioux among you?" The Cheyennes pointed out a Sioux sitting there, and when he was asked about the arrows he agreed that they were Sioux arrows.

A little later some of the young men who were present, looking out of the window, saw half a dozen soldiers approaching the building, and most of the Cheyennes, fearing trouble, got up and went out. Three men, Big Head, afterward a chief of the Cheyennes, Good Bear, living in 1914, Black Hairy Dog, afterward keeper of the medicine arrows, and the Sioux remained, and presently the guard entered and arrested the Sioux and took him out to be put in irons. Meantime the young men who had gone out of the office had run to their camp, mounted their horses and returned, and now called to the Cheyennes who were still in the post to come out and run away. The three men pushed aside the guard and ran out, and the guard fired at them. Big Head, being the last of the three, was hit by several bullets. The Cheyennes were helped on horses and rode away. The Sioux, who was being shackled with a ball and chain, also broke from his captors and ran out, carrying the ball in his hand, and was helped on a horse and escaped. Meantime the soldiers had been saddling their horses and rode down to the Cheyenne camp and there captured thirteen Cheyenne horses and drove them to the corral. After Big Head had gone a little way his companions helped him off with his coat and threw it on the ground, where it remained. It was covered with blood. The Cheyennes then went off to their main village.

A few days later another Cheyenne war party was journeying up the river toward the fort, but before reaching it they met a man named Heath, who had been the sutler at Fort Atkinson and was now sutler at Fort Kearny. He had a brother who later was a general in the Confederate army. Heath told them something of what had happened at the post, and advised them not to go there as they might get into trouble. Some of the young men, however, rode up near the post and found Big Head's coat and later saw, feeding with the government herd, horses recognized as Cheyenne horses belonging to Big Head's party. They made a charge on the herd and ran off the thirteen horses that the troops had captured from the Cheyennes but did not take any of the government animals.

During his absence Big Head had been made a chief, and some time after his return he requested the Cheyennes not to pay any regard to the injury that had been done him, but to ignore the whole matter.

In the autumn the Cheyennes, at the call of Colonel William Bent, went in to the new fort to receive their annuities, and there was no further trouble with the troops until the following July, 1857, when they were attacked by Colonel E. V. Sumner. The Southern Cheyennes declare that any depredations committed during the latter part of 1856 and the early part of 1857 were done by Sioux or Northern Cheyennes. They know nothing about them.

In September and October, 1856, Agent Thomas S. Twiss,[1] writing from Dripp's trading-post, then the Indian agency of the Upper Platte, explained at some length the dispute about the four horses which resulted in the killing of one Indian, the capture and subsequent death as a prisoner of Wolf Fire, and the death at the hands of the Indians of the old trapper Ganier and the attack on the mail rider and subsequent attacks on emigrant-trains. The delegation of Cheyennes who talked with the agent expressed deep regret at what had taken place, but said that they could not control the war party "when they saw their friends killed by the soldiers after they had thrown down their bows and arrows and begged for life."

The agent reported later: "The Cheyennes are perfectly quiet and peaceable and entirely within my control, and obedient to my authority." He then tells of the giving up to a surveying party of the white woman who had been captured, and complains with some bitterness of the obstacles thrown in his path by the military authorities.

After their troubles on the Platte all the Cheyennes, Northern and Southern, except the small camp of Wolf Fire's relations,

[1] *Report of Commissioner of Indian Affairs for* 1856, p. 87 *et seq.* Thomas S. Twiss—admitted 1822—graduated at West Point, second in his class, July 1, 1826, and was promoted brevet second lieutenant, engineers. Resigned 1829. Ware saw him in 1864.

gathered on the Solomon River, where they spent the winter. The people were uneasy and felt that they were not safe. It seemed to them that the white people wished to fight them, and many of those whose relations had been killed were angered by the injuries done to the tribe. Criers kept haranguing the camp telling what had happened, and the Indians talked much about these difficulties. On the whole, there was a growing feeling of injury and hostility and a disposition to fight back.

In the camp there were two medicine men who believed that in case war came they had the power to give the victory to their own people, and they persuaded the Cheyennes that they could do this. They were Ice, now White Bull,[1] and Dark,[2] long since dead. These two men were to use their spiritual power against the whites. One informant says that it was believed that if they made certain motions toward the enemy, the enemy would all fall dead. Another understood that their power would be used to check the balls coming from the white men's guns, so that the balls would drop harmless from the muzzles.

A council was held to consider the question of fighting the white men, and certain ceremonies were performed. Then the camp separated, the Northern people moving northward, and the Southern people to the south. After the northern section of the tribe had proceeded north for a few days they came upon some soldiers, and when they saw them did not stop to meet them, but ran away south and overtook the Southern people. Their report seemed to show that there must be fighting, and when the warm weather came the tribe set out to meet the soldiers and destroy them.

In the spring of 1857 Colonel E. V. Sumner left Fort Leavenworth with six troops of the old First Cavalry—now Fourth Cavalry—and three companies of infantry. Soon after starting the command divided but met again on the South Platte, July 4.

A little later Sumner was informed that the Indians were out "in force" intending "to resist." He left his wagons on the South Platte and started with pack-animals to look for the Indians.

---

[1] White Bull, Ho tŭá hwō′kō mǎ ĭs. He was not then living in the north.
[2] Dark, Āh nō kĭt′.

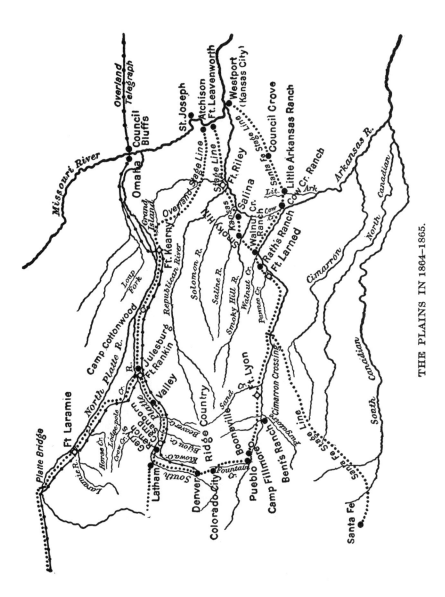

THE PLAINS IN 1864-1865.

He struck the trail July 24, and on the 29th overtook them. His report, which is extremely short and lacking in detail, says:

On the 29th of July, while pursuing the Cheyennes down Solomon's Fork of the Kansas, we suddenly came upon a large body of them drawn up in battle array, with their left resting upon the stream and their right covered by a bluff. . . . I think there were about three hundred. The cavalry was about three miles in advance of the infantry, and the six companies of the 1st regiment of Cavalry were marching in three columns. I immediately brought them into line and, without halting, detached the two flank companies at a gallop to turn their flanks (a movement they were evidently preparing to make against our right) and we continued to march steadily upon them. The Indians were all mounted and well armed; many of them had rifles and revolvers, and they stood with remarkable boldness until we charged and were nearly upon them, when they broke in all directions, and we pursued them seven miles. Their horses were fresh and very fleet, and it was impossible to overtake many of them.

There were but nine Indians killed in the pursuit, but there must have been a great number wounded. I had two men killed, and Lieutenant J. E. B. Stuart and eight men wounded.[1]

This charge was made with the sabre, perhaps the only occasion on which a large body of troops charged Indians with the sabre.

To this meagre account Agent Robert C. Miller,[2] who for some time travelled with Sumner, and undoubtedly often talked over the battle with him, adds:

The Cheyennes, before they went into battle with the troops, under the direction of their great medicine man, had selected a spot on the Smoky Hill, near a small and beautiful lake, in which they had but to dip their hands when the victory over the troops would be an easy one. So their medicine man told them, and they had but to hold up their hands and the balls would roll from the muzzles of the soldiers' guns, harmless, to their feet. Acting under this delusion, when Colonel Sumner came upon them with his command he found them drawn up in regular line of battle, well mounted, and moving forward to the music of their war song with as firm a tread as well-disciplined troops, expecting, no doubt, to receive the harmless fire of the soldiers and achieve an easy victory. But the charm was broken when the command was given by Colonel Sumner to charge with sabres, for they broke and fled in the wildest confusion, being completely routed. They lost, killed upon the field, nine of their principal men, and many more must have died from the effects of their wounds, as the bodies of several were found on the route of their flight.

[1] Brackett's *History of the U. S. Cavalry*, p. 175.
[2] *Report of Commissioner of Indian Affairs*, 1857, p. 141.

On the other hand, the Cheyennes declare that four Indians were killed. These were Coyote Ear, Yellow Shirt, Carries the Otter, and Black Bear. Coyote Ear was a brother of She Bear, now living, and the father-in-law of George Bent. Carries the Otter was the father of the well-known Two Moons. It is quite true, as Agent Miller declares, that the charge with the sabres wholly disconcerted the Cheyennes, who became panic-stricken, did not attempt to fight, and ran away as hard as they could. Sumner was somewhat criticised in military circles for the use of the sabre, for it was thought that had firearms been used many more Indians would have been killed.

At the camp—according to Cheyenne information—the Indians left their lodges standing and moved off with packs, going south of the Arkansas River, where they met the Kiowas, Apaches, Comanches, and a few Arapahoes. The troops followed the trail of the fleeing Indians, burned the abandoned lodges, and then marched up the Arkansas to Bent's Fort, where Sumner seized the Cheyenne annuities. Most of the goods he took for the use of his command, but a small quantity was distributed among the friendly Indians. Sumner now marched back down the river, intending to attack the Cheyennes again; but a little later, while on Walnut Creek, Sumner received orders to break up the expedition and send four companies of cavalry and three of infantry to join the Mormon expedition.

Percival G. Lowe, wagon-master of the expedition, was sent with Sumner's wagons to Fort Laramie. He gives a detailed account of the march thither, and his return to the South Platte and of his sojourn there, in his very interesting book.[1]

An interesting account of the Sumner campaign, which gives a far better notion of it than the brief reports by Sumner and Miller, was written by R. M. Peck, a private soldier of the First Cavalry, who served with that regiment on the plains from 1856 to 1861.[2]

After describing the two commands and their purposes and the planned routes, and adding that they had with them four mountain howitzers, Mr. Peck goes on to say that Sedgwick left Fort Leavenworth on the 18th of May and travelled westward. At the big

[1] *Five Years a Dragoon, and Other Adventures on the Great Plains.* (Kansas City, 1906.)

[2] *Kansas State Historical Collections*, vol. VIII, p. 484 *et seq.*, 1903–4.

bend of the Arkansas the command, with its beef-herd and mule-trains, was threatened by a stampeding herd of buffalo which swept down on them. The situation was critical, and Major Sedgwick, who had not had much experience on the plains, did not know what to do, and turned the command over to Captain Sturgis. The wagon-train was corralled, the beef-herd driven into the enclosure, and the troops opened fire on the approaching herd, splitting it, so that the two branches passed them on either side. It took this herd of buffalo about half an hour to pass the troops.

A little later the command passed old Fort Atkinson,[1] abandoned several years before, and after reaching the Arkansas followed up the river on the well-worn road then called the California trail. Bent's New Fort was the next place reached. It was a frontier trading-post, and "with its motley crew of retainers and hangers-on, of Mexicans, Indians, French Canadians, and white trappers and their various equipments and appurtenances, made an interesting picture of frontier life." At this time William Bent was the only survivor of the four brothers who had been engaged in the fur trade. The agency for Cheyennes, Arapahoes, Kiowas, Prairie Apaches, and Northern Comanches was at this post.

Sedgwick's command was accompanied by half a dozen Delaware scouts engaged at Leavenworth. The chief of these was named Fall Leaf, and they were efficient scouts, trailers, and hunters throughout the expedition. Sumner had with him a few Pawnees as guides and trailers.

After Sumner and Sedgwick had met at the South Platte, where they came together on the 5th of July, they prepared to start south with a pack-train and moved out July 13. The only wheeled vehicles taken were an ambulance for the use of the sick, and four mountain howitzers, which formed a four-gun battery under the command of Second Lieutenant George D. Bayard.[2]

---

[1] Fort Atkinson was built in 1850 and abandoned in 1853. It was one great sod building, and was called by the soldiers Fort Soddy, and later Fort Sodom. Fort Larned, at first called Camp Alert, was the next post built on the Arkansas, in 1859.

[2] *Life of George Dashiell Bayard*, by Samuel J. Bayard. (New York, 1874.)

In the valley of the Solomon River, July 29, the troops met with a large body of Indians which had apparently been for some time awaiting them, as many of the Indians had unsaddled and turned their horses loose to graze. No one knows how many Indians there were, but to the white troops the number seemed large, just as to the Indians the troops seemed many. A Cheyenne who took part in the battle told me that on this occasion he saw more white troops together than he had ever seen before. The battle was opened by a shot fired by one of Sumner's Indian scouts, and the troops were ordered to sling their carbines and to charge with the sabre. The Indians did not wait to receive the charge, but after one or two rather ineffectual volleys of arrows they scattered and fled. Two white men were killed and a few wounded. The troops estimated that about thirty Cheyennes were killed. One was taken alive, and after the battle the Pawnees tried to purchase this captive from Colonel Sumner, but of course he was not given up to them.

It has already been said that instead of thirty only four Cheyennes were really killed. There is no reason to suppose that the number of Cheyenne fighting men that appeared on the battle-field was over three hundred, and, notwithstanding the reference to rifles and revolvers, it is well known that at this time they had no guns except a few of the old-fashioned flintlock smoothbores, obtained from the traders. Most of the Indians were armed with bows and arrows.

That winter, 1857–8, Wolf Fire's relatives started south from the Black Hills, and when they reached Fort Laramie they were stopped and the four men arrested. The Cheyenne who had been captured by Sumner was taken to a post on the Platte described as below Fort Laramie. It was probably Fort Kearny. The four men arrested at Laramie were sent to this same post and confined there. The next spring, after the grass had grown, the five men were taken to Fort Laramie, and the same summer, after the Cheyennes had made a peace with the soldiers there, the prisoners were set free.

XI

GOLD IN COLORADO

1858–63

In the summer of 1858, according to Agent Miller, the Cheyennes and Arapahoes were in camp on the Pawnee Fork. He said that the Cheyennes were anxious for a treaty, having learned a lesson the fall before in their fight with Colonel Sumner; that they acknowledged that it was useless to fight against the white man, who would soon occupy the whole country; that the buffalo were disappearing and they wished peace and hoped that the Great Father would give them a home where they might be provided for and protected until they had been taught to cultivate the soil. This was not a new idea among the Cheyennes, for a dozen years before the famous chief, Yellow Wolf (Yellow Coyote), had expressed to Lieutenant J. W. Abert[1] the wish of many of the Cheyennes to have individual lands set apart for them and to be instructed in the art of raising crops from the ground.

The Kiowas and Comanches, on the other hand, were unwilling to treat, and Tohausen, the Kiowa chief, so well known as Mountain or Little Mountain, spoke with especial hostility to the whites.

In his report for 1859 Agent Bent said that the Cheyennes and Arapahoes wished to settle down and farm, and asked for a treaty to be held the next year by which lands might be provided for them. He said that "the Cheyenne and Arapaho tribes scrupulously maintain peaceful relations with the whites

[1] Of Yellow Wolf Abert said, August 29, 1846: "He is a man of considerable influence, of enlarged views, and gifted with more foresight than any other man in his tribe. He frequently talks of the diminishing number of his people, and the decrease of the once abundant buffalo. He says that in a few years they will become extinct; and unless the Indians wish to pass away also, they will have to adopt the habits of the white people, using such measures to produce subsistance as will render them independent of the precarious reliance afforded by the game." He proposed to pay the interpreter at Bent's Fort in mules, if he would build them a fort and teach them how to cultivate the ground and raise cattle.—(*Executive Document* 41, 30th Congress, 1st Session, p. 422.)

and with other Indian tribes, notwithstanding the many causes of irritation growing out of the occupation of the gold region and the immigration to it through their hunting grounds, which are no longer reliable as a certain source of food to them."

After the Sumner campaign all the Indians of the central plains, excepting the Kiowas, were quiet. In 1858, however, gold was discovered in Colorado and a rush of white emigrants set in up the Platte and the Arkansas and the Republican. In the spring of 1859 the travel up the Platte was very large. Bancroft in his history of Colorado states that about one hundred and fifty thousand people came up that river and up the Arkansas and the Smoky Hill, but of these only forty thousand remained. The rest, discouraged by the hardships of an unaccustomed life, and by the failure at once to find gold, came trooping back through the Indian country, frightening the game and exciting the Indians. The same year the Leavenworth and Pike's Peak Express Company[1] established a line of coaches up the Republican River through the very heart of the Cheyenne and Arapaho hunting-ground.

Richardson, who passed over this new route in May, declares that he saw not less than ten thousand gold-seekers between Leavenworth and Denver, and that thousands more were going toward the mountain by an unexplored route up the Smoky Hill.[2] In June, he found a thousand Arapahoes camped in the heart of what is now Denver.[3] They left their camps there with the women

---

[1] Root, *The Overland Stage to California*, p. 153. (Topeka, 1901.)

[2] George Bent says the Indians were greatly astonished at the sudden appearance of this swarm of gold-seekers. They thought the whites were insane. Some of them really became so, for the Cheyennes found not a few of them wandering about in the waterless country between the heads of the Smoky Hill and Republican Rivers and the foothills. Many of these men were delirious from hunger and thirst. The Cheyennes took them to their camps and fed them until their strength returned.

[3] Richardson speaks of them as being camped in Denver in 1859 and 1860, *Beyond the Mississippi*, p. 300. (Hartford, 1867.) Bancroft, *History of Colorado*, p. 458, note, speaks of them as being still camped in the town at times in 1862-3. They left their women and children in Denver and went to war against the Utes and a little later came hurrying back, declaring that the Utes were coming after them. The whites were irritated, fearing that the Arapahoes would cause a Ute attack on Denver or some other settlement. In 1863 the Agent persuaded the Cheyennes not to make war on the Utes, and a result was that the Utes came and ran off a Cheyenne herd at Fort Lyon, within sight of the garrison.

and children and went to war against the Utes. They were still there in 1860, and in 1863 were on very friendly terms with the miners.

In September, 1860, the Cheyennes and Arapahoes and Comanches met the Commissioner of Indian Affairs and other special commissioners at Bent's Fort. The Kiowas were still at war, and did not attend the council. The Indians were given medals bearing the portraits of the President. Apparently the Cheyennes there present were only the Arkansas bands. Those which ranged on the Republican and Smoky Hill still had plenty of buffalo, did not desire a treaty, and did not come in. For the making of this treaty with the Cheyennes, Arapahoes, Kiowas, and Comanches, Congress had appropriated $35,000. There was much delay in the proceedings and finally Commissioner Greenwood, being unable to remain longer, went away, leaving the treaties to be signed by the Indians later. A. G. Boone, a son of Daniel Boone and the founder of Booneville[1] on the Arkansas above Bent's, was the special agent, and in February, 1861, succeeded in inducing a part of the Indians to sign the treaties.[2] Nevertheless, many of the Cheyennes, including the Dog Soldiers, refused to sign, saying that they would never settle on a reservation.[3] In fact, much dissatisfaction over this treaty was felt by all the Indians, and when Governor Evans arrived in Colorado in 1862 the first Indians he met, a band of Arapahoes, complained about the treaty, saying that they had not been present and had received nothing for their "land and their gold." However, in his report for 1862 Evans states that he believes he can quiet the discontent if authorized to hold a council with the Indians who did not sign the treaties. One band, the Arapahoes

---

[1] Now known as Boone, a small railroad town on the north bank of the Arkansas at the mouth of Haynes Creek, about twenty miles below Pueblo, Colorado.

[2] Little Raven, the Arapaho chief, said at the council of the Little Arkansas, 1865: "Boone came out and got them (the Indians) to sign a paper, but (they) did not know what it meant. The Cheyennes signed it first, then I; but we did not know what it was. That is one reason why I want an interpreter, so that I can know what I sign."—Report Secretary of Interior, 1865–6, p. 703.

[3] "Tenure of Land Among the Indians," American Anthropologist, N. S., vol. IX, No. 1, p. 1.

above mentioned, had already promised to sign the treaty if a council was held.

In 1861 the regular troops were removed from the Indian country and sent South, and at this time, if the Indians had desired to cause trouble, they could have done so, but although the attitude of the Kiowas and Comanches was rather threatening, no serious hostilities occurred, and the Cheyennes and Arapahoes seem to have been very friendly. In August of that year Colonel Leavenworth reported from Fort Larned to the same effect, but added that all the Indians, friendly and unfriendly, had left the road to hunt. Among the whites there was little apprehension of Indian hostility, the only fear being that the Confederates might stir up the tribes to war or might even enter the country and attack the posts on the Arkansas.

That some such plan existed among the Confederates seems very probable. In May, 1861, F. J. Marshall, of Marysville, Kansas, wrote to President Jefferson Davis proposing a plan for seizing the western posts by occupying with a Confederate force the Cheyenne Pass above the forks of the Platte and operating thence to seize Forts Laramie and Wise, capture the overland mail line and cut off communication between the East and California. This scheme was indorsed by Colonel Weightman.[1]

In May, 1862, the commanding officer at Fort Larned reported that Poor (Lean) Bear, a friendly Apache chief, had informed him that young Kiowas had recently returned from the Comanche country where they had been told that the Comanches had made peace with the Texans, as the Indians called all Southerners. These young Kiowas had gone with the Comanches to a fort where they saw Indians from many tribes, and the commandant, a Confederate, received them very well, gave each one a good gun and gave to Bird Bow, their leader, a gun and a suit of uniform. He had said to them: "There are on the Arkansas two forts, Larned and Wise, belonging to your Great Father; what do you get from those forts or what do they do for the Kiowas, Comanches, Apaches, and Arapahoes? Keep nothing covered up or nothing hidden, but tell me truly in what you are benefited by those two forts."

The Kiowa leader answered that the tribes were not allowed

[1] *Official Records of Union and Confederate Armies*, vol. 1, p. 579.

about those forts but were driven off.   The commandant told the Indians that the Texans were angry and that as soon as their horses had shed their winter coats and the grass had become good he was going up on the Arkansas to capture Forts Larned and Wise.   He did not ask the Indians to help him, but said that they must not help the Americans, the Northerners.   He would be on the river July 4, and the Indians had better keep out of the way, for the Texans were angry and might hurt even the Indians.

This officer was General Albert Pike, C. S. A., the author of the song "Dixie," so popular in the South during the Civil War. On May 4, 1862, General Pike reported that he had ordered Lieutenant-Colonel Jumper, a Seminole, with his Indian soldiers to march to Fort Larned and take it.   The Kiowas and Comanches often came in to Fort Cobb and were friendly.   They had even signed treaties with Pike, who had promised to meet the two tribes and also the Indians of the reserve at Anadarko, the Agency, on July 4.

Pike's plan failed.   The Seminole forces under Jumper melted away and the men all went home.   The reserve Indians, Caddos, Delawares, Wichitas, Kichai, Wacos, Shawnees, Kickapoos, and a few Cherokees became hostile and attacked the Confederates, and the plains Indians also became hostile.   Nevertheless the authorities on the Arkansas were in constant fear of an attack from the south.   In 1863 a party of Confederate officers went north toward the Arkansas and were killed to a man by the Osages.[1]

There was thus some ground for the well-nigh universal alarm concerning a Confederate plot to bring about a rising among the plains Indians, but such alarm would have been felt only by people ignorant of Indians' ways and ways of thought.   Those better acquainted with these primitive people would have understood that there was so little cohesion among Indians and so little idea of united action that there never was any danger of a general uprising.

In the late summer of 1862 the white people on the plains and in Colorado had another fright.   About the end of August news reached the plains of the terrible Sioux uprising in Minnesota

[1] "Massacre of Confederates by Osage Indians in 1863," *Kansas Historical Collections*, vol. VIII, p. 62.

and commandants of posts, governors, and legislators at once raised a cry of alarm. Official records are full of these alarmists' reports and appeals for aid. The white people felt quite certain that a great force of savage Minnesota Sioux were marching upon them. They clamored for troops and at the same time began to regard with suspicion the Indians in their own neighborhood and to fear that the most peaceful tribes were plotting deep treachery.

In September nearly all the settlers on the Nebraska frontier were seized with the fear of an Indian attack and rushed to the town of Columbus. A war party of Yanktons and Brulés attacked the Pawnee village on the Loup Fork in Nebraska, and the Pawnee agent at once surmised that the event portended a general attack on the whole frontier. People were thoroughly frightened and the most trivial happenings were taken to be the signs of an Indian uprising.

The war party which attacked the Pawnee village killed a man—Adam Smith—who was putting up hay near what is now Genoa, and the people east of Kearny abandoned their farms and left the country. A few of them stopped in Columbus and later returned to their ranches, but many never came back. The settlers drove their cattle and hogs with them, and loaded into their wagons all their household goods. The people at Columbus built a stockade around the town, and for a time it was rumored that the Indians were coming down in great force.

In Colorado, then the greatest centre of population of all the plains country, a like fear was felt that the Indians generally would follow the example of the Minnesota Sioux.

In 1862 Governor Evans[1] reported the Cheyennes and Arapahoes restless, but declared that he had no doubt that the arrival of the Colorado volunteers, who were then under orders to return to the territory, would have the effect of keeping the Indians quiet. He had no thought of war and was busying himself with plans for settling the Indians on reservations.

In August, 1862, the Cheyennes, Arapahoes, and Apaches were induced by designing white men to attempt to seize their annuities near Fort Larned, but Colonel Leavenworth, an officer who knew Indians well, induced the tribes to leave the train alone and to move away from the road. If there had been more men

[1] *Report of Commissioner of Indian Affairs for the Year* 1862, p. 229.

like Colonel Leavenworth in the country there would have been less trouble.

The record of the years 1862–3 for the Indians of the central plains shows that, considering their grievances and the opportunities they had for taking matters into their own hands, the tribes were exceedingly peaceful and forbearing. At this time almost all the troops had been withdrawn from the frontier to fight the Confederates. There were left on the Arkansas thirty-nine men of the Second Infantry at Fort Larned, thirty-three men of the Tenth Infantry at Fort Wise, while on the Platte there were at Fort Kearny one hundred and twenty-five men of the Fourth and Sixth Cavalry and of the Eighth Kansas Cavalry, and at Fort Laramie ninety men of the Second and Tenth Infantry. Thus over all that great country there were scattered less than three hundred men at four posts. If the Indians had desired a war these petty garrisons would have been driven from the country or killed or penned up within their posts and rendered entirely useless as protectors of the travellers through the country, or for the few future settlers in it.

In the spring of 1863 S. G. Colley, the United States Indian Agent for the Upper Arkansas, declared that the Indians were quiet, though some of the young Kiowas were exacting presents from small trains that passed near their camps. At that time he declared that the Cheyennes and Arapahoes on the one side and the Utes on the other were constantly making war journeys against each other, and that when they were on the war-path they were very likely to make trouble for any one they might meet. He added that there was not a buffalo within two hundred miles of the reservation and but little game of any kind, and that starvation caused most of the depredations committed by the Indians. "Thousands and thousands of buffalo are killed by hunters during the summer and fall merely for their hides and tallow, to the displeasure and injury of the Indians." He expressed the opinion that there was some danger that the Sioux of the Upper Missouri might exert a bad influence on the Indians of the plains.

The intertribal warfare which was constantly going on between the Cheyennes and Arapahoes and the Utes was troublesome. War parties of each tribe made frequent journeys into the territory of the other tribe to take horses, and these war parties often gave trouble to the whites. A returning war party, if unsuccessful, was very likely to steal horses from the whites, and as they were often hard pushed for food when they came back from the enemy's country they often levied contribution on the white settlers on the way. Governor Evans early recognized the danger of this situation and in 1862 wisely attempted to stop these wars.[1] At first his efforts were not well received. Later the chiefs agreed that he was right, but the young men were not disposed to give up their time-honored practises, and in 1863 some depredations were charged to these war parties returning from the Ute country.

In the early summer of 1863 some soldiers returning from a visit to an Arapaho camp on the Cache la Poudre reported that these Indians said that the Sioux had come south and offered them the war pipe, but that they had refused to have anything to do with the Sioux. Evans thereupon sent a letter by Agent Loree,[2] of the Upper Platte Agency, to the Commissioner at Washington asking permission to hold a council with those Indians who had not signed the Fort Wise treaty of 1861. He appears to have believed that those bands were the ones likely to make raids, but, as already pointed out, those were the least discontented of the plains Indians, for they lived on the headwaters of the Republican and Smoky Hill where there were still buffalo.[3] If any danger was to be feared it was from the hungry Indians of the Arkansas and the Platte.

Loree returned from Washington in June authorized to hold a council with these Indians, and he, Governor Evans and Agent Colley, of the Upper Arkansas Agency, had been appointed commissioners. Evans now endeavored to collect the Indians for a council and wrote to Colley to get together the Indians on the Arkansas who had not signed the treaty. August 22 Colley reported from Fort Lyon that the Cheyennes "and Chippewas"

---

[1] *Report Commissioner Indian Affairs for* 1862, p. 230.

[2] This seems to be the proper spelling of the name, though it is written Laree, Lorry, and even Lovee.

[3] Even these bands had cause for complaint. An officer at Salina, at the mouth of Saline Fork on the Smoky Hill, 1864, reports one hundred men on Saline alone make a living by killing buffalo for hides and tallow and recommends that an order be issued forbidding such slaughter of game, as it angers the Indians.

(*sic*) refused to attend the council, saying that their horses were worn out and that there was no water in the country they would be obliged to pass through on their way to the council ground on the Arickaree Fork. Probably the real reason for their refusal was that shortly before a Cheyenne had been killed by a soldier at Fort Larned, and the Indians had been at the time very angry, but the agent had at last succeeded in pacifying the chiefs who said that they were satisfied. The Indian killed was Little Heart, son of the famous bowman, Sun Maker, and a member of the clan Ō ĭ'vĭ mănāh'. Little Heart was drunk at the time and was going from the Arapaho village to the fort to procure whiskey. The sentry who killed him declared that the Indian tried to ride over him, and it was established that this was the fact. For this reason the Cheyennes regarded the killing as in a measure justifiable. When the Cheyennes went in to Fort Larned to talk with the commander at the fort he and the agent gave them many presents to pay for the death.

Antoine Janisse,[1] a Frenchman with a Sioux wife, was directed to go in search of a band of Cheyennes said to be up near the Yellowstone, but Janisse was taken ill, and another man went in his place from whom no report was received.

---

[1] Antoine and Nicholas Janisse were born in Saint Charles County, Missouri, not far from where was born James Bordeaux, who later was chief factor of a trading-post on the North Platte belonging to the American Fur Company. This post was sold by James Bordeaux to the War Department and subsequently became the military post Fort Laramie. The Janisses and Bordeaux knew each other from childhood. They were French Creoles and spoke the French language. James Bordeaux brought Antoine and Nicholas Janisse, Sefray Iyott, and Leon Palladay to the Platte country as employees of the American Fur Company.

Both Janisses married Ogallala Sioux women at Fort Laramie, and brought up large families. Soon after his marriage Antoine Janisse, with other white men who had married Sioux women, moved with their families to a place called La Bonté, Colorado, not very far distant from Fort Collins. After the treaty of 1868 all these people returned to the Platte.

Sefray Iyott had married a sister of the Janisses at the time when the Ogallala Sioux moved from Fort Laramie to the Whetstone Agency on the Missouri River. Iyott was perhaps the man who was appointed agent for the Upper Platte in 1864–5, and who is called Jarrot in the reports. The Janisses accompanied the Ogallalas to Whetstone, and thence to Pine Ridge where they remained until they died.

Antoine, the elder of the two brothers, died on Pine Ridge Reservation about the year 1897, while Nicholas died there about 1905.

Elbridge Gerry, a trader on the South Platte, was now asked to collect the Indians ranging on the heads of the Republican and Smoky Hill Rivers. He set out early in June to find the northern bands of Southern Cheyennes—the Dog Soldiers—and other bands that lived north of the Arkansas. He spent some time searching for them, during which he travelled six hundred miles, but at last discovered one hundred and fifty lodges of Cheyennes on the head of the Smoky Hill River. The Indians were hunting buffalo and were not disposed to stop for a council. They believed that the buffalo would never become scarce and declared that they would not give up the hunter's life.[1]

However, Gerry, who understood Indians and was popular with the Dog Soldiers, succeeded in persuading a number of men to agree to meet him on Beaver Creek and to go to the council. Meeting the commissioners, he brought them to the council grounds where he left them to go to Beaver Creek to meet the chiefs who were not there, and returning to the Cheyenne village he found it increased to two hundred and forty lodges. The Indians, however, complained that they could not go to the council as their children were dying; that they would be glad to see the commissioners and desired to be on friendly terms with the whites, but they would not cede any of their lands until the whole tribe had come together to see and hear for themselves. They said that the treaty of 1861 was a swindle. White Antelope declared that he had never signed the treaty and Black Kettle was said to have denied having signed it. The killing of an Indian by a soldier at Fort Larned was resented; they said the white man's hands were dripping with blood. They denied that their country— that on the heads of the Republican and Smoky Hill—had been ceded by the treaty of 1861, and declared that they would never give it up. Gerry told them that it was likely a railroad would be built through it, but they answered that they did not care, but that the whites should never settle along the railroad. This was their country. The whites had taken that on the South Platte and they did not expect to recover it. A party of them had been up on the North Platte to hunt the winter before, but they had had a hard time and would not go up there again. The Indians spoke with great positiveness and made what they wished very

---

[1] *Report of Commissioner of Indian Affairs for the year* 1863, p. 129.

clear, but they did not speak with any hostility toward the whites. Bull Bear, the chief of the Dog Soldiers, expressed a willingness to go with Gerry if the Indians would consent, but they held a council and forbade him to go.   It is apparent that they did not trust their chiefs and that they thought that they had been bribed or cajoled into signing the treaty of 1861, parting with the lands without the knowledge of their people.

During the war of 1864 Governor Evans stated that at the time he considered the failure of the Indians to meet him in council a sign of their hostility, but his reports of 1863 show no such feeling on his part.

In his report of October 14, 1863,[1] he states that some depredations have been made during the year by "single bands and small parties" acting independently, but that now the Indians are quiet and that the northern bands, meaning those of the Republican and Smoky Hill, now denounce anyone who speaks for war.   He concludes by saying that he is confident that no hostility on the part of the tribes—Cheyennes, Arapahoes, Sioux of the Platte—need be apprehended in the future.   Agent Colley, in his annual report, dated September 30, 1863, also expresses the opinion that the Indians generally are friendly, and that only a part of the younger Kiowas are giving any trouble.   These often stop wagon-trains and demand or forcibly take goods.   He refers to the lack of buffalo and game generally anywhere near the reservation.

Affairs stood in this way when, on November 10, 1863, Robert North,[2] a white man who had been living among the Indians as one of themselves and who could neither read nor write, sub-

---

[1] *Report Commissioner Indian Affairs for* 1863, p. 121.

[2] Robert North was the "murderous white chief of an outlawed band of the Northern or Big Horn Arapahoes" (supposed to have been insane).   He had two wives, an Arapaho and a Gros Ventre, daughter of Many Bears, head chief of the Gros Ventres of the Prairie.   He was accused of assisting in the destruction of ten miners on the Yellowstone near the mouth of Powder River in 1863, and was leader of the Arapaho contingent of hostiles who assisted at the massacre of the eighty soldiers near Fort Phil Kearny in 1866. North, with his Arapaho wife, was hanged in Kansas in October, 1869, by vigilantes or robbers, while heading for the camp of the Southern Arapahoes. —"Sketches of Frontier and Indian Life on the Upper Missouri and Great Plains," by Joseph H. Taylor, in *The Renegade Chief*, pp. 224 *et seq*. (Bismarck, N. D., 1897.) [Some of these statements are certainly untrue.—G. B. G.]

mitted to Governor Evans a statement that the Comanches, Apaches, Kiowas, the northern band of Arapahoes, and all the Cheyennes, with the Sioux, had pledged one another to go to war with the whites as soon as they could procure ammunition in the spring; that the chiefs had agreed to be friendly until they procured ammunition and guns and that they had asked him, North, to join them in their attack on the whites.

This statement Evans seems to have accepted without investigation, and it apparently made him lose his head. In October he had reported that he was confident that no hostility on the part of the Indians need be apprehended in the future. A little more than a month later he sent North's statement to the Commissioner in Washington and declared his belief that the Indians contemplated war. On December 14 he wrote to Secretary of War Stanton asking for military aid, authority to call out the militia of Colorado, and requesting that troops should be stationed at proper intervals along the great routes of travel across the plains. He stated also that he had written Agent Colley, urging him to keep the Indians at peace but that the tribes could not be found; that they were far away from "their usual peaceful haunts," and could not be watched. As a matter of fact, a number of Cheyenne villages were camped on Ash Creek near Fort Larned all the winter and were constantly coming into the post.

H. T. Ketcham, Special Agent, reported for the fourth quarter of 1863 that the Indians were poor, sick, and starving on the Arkansas River, on Pawnee Fork, and on Walnut Creek. Ketcham had been sent to the plains to vaccinate the Indians, who were suffering greatly from smallpox. Wherever he appeared the Indians were glad to see him and treated him with great kindness. Many were living on the cattle of the emigrants that had died of disease. Buffalo were very scarce on the Arkansas and the Indians were bitter against certain white hunters who had been shooting down buffalo for their hides and tallow. Traders were swindling the Indians and were buying a few robes that they had for whiskey. All the Indians he saw were friendly.

The only depredation of which we have any record is that where a party of young Arapahoes ran off some horses belonging to Van Wirmer, a ranchman living east of Denver. When the chief of the party learned of this he at once took the horses away from the young men and returned them to the whites.

Governor Evans was quite ignorant of Indians and it is perhaps not strange that he was imposed on by North. He had the business of the territory of Colorado on his hands and this included the Utes of the mountains on one side and the Indians of the plains on the other. The work that he had to do was so much and so varied that little of it was done well.

XII

HARRYING THE INDIANS

1864

An examination of reports for the plains seems to show that up to March, 1864, no information had reached headquarters that the Indians were considered unfriendly. General Curtis, who had charge of the plains and of the Missouri and Kansas Indians, was occupied in fighting bushwhackers and evidently had no idea that an Indian war was impending. Some of the officers in command of posts expressed the view that the rush of men to the gold mines in the spring and summer might cause trouble, as miners were likely to be turbulent.

On the 16th of March Governor Evans wrote to Colonel Chivington, commanding the district of Colorado, that Colley reported the Indians quiet and friendly, but that they repeated former statements that the Sioux to the north intended to begin war in the spring. The Cheyennes and Arapahoes were busy fighting the Utes; the Arapahoes had quarrelled with the Kiowas, whom they charged with killing four young Arapahoes who had gone to war with the Kiowas and had not returned. On March 24 General Mitchell, commanding the district of Nebraska, reported that he had then had a talk with John Hunter, a well-known and honest interpreter, who stated that the Sioux and other tribes of the Upper Platte were friendly and were satisfied with their treatment by the government. On March 26 General Curtis wrote to Governor Evans that he should be obliged to draw every available man from the plains to fight the Confederates.

On the 9th of April, however, Colonel Chivington reported to the Adjutant-General of the Department of Kansas that a party of Cheyenne Indians had stolen one hundred and seventy-five head of cattle from the government contractors, Irwin, Jackman

& Co., from the headwaters of the Big Sandy on the Smoky Hill route of the overland stage line.[1] This report came from the herders in charge of the cattle, but when the matter was investigated a year later these herders were never mentioned; their names were not given and their testimony was never offered to prove that the Indians had committed this depredation. On the other hand, the Indians declared that the cattle were not run off. It is quite likely that they stampeded, as stock often does, and that the herders threw the blame on the Indians to excuse their own carelessness. It was never shown that the Indians had anything to do with the running off of the stock. A number of men who testified in the matter later spoke of the dispersal of the stock merely as a rumor, something that had been heard, while Kit Carson in his testimony before the Joint Commission declared that herders often let their cattle go by negligence and then when anything was lost the cry was raised that the Indians had stolen it.[2]

The Indians state that at the time when Irwin, Jackman & Co.'s herd was lost from Sand Creek the Cheyennes were encamped in the sand hills to the eastward on the headwaters of the Republican and Smoky Hill. The scattered oxen came drifting down toward their camps and some of the young men who were out after buffalo found small bunches of the cattle and drove them into the camp.

When the report was received Lieutenant George Eayre, with a detachment of troops and a howitzer, was sent out from Camp Weld, two miles from Denver, to recover the cattle. His report is very brief and merely states that he went to a branch of the Smoky Hill and there found a trail a few days old coming from the Republican. He then returned to Denver for lighter transportation and supplies, intending to follow up this trail. Evans in

---

[1] So says the official report, but Bancroft and other writers say the cattle were being wintered in Bijou Basin, which is a valley in the ridge country lying between the head of Bijou Creek and the bend of Sand Creek. This was a famous wintering-place, with fine grass and a milder climate than on the adjacent plains. Part of Chivington's command had gone into winter quarters here in October, 1864, and it was from here he began the march that ended in the Sand Creek massacre.

[2] *Report of the Joint Special Committee Appointed under Resolution of March 3, 1865*, p. 96.

his report of June 15 states that Eayre went out after the cattle and that one of his men separated from the command and was wounded by two Indians. The testimony of Private Bird of Company D, First Colorado Cavalry, says that Eayre's expedition encountered a camp of five lodges; that two of the Indians came toward them armed with rifles; that an advance guard when within sixty yards of them called out in salutation and the Indians replied. Before the two parties came together the Indians saw the command coming up at a gallop in the rear and, frightened, ran off to their village, took their women and left. Lieutenant Eayre apparently rode around a hill to head the Indians off and sent two men to capture a single Indian on the left. The Indian shot one of the men and the other ran away. The troops captured the camp, took all the dried buffalo meat, and burned the lodges.

Bird says that they pursued the Indians next day and recovered twenty of the stolen cattle and then returned to Denver. Chivington advised General Curtis, April 25, that Eayre had recovered a hundred head of cattle. If a hundred were recovered they must have been picked up on the prairie, since it is inconceivable that the Indians could have been driving off with them any such number.

Bird says that no attempt was made by Lieutenant Eayre to hold a talk with the Indians.

George Bent, speaking of Eayre's expedition, says that the command came upon Crow Chief's band encamped on the head of the Republican, where they had been through the winter hunting buffalo in entire ignorance of any trouble with the whites. One morning a man named Antelope Skin rode to the top of a nearby hill to look for buffalo and saw at a distance a column of cavalry rapidly moving down the valley toward the Cheyenne camp. He rode back to camp and warned the people to get on their horses for soldiers were coming, but the troops were so close behind him that he was obliged to turn aside and hide to avoid being overtaken. The Cheyenne horses had all been driven in earlier in the morning and the people, mounting them, ran away so that when the troops reached the lodges no Indians were in sight. They plundered the camp, destroying what they did not care to take with them. They now set out to look for some hostiles and before long came upon the trail of a small camp of Cheyennes under Raccoon,[1] which they followed toward Beaver Creek, a tributary of the Republican from the south. A party of young men belonging to this camp lingered behind and saw Eayre's troops following the trail and, hurrying forward, alarmed the camp. The people had time to pack up everything and get away, leaving their lodges standing. Eayre set fire to the lodges and returned again to Denver.

About the same time, April 12, a fight took place between Lieutenant Dunn of the First Colorado Cavalry and a small party of Cheyenne Indians on the north side of the South Platte River near Frémont's Orchard.[2] Here four of the troops were badly wounded, of whom two died later. This party consisted of some young men from the Southern Cheyennes who were on their way north to join the Northern Cheyennes. The previous summer the Crow Indians in a fight with the Northern Cheyennes had killed Brave Wolf, and the Northern Cheyennes had sent word south saying that they would mourn all winter for Brave Wolf and the following spring would send a war party against the Crows to avenge his death. If any young men of the Southern Cheyennes wished to come they would be welcome.

Accordingly, early in April, fourteen young men, all Dog Soldiers, left the camp on Beaver Creek and started north to take part in the expedition against the Crows.[3] Before they reached the South Platte they found four stray mules on the prairie and drove them along with them. That same night a white man came into their camp and claimed the mules. The Indians who had found them told him that he could have them if he would give

[1] Măts kūmh'.

[2] Frémont's Orchard, so called because Frémont saw a grove of cotton-woods on the south bank of the Platte at this place, which from a distance had the appearance of an old apple orchard. Frémont's Orchard was eighty-four miles from Denver (official distance). There is now a Union Pacific railroad town at this place which is set down on the maps as Orchard. It is sixteen miles above Bijou Creek.

[3] These Cheyennes were going north on the route used by the Kiowas in early days, before they were driven south of the Arkansas, and later by the Cheyennes. They crossed the Platte at mouth of Beaver Creek or of Bijou or of Kiowa Creek, go up Crow Creek to "Cheyenne Pass," and thence to head of Horse Creek, down it to North Platte; up Rawhide Butte Creek, over a little divide, down Old Woman's Fork to South Fork of Cheyenne River, and thence to the Black Hills or to Powder River. Cheyenne Pass is a broad, shallow valley at the head of Lodge-pole Creek, between the North and South Platte.

them a present to pay them for their trouble. The man went away to a camp of soldiers nearby and told the officer that a party of hostile Indians had driven off his animals.

Captain Sanborn sent Lieutenant Dunn, with forty men, after the Indians. Then, according to the accounts, after marching sixty miles Dunn overtook the Indians on the north side of the South Platte. He divided his men so that at last he had but fifteen with him. He met the chief, from whom he demanded the mules. The chief said that he would fight rather than give up the stock. Then the chief defied Dunn, gave a signal, and the Indians fired upon the troops.

This is the statement of Colonel Chivington, but Major Downing, Chivington's right-hand man, testified before the Joint Commission of 1865 that Dunn reached the South Platte at four o'clock in the afternoon and found the Indians crossing the river. Dunn halted to let his horses drink and Ripley, the claimant for the mules, and a soldier crossed the river and alone went among the Indians to see if Ripley's stock was in the herd. When they returned Ripley reported that they were. Dunn crossed the river and found the Indians driving their horse herd toward the bluffs. He sent Ripley and four men to stop the herd and rode forward alone to talk with the Indians. They came to meet him and he concluded that they were determined to fight, and rode back to his men, and when the Indians were within "six or eight" feet he ordered his men to dismount and disarm them. The fight lasted about an hour, when Dunn drove the Indians into the bluffs and followed them about twenty miles. This statement does not agree with Chivington's report. Both Downing and Chivington state that at the time it was not known to which tribe these Indians belonged. It is stated that bows and other arms picked up after the fight were sent to Denver to be examined by old frontiersmen so that the tribe might be

Crow Creek, which flows into the South Platte above Frémont's Orchard, heads in and near this valley, and Horse Creek, which flows into the North Platte below Laramie, also heads here. This route was a famous one, used by Kiowas before the Cheyennes moved south and used by Cheyennes from the time they moved south to live, about 1825–30, until 1865. This was evidently the route the party which Dunn attacked intended to use. They crossed the South Platte near the mouth of Kiowa Creek and struck northwest toward the head of Crow Creek and Cheyenne Pass.

identified, yet Chivington and Downing both say that the Indians talked to Dunn. If they had talked to Dunn he would have known the tribe, and, besides, it is stated that he went forward alone without an interpreter.

According to the statements of Indians who were of the party the troops charged on them without any warning. Four men were shot by the Indians, one of whom they supposed to be an officer. Of the Indians Bear Man, Wolf Coming Out, and Mad Wolf were wounded. The soldiers retreated and the Indians, thoroughly frightened, gave up their expedition to the north and returned to the camp on Beaver Creek. They took with them the head of the officer, which they had cut off, and his jacket, field-glasses, and watch.[1]

These frequent attacks coming all together and not at all understood by the Cheyennes made them uneasy and angry, and this feeling was increased by the arrival in the camp a few days later of Crow Chief and his people who had been driven from their camp on the head of the Republican by Eayre's troops.

This was the beginning of the war of 1864–5, which cost so many innocent lives. Nevertheless, during this month Gerry reported to Lieutenant Dunn that two lodges of Cheyennes had come into his place from the North Platte who did not know that there had been a fight. Three Southern Cheyennes also came in, who reported that they had camped on the head of Beaver Creek

---

[1] As the official reports mention no officer hurt in this fight and no men killed on the spot, although two were mortally wounded and died later on, it was thought for a time that the Indians were mistaken. They were right, however. Lieutenant Ware, then stationed at Camp Cottonwood, below the forks of the Platte, mentions this, although he knew nothing about the Fré-mont Orchard fight and heard nothing of any of these fights on the South Platte. He says, *Indian War of* 1864, p. 194, that on the 21st of May (he is quoting from a diary written at the time) Gilman, the Indian trader near Cottonwood, came in and said that a Brulé Sioux had visited his ranch and informed him that recently a Cheyenne chief had come up north of the Platte where he was visiting the Brulé camps, showing a cavalry *sergeant's* jacket, watch, and paraphernalia (*sic*) as trophies, and that he was starting war dances and trying to induce the Brulés to join the Cheyennes in the war. This note from Ware proves the Cheyennes' statement to be nearly correct and the official reports and stories of the officers untrue. If the troops had driven the Indians off the field and taken the wounded soldiers back to Camp Sanborn the Indians could not have cut off this sergeant's head and taken his jacket.

and that no soldiers had gone out from there. Sioux were reported camped at various points on the South Platte.

On April 20 Downing reports that the Cheyennes the day before came to a ranch on the Platte east of Camp Sanborn, took what they wanted and forced the people to abandon the place. One man was killed near this ranch, which was Morrison's, fifty-five miles east of Sanborn. Downing says that he understands that the Cheyennes discountenance these raids, but that nevertheless he shall attack any Cheyennes he meets. He instructed Gerry, who had reported the arrival of friendly Indians at his trading-store, to send them away and to warn them that he intended to attack every Cheyenne that he met, friendly or hostile.

A few days later he reported that his troops were all after the Indians, who were frightened and doing their utmost to get away, and then that the Indians had run off some more stock and had been pursued toward the Republican. May 1 he reported again to Chivington, excusing himself for not killing a Cheyenne he had captured, having apparently had an understanding with Chivington that no prisoners were to be taken. This Indian, who was half Sioux and half Cheyenne, was kept alive for the purpose of getting information from him as to the whereabouts of the Cheyenne camp. Colonel Chivington, then and afterward, as shown by his speeches, believed also in killing all Indians seen, "little and big."

A few years ago in the Denver *News* Major Downing referred to securing information about the position of the hostile camp from an Indian whom he had captured by "toasting his shins" over a small blaze.

In May Downing, guided by this Indian and by Ashcroft, a white man, moved toward Cedar Canyon, north of the South Platte, and there came upon a camp of Cheyennes. These people did not know that there had been any trouble with whites; the men were all away and only old women and children were in the camp. He surprised the village about daylight, and "ordered the men to commence killing them."[1] The fight lasted three hours, and Downing claimed that twenty-six Indians were killed and thirty wounded. His own loss was one killed and one wounded. He took no prisoners. He ran out of ammunition

[1] *Report of Joint Committee*, p. 69.

and so could not pursue the Indians. About a hundred head of stock was captured, which was distributed among "the boys." General Curtis afterward objected to this distribution of plundered property to "the boys," but the captured horses were never returned to the government.

General Curtis, who commanded the department, feared that the Confederates intended to make a raid upon the Arkansas in southeastern Colorado, and instructed Chivington to concentrate his forces near Fort Lyon, and Chivington ordered Downing to prepare to move all the troops from the Platte to the Arkansas. Thus, after having thoroughly stirred up the Indians on the plains and begun a war, the troops were all withdrawn from the roads and settlements and travellers were left unprotected and at the mercy of the enraged Indians. Chivington treated the matter lightly enough, declaring that he did not believe the Indians would long remain hostile. But this war from April, 1864, to the treaty of 1865 cost the government thirty million dollars.

Though most of the troops were withdrawn from the region of the Platte, Lieutenant Eayre, with the Independent Battery of Colorado Volunteer Artillery, remained in the field. He marched from Camp Weld, at Denver, seized wagons on the streets of Denver, loaded them with supplies, and set out to look for the Cheyennes. All these had now come together in one large camp on the Smoky Hill, while the Sioux were camped east of them on the Solomon River. Eayre appears to have passed between these two camps without discovering them or being seen by the Indians. He then moved southeast toward Fort Larned and when within a day's march of that post met a large body of Cheyennes moving north. These were those already spoken of as having been camped near the post all winter, hunting on Ash Creek and trading. News of the fight between their tribesmen and the soldiers on the Platte appears to have reached them about the middle of May, and after holding a council about this they started north. The commanding officer at Fort Larned was told by Indians there that these Cheyennes were about to join their people in the north and begin war. According to the report of the Indians, the soldiers attacked them. Evans, on the other hand, says that Eayre reported that the Indians charged him. Bird, of Eayre's command, says that no effort was made to hold a talk with the Indians. The military authorities declare that twenty-eight Indians were killed, while of the troops four were killed and three wounded.

Major T. I. McKenny, of General Curtis's staff, visited Fort Larned and talked with Eayre's men just after the fight. From Lieutenant Burton, who was in the fight, he learned that "fifteen wagons were purchased on the streets of Denver City; that Lieutenant Eayre with two mountain howitzers and eighty-four men all told went in search of the Indians with instructions to burn bridges (villages) and kill Cheyennes whenever and wherever found. . . . He wandered off out of his district and to within fifty miles of this place. The Indians, finding his command well scattered, his wagons being behind without any rear guard, artillery in the centre, one and a half miles from them, and the cavalry one mile in advance, made an attack, killing three instantly and wounding three others, one dying two days afterwards." The Colorado troops retreated to this post.

There is additional white testimony which goes to show that Eayre attacked the Indians. Major Wynkoop declares that the Indians were hunting buffalo; that a sergeant rode out from the command and met Lean Bear, the chief of the camp, and took him into the column, where he was presently killed, and that then the troops attacked the Indians. The testimony of the Indians has always been that Eayre made the attack. George Bent says that the Cheyennes came north to hunt and were at Ash Creek, twenty miles from Pawnee Fork, when soldiers were discovered by hunters, who reported the discovery at the camp. The crier announced that soldiers had been seen—soldiers with cannon. He called upon the chiefs to go out and meet the soldiers and tell them that the camp was friendly. Wolf Chief, still living, says: "A number of us mounted our horses and followed Lean Bear,[1] the chief, out to meet the soldiers. We rode up on a hill and saw the soldiers coming in four groups with cannon drawn by horses. When we saw the soldiers all formed in line, we did not want to fight. Lean Bear, the chief, told us to stay behind him while he went forward to show his papers from

[1] So called by the whites. His real name was Starving Bear—Ā'wŏn Ì nāh'kū. He was born 1813 and died 1864, and was one of those taken to Washington in 1862.

Washington which would tell the soldiers that we were friendly. The officer was in front of the line. Lean Bear had a medal on his breast given him at the time the Cheyenne chiefs visited Washington in 1862. He rode out to meet the officer, some of the Indians riding behind him. When they were twenty or thirty feet from the officer, he called out an order and the soldiers all fired together. Lean Bear and Star were shot, and fell from their ponies. As they lay on the ground the soldiers rode forward and shot them again."

The troops now opened fire with the howitzer, loaded with grape, the balls striking all about the Indians. A number of the troops and Indians were killed and they fought for some little time, until Black Kettle, who was always in favor of peace with the whites, came riding up from the camp and stopped the fight. "He told us we must not fight with the white people, so we stopped," said Wolf Chief.[1]

This evidence from the Indians, taken in connection with what the official papers say, is pretty good proof that Eayre made the attack.

The day after this fight the Cheyennes made a raid on the stage road between Fort Larned and Fort Riley. They went to a ranch on Walnut Creek, where lived a man who had a Cheyenne wife. They took his wife from him and warned him to leave the country, telling him that the soldiers had attacked them and killed their chief and that they were going to kill every white man in the country.[2] This raid was clearly made in revenge for the killing of Lean Bear, but is often spoken of as another proof that the Cheyennes were hostile and had been planning war all winter.

After the raid on the stage road a posse of citizens, gathered at Salina, went on the road toward Larned. All the stations and ranches along the road were abandoned and had been ransacked by the Indians. At Fort Larned Eayre's command was in camp, having just arrived. The posse learned from friendly Indians at

---

[1] Wolf Chief says some of the Indians were so angry that they would not listen to Black Kettle but pursued the troops several miles. This is probably the basis for the statement I have seen in some accounts that the Indians "chased Eayre's outfit into Fort Larned."

[2] *Official Records Union and Confederate Armies*, vol. 63, p. 661; also a better report in vol. 64, p. 150.

the post that the Cheyennes that Eayre had attacked were still in camp where the fight had taken place. They had lost seven Cheyennes and ten Sioux.

Soon after Eayre reached Larned the Kiowas came in. Captain Parmeter, in command at the post, had been warned by Left Hand, chief of the Arapahoes, and by other Indians, that the Kiowas intended to run off the horse herd but Parmeter paid no attention to these warnings. He is said to have been drunk on the day the Kiowas visited the post. Satanta, a Kiowa chief, came in and talked with the Captain, and the Kiowa women held a dance to amuse the soldiers, and while this was being done the Kiowa warriors quietly ran off the herd, including two hundred and forty of Eayre's horses and mules.

The next day Left Hand, the friendly Arapaho chief, came to the post bearing a white flag. He wished to assist in recovering the horses from the Kiowas, but when he approached the post Captain Parmeter ordered the soldiers to fire on the Arapahoes, who escaped without injury, but not without losing their tempers. Hitherto they had been friendly, but they now went up the Arkansas and made a raid. From their own agency at Point of Rocks they ran off twenty-eight horses, and so frightened the settlers in their neighborhood that all abandoned their homes; and while some fled to Fort Lyon the rest went up the river into the mountains.

Thus war was begun both on the Arkansas and on the Platte. Yet there were some people who thought that the Indians could be won back to friendship by judicious action. Major H. D. Wallen, of the Seventh Infantry, wrote, June 20, 1864, to the Adjutant-General "that an extensive Indian war is about to take place between the whites and the Cheyennes, Kiowas, and a band of Arapahoes. It can be prevented by prompt management."

Major T. I. McKenny, confidential staff-officer of General Curtis, sent to investigate conditions, reported: "In regard to these Indian difficulties, I think if great caution is not exercised on our part, there will be a bloody war. It should be our policy to try and conciliate them, guard our mails and trains well to prevent theft, and stop these scouting parties that are roaming over the country, who do not know one tribe from another and who will kill anything in the shape of an Indian. It will require only a few more murders on the part of our troops to unite all these warlike tribes."

The tribes were already united. Even as Major McKenny was writing this, war parties of angry Cheyennes, Arapahoes, and Sioux were setting out to clear the Platte and Arkansas roads of whites, and terrible work they made of it.

XIII

BEFORE SAND CREEK

1864

SOME months before any of this fighting had taken place the difficulties certain to arise from the invasion by the white people and the consequent killing of the game and depriving the Indians of their means of subsistence had been brought to the attention of the government at Washington.

In January, 1864, H. P. Bennett, delegate to Congress from Colorado Territory, wrote to the Commissioner of Indian Affairs as follows:

In 1861 a treaty was made with the Upper Arkansas band of Arapaho Indians by which they relinquished all their right and title to a large tract of valuable land for certain considerations, among which was one that they should be protected in the peaceful possession of their homes—on a reservation upon the Arkansas River. Three years have elapsed and they are still wanderers from their lands; the buffalo on which their forefathers depended for subsistence are passing rapidly away, by the encroachment of the whites upon their hunting grounds, and already the Red Man finds hunger and starvation staring him and his in the face; for this and many other reasons this band of Indians are anxious to commence the cultivation of their lands, but this they cannot do, as a military reservation has been made by the War Department within a few months and so located as to deprive them of the very lands they wish to occupy. Therefore, they ask that the troops stationed at Fort Lyon, C. T., may be removed from their reservation to some other point where they will be of more service in preserving the peace and preventing any outbreak between them and the whites.

The delegate recommended that the troops should be posted on Indian lands just above the Cheyenne and Arapaho Reservation between the whites and the Indians. This would keep the Indians from going into the settlements and the whites from encroaching on Indian lands and prevent the young men from getting whiskey.

143

The Commissioner of Indian Affairs forwarded Mr. Bennett's letter to the Secretary of the Interior with the recommendation that the subject be laid before the War Department, but there is no evidence that any further action was taken in the matter.

The effect of the attacks on the Cheyennes on the South Platte was soon apparent. General Mitchell, of the District of Nebraska, reported on May 27 that the Indians were becoming hostile and asked for a thousand men and a battery of artillery to guard the Platte road. The next day Governor Evans wrote to General Curtis asking protection for the settlements on the South Platte, the Arkansas, and their tributaries. This was a request that could not possibly have been granted, since a garrison would have been required for each ranch-house or a great body of men to constantly patrol the region in question. The ranch-houses were four or five miles apart and all exposed to attack. All this should have been thought of before the attempts had been made to "punish" the Indians. They might easily have been kept quiet, but it was now too late.

Chivington, after having done all the harm he could, had withdrawn his troops from the Platte and now on the Arkansas was awaiting the carrying out of the Confederate plan to capture Forts Larned and Lyon and raid into Colorado. It was not until some time later that he discovered that the story of a Confederate advance was a mere rumor. While he was waiting, the Cheyennes and the Brulé Sioux were making small raids on the Platte. Governor Evans reported, June 11, that the Indians had run off stock from Coal Creek, ten miles from Denver, and afterward had gone east to Box Elder Creek, had run off all of Van Wirmer's stock, burned the ranch, attacked a family of emigrants near the ranch, killing the emigrant Hungate and his wife, two children, and another man. This raid, almost within sight of Denver, created a panic. The ranches in the neighborhood were abandoned. Everyone fled to Denver and a rumor being circulated that the Indians were advancing on the town the people became panic-stricken, forced the doors of the ordnance storehouse and took possession of the arms and ammunition belonging to the United States. There were no troops in Denver except a handful of soldiers who, with a body of militia, started to look for Indians, but returned without having accomplished anything.

The bodies of the murdered emigrants, badly mutilated, were brought into Denver and placed on public view. People crowded to look at them and from that time most of the people of Colorado were in favor of exterminating all Indians.

Up to this time all the Sioux, except a small band that usually lived with the Cheyenne Dog Soldiers, had been peaceful. On June 19 General Mitchell forwarded to headquarters the report of a council held with the Brulé Sioux near Cottonwood Springs on the Platte. These were part of the Indians whom Harney had attacked at Ash Hollow and they were exceedingly anxious to avoid trouble with the soldiers. Owing to the scarcity of game north of the Platte, they wished to go south of that river to hunt, but were afraid they would be taken for hostile Indians and attacked. They asked that a white man be sent to live with them to tell the soldiers who they were. Some of the young men were reported to be with the Cheyennes, but it was said that they had been ordered to return to the main camp. General Mitchell warned them to keep away from the emigrant road, to avoid the hostiles, and to make no raids on the Pawnees. Nevertheless a few days later a small party of young men, either from this camp or from the Sioux who were camped near the Dog Soldiers, went east of Kearny to attack the Pawnees. They came upon a party of whites whom it is believed they mistook in the darkness for Pawnees. At all events, they charged them and killed some of the whites. General Mitchell at once ordered out troops to hunt down the Sioux and soon forced the tribe into the condition of hostility.[1]

On the road along Lodge-pole Creek, between Julesburg and Fort Laramie, on June 28, a train of thirty wagons was attacked by Indians, and all the mules run off, and the same day a coach was attacked on the Arkansas between Fort Larned and Fort Lyon.

[1] Lieutenant Ware in his book describes three councils Mitchell had with the Brulés at Cottonwood that spring and summer. The Indians came back three times in their eagerness to avoid trouble. At the last meeting a company of Pawnee scouts was at Cottonwood and Mitchell brought them and the Sioux together and attempted to make peace between them, but had to rush cavalry and guns between the two parties to prevent their fighting. He made a peace talk, but the Sioux and Pawnees kept yelling taunts at each other and Mitchell at last broke up the council and ordered the Sioux to get away in a hurry. They did not come back again.—*The Indian War of 1864*, p. 219 *et seq.*

The following day General Curtis reports that he is starting with a large force to march along the road from Salina to Fort Larned, leaving small garrisons along the way to guard the stage line. The war had now really begun. Every possible motive had been given the Indians to induce them to fight and raid—and they were doing both. A short time before this Governor Evans had sent out a circular to friendly Indians calling upon them to come in and encamp near the posts, where they could be watched by the troops and kept out of the fight. He wrote to Curtis on June 16, telling him that he had issued this circular, but he did not send a copy to Agent Colley until June 29. According to the circular the Cheyennes and Arapahoes were to come to Fort Lyon, the Kiowas and Comanches to Fort Larned, and both camps of Indians would be fed by the troops. A part of the Cheyennes, those living on the Arkansas, were at this time encamped at Salt Plain or Salt Spring on Medicine Lodge Creek south of the Arkansas and near Fort Larned.

A few days after the fight with Eayre's troops the main camp of the Cheyennes on the Smoky Hill had moved south and joined the Indians Eayre had attacked on Ash Creek. A few days later a part of the Indians moved on south, crossed the Arkansas above Larned and camped on Medicine Lodge Creek. They reached here in May and found the Kiowas, Comanches, and Apaches encamped in that vicinity. Not long after this George Bent went to an Arapaho camp near Larned and found his father there. William Bent had been sent down here with Evans's circular to the Indians, and the time when he was seen there must have been in June or early in July. George Bent says that his father induced the chiefs to visit Captain Parmeter, who, being either angry or drunk, treated them badly.[1] Later the Cheyennes were taken in to see Major Anthony, who had succeeded Parmeter in command. A council was held at which Major Anthony treated the Indians cordially but nothing was decided. The tribe remained near Salt Plain until they had held their medicine-lodge and then

[1] A few days later the Kiowas ran off the herd and then the Arapaho chief went in with a white flag, was fired on, and the Arapahoes made the raid up the Arkansas. This was all apparently in June. Eayre was still at Larned and the Cheyennes had just come south of the Arkansas. See also W. W. Bent's testimony before Joint Commission.

the Cheyennes moved north again. At the crossing of the Arkansas they were met by runners from a Sioux camp on the Republican, who notified them that the Indians up there had been making raids on the overland stage on the Platte. The Cheyennes moved up to the Republican River and began to send out raiding parties from there.

The war that was now in progress was chiefly confined to the Platte route, though the Kiowas, Comanches, and Apaches made a few raids on the Arkansas. Now and then a small party of Cheyennes or Arapahoes also struck this road, but there was far less travel on the Arkansas than on the Platte and fewer ranches, so that orders were given to call back the troops sent to the Arkansas in order to get a force effective for work on the Platte. Between Larned and Lyon, a distance of two hundred and sixty-four miles, there was only one station, and this was abandoned early in the year. The few ranches above Fort Lyon were abandoned when the Indians began their raiding.

Conditions on the Platte road were quite different. Here the travel was much heavier and the road was better protected. In Central Nebraska was Fort Kearny, Fort Cottonwood was farther up the Platte, and Julesburg above the forks.[1] The overland mail ran up the Platte and there were stations every ten or twelve miles. Between the stations there were ranches, and at almost every ranch a store and "Pilgrim Quarters" where travellers could sleep. This was also a great route for freight. All the goods imported to Colorado, including supplies of food, were taken up the Platte, and great freight-trains bound for Utah, for the new mines in Montana, and even for California and Oregon, also passed up that stream, along which too was the great emigrant road. Early in 1864 the rush of emigration on the Platte was very large; people were hurrying as never before since the days of

[1] The Overland Telegraph ran up the Platte, with a branch line up the South Platte to Denver, the main line running up the North Platte past Laramie. The posts on the Platte were: Fort Kearny, 190 miles west of Omaha, at the upper end of Grand Island; Camp Cottonwood, or Camp McKean, later Fort McPherson, at Cottonwood Springs, 47 miles above Fort Kearny; Camp Rankin, later Fort Sedgwick, built in the fall of 1864, one mile above Julesburg, 104 miles above Camp Cottonwood; Camp Sanborn, 7 miles above Frémont's Orchard and about 120 miles above Julesburg—the most eastern post garrisoned by Colorado troops. Late in the summer small detachments were placed at many stage stations.

'49; among them large numbers of men who had left the States for fear of being drafted and forced into the army. The rush was so great that the Julesburg Ferry across the Platte was blocked and many were obliged to go up to the Latham Crossing and other fords. To this great overland highway, "the finest natural road in the world," crowded with mail-coaches, freight-wagons, and emigrant trains, the Cheyennes and Sioux sent their raiding parties. The attacks began in July and their effects were soon felt all along the road.

On the 17th of July the Indians ran off the horses belonging to an emigrant train near Camp Sanborn on the South Platte, and took away the stock at the Bijou Ranch. They killed two men and wounded a third. They also took all the stock from Junction Ranch and Murray's Ranch, and killed five emigrants. The troops sent out surprised five Indians on Beaver Creek near Murray's place, and recovered one hundred and twenty-five head of stolen stock. The 7th of August Indians supposed to be Kiowas attacked a train below Fort Lyon, and on the same day a party of Kiowas headed by Satanta visited Bent's Ranch on the Arkansas. The same day five men were reported killed at the Cimarron Crossing. August 11 fifteen Indians, supposed to be Kiowas or Arapahoes, chased a soldier riding into Fort Lyon. Major Wynkoop mounted some men and drove the Indians off. He declared that he would kill every Indian he saw until otherwise ordered. Early in August Governor Evans issued a proclamation and advised parties of citizens to hunt down the Indians and to kill every hostile they might meet. The result of this proclamation was to put the friendly Indians at the mercy of any revengeful emigrant who had been attacked by hostiles, and any man who coveted an Indian's pony or other property could shoot him as a hostile and seize the property as his lawful prize.[1]

On August 8 the Cheyennes, with some Sioux, attacked a train near Plum Creek on the Platte, killed eleven men, burned the train, and carried off a woman and a boy. Two days later they raided the valley of the Little Blue, capturing trains and ranches and carrying off from the Liberty Farm Mrs. Eubanks, her two children, her nephew, and Miss Roper.[2]

---

[1] *Report of Secretary of the Interior for 1864–5*, p. 374.
[2] *Official Records, Union and Confederate Armies*, vol. 84, pp. 612 *et seq.*

This raid caused a panic on the Nebraska frontier. The settlers all fled eastward. General Mitchell gathered a large force and marched against the Indians. He went up the Platte and scouted south to the Republican, but found no hostiles. At this time, according to George Bent, there was an immense camp of hostiles on the Solomon. Here were the Southern Cheyennes, the Arapahoes, and the Sioux under Spotted Tail and Pawnee Killer. From this camp, according to the testimony of those who occupied it, little war parties were constantly starting out, most of them raiding on the overland route. The Sioux made their raids east of Fort Kearny, in Nebraska, and it was from there that they made this famous Little Blue raid. The Cheyennes visited the overland road west of Kearny, while the attacks of the Arapahoes were made on the same road but farther west and on the South Platte up near Denver. These raids on the overland road were terribly destructive. Many people were killed, horses were run off, coaches attacked, ranches burned, and whole wagon-trains captured. For over a month the Indians completely closed the road. The mail for Denver had to be sent to Panama, across the Isthmus and up the Pacific coast, and from San Francisco overland by stage to Denver.

George Bent writes:

At this time, as I rode from one camp to another in this great village, I saw scalp dances constantly going on; the camps were filled with plunder taken from the captured wagon-trains; warriors were strutting about with ladies' silk cloaks and bonnets on and the Indian women were making shirts for the young men out of the finest silk.

One morning in August, while most of the men were out after buffalo, firing was heard up the river in the direction in which a Sioux hunting party had gone. It was thought in the camp that these Sioux were killing buffalo, but presently a Cheyenne man named Hawk came rushing over the hills at full speed, signalling with his hands that the soldiers were after the Sioux hunters.

About fifty of us ran for the herd and as soon as we were mounted, dashed over the hill and came in sight of the Sioux all scattered out with little bunches of cavalry pursuing them. As soon as the soldiers saw us they got together and started to retreat. We followed them, and from over the hills from every direction came the buffalo hunters to join in the fight. No fight took place, for the cavalrymen had a good start of us and did not spare their horses.

Two troopers on worn-out animals kept falling behind and were overtaken by some of the Indians and killed. The rest of the soldiers got away and when they reached Fort Kearny on the Platte, the officer in command reported that he had attacked five hundred Indians near the Republican and chased them ten miles, after which the Indians had turned around and chased him thirty.

This was the fight reported by Captain Mussey, of which General Mitchell writes August 18.

Through August the raiding grew more and more vigorous. The overland stage agent wrote a letter complaining of the raids.[1] On August 15 the last coach from the East reached Colorado. Coaches from the West gathered at Latham Station on the South Platte and remained there awaiting the opening of the road.[2] About a hundred passengers had gathered here when a rumor arose that the Indians were coming up the Platte to "clean out Latham," and threw these people into a panic.

The freighters continued their trips for some time after the stages had ceased to run. They moved in large bodies, strongly armed, and could defy small war parties, yet about the middle of the month conditions grew so bad that the freighters were obliged to corral their outfits and wait for better times. Meantime, since no supplies could arrive, food grew scarce in Denver and prices soared. Flour jumped from nine dollars to sixteen dollars per hundredweight and then to twenty-five dollars. At the same time a plague of locusts settled down over the land and devoured the crops on the South Platte and its tributaries. On August 18 Governor Evans, by telegraph, notified General Curtis that the Indians were killing people within thirty miles of Denver; that large parties of Indians were close to the town; that the roads were blocked; crops could not be gathered for fear of Indian attacks and the whole territory was in a state of starvation. Flour was now twenty-four dollars a hundredweight. Evans asked that the Second Colorado Cavalry, then serving in Kansas, be sent home to protect the people.

On the 20th of August Gerry, the Indian trader, stated that

---

[1] *Report of Secretary of the Interior*, 1864–5, p. 398. General Superintendent Otis of the Overland Stage Company reports August 11, the day after the Little Blue raid, that he has ordered the stock drawn off the Platte line.— *Official Records*, vol. 84, p. 661.

[2] Root's *Overland Stage*, p. 330.

two Cheyennes, Long Chin and Man Shot by the Ree,[1] had come to his house[2] and advised him to take his stock away from the river; that between eight hundred and a thousand Apache, Comanche, Cheyenne, and Arapaho warriors were camped by Point of Rocks, on Beaver Creek, about one hundred and twenty-five miles from Denver, and that in two nights they would make a raid on the river. There were said to be no lodges with this party, which was out on the war-path. The old men of the tribes mentioned were said to be in favor of peace, but the young men could not be controlled.

Gerry rode sixty-five miles without stopping to bring this news to Denver. The settlers on the Platte were warned. On the night mentioned by the two Indians the hostiles appeared all along the river. They found the settlers on their guard and did not make many attacks, but at some places they ran off the stock, among them all of Gerry's herd.[3]

Acting on the invitation conveyed in Evans's circular of the previous June a camp of friendly Arapahoes had come in and established themselves on the Cache la Poudre near Latham. They were in charge of Agent Whitely. After the settlers on the South Platte had to some degree recovered from the frantic terror into which they had been thrown by the raids of late August they felt a great longing for revenge. No hostiles were within their reach, but here were some Indians, friendly to be sure, but Indians. Vengeance might be taken on these. A party of a hundred armed men set out to attack these friendly Arapahoes on the Cache la Poudre. No doubt they would have massacred them, but fortunately while on their way the whites heard of a small raiding

---

[1] Long Chin, Tsĭs' stō' ōn ah"; Man Shot by the Ree, O nōn' ĭ ā mō' ō. An earlier name for this last man was Pushing Ahead, Mā ĭt' ĭsh ĭ mĭ' ō. He had been a great warrior, but at this time must have been about sixty-four years old. Long Chin also was an old man at this time.

[2] Gerry's Ranch was seven miles below Latham, at the mouth of Crow Creek, on the south bank of the South Platte.—*Official Records*, vol. 84, p. 843.

[3] *Report of the Secretary of the Interior for* 1864–5, p. 363. August 21 a party of Cheyennes ran off Gerry's and Reynal's stock. Only ten Indians were in the party. They came from the south, ran off the stock, crossed the Platte at Gerry's, at the mouth of Crow Creek, went up Crow Creek twenty miles, then turned east and then south, recrossing the Platte near Frémont's Orchard and going south up Bijou Creek.—*Official Records*, vol. 84, pp. 843, 845.

party of hostiles, and turned toward them, hoping to meet them. Thus the Arapahoes escaped.

The Indians held the road from August 15 to September 24. It was not until the 24th of September that the first east-bound coach left Latham, Colorado.

While the large Indian village was still on the head of the Solomon River the Cheyenne chiefs received a letter from William Bent urging them to make peace with the whites. They held a council and, after talking it all over, decided that they would make peace. They wrote a letter to their agent announcing this decision, as follows:

CHEYENNE VILLAGE, August 29, 1864.

MAJOR COLLEY:

We received a letter from Bent wishing us to make peace. We held a council in regard to it. All come to the conclusion to make peace with you, providing you make peace with the Kiowas, Comanches, Arapahoes and Apaches and Sioux. We are going to send a message to the Kiowas and to the other nations about our going to make peace with you. We hear that you have some (Indian prisoners) in Denver. We have seven prisoners of yours which we are willing to give up, providing you give up yours. There are three war parties out yet and two of Arapahoes. They have been out for some time and are expected in soon. When we held this council there were few Arapahoes and Sioux present. We want true news from you in return. That is a letter.

(Signed)   BLACK KETTLE AND OTHER CHIEFS.

Agent Colley reported from Lyon on September 4 that some Indians had come in from the hostile camp with a letter.[1] Of this letter there seem to have been two copies, one written by George Bent, the other by Edmond Guerrier. One was addressed to Major Colley, the other to Major Wynkoop, the commanding officer. Later, both Colley and Wynkoop tried to show that at this time the Cheyennes were friendly, but the raids made at the time proved the Indians hostile. Wynkoop treated the messengers who brought the letter with severity, locking them in the guard-house and keeping a strong guard over them. That most of the Indians were still hostile is quite certain. The two old men who had warned Gerry of the raid in August told him that the old men were for peace, but the young men were all for war. The

[1] *Report of the Secretary of the Interior for* 1864–5, p. 377.

letter is dated August 29, and made reply to Evans's circular which was delivered to the Indians not later than July 15 by William Bent. On the other hand, it is possible that Bent had sent them a message later, of which we have at present no record.

Major Wynkoop, who was anxious to recover the white prisoners, set out for the Indian village, taking with him a force of one hundred and thirty men, including one section of a battery and the Indian messengers under guard. When he reached there—on Hackberry Creek, south branch of the Smoky Hill River—he found six or eight hundred warriors drawn up in line of battle and prepared to fight, but putting on a bold front he advanced toward the Indians, sending forward one of the men that he had under guard, telling them that he had come to hold a consultation with Cheyennes and Arapahoes; that he did not wish to fight, but would fight if necessary. Black Kettle and other chiefs prevented a fight. A council was held at which Wynkoop stated that he was not authorized to conclude terms of peace, but that if they would bring in and turn over to him their prisoners he would take such chiefs as they might select to the governor of Colorado and try to make peace for them. The Indians brought in four children, the oldest sixteen, three of whom had been captured at the Liberty Farm on Little Blue River, and one on the South Platte. The other prisoners were not in this camp, but with other sections of the tribe. The Indians agreed to deliver them as soon as it was possible to procure them.

Wynkoop brought the chiefs to Denver,[1] where they had a talk with Evans, Chivington, and others at Camp Weld. The chiefs present were Black Kettle, White Antelope, Bull Bear, Neva, and a number of Arapahoes. There seems no reason for supposing that either Evans or Chivington promised peace to the Indians. Evans's annual report,[2] dated October 15, 1864,

[1] Old men say that when the chiefs reached Fort Lyon Colley gave them their annuities and Wynkoop a lot of army rations. Before starting for Denver the chiefs sent these goods out to the camp on Hackberry Creek with word that "everything was all right and that they were going up to Denver to make peace." The Indians then started for Fort Larned, intending to winter near the post as they had the winter before, but they ran into Blunt.

[2] Evans's report, October 15, pp. 360–5 in *Report of the Secretary of the Interior for* 1864–5. Evans here makes a distinction between "surrender" to the military and securing "peace" by a treaty, but the Indians, of course, did not understand this distinction. He says he told them he could not give them peace but that he strongly advised them to surrender and has since

says that he told the chiefs that they were in the hands of the military and had better make peace, and gives a letter dated September 29, just after the council, written to Colley, telling Colley to make it plain to the Indians that he can promise them nothing; that they are in the hands of the soldiers. He says: "You will be particular to impress upon these chiefs the fact that my talk with them was for the purpose of ascertaining their views and not to offer them anything whatever." Nevertheless, his reported talk to them does not bear out this statement, for he definitely told them that his circular calling the friendly Indians to the posts still held good. He said in his report of October 15 that a few of them were for peace, but the great body was hostile. They must be conquered. Peace without conquest would be the most barbarous of humanity. Commissioner Dole reproved Governor Evans for this report and told him that if any of the Indians wished for peace it was his duty as superintendent of Indian Affairs to foster the spirit, and do all that he could for peace.[1] Evans had already gone East, and took no further part in affairs. Chivington, however, was eager to fight, and October 26 telegraphed Major Charlot: "Winter approaches, 3rd regiment is full and they (the Cheyennes) know they will be chastised for their outrages and now want peace. I hope the Major-General will direct that they make full restitution and then go on their reserve and stay there."

learned that four hundred lodges have actually surrendered at Fort Lyon. So this was the status of Black Kettle's camp and the Arapahoes—they were surrendered Indians waiting in the hands of the military until a peace was arranged. Chivington did not promise the chiefs peace either, nor accept their surrender, but Wynkoop, Chivington's subordinate, did accept their surrender, and Bent says that after the Blunt fight the chiefs from Denver came to the camp on the Smoky Hill and assured the Indians that everything "was all right" and that Wynkoop had told them to bring their people in near Lyon. Evans says, p. 364, the council was held September 28; the chiefs very anxious for peace, even offered to join the troops in fighting the hostiles; he, however, reminded them of their refusal to meet him in council in fall, 1863, of their failure to come in when he issued the circular to friendlies in June, 1864; told them their hands were red with blood, that they were in the hands of military, advised them to submit to the military under any terms they could secure. He "left them in the hands of Major Wynkoop," and has since learned that about four hundred of them have surrendered to Wynkoop. On page 366 Evans states his hope that the War Department will organize a winter campaign to punish the plains tribes.

[1] *Report of the Secretary of the Interior*, 1864–5, p. 400.

This telegram shows where the enmity between Chivington and Wynkoop originated. Wynkoop wished to make peace, while Chivington wrote that his new regiment of hundred days' men was anxious to make a winter campaign. Chivington's complaint to headquarters resulted in the relief of Wynkoop from his command and the detail of Major Anthony to command at Fort Lyon. From that day forward Wynkoop and Chivington were at enmity.

General Curtis replied to Chivington's telegram saying: "I fear Agent of Interior Department will be ready to make presents too soon. It is better to chastise before giving anything but a little tobacco to talk over. No peace must be made without my directions." [1]

Of all these men who were dealing with this group of Indians Wynkoop seems to have known much the most about Indians.

Two days before the council at Denver General Blunt, who had left Fort Larned, was moving up Pawnee Fork with a strong body of cavalry, when his advance guard under Major Anthony ran upon a small party of Indians and attacked them. Other Indians came up and surrounded this advance guard, which was badly threatened.[2] Blunt came up with the main body of troops and the Indians withdrew, Blunt pursuing them for several days. One soldier was killed, seven wounded, and one missing, and nine dead Indians were left on the field. Anthony had some Dela-

[1] From Fort Leavenworth, September 28.—*Report of Secretary of the Interior*, 1864–5, p. 365.

[2] The accompanying sketch and account from Cheyenne sources will, I think, make clear the way in which this fight took place. Blunt in his report says he marched up Pawnee Fork from Fort Larned, near its mouth. The Cheyenne village was on Walnut Creek, some distance west of its mouth. The war party was camped farther down Walnut Creek, east of the main village. Anthony left Blunt on Pawnee Fork and struck north, encountering the war party on Walnut Creek and driving them up the stream toward the main village.

Meantime a party of Cheyennes had left the main village and struck across toward Pawnee Fork, intending to visit Fort Larned. They met Blunt, shook hands, and turning about started to take him across to the main village, which did not intend to camp near Fort Larned but on what was called the Cheyenne Bottom, on Walnut Creek some miles northeast of Larned. This Cheyenne Bottom was a famous wintering ground often occupied by the Indians. The Kiowas sometimes wintered on the Arkansas opposite the mouth of Walnut Creek, and the gathering of the Indians in this general

ware Indians with him. The report of the Indians is somewhat different. Wolf Robe, who was present, tells the following story:

> With five others I started to war against the Pawnees, for we had heard from the Sioux that the Pawnees were having a big buffalo hunt near the Red Shield River. White Leaf was the leader. He took us down the stream about ten miles below the main camp and there we stopped for the night, for we expected some young men to join us in the morning. At daylight one of the party went out to look at the horses, but soon returned, saying that he had seen soldiers riding toward the camp. As soon as he had roused us we all sprang up and ran to get our horses. We had hardly time to mount before the troops came charging down on us. White Leaf's pony broke away and he followed us on foot, the soldiers shooting at us as we ran. As I looked back I saw that some of those who were after us were Indians dressed like soldiers. I could tell that they were Indians by their long hair. White Leaf fought them on foot and we were on our horses.

Presently, from the main camp where the firing was heard, warriors began to mount and ride toward the firing and soon there were too many Indians for the troops, who began to fall back. Gradually the troops became frightened and they would have run had it not been for the fact that with them were some

neighborhood led to the establishment of whiskey traders' ranches near the mouth of Walnut Creek. One of these was kept by Allison, a one-armed man, and it is reported that the Kiowas named Walnut Creek No Arm's Creek.

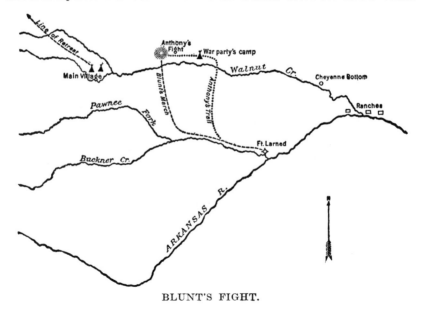

BLUNT'S FIGHT.

Delaware and Shawnee scouts. The chief, who was probably Fall Leaf, advised the officer to take up a position on the hill, and here they kept the Indians off, though they kept circling around them, shooting at them with arrows and their few guns, making a great dust and some noise.

Meantime General Blunt was coming up the valley, having no idea of what was going on. Early in the morning about fifty Cheyennes had left the camp and gone down-stream. In some way they had missed the advance guard but farther on met the general and the main command. He shook hands with them and received them kindly and the warriors turned back and rode with the column toward their camp. As soldiers and Indians were riding along on the best of terms they suddenly heard distant firing, and then came in sight of the hill on which the advance guard had taken refuge, and saw several hundred Indians circling around its base.

The general and his troopers halted and sat in their saddles staring at this unexpected sight, while at the same time the fifty Cheyenne warriors, fearing some treachery from the soldiers, slipped away and took a shelter behind the banks of the stream, where they began to prepare for a fight. General Blunt was too much interested in what he saw before him to pay any attention to the Indians who had just left him, and, putting his column in motion, he hurried to the relief of the advance guard. The Indians, seeing this larger force, fled. Blunt pursued them, but the Indians hurried to their camp, had the women take down the lodges and pack their things, and in a few moments were in full retreat. The troops kept after them for two or three days, but failed to overtake them. It was during this fight with the advance guard on the hill that a young Mexican captive, who had been carried off by the Arapahoes as a boy and adopted, was killed and scalped by the Delawares. This young man was thought to be George Bent, whose death was therefore reported. A few weeks later he was again reported killed at Sand Creek, and the following summer General Sanborn reported him killed again.

Anthony's attack on the little party who were on their way to the Pawnees thus stirred things up again and renewed the doubt of the Indians.

General Curtis, referring to this affair with Blunt, telegraphed to Colonel Chivington, October 7: "These are probably the Indians whom Major Wynkoop represents erroneously and unfortunately out of his command." This telegram has no meaning, but perhaps intends to say that these are probably the Indians whom Major Wynkoop represents erroneously as peaceful, and who were out of his reach. Curtis was right; they were the Indians, now attacked, whose chiefs were at Denver trying to make peace.

XIV

THE SAND CREEK MASSACRE

1864

OF what Major Wynkoop did after he returned with the chiefs from Denver to Fort Lyon or what he promised them I find no official record, but there is evidence in the testimony given before the Joint Special Committee of Congress in 1865.[1] From this testimony it seems clear that Wynkoop did promise the chiefs protection and that relying on this promise, and on the circular to the friendlies sent out by Governor Evans, they moved in to Sand Creek, believing that peace had been made or soon would be made. Agent Colley, testifying before this Commission, says that the coming in of the Cheyennes and Arapahoes was a direct consequence of Governor Evans's circular. He says also that the Cheyennes had purchased from the hostiles the prisoners they gave up. John Smith declares that the Indians went to Sand Creek with every assurance of peace promised by the commanding officer, Major Wynkoop.[2] Smith was interpreter at the Denver council. His name is familiar in all Cheyenne matters of those early times. Edmond G. Guerrier testified that Wynkoop had asked the Indians to come in and had promised them protection. They had promised to do so. Nevertheless, before all of them had come in Wynkoop was relieved of his command.

Wynkoop's action with regard to the Indians was strongly disapproved at headquarters. By Special Orders No. 4, dated October 17, Major Scott Anthony was relieved from the command at Fort Larned and ordered to proceed to Fort Lyon and take command of that post and "to investigate and report on the rumor in regard to the treaty made at Fort Lyon" and "investigate

[1] *Report of Joint Special Committee under joint resolution of March 3, 1865, with an appendix*, Washington, 1867.

[2] *Report of the Joint Committee*, p. 51.

159

and report upon unofficial rumors that reached headquarters that certain officers had issued stores, goods, or supplies to hostile Indians in direct violation of orders from the general commanding the department." This and subsequent correspondence indirectly criticised Wynkoop, intimating that he had acted foolishly, had permitted Indians to approach the post against General Curtis's explicit orders and had left his district—going to Denver—without orders. This order is from Major Henning, who was in temporary command of the district of the Upper Arkansas. Curtis and Major Henning in their apparent ignorance of Indians and Indian matters seemed possessed of the idea that punishment must be meted out to the Indians at large but did not seem to realize that it was in the power of the Indians to inflict far greater loss of innocent blood on the whites than the whites could inflict on them. These letters in fact show the spirit at headquarters, and it was in this spirit that Major Anthony took command at Fort Lyon on November 2. His orders were not to make peace, and yet he found a camp of six hundred and fifty-two Arapahoes within a mile of the post and a camp of Cheyennes on Sand Creek. Anthony says that he told these Arapahoes that he could not feed them, nor permit them to visit the post, but that if they gave up their arms and submitted to being treated as prisoners of war they might remain where they were. They acceded to these terms and turned over about twenty head of stolen animals and some old arms, most of them worthless. Anthony fed them for about ten days, which was in direct disobedience of his orders, and then told them he could feed them no longer and, returning their arms, advised them to go hunt buffalo. He says also that before leaving the Arapahoes sent word to the Cheyennes that he was not very friendly toward them. A part of these Arapahoes had been receiving rations here all summer, having apparently come in and surrendered when they received Evans's circular to the friendly Indians. A delegation of fifty or sixty Cheyennes came in from the Sand Creek camp soon after the Arapahoes went away and Anthony and Colley bought some tobacco for them. They said that they had no desire to fight; that they wished to be at peace. The meeting was held in the old stone building of Bent's Fort. Anthony says he told them that he had no authority to make peace, as they requested, but that if he received such authority he would come out and tell them. Meantime he was constantly writing to district headquarters stating that there was a small band within forty miles and that if he had the force to do so he would go out and attack them.[1] This shows clearly that he told the Cheyennes to camp on Sand Creek only in order that he might have them within reach if he could get a chance to attack them. He had no idea of making peace nor of asking headquarters for permission to make peace. Colley, in his testimony in 1865, says that Black Kettle and his delegation for whom Anthony and he bought tobacco were at the post only three days before the attack. At this time, according to Wynkoop, Little Raven, with most of the Arapahoes, went down the Arkansas to Camp Wynkoop, fifty-five miles below Fort Lyon, while Left Hand, with a few lodges, joined the Cheyennes on Sand Creek.

Anthony and Chivington have always been blamed for the attack on the Indians, and in a sense no doubt they were to blame, but the reports seem to indicate that they were encouraged by their superior officers. Chivington and Anthony naturally arranged the details. On the other hand, it seems clear that Anthony was lying to the Indians and trying to keep them in a situation where it would be possible for him to get at them at once if he wished to make an attack.

In October Major-General Halleck had ordered Brigadier-General P. E. Connor to give protection to the overland stage between Salt Lake and Fort Kearny, Nebraska. In order to do this Connor purposed to go East, as shown by telegrams from him printed in the *Official Records of the Union and Confederate Armies*. He also telegraphed to Chivington: "I am ordered by the Secretary of War to give all protection in my power to overland stage between here and Fort Kearny. . . . Can we get a fight out of the Indians this winter? . . . How many troops can you spare for a campaign?" This indicated to Chivington that another eager to kill Indians was likely to take the field and perhaps spurred him on to action.

On November 19 General Blunt, the commander of the district of the Upper Arkansas, wrote to Curtis urging a winter campaign and enclosing a clipping from a Kansas newspaper, which

[1] *Report of the Joint Committee on the Conduct of the War*, vol. III, p. 18. (*Massacre of Cheyenne Indians*.)

said that it would be an outrage to make peace without first punishing the Indians severely. On November 24 Curtis wrote to Evans, then about to start for Washington, to urge the War Department to send out more troops in view of the winter campaign against the Indians. Meantime, however, Chivington had taken the field and had telegraphed Curtis that the Indians had attacked two trains below Fort Lyon and he would clean them out.

During the raids in August the War Department had authorized the raising of a regiment of hundred-days men in Colorado. This was the Third Colorado Cavalry. Early in the autumn this regiment marched down the Platte to open the road which the Indians had blocked with their raiding parties, and on its return camped in the Bijou Basin east of Denver. From here it marched in November to join the expedition against the Cheyennes. A part of the men who had no horses remained behind. The snow was two or three feet deep in the Bijou Basin, but when the Arkansas was reached the ground was nearly bare. Chivington reached Booneville on the Arkansas November 24, and for some time stopped all travel down the river, holding back even the mail for fear that news of his movement would reach the Indians and thus let them escape.

After a few days Chivington moved down to William Bent's stockade on the south side of the river, where he left a guard to see that no one left the ranch to warn the Indians. From here he marched to Fort Lyon, reaching that place on the morning of the 28th, and again throwing out a line of pickets about the post to stop anyone who might attempt to leave. Major Anthony was evidently glad at the time that Chivington had come to attack the Indians. He states[1] that he had warned the Cheyennes to keep away from the fort, but they persisted in coming and his guard had fired on them several days before Chivington arrived. In the same testimony, however, Anthony declares that he "made some very harsh remarks" to Chivington about attacking the Indians, not because he considered them friendly but because he thought the force was not large enough to protect the roads from the raids which would certainly follow an attack. He quotes remarks said to have been made by the Indians on Sand Creek

[1] *Report of the Joint Committee on Conduct of the War*, vol. III, p. 21. (*Massacre of Cheyenne Indians.*)

a few days before Chivington's arrival, which imply that the Indians were ready and willing to fight. His report on the arrival of Chivington's force, dated November 28, shows that he fully approved the attack on the friendly camp.

The command left the post about dark. There is much uncertainty as to what troops were present, but besides the Third Colorado Regiment there was certainly a battalion of the First Regiment, which Chivington had brought with him and Anthony joined with the Second Battalion of the First Regiment and twenty-five men and two more howitzers. Some say that Chivington reached the post with six hundred men, others say seven hundred. Possibly he had six hundred of the First Cavalry, or he may have had six hundred men in all, and something over seven hundred when Anthony's command joined him.[1]

The country passed over was rolling prairie with short grass. Of the march Dunn says: "The night was bitter cold; Jim Beckwith,[2] the old trapper who had been guiding them, had become so stiffened that he was unable longer to distinguish the course, and they were obliged to rely on a half-breed Indian. About one-third of the men had the appearance of soldiers who had seen service; the remainder had a diversity of arms and equipment, as well as of uniforms, and marched with the air of raw recruits. About half a mile in advance were three men, the half-breed guide[3] and two officers, one of the latter of such gigantic proportions[4] that the others seemed pygmies beside him. Near daybreak the half-breed turned to the white men and said: 'Wolf he howl. Injun dog he hear wolf, he howl too. Injun he hear dog and listen; hear something, and run off.' The big man tapped the butt of his revolver in an ominous way, and replied: 'Jack, I haven't had an Indian to eat for a long time. If you fool with me, and don't lead us to that camp, I'll have you for breakfast.' They found the camp."[5]

[1] Bancroft, *History of Colorado*, p. 466, says he had nine hundred men, and in note on next page says six hundred and fifty hundred-days men, one hundred and seventy-five First Colorado Cavalry, and a few New Mexico Infantry.

[2] James Beckwourth, a mulatto trapper of early times, who lived long with the Crows.

[3] This is said to have been Robert Bent, the oldest son of Colonel Bent by his wife Owl Woman, a daughter of White (Painted) Thunder.

[4] This is said to have been Chivington.

[5] *Massacres of the Mountains*, p. 396. (J. P. Dunn, N. Y., 1886.)

The camp was at the big bend of Sand Creek and the place is also called the Big South Bend. Guerrier in his testimony in 1865 says there were eighty lodges with four or five persons in each lodge. John Smith, who was also in the camp, says one hundred lodges, two hundred men, and five hundred women. There were ten lodges of Arapahoes and the rest were Cheyennes. Very likely Guerrier counted only the Cheyennes, as the Arapahoes were camped a little apart. The creek bed was two hundred yards wide and sometimes much wider; the banks were from two to ten feet high and the bed of the stream was perfectly level dry sand, with an occasional pool here and there. The officers, dealing with a new and unknown country, were confused as to directions, and their statements as to movements made cannot be followed.

John Smith says that the attack occurred between dawn and daylight, nearer sunrise than daybreak. The Indians discovered a large body of troops approaching. Some of the women at first thought they were buffalo, but others recognized them as troops and ran to Smith's lodge and called him out, asking him to go and see what the troops were and what they wanted. At the council of 1860 Black Kettle had been given a large American flag, and now he ran it up on a long lodge-pole before his lodge, with a small white flag under it as a sign that the camp was friendly. Smith started toward the body of troops, but firing began almost at once and he ran back to the village. The shots were from Wilson's battalion of the First Regiment, which had been sent out to cut off the herd. Wilson says that in carrying out this order he was obliged to open fire on the Indians. He detached Company H, which fired for about five minutes. This firing led the Indians to huddle together about Black Kettle's lodge. Lieutenant Cramer says that Wilson took a position on the northeast bank of the stream. Wilson says the remainder of the command was on the southeast side. The troops on the southeast side were Anthony's battalion mounted, and behind them the Third Regiment on foot, firing over and through Anthony's men. Cramer says that when Smith ran out toward the troops an officer called out to his men to shoot that man. Smith, when fired on, ran back. Anthony's men now started to charge, but as the Third Regiment under Chivington kept up its firing over the mounted men, Anthony

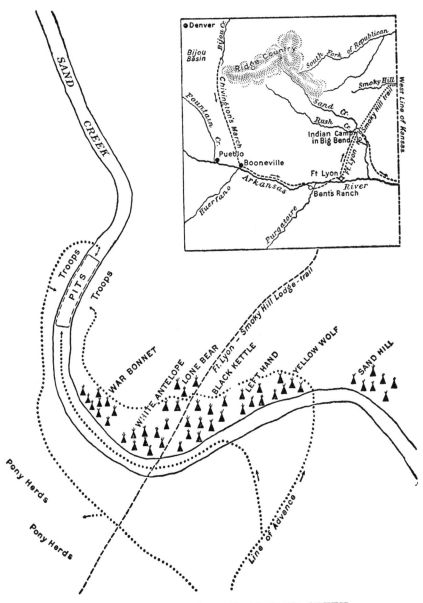

PLAN OF CHEYENNE CAMP AT SAND CREEK.

had to move to get out of the line of fire. A general advance was now made, the mounted men following up both banks, while Chivington, with the Third Regiment on foot, advanced up the dry stream bed. The Indians, who had stood there confused and seemingly unable to believe their senses, broke and fled up the stream bed.

The first Indians killed were White Antelope, then an old man about seventy-five years of age, and Left Hand, an Arapaho. As the Indians ran up the creek the soldiers followed them, the mounted men riding along the bank, while Chivington with his foot force moved slowly up the bed of the stream. As Chivington's men entered the camp John Smith came out of his lodge. Colonel Chivington saw him and called out: "Run here, Uncle John," and Smith, evidently greatly frightened, lost no time in obeying. He caught hold of a caisson and marched on with the troops. At length they came to a place where about a hundred Indians, as Smith thought, had stopped and taken refuge in the high bank of the stream. A part of the troops—no doubt the mounted men—had gotten above these Indians and rushed down into the stream, thus cutting off their retreat. The Indians had dug rifle-pits in the foot of the bank and thus partly sheltered began to fight for their lives. A large number of the soldiers gathered here, firing at the Indians, and it seems that even howitzers were used. All over the broad valley little parties of soldiers who had been pursuing stray Indians into the sand hills kept coming up to join the fight, and the firing grew constantly hotter.

Anthony believes that the Indians defended themselves for about four hours, and in a letter written to a friend after the fight he says: "I never saw more bravery displayed by any set of people on the face of the earth than by these Indians. They would charge on the whole company singly, determined to kill someone before being killed themselves. . . . We, of course, took no prisoners. . . ." Smith thinks there were two hundred soldiers here and that the rest were scattered, pursuing small bodies of Indians among the hills and plundering the camp. He does not think that half the Indians had time to arm when the attack began.

At last, after most of the Indians hiding in the pits had been killed, the soldiers drew off and returned to the village. The time occupied in the fight is variously estimated, some of the officers saying that they left the Indians before noon, others that they left them just before sunset, but as the fight began at dawn and did not last many hours it is probable that the soldiers left them before noon.   After they did so the Indians who were still alive came out of the pits and retreated up the stream.   John Smith later visited these pits where the main fight had taken place, and says that he saw there about seventy bodies, chiefly women and children.   The entire number killed in the attack was variously estimated by the officers of troops at from one hundred to eight hundred.   Chivington reported five hundred killed.   Bent says over a hundred and fifty were killed.   Of the ten lodges of Arapahoes under Left Hand, they estimated that a chief and about forty-six people were killed; four escaped.   Of the killed two-thirds were women and children.   Smith says that after the fight Chivington took him over the field to identify the chiefs.   Bodies were lying in the creek bed, many partly in the water and covered with sand, and so badly mutilated and cut up by the troops that Smith could not recognize many of them.   He thus made the mistake of reporting Black Kettle among the dead.   Among the Cheyenne chiefs killed the most important ones were: White Antelope,[1] Standing Water,[2] One Eye,[3] War Bonnet,[4] Spotted Crow,[5] Two Thighs,[6] Bear Man,[7] Yellow Shield,[8] and Yellow Wolf.[9]

The soldiers scalped the dead, cut up and mutilated the bodies and took back to Denver over a hundred scalps, which were exhibited in triumph between the acts of a theatrical performance one evening.   It was understood that no prisoners were to be taken and none were taken, except the two young half-breeds, Charlie Bent and Jack Smith.   Women and children who had asked the soldiers for pity and protection were killed.   Lieutenant

[1] White Antelope, *Wō' kāī hwō'ko mǎ ǐs.*
[2] Standing Water, *Mǎp ē'vǎ nī ǐsts'.*
[3] One Eye, so-called by the whites; his real name was Lone Bear, *Nah'kū ǔk'ǐ yū ǔs.*
[4] War Bonnet, *Kǎ kō yū'ǐ sǐ nǐh".*
[5] Spotted Crow, *Ōk ǔk'ǐ wō wō'āǐsts.*
[6] Two Thighs, *Nǐsh'ǐn o mǎh"*, also called Two Buttes, *Nǐs'so o mǐn'.*
[7] Bear Man, *Nāh'kū māhā".*
[8] Yellow Shield, *Ē hyō vō'hǐ vā hěh".*
[9] Yellow Wolf (really Yellow Coyote), *Ōh'kōhm hkō'wāǐs.*

Olney,[1] of the First Colorado Cavalry, swore at the investigation in 1865 that he saw Lieutenant Richmond, of the Third Colorado Cavalry, shoot and scalp three women and five children who had been captured by some soldiers and were being conducted to camp.[2] The women and children screamed for mercy, while Richmond coolly shot one after another, and the soldiers, whose prisoners they were, "shrank back, apparently aghast."

Amos C. Miksch, a corporal of the First Colorado Cavalry, saw a major in the Third Regiment blow out the brains of a little Indian child and saw Lieutenant Richmond scalp two Indians.[3]

Chivington's first report of the affair reads as follows:

HEADQUARTERS DISTRICT OF COLORADO,
      In the Field, Cheyenne Country, South Bend, Big Sandy, Nov. 29.
GENTLEMEN:
      In the last ten days my command has marched three hundred miles— one hundred of which the snow was two feet deep. After a march of forty miles last night I at daylight this morning attacked a Cheyenne village of one hundred and thirty lodges, from nine hundred to a thousand warriors strong. We killed chiefs Black Kettle, White Antelope and Little Robe, and between four and five hundred other Indians; captured between four and five hundred ponies and mules. Our loss is nine killed and thirty-eight wounded. All did nobly. I think I will catch some more of them about eighty miles on the Smoky Hill. We found a white man's scalp not more than three days old in a lodge.

J. M. CHIVINGTON,
      Col. Commanding District of Colorado and First Indian Expedition.
Maj.-Gen. S. R. Curtis, Fort Leavenworth.

The white man's scalp here mentioned has constantly been spoken of by Chivington's defenders as a proof that the Indians were making raids just previous to the attack. No one examined the scalp closely, except a surgeon, who testified that "it looked fresh."

The day following the battle Chivington remained at the captured village and, then sending Major Anthony to escort the wounded and take the dead and the captured property to Fort

---

[1] *Report of Joint Special Committee*, p. 61.

[2] It was the New Mexican troops, many of them sons of old trappers and fur traders, that protected the few prisoners taken. The First Regiment men also acted kindly and took little or no part in the scalping and mutilating.

[3] *Report of Joint Special Committee*, p. 74.

Lyon, Chivington set out to attack another Indian camp believed to be near the Arkansas below Fort Lyon. This was Little Raven's camp of Arapahoes. Anthony, after going to Fort Lyon, set out to rejoin Chivington, and December 15 reported that he had found Chivington's command sixty-five miles below Lyon on the Arkansas. On the following day the Larned coach came along and passengers spoke of a band of Indians fifteen miles below. The troops moved seventeen miles down the river finding no Indians, but coming upon the camp of the night before. Scouts sent out returned in the middle of the night with a report that Indians were fifteen miles below. The troops followed them and at daylight came upon the camp of the Indians, abandoned but a short time before. The troops remained here two days and then returned to Lyon, which they reached December 11.

Chivington's troops now returned to Denver, where they were received in triumph, exhibiting the scalps that they had taken and the trophies from the captured camp. Of the four or five hundred ponies and mules taken not one head was turned in to the government. It was testified that the ponies were distributed "among the boys." Everything in fact that had been captured disappeared.[1]

In Colorado Colonel Chivington and his men were heroes and in the East they were at first highly praised for the heroic manner in which they had fought and conquered the Cheyennes, but a letter from Agent Colley, printed in the Missouri *Intelligencer*, January 6, 1865, soon caused a change of feeling toward Chivington in the States. Colley explained the temper of the Indians and the good prospects that there had been for a peaceful outcome "when Colonel Chivington marched from Denver, surprised the fort, killed half of them, all women and children, and then returned to Denver."

General Halleck, Chief of Staff of the Army, at once ordered Chivington's conduct investigated and General Curtis attempted to have him court-martialed, but Chivington's term of service

---

[1] The War Department later made an effort to recover the animals, but Colonel Moonlight, then in command at Denver, reported in January, 1865, that only about one hundred broken-down and useless ponies were returned to him and that about five hundred more could not be recovered or traced; they had simply "disappeared."

had expired; he had been mustered out of the service and therefore was beyond the reach of a military court. Nevertheless, an
investigation was set on foot and Major Wynkoop was sent to
Fort Lyon to take testimony of officers and soldiers.

By a joint resolution passed by Congress March 3, 1865, a
Joint Committee of both houses was appointed to inquire into the
condition of the Indian tribes and their treatment by the authorities and to submit a report. The committee met March 9 and
divided up the country where the inquiry was to be made, among
subcommittees, of which one consisting of Messrs. Doolittle,
Foster, and Ross was assigned to the duty of inquiring into Indian
affairs in Kansas, Indian Territory, Colorado, New Mexico, and
Utah. The report of the committee, signed by J. B. Doolittle,
Chairman of the Joint Committee, was received January 26, 1867.
It contains much testimony about the Sand Creek massacre and
states among other things that the Indians, excepting in the Indian Territory, are rapidly decreasing in numbers and that "the
Committee are of the opinion that in a large majority of cases
Indian wars are to be traced to the aggressions of lawless white
men always to be found upon the frontier or boundary lines between savage and civilized life."

Such is the testimony of white onlookers and participants in
this unprovoked attack on an unsuspecting community that had
been promised protection by government officials, and on the faith
of that protection had put themselves in the hands of the troops.

We have a little testimony from the other side, for George
Bent was in the village at the time and has given me an account
of what happened as he saw it.

Three days before the attack he had returned from his father's
ranch on the Purgatoire to Black Kettle's camp. On the morning of the 29th he was awakened by a great noise in the village;
people crying out that soldiers were coming. He sprang out of bed
and ran out of the lodge. It was not yet day, but through the
dim gray of the winter twilight he saw two bodies of horsemen,
one on each side of the creek, charging down toward the camp.

When I looked toward the chief's lodge [he says] I saw that Black Kettle
had a large American flag up on a long lodge-pole as a signal to the troop
that the camp was friendly. Part of the warriors were running out toward
the pony herds and the rest of the people were rushing about the camp in
great fear. All the time Black Kettle kept calling out not to be frightened;

that the camp was under protection and there was no danger. Then suddenly the troops opened fire on this mass of men, women and children, and all began to scatter and run.

The main body of Indians rushed up the bed of the creek, which was dry level sand with only a few little pools of water here and there. On each side of this wide bed stood banks from two to ten feet high. While the main body of the people fled up this dry bed, a part of the young men were trying to save the herd from the soldiers, and small parties were running in all directions toward the sand hills. One of these parties, made up of perhaps ten middle-aged Cheyenne men, started for the sand hills west of the creek, and I joined them. Before we had gone far the troops saw us and opened a heavy fire on us, forcing us to run back and take shelter in the bed of the creek. We now started up the stream bed, following the main body of Indians and with a whole company of cavalry close on our heels shooting at us every foot of the way. As we went along we passed many Indians, men, women and children, some wounded, others dead, lying on the sand and in the pools of water. Presently we came to a place where the main party had stopped, and were now hiding in pits that they had dug in the high bank of the stream. Just as we reached this place I was struck by a ball in the hip and badly wounded, but I managed to get into one of the pits. About these pits nearly all Chivington's men had gathered and more were continually coming up, for they had given up the pursuit of the small bodies of Indians who had fled to the sand hills.

The soldiers concentrated their fire on the people in the pits and we fought back as well as we could with guns and bows, but we had only a few guns. The troops did not rush in and fight hand to hand, but once or twice after they had killed many of the men in a certain pit they rushed in and finished up the work, killing the wounded and the women and children that had not been hurt. The fight here was kept up until nearly sundown, when at last the commanding officer called off his men and all started back down the creek toward the camp that they had driven us from. As they went back, the soldiers scalped the dead lying in the bed of the stream and cut up the bodies in a manner that no Indian could equal. Little Bear told me recently that after the fight he saw the soldiers scalping the dead and saw an old woman who had been scalped by the soldiers walk about, but unable to see where to go. Her whole scalp had been taken and the skin of her forehead fell down over her eyes.

At the beginning of the attack Black Kettle, with his wife and White Antelope, took their position before Black Kettle's lodge and remained there after all others had left the camp. At last Black Kettle, seeing that it was useless to stay longer, started to run, calling out to White Antelope to follow him, but White Antelope refused and stood there ready to die, with arms folded, singing his death song:

> "Nothing lives long,
> Except the earth and the mountains,"

until he was shot down by the soldiers.

Black Kettle and his wife followed the Indians in their flight up the dry bed of the creek. The soldiers pursued them, firing at them constantly and before the two had gone far the woman was shot down. Black Kettle supposed she was dead, and, the soldiers being close behind him, continued his flight. The troops followed him all the way to the rifle-pits, but he reached them unhurt. After the fight he returned down the stream looking for his wife's body. Presently he found her alive and not dangerously wounded. She told him that after she had fallen wounded the soldiers had ridden up and again shot her several times as she lay there on the sand. Black Kettle put her on his back and carried her up the stream, until he met a mounted man and the two put her on the horse. She was taken to the Cheyenne camp on the Smoky Hill. When she reached there it was found that she had nine wounds on her body. My brother Charlie was in the camp and he and Jack Smith, another young half-breed, were captured. After the fight the soldiers took Jack Smith out and shot him in cold blood. Some of the officers told Colonel Chivington what the men were about and begged him to save the young man, but he replied curtly that he had given orders to take no prisoners and that he had no further orders to give. Some of the soldiers shot Jack and were going to shoot my brother also, but fortunately among the troops there were a number of New Mexican scouts whom Charlie knew and these young fellows protected him. A few of our women and children were captured by the soldiers, but were turned over to my father at the fort, with the exception of two little girls and a boy, who were taken to Denver and there exhibited as great curiosities.

Soon after the troops left us, we came out of the pits and began to move slowly up the stream. More than half of us were wounded and all were on foot. When we had gone up the stream a few miles we began to meet some of our men who had left camp at the beginning of the attack and tried to save the horses which were being driven off by the soldiers. None of these men had more than one rope, so each one could catch only a single horse. As they joined us, the wounded were put on these ponies' bare backs. Among these men was my cousin, a young Cheyenne, from whom I secured a pony. I was so badly wounded that I could hardly walk.

When our party had gone about ten miles above the captured camp, we went into a ravine and stopped there for the night. It was very dark and bitterly cold. Very few of us had warm clothing, for we had been driven out of our beds and had had no time to dress. The wounded suffered greatly. There was no wood to be had, but the unwounded men and women collected grass and made fires. The wounded were placed near the fires and covered with grass to keep them from freezing. All night long the people kept up a constant hallooing to attract the attention of any Indians who might be wandering about in the sand hills. Our people had been scattered all over the country by the troops and no one knows how many of them may have been frozen to death in the open country that night.

We left this comfortless ravine before day and started east toward a Cheyenne camp on the Smoky Hill, forty or fifty miles away. The wounded were all very stiff and sore, and could hardly mount. My hip was swollen with the cold, and I had to walk a long way before I could mount my horse. Not only were half our party wounded, but we were obliged also to look out for a large number of women and little children.   In fact, it was on the women and children that the brunt of this terrible business fell.   Over three-fourths of the people killed in the battle were women and children.

We had not gone far on our way before we began to meet Indians from the camp on the Smoky Hill.   They were coming, bringing us horses, blankets, cooked meat and other supplies.   A few of our people had succeeded in getting horses when the soldiers began the attack, and these men had ridden to the Smoky Hill River and sent aid back to us from the camp there.   Almost everyone in that camp had friends or relatives in our camp, and when we came in sight of the lodges, everyone left the camp and came out to meet us, wailing and mourning in a manner that I have never heard equalled.

A year after this attack on our camp a number of investigations of the occurrence were made.   Colonel Chivington's friends were then extremely anxious to prove that our camp was hostile, but they had no facts in support of their statements.   It was only when these investigations were ordered that they began to consider the question; at the time of the attack it was of no interest to them whether we were hostiles or friendlies.   One of Chivington's most trusted officers recently said: "When we came upon the camp on Sand Creek we did not care whether these particular Indians were friendly or not." It was well known to everybody in Denver that the Colonel's orders to his troops were to kill Indians, to "kill all, little and big."

XV

RAIDING ALONG THE PLATTE

1865

Soon after the fugitives from Sand Creek had reached the Cheyenne camp on the head of the Smoky Hill[1] a council was held and it was decided to send a pipe to the Sioux and Northern Arapahoes and invite those tribes to join the Cheyennes in a war against the whites. The Cheyenne pipe bearers went first to the Sioux camp on Solomon Fork and then visited a camp of eighty lodges of Northern Arapahoes. These Arapahoes had come south in the fall, intending to visit their kinsmen the Southern Arapahoes, but on reaching the Republican they had learned that the Southern Arapahoes had retired far south of the Arkansas, to avoid the troops, and as it was very dangerous to attempt to cross the Arkansas at that time the Northern Arapahoes had decided to remain near the Republican during the winter and return home to the north in the spring. The leaders of the Sioux and Arapahoes all smoked the Cheyenne pipe and agreed to join in the war. This was early in December.

George Bent and Edmond Guerrier, both of whom had been in the camp at Sand Creek, where Bent was wounded, set out for William Bent's ranch on the Purgatoire. On reaching the vicinity of Fort Lyon, they saw a number of wall and Sibley tents by the river bank above the fort. This sight discouraged Guerrier, who thought that they could not reach Bent's ranch without being pursued and fired upon by the troops, and announced that

---

[1] Măn ō′ĭ yō′hē′, Bunch of Timber, or Grove of Trees, River; the Smoky Hill River was so called by the Cheyennes because at the stream's head there was a large grove of cottonwood trees, among which grew no underbrush. This grove was called by the whites the Big Timbers of the Smoky Hill and was on the South Fork of that river, about on the west line of Kansas. Lieutenant Fitch's report, 1865, gives a good description of this grove. This fork of the Smoky Hill was sometimes called by the whites Burnt Timber Creek, an evident corruption of Bunch (of) Timber Creek.

he was going down to give himself up. He rode down into the camp and surrendered. He was not badly treated. Bent and the young Indian who was with them made their way safely to Bent's ranch and remained there in hiding four or five days, until Bent's wound had improved. They then set out to rejoin the Indians and found them encamped together on Cherry Creek— Cheyennes, Dog Soldiers, Spotted Tail's and Pawnee Killer's bands of Sioux, and the Northern Arapahoes. Some small raids had already been made on the South Platte and an attack in force was being planned.

The chiefs waited until all the small war parties had returned from the Platte and then held a council, at which they decided to make an attack on Julesburg. A party of perhaps a thousand warriors—Cheyennes, Sioux, and Arapahoes—was made up, and, accompanied by a number of women with extra ponies on which to bring back plunder, they left the camp on Cherry Creek January 5 or 6, and set out in a northwesterly direction for Julesburg. The march was an orderly one, bands of Indian soldiers being thrown out in front, rear, and on both flanks of the column, to prevent straggling or any attempt on the part of young warriors to make a premature attack which would warn the whites that Indians were in the vicinity. The Sioux led the march because they knew the location of the ranches and stations near Julesburg better than the Cheyennes, who did not often visit that region. Besides this, the pipe had been first offered to the Sioux and accepted by them, and therefore, according to custom, they were entitled to be treated with respect and to be given the lead in all movements. Thus the marching column was led by the chiefs of the Sioux. The Arapaho and Cheyenne chiefs followed them, and the warriors, young men, and women came behind, guarded by the soldiers.

On the night of the 6th–7th of January the Indians reached the vicinity of Julesburg and camped some miles south of the Platte, among the sand hills. The Indian soldier bands, still on duty, permitted no noise in the camp and kept close watch on the young men to prevent any attempts to slip off and make independent attacks.

At this period Julesburg was a small settlement. At this point the overland stage had formerly forded the South Platte and proceeded up the Pole Creek and Ridge roads to the North Platte and up that stream by way of Fort Laramie and on into the mountains; but in 1862, because of Indian raids on the North Platte, that road had been abandoned, and a new road established up the south bank of the South Platte, from Julesburg to Latham, crossing the Platte at Latham and going on thence west to Salt Lake City. The Julesburg station was built of cedar logs hauled from Cottonwood Canyon, one hundred miles below on the Platte. Besides the station there were also the express and telegraph office, stables and corrals, a large store and a warehouse filled with the stage company's supplies. One mile west of Julesburg was a small post, Fort Rankin,[1] surrounded by a strong stockade and garrisoned by a company of the Seventh Iowa Cavalry. This post was on the site later occupied by Fort Sedgwick.

The Indian plan was to draw the soldiers of the garrison into the sand hills and there surround and annihilate them. Before daylight on the 7th of January Big Crow, the chief of the Cheyenne Crooked Lance Soldiers, selected seven men, five Cheyennes and two Sioux, to go out and show themselves near the fort, in the hope that the soldiers would pursue them into the sand hills, where the main body of warriors was to be concealed. The seven men led their ponies down a small ravine which ran from the sand hills south of the river out across the flat bottom-lands and entered the Platte below the post. Keeping under the cover of the banks of this ravine, the party arrived near the fort and there waited until dawn. As day came they saw some men walking about outside the stockade, and mounting their ponies they rode up out of the ravine and charged these men, driving them inside the fortifications. A few minutes later Captain O'Brien came out with a body of cavalry and some mounted citizens and attacked the Indians. Big Crow and his men then retreated toward the sand hills, two or three miles south of the fort, drawing the troops after them.

Meantime the main body of warriors was still in camp behind the hills. About daylight they heard distant firing, and presently

[1] Established August, 1864. Originally known as Camp Rankin, but the designation was changed to Fort Sedgwick in orders issued by Brevet Major-General Wheaton, September 27, 1865, presumably in honor of Major-General John Sedgwick, who was killed at the battle of Spottsylvania Court House, May 9, 1864. Troops were withdrawn from Fort Sedgwick May 31, 1871.

the Indian soldiers informed them that the troops had come out of the fort and were pursuing Big Crow's party toward the hills. All began to prepare for the fight, painting themselves, putting on war bonnets, and taking covers from shields.   As soon as all were ready the Indian soldiers formed the warriors into a column and marched them up behind the sand hills.   Here they sat on their ponies, guarded on all sides by bands of soldiers.   As the sound of firing came nearer the warriors grew excited and impatient of restraint, and at length a body of young men broke through the line of soldiers and charged out from behind the hills.   Thus the plan of drawing the troops in among the hills and there surrounding them was spoiled, and as further attempts at concealment were now useless, the signal was given and all the warriors charged.

At this time the troops were still half a mile or more from the hills.   The moment he saw the Indians come swarming out of the hills, Captain O'Brien faced his command about and started it back toward the post at a gallop.   Big Crow and his seven warriors at once turned and rode after the soldiers, hanging on their rear.   These warriors were soon overtaken by a number of men on fast ponies, who attacked the troops fiercely and attempted to hold them until more of the Indians could come up.   Some of the soldiers threw themselves off their horses to fight on foot, but they were at once surrounded and in a few minutes were all killed. The remaining troops continued to retreat, but before they could reach the stockade the Indians were circling all around them, firing and yelling.   The warriors, however, were not in force sufficient to hold the troops, and before the main body came up the remnant of O'Brien's command had cut its way through and reached the stockade.

The published versions of this affair differ as to the number of Captain O'Brien's force.   Palmer says O'Brien had thirty-eight men, of whom fourteen were killed.   Lieutenant Ware, who belonged to the Fort Rankin garrison, but was not present at the fight, states that O'Brien had sixty men, and that one sergeant, three corporals, and ten privates were killed.[1]   A newspaper

---

[1] *The Indian War of* 1864, by Eugene F. Ware, p. 448.   Ware's account of this affair is unsatisfactory.   His account of the second attack on Julesburg, during which he was present, is much better.

version published soon after the fight states that a number of citizens joined the soldiers in the charge and that fourteen soldiers and four citizens were killed. This would make eighteen men killed, the exact number of graves which George Bent counted near the stockade when the Indians attacked Julesburg a second time some weeks later.

Just before the Indians charged out of the hills the west-bound coach came up the road and stopped at Julesburg station, where the driver and his passengers alighted to get breakfast. Just as they were entering the station they saw the main body of warriors, a thousand strong, come swarming out into the valley. The Indians were still perhaps two miles away, but some of them saw the coach, and charged down toward the station. The driver and his passengers, the station hands, the storekeeper, and operator saw them coming, and, leaving the station, they ran as hard as they could toward the fort which they reached just before the soldiers entered the gate.

A large body of Indians soon reached Julesburg where some of them at once broke into the warehouse and store and began to plunder, while others entered the stage station and ate the breakfast which was set out on the table and still hot. Bent saw an old Indian take from the table a sugar bowl, which he seemed greatly to admire, and tie it to his belt, after which he rode off with the bowl dangling behind him. The warriors who had driven the troops into the stockade continued for some time to ride about the post, yelling and shooting, but after a while they joined their fellows at Julesburg station. The plundering was now in full swing; the women had come to the station with extra ponies, and these animals, laden with articles taken from the store and warehouse, made trip after trip to the Indian camp among the hills. The warehouse was filled with sacks of shelled corn, but there were also bags of flour and sugar; and these the Indians dragged outside and loaded on the ponies. In the store they found the shelves full of canned goods and groceries. The canned goods puzzled the Indians. They had not seen such things before, did not know what was in the cans, and left them on the shelves. The store was well located for all the plains trade and the stock was large and complete. There was even a glass case containing gold and silver watches. The business must have been a valuable one. Some years ago it was reported that the widow of the man who owned this store had put in a claim for forty thousand dollars against the government for damages caused by the Indian raid and had secured, in partial payment, twenty thousand dollars.

On the other bank of the river, about opposite Julesburg, a herd of cattle was grazing, and while the plundering was going on a number of Indians rode across the river to round up this herd. The troops at Fort Rankin opened fire on these Indians with their howitzers, but without effect. They next turned the guns on the crowd of Indians gathered about the station, store, and warehouse, the shells passing high overhead without doing any harm. This was an attempt to frighten the Indians off. The troops did not fire into the crowd for fear of setting the buildings on fire.

One of the passengers in the coach which had driven up just before the Indians charged the troops was a United States paymaster on his way west to pay the Colorado troops. He had with him a large metal money box, and when he fled to the fort with the rest of the people from the station he abandoned the box. The Indians found this box and knocked it open with their tomahawks. They were greatly disappointed to find that it contained nothing but bundles of "green paper." None of them knew what it was, and they emptied the paper out on the ground. Bent secured as much of the money as he could comfortably carry. He saw a warrior take a thick bundle of the money, chop it into three or four pieces with his tomahawk, and then throw it up into the air. He shouted with delight as the bits of paper were whirled away and scattered by the wind. After the Indians had gone, the paymaster ordered out the garrison and had the men search the whole valley for this money. They found bills scattered all over the valley, but did not recover half of what the box had held.

The Indians remained until late in the day, plundering the store and warehouse and taking load after load of goods into the hills. At length, when they had secured all that the ponies could carry, they withdrew and assembled at the camp among the hills. From here they set out on their return to Cherry Creek, but their ponies were so heavily burdened that it took three days to reach the village.[1]

---

[1] The brief official notices of this Julesburg affair attempt to make it appear that the Indians were driven away by O'Brien's little force and that no

Some days after their return from Julesburg the Indians broke camp on Cherry Creek and moved north to a stream which they call White Butte Creek, between the Republican and the South Platte.[1] Ever since Sand Creek the Cheyennes had been in mourning for the dead; but now the camps were full of plunder, scalp-dances were going on all the time, and every one began to feel more cheerful. Among the Cheyennes was a large faction headed by Black Kettle, which still opposed making war on the whites. These Cheyennes had always been opposed to the war, and even after the Sand Creek massacre they still held firm for peace. Here in the new camp on White Butte Creek the chiefs of the three tribes held another council and decided to make a great raid along the South Platte, and then move north to Powder River and join the Northern Cheyennes and the Ogallala Sioux, who also were hostile to the whites. When Black Kettle and his party heard of this decision they announced that they intended to return south of the Arkansas and remain in camp there until a new peace could be arranged. There were eighty lodges in this band under Black Kettle, and they started south the same day that the rest of the Indians began their march toward the Platte.

About the 26th of January the Indians broke camp on White Butte Creek and started north toward the South Platte.[2] The village with the women and children and part of the men struck due north, intending to reach the river about twenty-five miles west of Julesburg, while a Cheyenne war party went northwest to

plundering was done. Lieutenant Ware, who returned to Julesburg a day or two after the fight, states that the Indians were greatly alarmed by the Sand Creek affair; that they fled north and attempted to cross the Platte at Julesburg, but were attacked and driven back south by O'Brien and his cavalry. Ware does not say a word about any plundering being done; he implies that the Indians fled south immediately after their fight with O'Brien. Root's list embraces damages suffered in both Julesburg raids.

[1] Perhaps the stream now called Frenchman's, or Whitemen's, Fork.

[2] Immediately after the Julesburg raid, January 7, General Mitchell, commanding on the Platte, stripped the stage line of all troops and collected some five hundred cavalry and several guns at Camp Cottonwood. From here he set out, January 16, to attack the Indians in their camps on the Republican. On the 19th he went into camp at a place he calls the Big Timbers of the Republican, where he found signs of a large Indian village recently abandoned. This appears to have been the very camp on Cherry Creek the Indians occupied before and after the Julesburg raid, and which they abandoned only a few days before Mitchell reached the Republican. The precise

raid above Julesburg, a Sioux party northeast to raid below Julesburg, and an Arapaho party about north to raid near Julesburg. The village and these war parties all struck the road the same day, January 28, and in a few hours completely wrecked about seventy-five miles of road, burning stations and ranches, capturing wagon-trains, and destroying the telegraph line.

The village struck the South Platte at Harlow's ranch, twenty-three miles west of Julesburg, and while it was being crossed to the north bank of the river on the ice, the warriors attacked and burned the ranch. This ranch, like most of those along the Platte in those days, had attached to it a store at which the emigrants and freighters traded. The store was a frame structure, built in front of a strong log building, in which the family lived, with a corral back of it. When the Indians appeared, the people at the ranch ran into the log building and opened fire through loopholes. The Indians gathered in front of the store and set it on fire. As the flames spread the log building took fire, and soon after two white men and a woman ran out. The men were killed and the woman was taken alive. She was captured by a Sioux named Cut Belly, and the Cheyennes believe that she is the woman who was taken into Fort Laramie in the spring of 1865 and surrendered by two Sioux chiefs, named Big Crow and Blackfoot, but this appears to be a mistake.[1] During the attack on this ranch the Indians secured some whiskey and many of them became drunk. An Arapaho was shot in the head and fatally wounded by a

location is uncertain, but the Arickaree Fork of the Republican was sometimes called Timber Creek or Thickwood. The Pawnees called it Lŭk'ĭs tĭ'kŭrĭ— "much wood," or "timber is abundant." Mitchell's scouting parties examined the country in every direction, but failed to locate the Indians, who were then encamped on White Butte Creek, not more than a day's march northwest of Mitchell's main camp. Failing to find the Indians, Mitchell returned to the Platte, reaching Cottonwood January 26. Two days later, before he had had time to redistribute his troops along the line, he received news by wire that the Indians had struck the road above him and had "cleaned out" nearly a hundred miles of it. See *Official Records*, vol. 101, reports, January 16–28; also Ware.

[1] The official reports all agree that the woman surrendered at Laramie was Mrs. Eubanks, captured on the Little Blue, August 11, 1864. The two Sioux, Two Face (*sic*) and Blackfoot, were friends of the whites. They had bought the woman and her child at their own expense from the Indians who had captured them and had brought them to the fort and given them up to prove their friendliness. The drunken officer in command of the post ordered the two Indians hanged in chains, and this was done.

drunken Cheyenne. While the men were fighting and drinking at this ranch, the women and children had crossed the river and set up the lodges on the north bank. The camp was a very large one, extending three or four miles along the river. Below it a small stream, Moore's Creek, flows into the Platte from the north, and above it another unnamed creek enters it also from the north.

Early on the morning of the day on which the village crossed the Platte at Harlow's ranch, a war party of one hundred Cheyennes, which George Bent had joined, struck the road at the Washington ranch, about fifty miles west of Julesburg and three miles east of Valley stage station. At this ranch the Indians ran off some mules and five hundred head of cattle, at the same time setting fire to a stack of one hundred tons of government hay, valued at fifty dollars a ton. There was a company of cavalry at Valley Station, but the troops made no attempt to interfere with the Indians, who moved off down the valley, driving the cattle ahead of them. They abandoned the lean animals and kept only the best ones. These they crossed over on the ice to the north bank and went into camp among the bluffs, about ten miles below the ranch. Lieutenant Kennedy at Valley Station reported that he attacked the Indians with his company, killing twenty warriors and recapturing four hundred head of cattle. The Indians, however, state that the troops came down the river during the night and rounded up the lean cattle that had been abandoned. In the morning the Indians saw the troops returning up the river, and some of the warriors crossed on the ice and attacked the soldiers, wounding two of them. The Cheyennes speak of this as a small brush in which no one was killed on either side.

At this time the South Platte road was the most thickly settled part of the plains. Besides the stage stations placed along the road at distances of ten to fifteen miles apart, there were many ranches and stores. The branch telegraph line to Denver followed this road, and many large wagon-trains loaded with goods for Denver and Salt Lake were proceeding west on the day the Indians struck the line. The Indians remained encamped on the north bank of the river from January 28 to February 2, and during these six days the war parties swept up and down the road, burning stations and ranches, destroying the telegraph line, capturing trains, and running off cattle. From the first day of the raids the coaches ceased to run, and none of them was captured. Except one company at Julesburg and another at Valley, fifty miles west, there were no troops along the line when the raids began, and of these companies neither was strong enough to check the Indians.

The villages were now filled with plunder. The Indians had never before lived so well. In the camps of the three tribes were many fat beeves and great quantities of flour, sugar, bacon, coffee, and all kinds of white man's food. In the past the Indians had tasted such things only on rare occasions. In speaking of this camp on the South Platte, George Bent says: "I never saw so much plunder in an Indian camp as there was in this one. Besides all the ranches and stage stations which had been plundered —and most of these places had stores at which the emigrants and travellers traded—two large wagon-trains had been captured west of Julesburg. The camp was well supplied with fresh beef, and there was a large herd of cattle on the hoof. The Indians had hitched their ponies to some of the wagons and brought them to camp loaded with sacks of flour, corn-meal, rice, sugar, and coffee; they had crates of hams and bacon, boxes of dried fruit, and big tins of molasses. Then there were boots and shoes, clothing, bolts of cloth and silks, and also hardware. About the only thing the Indians did not take was a wagon-train loaded with heavy mining-machinery. Most of these articles were new to the Indians and they were constantly bringing things to me, to ask what they were for. I remember an old man bringing me a box and asking what was in it. It was full of candied citron." During these raids the war parties were often out at night, and when they missed their way they would ride to high ground and look for the camp-fires in the big village. These fires could be seen for many miles up and down the river. When the fires were not in sight, the warriors would halt and listen for the drums beating in the village, where the scalp dances were going on. On a still night these drums could be heard miles away.

During these raids a party of young Cheyennes met with nine men who had belonged to the Third Colorado Cavalry (hundred-days men) and had taken part in the Sand Creek affair. These men had been mustered out of service and were on their way east when the Cheyennes met them on the South Platte and killed them all. After the fight the Cheyennes found in the valises belonging to these men the scalps of two Cheyennes, White Leaf and Little Wolf[1]—son of Two Thighs—who had been killed at Sand Creek. Little Wolf's scalp was recognized at once by a peculiar little shell which he had always worn, still attached to the hair. White Leaf's scalp was known by the light color of the hair. The white men had many other trophies from Sand Creek, which they were taking home to the States, and when the Indians saw all these things they were so angry that they cut the bodies of the dead men to pieces. Little Bear and Touching Cloud, the latter still living in 1909, were with this war party.

The Indians remained but six days in the camp on the north bank of the South Platte, but old people who were there say that so many strange events were crowded into these days that the time seemed much longer than it really was.[2] On the morning of February 2 the camp was broken up and the village started for the North Platte, moving about due north toward Lodge-pole Creek, and while it was moving in that direction a war party of about a thousand men rode down the South Platte to make a second attack on Julesburg. The Indians employed the same tactics as on the first visit to Julesburg, sending a small party of warriors close to the fort to draw the soldiers out; but the soldiers had learned caution and all attempts to lure them outside of their stockade failed. The main body of Indians now came out of their concealment, and after circling around the post for some time, shooting and yelling, they all rode down to Julesburg and began to plunder the store and warehouse again. In the warehouse

---

[1] Ōh'kūm hkā'kīt, Little Coyote.

[2] Colonel Livingston's report of February 5 gives the following partial list of depredations committed by the Indians during these raids along the Platte: "Beaver Creek stage station burned Jan. 14; Godfrey's Ranch attacked Jan. 14; Morrison's American Ranch burned Jan. 15; seven whites killed; Mrs. Morrison and child missing; Wisconsin Ranch burned Jan. 14; Washington Ranch attacked Jan. 27; Lillian Springs Ranch attacked and burned Jan. 27; Gittrell's Ranch burned Jan. 25; 500 cattle run off and 100 tons of government hay burned at Moore's Ranch near Valley Station Jan. 28; Harlow's Ranch, Buffalo Springs Ranch and Spring Hill Station burned Jan. 28. Buler's Ranch and Julesburg burned and a train of 22 wagons captured Feb. 2; telegraph line destroyed and all the cattle—1,500 head—between Julesburg and Washington Ranch run off."—*Official Records*, vol. 101, pp. 40, 41. Lieutenant Ware gives further details and mentions three more trains captured. Root mentions other depredations.

they found a large supply of shelled corn in bags, and this they
packed on their ponies and took across to the north side of the
river, sanding a road across the ice so that the unshod ponies
should not slip. After they had plundered the buildings they
set them on fire, burning them slowly, one by one, in the hope of
exasperating the troops into coming out to fight; but the troops
contented themselves with firing shells into the crowd gathered
about the burning buildings.

After the buildings had been burned, most of the Indians
crossed to the north bank of the river and went into camp a mile
above Julesburg, and just opposite Fort Rankin; while at the
same time a large war party of Cheyennes and Arapahoes started
up the river on a raid and a second large party of Sioux went down
the river.   Near the ruins of Gittrell's ranch, nine miles above
Julesburg, the Cheyennes captured two large wagon-trains bound
for Denver, one loaded with heavy mining-machinery, the other
with bottled liquors. After making this raid the Cheyennes and
Arapahoes crossed the Platte and rejoined the village at the
crossing of Lodge-pole Creek on February 3. The main body of
the Julesburg raiders camped on the north side of the river opposite Fort Rankin during that night, holding scalp dances
around a large fire in their camp, keeping up the drumming and
singing until nearly daylight, while the anxious soldiers across the
river watched them from the roofs of the buildings inside the
stockade. About dawn on the 3d the Indians broke camp and
moved up Lodge-pole Creek, destroying the telegraph line that
ran up that road and rejoining the village at Pole Creek Crossing.

When the village left the South Platte on the morning of
February 2 and started north, the Sioux led the way. The Cheyennes did not know the country in this vicinity very well, but the
Sioux were familiar with it and knew all the best routes and camping places. The Sioux knew that soldiers were stationed on the
North Platte, and when the village started north a body of scouts
was sent on ahead to watch for these troops, while another body
was left behind to act as rear guard and warn the village if troops
from the South Platte made their appearance. The Indians did
not move in "Indian file," as most white people have been taught
to think is the ordinary Indian mode of travel; they moved in a
wide, irregular column, scattered out all over the country, making

a trail a mile or more broad. Some of the old men or chiefs always headed the march. They knew the whole country, and travelling by landmark and direction, they struck across it from point to point, without regard to trails or roads. When the old men at the head of the column reached a good camping-place, they halted and dismounted, calling out: "Camp here," and as the women came up they unpacked the ponies and put up the lodges. If the camp was only for a single night, the old men would say: "Camp here, one sleep," and then the women would unpack but a few things; just what was required for the one night. During this move to the north they had a large number of wagons loaded with plunder. They had tied ponies to the wagons, using long rawhide and twisted buffalo-hair lariats in place of harness; but as the Indians had had no experience in driving and the ponies were wild and unused to drawing wheeled vehicles, the wagons caused much trouble. They kept zigzagging all over the prairie, and the Indians soon abandoned them and packed the plunder on the ponies' backs.

The night of February 2 the village encamped on the little divide between the South Platte and Lodge-pole Creek. On the 3d they reached Lodge-pole Creek at a point about twenty-five or thirty miles northwest of Julesburg, and here the warriors who had burned Julesburg and raided the road came in with their plunder. On the morning of the 4th the stream was crossed two miles below the old Overland Stage Road Crossing of Pole Creek. This day a hard march was made over the high, dry ridge which lies between Lodge-pole Creek and the North Platte. That night the lodges were set up on a small stream not far east of Mud Springs, and near the old overland stage station and ranch which stood in a little hollow near the head of a small eastern branch of Pumpkinseed Creek, known to the Sioux as Muddy Spring Creek.[1] The ranch was the only place at the time occupied by whites between the South and North Platte. There were here a telegraph station, a few soldiers, and some herders who had charge of a herd of cattle and some horses and mules. On the morning of the 4th the advance party of Indian scouts came upon Mud Springs and ran off the herd of cattle

[1] Mud Springs ranch was at or very near the site of the present town of Simla, Nebraska.

and twenty head of horses and mules from a creek some distance from the ranch. They made no attack this day.

The operator at once telegraphed to Camp Mitchell and Fort Laramie for aid, and troops were immediately started from both posts, marching night and day, to the relief of the men at the ranch. Lieutenant Ellsworth left Camp Mitchell, fifty-five miles west of Mud Springs, with thirty-six men of the Eleventh Ohio Cavalry, and after marching all night reached the ranch about daylight on the 5th.

Before day that morning, February 5, a small party of warriors left the Indian village and went to the ranch. Later a larger force followed them, and when this second body came up they found the first party engaged with the troops. A number of horses and mules were shut up in the corral and the white men were inside the log ranch building, firing on the Indians through loopholes. The Indians crept up as near to the building as they could get, keeping under cover, and opened fire with arrows and bullets. The firing went on until about noon, neither side being able to see what damage was done to the other. At last the troops ceased fire—the Indians thought they had run out of ammunition—and in order to divert attention from themselves turned all the stock out of the corral. The horses and mules rushed off, scattering in every direction; the young warriors pursuing them, each man doing his best to touch as many animals as he could. If a man touched a horse with his whip, bow, or any other implement held in his hand, that animal belonged to him, and all the Indians recognized his claim. Satisfied with the capture of the stock—all of the animals were branded U. S.—and having little hope of taking the ranch, the Indians now returned to the camp, which in the meantime had been moved farther to the north and was now at some springs on the head of a stream known at that time as Rush Creek, but at the present day called Deep Holes Creek.[1]

During that night Colonel Collins reached Mud Springs with twenty-five picked men from Fort Laramie. About dawn the Indians came riding over the hills from every direction and down

[1] This camp was on a small eastern branch of Deep Holes Creek, still known as Camp Creek. Camp Creek Springs (old Rush Creek Springs), at which the village was located, are near the head of this small branch.

into the Mud Springs hollow. Here they attempted to cut off some of Collins's men who had lagged on the road, but soon after a hundred more of the Colonel's command came up, and all reached the ranch in safety. The Indians now attacked in force, creeping up under cover to points very near the ranch and corral. A body of about two hundred came up under cover of a hill and some ravines and began to fire arrows into the air, which came down upon the corral at an angle, striking many men and horses. The troops made a sally, drove the Indians off and, near the top of the hill, dug a rifle-pit which they held. At 2 p. m. the Indians began to retire into the hills, but many were in sight until dark. During the day some Mexicans or whites were noticed among the warriors.

During this day, the 6th, the Indians removed their villages across the North Platte and formed a new camp some miles north of the river, among the high bluffs at the head of Brown's Creek. On the 7th Colonel Collins sent out a scouting party to look for the Indians, and on the 8th he set out with his whole command and the wagon-train. He found the abandoned camp of the Indians at Rush Creek Springs. Here a hundred cattle had been killed and the ground was strewn with empty oyster cans and other débris. Collins followed the trail down the creek to the North Platte at the point where the village had crossed. In his report he implies that he was pursuing the Indians, but, of course, he was not doing that. He had less than two hundred men, the Indians at least a thousand, and, according to his own report, nearer three thousand. On reaching the North Platte he was at once discovered by the Indians, who recrossed the river on the ice and attacked him.

The Indians, having camped among the high bluffs on the north side of the river, thought that they had seen the last of the soldiers, and began preparing for their march to the Black Hills. Criers passed through the camps to announce that the chiefs had decided to remain here four days to rest the ponies, because the next camping-place was far away to the north, to be reached only by a long hard march through the sand hills. That night, as usual, dances were going on in every part of the village. The moon was full. The drums were beating and the echoes coming back from the high hills among which the camp stood. Some time after noon the next day a mounted warrior was seen on the bluff south of the camp, signalling with his robe that soldiers were in sight in the Platte valley. He kept signalling, "Enemies," and then "Across the river."

There was a rush for the horses, each man anxious to start as soon as possible, and a few moments later the mounted men in groups were rushing across the bluffs and down into the valley. George Bent says: "When I had mounted I rode to the bluffs, whence I had a fine view of the valley, here several miles wide, perfectly flat, with the frozen Platte winding through it. On the south side of the river I saw a train of white-topped wagons moving along the road under an escort of cavalry, and toward this train the Indians were hurrying, looking like a swarm of little black ants, crawling across the river on the ice. Looking through my field-glasses I could see that there were four groups or companies of cavalry escorting the wagons. I watched them move on until they reached the stream on whose head our camp had stood the day before, and here in the angle formed by the junction of the creek with the river, they halted, corralled the wagons, and began to prepare to fight."

The wagons had been corralled by Colonel Collins on a piece of level ground surrounded by ridges and knolls among which the soldiers dug rifle-pits, forming a circle around the wagons. When the Indians first crossed the river they dashed up boldly, apparently bent on stampeding the horses and mules, but the soldiers in the rifle-pits soon drove them back, and they then took cover behind the ridges and knolls, creeping up as close as they could to the wagons. The fight now settled down to firing by both sides, from cover. A party of Indians had crept along the ice on the river, under cover of the high banks, and reached a position in rear of the troops. They opened a galling fire on the wagons. The troops stood the fire for some time; then a detachment of cavalry came out of the corral, leading their horses, mounted, formed in line, and charged toward the Indians hidden behind the bank. The warriors saw the troops coming and at once mounted to get out of the way of the charge. Yellow Nose,[1] always a little man, and at that time a mere boy, was too

[1] Yellow Nose was a Ute captive taken with his mother on the Rio Grande about the year 1854. He was brought up by old Spotted Wolf of the Northern

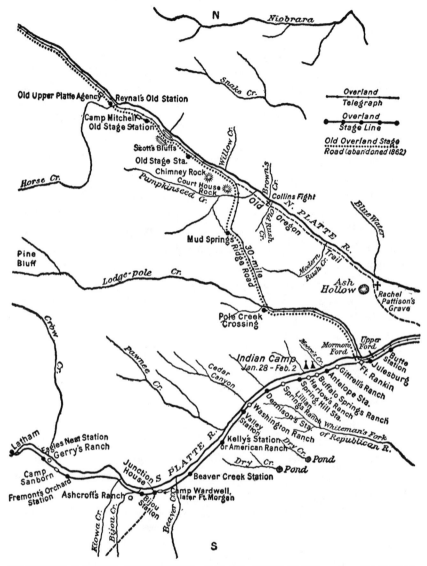

COUNTRY RAIDED DECEMBER, 1864, TO FEBRUARY, 1865, SHOWING
STAGE AND TELEGRAPH LINES AND RANCHES.

COUNTRY RAIDED DECEMBER, 1864, TO FEBRUARY, 1865, SHOWING STAGE AND TELEGRAPH LINES AND RANCHES.

The stage stations going west were:

O'Fallon's Bluffs.
Alkali Lake, 15 miles west.
Diamond Springs, near old Lower Crossing, 25 miles west.
Elbow Station and Butte Station, probably then abandoned.
Julesburg, or Upper Crossing, was 1 mile east of the mouth of Lodge-pole Creek, about a mile east of Fort Rankin, 456 miles west of Atchison, Kansas, and 197 miles east of Denver.

Distances from Julesburg west:

Gittrell's Ranch, 9 miles.
Antelope Stage Station, 12 miles, according to stage company; 16 miles according to Colonel Livingston's report.
Buffalo Springs Ranch—burned at end of January—19 miles.
Harlow's Ranch, 23 miles west of Julesburg and 27 miles east of Valley.
Spring Hill Station, 25 miles west of Julesburg.
Lillian Springs Ranch, 34 miles.
Dennison's Station, 38 miles.
Moore's Washington ranch, about 3 miles east of Valley Station.
Valley Station, exactly 50 miles west of Julesburg. Small garrison here January–February.
American Ranch—a stage station—65 miles west of Julesburg. This was called Kelly's American Ranch, also Morrison's American Ranch.
Junction House, 15 miles west of Beaver Creek, 5 miles east of Bijou Creek. At this place the Denver "cut-off" road leaves the overland stage road and strikes southwest toward Denver.
Junction House to Denver, 90 miles.
Beaver Creek Station, 77 miles west of Julesburg.
Bijou Creek Station, 97 miles west of Julesburg.
Fremont Orchard Station, 113 miles.
Camp Sanborn, abandoned before January, 1865.
Eagle's Nest Station, 125 miles west of Julesburg.
Latham Station, 135 miles from Julesburg, 61 miles from Denver. Here the coaches crossed the Platte and ran west to Salt Lake.
Big Bend Station, 15 miles south of Latham, 46 miles from Denver.
Camp Living Springs, where there were troops in January, 1865, 29 miles from Denver.
Fort Lupton Station, 29 miles from Denver.
Pierson Station, 14 miles from Denver.
Denver, 197 miles from Julesburg, 400 miles from Fort Kearny, 653 miles from Atchison, according to official stage company statistics.
Pole Creek and North Platte road. This is the old Overland Stage Road abandoned in 1862. In 1864–5 the stages ran up the South Platte to Latham, crossed the river there, and ran due west to Salt Lake. The Pole Creek and North Platte road was used by emigrants and the military only; the Overland Telegraph Line ran along this road, with a branch line up the South Platte to Denver.
From Julesburg. Cross the river at Mormon Ford and go up the south bank of Pole Creek. Pole Creek Crossing, 35 miles from Julesburg. Cross Pole Creek here and go across the dry divide called the Thirty-Mile Ridge or Jule's Stretch to Mud Springs, 32 miles (about) from Pole Creek Crossing. From Mud Springs the road strikes northwest, fords Pumpkinseed Creek below the forks, and, entering the North Platte valley, passes between Court House Rock and the river. Here the old Oregon Trail, coming up the Platte from Ash Hollow, joins the road. Pass an old stage station near Chimney Rock, cross Scott's Bluffs through Mitchell's Pass, and reach Camp Mitchell, established in 1864. Camp Mitchell was 55 miles west of Mud Springs and 3 miles west of Mitchell Gap in Scott's Bluffs. Horse Creek, 37 miles east of Fort Laramie. Reynal's Ranch (trading-house and old stage station), on west bank of Horse Creek. Upper Platte Agency or Owakipamni (place of distribution), 9 miles west of Horse Creek and 28 miles east of Fort Laramie. Bordeaux's trading-house, site of the Grattan fight, 9 or 10 miles east of Fort Laramie (was still in existence in 1864). Beauvais's Ranch and trading-house, 5 miles east of Laramie. Fort Laramie, about 184 miles, by this road, from Julesburg.

small to mount his horse in a hurry, and while he was still trying to get on the horse a soldier rode up and shot him in the breast. At that moment Yellow Nose succeeded in mounting, and followed the rest of his party, who were in full flight for a nearby sand hill. The cavalry were close after them, seemingly about to overtake them, when suddenly a large party of Indians rode out from behind the sand hill and charged the troops, who turned and galloped back toward the corral. The Indians rode into their rear ranks and killed about half of them before they reached the wagons. A soldier mounted on a very fast horse dashed right through the charging Indians and got away along the Laramie road toward the west. A few Indians on fleet ponies followed him, and after a long chase overtook and killed him. In his saddle-bags they found a paper which they brought to George Bent after the fight. It was a message from Colonel Collins to the officer commanding at Fort Laramie, stating that he had been attacked by three thousand warriors and forced to corral his wagons, and requesting that aid be sent to him at once. Many years later George Bent met Sergeant MacDonald, who died at Teluga, Oklahoma, about 1900. He told Bent that he was an enlisted man with this train when it was attacked and that Colonel Collins had given copies of this message to two men, with orders to ride through the Indian lines and take it to the fort. Colonel Collins, however, says nothing in his report about this, but states that the charge was made to drive some Indians from a knoll about four hundred yards from the corral.

The fighting continued until nearly evening; but it was not very interesting. Both sides stuck close to their cover, exposing themselves as little as possible. Toward dark most of the Indians withdrew in little parties and recrossed the river to their camp. In the morning some of them returned and fired a few shots at the soldiers, then returned to camp again. Colonel Collins declares that at noon the last stragglers were seen crossing the bluffs

Cheyennes, who died about 1896. Spotted Wolf married Wind Woman, a sister of Gentle Horse and Black Kettle. Yellow Nose became a great warrior and took a prominent part in many of the old battles with the whites, such as Crook's fight on the Rosebud and Custer's fight on the Little Big Horn a few days later. He still (1909) is living not far from Geary, Oklahoma. He captured a flag—guidon—in the Custer battle. He was in Dull Knife's village when it was captured in 1876.

and hurrying in among the sand hills, a few scouts remaining behind to watch the troops.

Early that morning (February 9), according to Indian accounts, the women took down the lodges and the village started north into the rough sand-hills country, where there was no wood and water was very scarce. After having travelled about forty miles they camped that night on a small stream called by the Indians Snake Creek.[1] There was no wood here, but fires were made of buffalo-chips. The next day another long march was made and the Indians encamped on Niobrara River, called by them Sudden or Unexpected River, sometimes Surprise River.[2] The next camp was on a small sand creek, evidently near White River, where there was plenty of wood, and here the village rested four days, killing antelope and elk.

At this camp on the sand creek, runners came in with news that the Northern Cheyennes and the Ogallala Sioux were encamped on Powder River,[3] west of the Black Hills, and the Northern Arapahoes near Tongue River,[4] farther west. These runners were Cheyenne men who had been sent north from the camp on White Butte Creek, the day that Black Kettle's band moved south and the rest of the village north, to raid the South Platte road. With them came a number of Northern Cheyennes. From this camp the Indians moved up to Bear Lodge River, a fine stream flowing through the northeastern part of the Black Hills, on whose forks the Indians loved to make their winter camps. The Sioux who were in the village, Brulé or Burnt Thigh Sioux, of Spotted Tail's and Pawnee Killer's bands, now left the camp and moved off to the east, and about the same time the Northern Arapahoes left and moved west toward Tongue River to join their people. This left only the Southern Cheyennes in the camp on Bear Lodge

[1] Snake Creek—Shĭ shĭ'nĭ ĭ'yo he.

[2] Hĭs sē'yŏvi'yoē. It is said that the Cheyennes crossing a wide flat on which no timber nor willows grew were astonished when they came on the stream flowing through this flat. This is said to be the character of the Niobrara River between the headwaters of Snake Creek and White River to the north. This was called by the early trappers "Running Water."

[3] Paiyō'hē, from Pai, gunpowder, coal or any black dust + ohe, so named from the seams of lignite found along its banks. The word is said to have been used for lignite or black powder of any sort long before gunpowder was known.

[4] Tongue River, Wĭt'ăno ĭ'yohē', river of tongues.

River, and they also soon broke camp and moved around the northern side of the Black Hills, camping on Red Paint River,[1] at the northwest side of the hills; thence they moved west, camping on Antelope Pit River,[2] where in early days the Indians had caught antelope in pits. Their next move brought them to Powder River, and there they found the Northern Cheyennes and a big camp of Ogallalas camped near each other in a good place, with plenty of wood and grass and with buffalo abundant.

[1] Red Paint River, Mā'ĭ tŭm ō nī'yohē, a stream from whose banks in ancient days the Indians used to dig the red clay used in painting.

[2] Antelope Pit River, Wō kai hē'yūniō i'ohe. It was on this stream especially that the Cheyennes captured antelope in pitfalls.

XVI

THE POWDER RIVER EXPEDITION

1865

THE raids during the winter of 1864–5 led General Grenville M. Dodge, who commanded the department of the Missouri, to believe that one sure way to protect the frontier from Indian depredations was to strike some hard blows in the enemy's country. He planned to send into the Powder River country, where the Sioux, Cheyennes, and Arapahoes were thought to be in camp, four columns of troops—one under General Sully and three under command of General P. E. Connor—and to attack the Indians there.

General Connor took command of the District of the Plains, which had been created for him, March 30, 1865. Returning from the East, where he had gone to consult General Dodge, he reached Julesburg May 15, and at once began to prepare for the expedition to the Powder River and Yellowstone country. Sully failed to get his men ready and Connor acted alone.

It was determined that the right column of the command, under Colonel N. Cole,[1] should march from Columbus, Nebraska, northwesterly, passing north of the Black Hills. From Fort Laramie Colonel Walker, of the Sixteenth Kansas Cavalry, with about six hundred men and a pack-train was to march north, through the Black Hills. He did this, joining Cole north of the Black Hills and east of the Little Missouri River. Connor commanded the other column. He had a detachment of the Seventh Iowa Cavalry, the Second California Cavalry, a signal corps, a company of ninety-five Pawnee scouts, under Major Frank North, and about the same number of Omaha and Winnebago scouts.

When Connor reached Fort Laramie and established temporary headquarters there he found great dissatisfaction prevailing among the volunteer troops. Most of these men had enlisted

[1] Connor's orders to Cole and Walker are in *Official Records*, vol. 102, pp. 1045–9. Connor orders Cole to kill all males over twelve years.

for three years, or during the War of the Rebellion. Many were veterans who had re-enlisted. At the close of the Civil War, instead of being discharged and sent home, as they felt they should have been, they were ordered out on this Indian campaign. Desertions were constantly taking place, and when Colonel Walker's order was read to the troops, the volunteers mutinied and declared they would not go on the expedition. Connor at once formed the remainder of his troops in line of battle, brought his artillery to bear on the mutineers, and just as he was about to order an attack the men consented to go. They left Fort Laramie on the appointed day, July 5, under command of Colonel Walker. The regiment that mutinied was Colonel Walker's own, the Sixteenth Kansas Cavalry.

On August 2, with a force of about six hundred and seventy-five men, Connor crossed the Platte near the La Bonté crossing and marched up the north bank of the river to a point not far from where Fort Fetterman afterward stood. Here he turned north and marched across the dry country between the Platte and the headwaters of Powder River, and then on down Powder River. Long before they reached Powder River the Big Horn Mountains began to be visible. "The sun so shone as to fall with full blaze upon the southern and southwestern sides of Cloud Peak . . . and the whole snow-covered range so clearly blended with the sky as to leave it in doubt whether all was not a mass of bright cloud. . . . In front and a little to the northeast could be seen the four columns of Pumpkin Buttes, and fifty miles further east Bear Butte, and beyond, a faint outline of the Black Hills. The atmosphere was so wonderfully clear and bright that one could imagine that he could see the eagles on the crags of Pumpkin Buttes full forty miles away." [1]

The command reached Powder River August 11, and began the construction of a post called Camp Connor, which later became Fort Reno, twenty-three and one-half miles above the mouth of Crazy Woman's Fork. Scouting and picket duty was done chiefly by the Pawnee scouts. From the official record and Palmer's account, the expedition seems to have been more or less a picnic or pleasure excursion. The troops ran their horses

[1] *Transactions and Reports, Nebraska Historical Society*, vol. II, p. 206. (Lincoln, 1887.)

almost to death chasing buffalo and jack rabbits, although General Curtis while commanding this department had issued orders forbidding this practise. Connor had better control over his men, but his officers seem to have done about as they pleased. Even on the very day that the Pawnees had a fight with the Cheyennes a few officers rode after game far from the column and came near being attacked by Indians.

A few days after the command reached Powder River scouts reported an Indian trail, and the whole company of Pawnees was ordered to follow it. According to their practise when expecting a fight they stripped themselves and their horses, and started out. The trail seemed to have been made by thirty-five or forty animals, one of which was dragging a travois. The Indians travelled fast, but the Pawnees followed at a gallop. At night about half the men, whose horses had become exhausted, were sent back to camp, but the remainder followed the trail until it became too dark to see it, when two Pawnees dismounted and followed on foot. At daylight a smoke was seen—at the camp of the Cheyennes, who were then just moving out.

These, because the Pawnees were riding in column, at first took them for white troops and prepared to fight, but when they heard the war cry of the Pawnees they sprang on their horses again and took to flight. A running fight took place, in which, according to Major North's statements and the official report, the whole party of Cheyennes, twenty-four or twenty-seven, was killed. Connor's report is as follows:

HEADQUARTERS,
POWDER RIVER, August 19th, 1865.

MAJOR-GENERAL G. M. DODGE:

A detachment of my Pawnee scouts on the 16th inst. discovered and pursued a party of 24 Cheyennes returning from the mail road with scalps and plunder. They overtook them about sixty miles northeast of here on Powder River, and after a short engagement killed the whole party. Loss on our side, 4 horses killed. We captured 29 animals, among which were 4 Government and one overland stage line horse, besides two Government saddles and a quantity of women's and children's clothing, and two of the infantry coats issued by Col. Moonlight last spring to the Indians, who subsequently killed Capt. Fouts and four soldiers of the Seventh Iowa.

P. EDW. CONNOR,
Brigadier-General.

These Cheyennes are believed to have been a part of those engaged in the attack on the Platte Bridge when Lieutenant Collins and Sergeant Custard with their men were killed. There were said to have been scalps of white soldiers found in the packs of the Indians.[1]

The Southern Cheyennes do not appear to know of any fight in which twenty-four or twenty-seven Cheyennes were killed. It seems probable therefore that this whole Cheyenne party of twenty-four was killed and that the Southern Cheyennes know nothing of it. Palmer's detailed account of the fight agrees with all the others that are given.

Only a few days later Major North came near being killed by the Cheyennes. He had ridden ahead of his Pawnees, whose horses were giving out, and was charged by a dozen Cheyennes. His horse was shot in the first encounter, and so badly wounded that it could not be ridden. He started to retreat, leading his horse, and then found that he was almost out of ammunition. By judicious use of his gun—by always threatening to fire at the approaching Indians and never firing—he kept the Indians from coming close to him, and at length met some of the Pawnees, when the Cheyennes left him.

Just west of Powder River there was a beaten trail along which passed many of the war parties returning from the mail road. Here little fights frequently took place, and every day or two the troops and the Pawnees killed one or more Cheyennes. Bent says that the Pawnees often showed themselves and acted like hostile Indians, thus getting close to the Cheyennes and Sioux before their identity was discovered.

That summer a party of engineers with a large wagon-train had started from the Missouri River up the Niobrara to open a wagon-road to the Montana mines. Colonel Sawyer, the leader of the expedition, had been given a military escort—Companies C and D, Fifth U. S. Volunteers. The soldiers of these companies were ex-Confederates released from military prisons on consenting to enlist to fight the Indians. The escort was commanded by Captain Williford, who, besides the infantry, had twenty-four men of the First Dakota Cavalry. At the head of the Niobrara the party struck across for Powder River, but on account of the

[1] *Pawnee Hero Stories and Folk Tales*, p. 326. (New York, 1889.)

rough country had great difficulty in reaching it. About twenty miles before they came to the stream they turned aside to avoid the broken country, and two days later were attacked by "several thousand" Indians, who kept them corralled for nearly four days and nights, fighting through the day and withdrawing at night, to renew hostilities in the morning. At last the Indians withdrew and the train moved sixty miles further south. South of Pumpkin Buttes the company struck Connor's trail and followed it to the new fort. Of this attack General Dodge said that "the Indians attacked Colonel Sawyer's wagon-road party, and failing in their attempt, they held a parley. Colonel Bent's sons, George and Joe Bent, appeared on the part of the Indians, and Colonel Sawyer gave them a wagon-load of goods to let him go undisturbed, Captain Williford, commanding escort, not agreeing to it. The Indians accepted the proposal and agreed to it, but after receiving the goods they attacked the party, killing three men. . . . He (George Bent) was dressed in one of our staff-officers' uniforms."

The Indian account of this affair is substantially the same. One day hunters rode into the village and notified them that soldiers were coming. Bull Bear, the camp crier, rode about calling out the news to the Cheyennes, while Red Cloud made the same announcement to the Sioux, and all the Indians drove in their horses. The men mounted their war ponies and went about twenty miles up Powder River, where they met troops, and a big wagon-train near the Gourd (Pumpkin) Butte. The soldiers were marching on each side of the wagons, and an officer with several soldiers and a Mexican interpreter rode out to meet the Indians, and made signs that four or five chiefs should come forward to meet them. Bull Bear and Dull Knife, George Bent and Red Cloud went to meet them.

The officer, evidently Colonel Sawyer, said that he was going to the Big Horn River to build a post, and had not come here to fight. Red Cloud said that if he would keep out of his country and would make no roads all would be well. Dull Knife said the same thing, and Red Cloud advised the officer to go due west, and then north on the Big Horn River and he would be out of the Indian country. The officer said, however, that that road was too long, and offered a wagon-load of sugar, coffee, rice, and other provisions if they would allow him to strike straight across the country. The chiefs agreed to this, and the officer told Bent to keep the Indians away while he had the wagon unloaded. This was about the middle of the day. The officer wished to get nearer the river and to go into camp. After he had moved down to the river and corralled his wagons, more Sioux came from the camp, and because they had received no share of the goods handed over they began to circle round the wagons and to fire on them. The soldiers had chosen a good place in which to fight— near to the water and with bare, level ground all about them— so that the Indians could not get near them. In this fight some horses were killed and five Sioux wounded, of whom two died later. Two soldiers and one Mexican were killed.

As General Connor's command moved down Tongue River the Pawnees came upon a heavy Indian trail over which a large camp had passed. When Captain North reported this to General Connor, he was ordered to take ten of his Pawnees and follow the trail. Only twenty-five or thirty miles from where he had left the command he found a large village of Indians, consisting of two or three hundred lodges. Messengers were sent back to General Connor, and the next day he came up with four hundred men and two pieces of artillery. The command was brought to within three-quarters of a mile of the Indian village before it was discovered. The troops charged on the camp, and dispersed its inhabitants, who were chiefly Arapahoes, under Black Bear, with some Cheyennes. The village, a large number of horses, and some women and children were captured, while a number of the Indians were killed. General Dodge says that six hundred horses were captured; Palmer says one thousand one hundred, and Major North says seven hundred and fifty horses and mules. The women and children captured were afterward set free. It was said that General Connor was inclined to give their horses back to the Arapahoes, but the Pawnees grumbled so about it that the idea was given up.

The utter heedlessness of Indians, even in time of war, could hardly be better shown than by something that happened just before Connor's attack on this village.

Ignorant of the fact that troops were near, a Cheyenne named Little Horse[1] with his wife and boy started from the Cheyenne

[1] Mŏ ĭn'ǎ hkā' kǐt. Very likely the same Little Horse who was a leader of the Northern Cheyennes at the Fort Phil Kearny fight.

camp to go to the Arapaho village. They were following the Arapaho trail. One of the packs got loose, and the wife dismounted to tighten it. She happened to turn her head and look back, and far behind saw people following the trail. She said to her husband, "Look over there," and Little Horse looked back and said: "Why, they are soldiers; hurry."

They went on, and when they had passed over the next hill and out of sight turned off the trail. Little Horse cut loose the travois on which the boy was riding, took the boy on behind him, and they cut across the country for the Arapaho camp, riding fast. When they reached the camp the wife of Little Horse told the crier to go through the camp and call out that soldiers were following. An Indian who heard this said: "Little Horse has made a mistake; he just saw some Indians coming over the trail, and nothing more."

Little Horse, however, went to his relations and said: "Now, you people would better get away from here; pack up whatever you wish to take along. We must go to-night." His brother-in-law, the Panther, said: "Oh, you are always getting frightened and making mistakes about things. You saw nothing but some buffalo."

"Very well," said Little Horse, "you need not go unless you want to, but we shall go to-night," and he and his relatives went on up the stream.

The Arapahoes had no belief that the troops were coming. On the morning of the attack they were about to move camp, and the women were pulling down the lodges. A man who had a fast horse and who was going to run a race with some one while the camp was travelling had gone up on the hill to give his horse a run, and as he passed over a ridge he saw before him the troops all ready to make a charge. He rode back as hard as he could and notified the camp. Many of the Arapaho men, women, and children ran out of the camp and down into the timber and brush on Tongue River and hid there. When the troops charged the village they followed only the people who were on horseback and running away, and did not think of those who had hidden in the brush. The Pawnees used to say that they did not care much about killing the people. They were after the horse herd of the camp, for General Connor had promised them that they could keep the horses they captured. Therefore they devoted themselves to catching the horses, and did not especially try to kill people.

Panther, Little Horse's brother-in-law, who had refused to heed his warning was killed in the village, and when Little Horse returned the day after the troops had gone away he found his body lying just in front of where the lodge had been.

Palmer's account of this affair is quite graphic, though written from the point of view of a man who knew nothing of Indians or Indian fighting, but wished to impress an audience. It is evident from the published accounts that after the Indians got over their first fright they made a good fight, and that, although the village had been captured and they had lost their horses and many of their people, nevertheless the troops could not get at them, and the Indians did not run far. In fact, after Connor and his command had turned about and were going back to their camp the Indians followed them and kept quite close to them, and, in bravado, gave some very extraordinary exhibitions of riding. General Connor burned the village and punished his own troops for stopping to plunder when they should have been fighting by destroying all the articles they had taken. The captives, eight women and thirteen children, were set free a few days later.

The command now moved down Tongue River, reaching the point where Cole should have been about the 1st of September, but no signs were found there of Cole or Walker.

On September 4 messengers from Sawyer's train came to the camp and reported the train corralled and surrounded on the Bozeman trail, west of Tongue River, and Connor sent troops to relieve Sawyer. It is supposed that Sawyer was attacked by the Arapahoes whom Connor had lately driven out of their camp.

The failure to hear anything of the columns under Cole and Walker made General Connor uneasy, and on the 8th of September Major North, with twenty Pawnees, was sent out toward Powder River to look for trails, while Connor turned about and proceeded up Tongue River. The Pawnees started out in a violent rain-storm, carrying only such provisions as they could tie on their saddles, and expecting to live chiefly on game. On the 11th of September North returned and reported that on Powder River they had found between five and six hundred dead cavalry horses, undoubtedly belonging to Cole's command. Most of them were dead on the picket line, and many fires were found in the camp, in the ashes of which were remains of saddles, bridles, and other equipment intentionally destroyed. This news troubled Connor greatly, and he again sent out scouts to try to locate Cole and order him to proceed up Powder River to Fort Connor.

Major North and his Pawnees finally found Cole and Walker on September 19. The men were starving and flocked about North and his Pawnees begging for food. The Pawnees gave them all they had, and refused to accept money for it, though some of the men offered five dollars for a single hardtack.

In passing through the rough bad-land country Cole was continually delayed by his inability to get his wagons along. Neither he nor Walker had had any experience on the plains, and they were without guides or any one familiar with the country or with Indian campaigning. After their meeting they had a very hard time because of the novel difficulties of prairie travel and of Indian fighting. Walker appears to have wandered about in the hope that he might meet Connor, and Cole followed after him. The command was several times attacked by the Indians, Sioux and Cheyenne, and Cole reported that his men had killed a large number. They were in constant fear that they would lose their horses, and so did not let them graze. The animals grew thin and weak, became unserviceable, and finally died in large numbers. Some horses were captured by Indians, and during one or two cold storms five hundred or six hundred died at the picket line. Cole was thus obliged to burn his saddles and wagons, and finally lost most of his live stock. It is altogether possible that if it had not been for his artillery the Indians might have killed his whole command. The big guns with the shells frightened the Indians, and it was usually practicable to disperse any gathering by firing the cannon at them.

When Major North and the Pawnees found the command of about one thousand eight hundred men all the cavalrymen were on foot. They had still about 600 horses, but none fit for service. The men were wholly without provisions, and if they had not been found must before long have died of starvation. Cole's loss was twelve men killed and two missing, besides several wounded. He estimated the loss of the Indians in the fights had with them as "from 200 to 500 killed" and a great many wounded. Major North took this command to Fort Connor, which Connor himself reached September 24. Connor reported Cole's command "as completely disgusted and discouraged an outfit of men as I ever saw."

At Camp Connor General Connor found orders from the Department Commander calling him in to Fort Laramie and relieving him of his command. He was greatly angered at this treatment, and felt that he had been grievously injured—as indeed he had. After he was mustered out he went to Salt Lake City, and never made any report on his expedition; the good work that he had done in the Powder River country came to nothing, and he was never given any credit for it.

Just as Connor failed to make a report, so neither Cole nor Walker made a written report at the time, but a year later Cole, exasperated by the charges made against him by General Connor and his officers, sent a long report to General Grant. From that[1] and from the stories told by the Cheyennes a clear idea may be had of the situation. It seems evident that, while Cole and Walker both showed themselves incompetent, General Connor, after all, was largely responsible for their troubles. He sent out two columns under two colonels, but did not put Walker under Cole's command. When the two men met they at once began to quarrel, and seem to have disagreed about everything and to have acted together only when attacked by Indians in force. Besides that, Connor had promised to be at a certain point on or near September 1, but appears to have felt little responsibility about this, and spent nearly two weeks building a fort and a week more fighting Arapahoes. Meantime Cole and Walker, absolutely unacquainted with the plains or with Indians, were at a loss what to do or where to go.

During the first days of September Cole and Walker, having already lost hundreds of animals through starvation, were attacked by a large body of Cheyennes and Sioux, and what the Cheyennes called Roman Nose's fight took place. Cole and Walker, who were marching up the valley of Powder River, were discovered by a small Cheyenne war party who sent back word to the

[1] *Official Records*, vol. 102.

camp and all the men came out to the fight. Roman Nose had requested the leaders not to make the charge until he came up, for usually it took him some time to perform the ceremonies required by the protective war bonnet which he wore—the one made for him by Ice, of the Northern Cheyennes, and the one he wore when he was killed in 1868. When Roman Nose came to the fight he put himself at the head of the Indians, who formed a line facing the troops, while Roman Nose, mounted on a fine war horse, rode the whole length of the line at a run within easy carbine shot of the soldiers. His war bonnet protected him, and he was not hit. He repeated this manœuvre several times, and then at a signal all the Indians charged. If the Indians had had a few guns they might have broken the line and killed many of the soldiers, but they had less than half a dozen guns among them and could not long face the heavy volleys from the Spencer carbines with which most of the troops were armed. The Indians soon withdrew to the hills, where they were shelled, but without injury. The only man hit was a very old Sioux, Black Whetstone, who was sitting behind a hill half a mile away when a shell came over the hill and dropped on him.

The Cheyennes now left the troops and went away toward the Black Hills to hunt buffalo. The command continued its slow progress up the river, and on September 8 reached the mouth of Little Powder River where they were attacked by "3,000 Sioux." This attack is said by the Indians to have been made to stop the troops, in order that the women of the Sioux camp might pack their lodges and move away. That night a cold storm came on, and many of the horses and mules that the troops still had died on the picket line. Wagons, saddles, supplies of all kinds, and even ammunition were now destroyed.

Finally, as stated, the command was found by Major North and his Pawnees, who led them, barefooted and in rags, into Fort Connor, which they reached September 20.

General Dodge had been receiving news from Fort Connor which had misled him into believing that Cole and Walker's retreat up Powder River had been a victorious advance. He speaks of battles in which the Sioux were driven, defeated, and pursued. On the 4th he says that they defeated the Sioux, killing two hundred. But this was the day the troops moved about a mile up the valley to get better grass for the starving animals and saw no Indians.

According to Cheyenne accounts the troops never took the offensive against the Indians. Their horses were in such condition that the troops could not make a mounted charge and were satisfied to fight off the Indians. Cole himself says that his men never fought except when forced to do so.

After the withdrawal of these troops there were no soldiers in the country until the following year, when General Carrington was sent up there to establish Fort Phil Kearny.

XVII

PLATTE BRIDGE FIGHT

1865

In March, 1865, the Southern Cheyennes who had gone north
to raid the overland stage road joined the Northern Cheyennes,
and the Ogallala Sioux under Old Man Afraid of His Horses, who
were encamped on Powder River. The two tribes were in separate camps a short distance apart, and the Southern Cheyennes
put up their lodges with their kinsmen, the Northern Cheyennes.
Many of the younger people of the Southern Cheyennes had
never before been in the northern country nor seen a great camp
of the northern tribe. Now that they met the Northern Cheyennes with the Sioux they found that the northern division had
some customs unlike those of the southerners and resembling those
of the Sioux.

The Northern Cheyennes and the Sioux gladly welcomed the
people from the south and feasted them daily. They had heard
something about the slaughter at Sand Creek and questioned the
southern people about that, as well as about their fights with the
troops on their way north. Not long after they reached Powder
River all the lodges were taken down and the villages moved a
short distance down the stream to camp again in a fresh place.
Here the lodges, instead of being arranged in a great circle, were
pitched in little clusters up and down the river, making a camp
that extended along the stream for about two miles. Indians who
were in the camp on the Little Big Horn River when it was attacked by Custer in 1876 say that it was much like this one on
Powder River, though the one on the Little Big Horn was far the
larger of the two.

It was thought that the camp would remain here for some time
and for this reason small groups, five or six families, joined in
building log corrals or pens in which to keep their best horses
at night. Each evening the more valuable animals were driven

into these corrals, while the wild ponies and old pack-horses were left to run loose on the prairie.

One morning a herder going out on the prairie to look at the horses found there a bow and quiver. He brought them into the camp and they were recognized as being made by the Crows. During the night a party of young Crows had come to the camp to capture horses. They had found the wild horses on the prairie, and in trying to ride one a Crow had been thrown and in the darkness had lost his bow and quiver.

The story told by the weapons was at once understood and young men mounted their horses and in small parties set out to look for the trail left by the Crows. It was soon found and the Cheyennes followed it rapidly, for it was easily read in the snow. Before long a party overtook four of the Crows and killed them. They had been unable to find any horses they could ride, and on foot they could not drive the wild animals swiftly enough to escape pursuit. They had therefore abandoned the horses and tried to get away on foot. The young man who had been thrown and had lost his bow and arrows had mounted a wild horse that belonged to Old Bull Bear. He must have been badly hurt by the fall, for while following his tracks they saw a number of places where he had sat down to rest. He was killed only a couple of miles from the village. The young Cheyennes who were following the horses' tracks at length came to the place where three of the Crows had ceased to try to drive the horses and had run off together through the snow, turning into the mountains and following up a canyon until they came to a hole in the rocks, into which they had gone. The Cheyennes could see the barrels of guns thrust out of this hole, and did not go very near to it.

As they were standing about Gentle Horse rode up and said: "Wait, be careful; get away from near the mouth of that hole. Do not take any risks." After he had spoken he looked about a little and saw, not far from the first hole, another one in the rocks higher up on the face of the canyon. He directed the young men to gather cedar and pine boughs, and said to them: "We will get those enemies out of that place, for we will smoke them out." They went around, and, getting to the upper hole, they stuffed into it cedar and pine and some sage-brush and set it on fire. The young men brought branches and threw them into the hole, and with their lances shoved the burning branches down to the bottom, which they now saw was connected with the cave in which the Crows were. When they were thrusting down the lances the Crows came up to the crevice below and struck the lances with their ramrods, thus counting a coup on the Cheyennes. Presently from the top of the canyon Gentle Horse and the others began to drop burning branches down in front of the cave so that there might be smoke on both sides of the Crows. Those who could see the mouth of the cave saw the Crows within hard at work throwing out earth to try to put out the fire.

A little later one of the Crows, holding his butcher-knife in his hand, ran out of the cave and up to Big Horse[1] and struck him on the breast with his knife, breaking the knife blade on the German silver breastplate which he wore. The Cheyennes who were watching shot down this Crow, and then the other two Crows jumped out and were killed; their hands were scorched and the strings of their bows were burned in two.

The Cheyennes returned to camp with the scalps of the four Crows and for a number of nights scalp dances were held by the Sioux and Northern Cheyennes. So great a drumming and singing went on that the buffalo were frightened away from the neighborhood of the camp. The Cheyennes believe that buffalo are afraid of a drum, but say that they do not mind singing.

It now became necessary to send out men to find the buffalo, and at length the scouts came in with news that the herds were on Little Powder River.[2] Camp was broken and two moves were made to that stream. In this new camp the Crazy Dogs, then acting as police, gave orders that no drumming should be done. From this time on the drums were silent, but the dancing and singing over the Crow scalps continued.

The Crazy Dogs[3] were one of several soldier societies, of which the others were Red Shields,[4] Dog Soldiers,[5] Crooked Lance Soldiers,[6] Kit-Fox Soldiers,[7] Bow String,[8] and Chief Soldiers.[9]

In a large camp one of these societies was always on duty to

---

[1] Still alive at Cantonment, Oklahoma, in 1908, about eighty years old.
[2] Pai'yo hē kĭs derivation is Powder River; + the diminutive suffix "kis."
[3] Ho tăm'i măs sau', Dogs Crazy.
[4] Ma ho hē'văs.
[5] Ho tămi'tăn'iu.
[6] Hĭm'o wē yŭh'k ĭs.
[7] Wōhk sēh'hē tăn'iu.
[8] Hĭm'o tăn o'hĭs.
[9] Wĭ'hĭū tăn'iu.

enforce the orders of the chiefs and generally to keep order in the camp. Neither the Chief Soldiers nor the Red Shields took part in this police work, for these two societies were composed of older men, but the principal duty of the other societies was the enforcing of order. It sometimes happened that the young men of these societies became arrogant and endeavored to exert undue influence on the camp, to carry out certain plans that their soldier band had determined on. Under ordinary conditions when one society had policed the camp for a certain length of time it went off duty, being relieved by soldiers of another band selected by the chiefs.

The powers of the soldiers were great and often they severely punished men who violated customs or camp rules. Sometimes they whipped men, beat them with their war clubs, or even killed their ponies. Under less provocation they might cut up robes, break lodge-poles or even cut up lodges. The soldiers took charge of the general hunts and directed the hunters, seeing to it that the rules governing the hunt were observed and that all men had an equal chance to kill food.

For some time the camp remained on Little Powder River, killing buffalo and frequently moving camp in order to find fresh grass for the horses, which must be put in good condition after the long, cold winter. In May the camp moved over to Tongue River and travelled up that stream by short marches until near its head at the base of the Big Horn Mountains. Here the chiefs of the tribes held a war council and it was decided that as soon as the horses were strong enough war parties should set out and raid the emigrant roads on the North Platte and the South Platte. It was determined also to make a general attack at some point on the road in midsummer. Now the camp moved back to Powder River, and from there parties began to set out southward to raid the white men's roads. The objective point of one large party was the emigrant road near the Platte Bridge. In this large force there were Northern and Southern Cheyennes and a body of Sioux warriors, led by Young Man Afraid of His Horses.[1]

---

[1] This famous Sioux warrior's name, like that of his father, has been misinterpreted. It really means, "They fear even his horses," or "Even his horses are feared." The significance is that the man is so brave that his enemies are afraid even of his horses.

The Northern Cheyennes, who had always lived up in this country, led their southern kinsfolk directly to the North Platte River, striking it at a point about thirty miles below the Platte Bridge, where the town of Casper, Natrona County, now is.[1] To the Southern Cheyennes this whole country was strange, although their forefathers had lived here up until the separation of the two sections of the tribe, about a generation before. The Cheyennes reached the river after three nights, forded it, and went west along the stage road until they came to a stockade. Here they fought the soldiers all day, running off a herd of mules, and toward evening retreating across the Platte River.

After some raiding along the stage road the Indians all gathered in the hills on the north side of the Platte River and in the neighborhood of the bridge which stood close to the fort there—sometimes called Camp Dodge. They went into camp on a little stream that flows into the Platte some distance east of the bridge, but the camp was far up the creek so that the high bluffs along the northern border of the river valley hid them from view. Here were gathered a great party of fighting Indians, estimated by people who were present at three thousand men. At all events, three tribes were represented, Sioux, Cheyennes, and Arapahoes, and there were present a large proportion of the fighting men of these tribes. Besides the men there were about two hundred women, chiefly Cheyennes.

It was now the middle of the summer, and they decided to attack the stockade at the Platte Bridge. A small force of Indians was to be sent down close to the fort to induce the soldiers to come out and pursue them, when the Indians would lead the troops to a place where a large force of Indians was hidden. After these decoys had been sent out the main body went to the bluffs overlooking the river bottom and the fort. During the march to this point the rear and both flanks were guarded by bands of the soldiers, the Crazy Dogs marching on the flanks, while the Dog Soldiers brought up the rear. These soldiers kept the warriors in compact formation, and the warriors followed

[1] This party attacked Deer Creek, an abandoned stage station then occupied by troops of the Eleventh Kansas Cavalry. The fight was May 20; two hundred Indians attacked Deer Creek and ran off twenty horses from the cavalry. Colonel Plumb reports one soldier killed.

close after the pipe-bearers, chiefs and older men, who rode in advance. The company moved slowly, so as not to cause the rising of a cloud of dust which might warn the troops of the presence of the Indians.

Before they had reached the tops of the hills the Crazy Dogs halted the Indians and a few men, some of whom had field-glasses, went up and looked over the crest of the hills. The warriors behind the hill were making final preparations for battle, taking their war clothing from the sacks, holding the different articles up to the four points of the compass, and to the sun, and then putting them on. The owner of a shield stripped off its cover, shook loose its various ornaments, held it four times toward the earth, and then shook it four times toward the sky, afterward hanging it on his left arm, where it should be carried in battle. All these ceremonies and the prayers made were supplications for protection and success in the fight that was to come.

The party which had been sent down to the neighborhood of the bridge rode about there, hoping to induce the soldiers to follow them into an ambuscade. The soldiers came out of the gate of the fort, but would not follow the Indians to any great distance beyond the bridge.

The troops had a howitzer, and when the Indians came back and rode up near to the soldiers some shots were fired from this big gun. The shooting greatly excited the Indians behind the hill, who finally broke through the soldiers, and in a mass ran up to the crest of the bluffs, and from there watched what was going on. It appears, nevertheless, that the troops did not see these people, who at length returned to their camp.

When it was seen that the soldiers would not follow the Indians and it began to get late in the day the chiefs sent High Backed Wolf,[1] a Cheyenne, to the men who were near the fort, ordering them to come back to the main body. One of these men spoke angrily to High Backed Wolf, and said: "Now, when I see anything and go to get it, I want to succeed in getting it." He wished to keep on fighting. High Backed Wolf said: "All right, I feel just as you do about that, but I am trying to do what the head men have asked me to do. Come on now, let us swim the river and get close to the soldiers." They did so.

[1] Hōh nĭh"o hkā'ĭ yō hōs.

A small party of soldiers was coming up the river, and had nearly reached the post. The Indians charged them and rode through the soldiers almost to the walls of the post, where they met other soldiers who had just come out to help those who were approaching. A young man named Iron counted coup on one of the soldiers, and here High Backed Wolf was shot, but clung to his horse for some distance before falling. The Indians say that he was shot by a musket ball, but others believe that the officer, near whom he rode, killed him with a revolver. The other Cheyennes now stopped fighting and recrossed the river, leaving the dead man on the south side. Next morning when his body was recovered by his father, Blind Wolf, and two or three others, it was found that he had a wound in the breast, apparently from an arrow, and a little piece of sinew was sticking out of the wound. This would suggest that he had been shot also by one of the Shoshoni Indians, of whom there were two or three at the fort.

Black White Man[1] says of the death of High Backed Wolf that before this fighting began White Bull[2] had told the Cheyennes that at this time they must not hold in the mouth any metal, especially no iron and no bullet. High Backed Wolf and his brother Horse Black[3] had chased the soldiers for some distance, but presently the soldiers stopped and High Backed Wolf, while loading his six-shooter, put a pistol bullet in his mouth and was killed.

Next morning early about one-half the men in the camp, keeping out of sight, went down to the river below the bridge and hid themselves in the brush and timber along the little stream and the other half, going around north of the river bottom out of sight, hid above the bridge. The small party of Indians acting as decoys had again been sent down to the fort to try to bring out the soldiers. After a time a party of troops on gray horses came out of the post and crossed the bridge. The Indians supposed they were pursuing the decoys, but they were going to the relief of a wagon-train that was coming down the river, of which the Indians as yet knew nothing. The Cheyennes were watching them from the tops of the hills and making signs to others

---

[1] Black White Man = Negro, Mŏhk stā'vĭ'hĭo.
[2] White Bull, Hō tū'ă'hwō' kō măs.
[3] Horse Black, Mō ĭn'ă mŏhk stā'văs.

who could not see so well to keep still and wait. Then as the soldiers rode off the bridge and started up the long flat the Indians signalled for half the party below the bridge to get behind the soldiers and cut them off from the bridge, while the other half should go around the other way and meet them. Those who had got between the soldiers and the bridge were the first to charge. The soldiers started up the road on a fast gallop, riding toward the hills and away from the bridge and the post, and then met the party that was ahead of the soldiers, who charged on them. For a short time the soldiers fought hard to go forward in the direction that they had been going, that is, away from the post, but at last overpowered by numbers they turned and rode straight for the bridge. A soldier seized the reins of the horse ridden by the brother of White Horse and beat him over the head with a revolver. White Bull charged on the man and struck him across the head with a sabre, knocking him off his horse. Most of the soldiers succeeded in crossing the river, but the officer and some other men were killed.

An Indian said: "The soldiers charged straight toward us as we rushed forward to meet them. I saw the officer sitting his saddle with a long arrow sticking in his forehead. His horse, a big gray, was running away with him. He passed me, and, looking back, I saw him go down among the crowd of warriors at my back. The smoke and dust hid everything."

Some of the Indians say that perhaps Lieutenant Collins might have crossed the bridge in safety except that his horse ran away with him, and he could not control it. It was captured by the Indians and lived long in the Cheyenne camp, but was always uncontrollable and constantly ran away.

Although the whites were so few by comparison with the Indians only eight men[1] were killed with Lieutenant Collins at this time. To this day it is impossible to make the Indians believe that the number was so small.

Soon after all this happened people on the hills began to signal that soldiers were coming down the north side of the river, and soon the white-covered wagons were seen coming. Quite a long distance before the troops reached the bridge they halted, corralled their wagons and unharnessed their teams. As the

[1] Coutant, *History of Wyoming*, p. 473.

drivers were taking the animals down to the river bank the Indians charged them and they at once left their mules and rushed back to the wagons. The Indians charged the wagon corral, but the troops had taken refuge in and behind the wagons and had cut loopholes in the wagon-boxes through which they fired and killed a number of Indians. Meantime the mules were rushing about, but a Cheyenne rode in and captured the bell-mare, and when he led her away the mules all followed her blindly and were taken into camp. The soldiers kept firing from the wagons, and now Roman Nose ordered the men who had guns to creep up as close as possible to the wagons and to shoot into the wagons. They fired a number of volleys in this way. Then Roman Nose and two or three others rode close to the troops to induce them all to discharge their guns, and presently charging the wagons found all the soldiers dead or badly wounded. Three soldiers cut off from the wagons ran to the river and swam across. One of these was killed later. Another carried his revolver across above the water. Left Hand, a brother of Roman Nose, and some other Indians followed him across the river. The soldier climbed the bank and hid among the willows, and as the Indian came out of the water the soldier killed him, and with his companion reached the stockade.

Among the Indians who had recently joined this great party, though only a portion of them were present at the fight at the Platte Bridge, was a large village of Brulé Sioux. Up to this time these people had taken no part in the war. They had been encamped at Fort Laramie, in charge of a white man named Elston, and had been subsisted by the troops. There had been complaint of the cost of this, and General Dodge ordered them sent east to a point where food was less costly. Colonel Moonlight, commander at Fort Laramie, sent them under guard to Fort Kearny, in Nebraska. It was a large village, about one hundred and eighty-five lodges, and Elston had them all in good control and had a uniformed and armed company of the Indians, whom he had been using to police the camp.

Fort Kearny was in the Pawnee country, and the Brulés feared that if they were sent there the Pawnees would attack them in great force. They were thus much frightened and dissatisfied—exceedingly loath to go. Captain Fouts left Laramie with these Indians June 11, 1865. He had one hundred and thirty-five men and four officers of the Seventh Iowa Cavalry. They had hardly started before the Indians began to complain that the escort treated them badly, and abused the young girls. The result of this added discontent was that before they had been more than a day or two on the road the Indians held a secret council and decided to attack their guard at the next camp, and to join the hostiles who were in the north. The next camp was made on Horse Creek,[1] a small stream on the Platte. Where the road crossed the creek, near its mouth, the troops put up their tents on the east bank, while the Indians camped on the west side near a bluff overgrown with willows. Early next morning a part of the troops and the wagon-train started down the road, while the soldiers who were to guard the Indians crossed Horse Creek and rode toward the lodges, to count the people and get them started on their way.

As the soldiers rode up, the women and children slipped in among the willows behind the lodges and hid, while the warriors came out and lined up to be counted, holding their bows and the few pistols they possessed hidden under their blankets. The plan was to let the soldiers approach very near, and then attack and kill them all, but the hot-headedness of some of the young men interfered with this plan. The officer was riding far ahead of his men, and as he rode close to the Indians the young men could not restrain themselves, and, leaping forward, killed the officer. No sooner had the troopers witnessed this than they wheeled about and galloped off as fast as they could go. The official record seems to show that the troops had no ammunition, for none had been issued the night before, though Lieutenant W. Haywood urged the commanding officer to issue ammunition to the men. Captain Wilcox, on learning what had taken place, followed the Indians, and found them just crossing the Platte, the women and children swimming the ponies, while the men were on the bank ready to fight. He did not attack them.

Colonel Moonlight at Fort Laramie, advised by telegraph from Camp Mitchell of what had happened, crossed the Platte with a strong force of cavalry and struck out northward in pursuit of the Indians. He followed their trail from where they had crossed

---

[1] Mōh ĭn'ŏ hăm ĭ'yō hē.

the Platte and camped on Dead Man's Fork, one hundred and twenty miles northeast of Laramie. He had no idea where the Indians were, and turned loose his horses to graze. The next day the Indians charged his camp and captured his horses. Moonlight says that the men got their horses and tried to mount, but that the animals broke away and ran straight at the Indians. The Indians say that the horses seem to have broken their picket-lines, and came rushing in a mass at the Indians, who thought that a large force of cavalry was charging them, and ran away. They very soon discovered what was happening, and closed in on the herd and carried it off. There was no fighting, but Moonlight was left afoot. He was obliged to burn his saddles and equipments, and march back on foot to Laramie, through a rough country, where there was little water. The soldiers reached Laramie after a hard march, and were more or less pestered by a few Indians who kept hanging on their rear. They were very angry at Moonlight, through whose carelessness they had lost their mounts.[1]

Moonlight was much censured for losing his horses, and shortly afterward was mustered out of the service by General Connor, who, however, gave no reason for the action.

After the fight at the Platte Bridge a small party of Indians went down the stage road toward Fort Laramie. They captured some ranches and burned some stage stations, killing a few soldiers, after which they returned north again. The village was found on Lodge-pole Creek[2] near Powder River. Soon all the

---

[1] Dead Man's Fork is a tributary of Hat Creek, which is a southern tributary of the South Cheyenne River. Dead Man's Fork is in the extreme northwest corner of Nebraska in the rough country, where much pine grows.

In the evening (June 17 ?) Moonlight camped one hundred miles northeast of Fort Laramie. Next morning before dawn he moved on, and after making twenty miles halted about noon in the valley of Dead Man's Fork. Here he turned his horses out to graze, but some California officers who had served against Indians under General Connor protested against turning the animals loose. Moonlight paid no heed to what they said, so these officers had the California men picket their horses near camp. The Indians soon appeared and stampeded the stock in broad daylight. Most of the California horses, on picket, were saved; the loose animals were all lost.

General Dodge reports that Moonlight permitted his camp to be surprised in broad day, and had most of his herd run off.

[2] Clear Creek of the whites.

war parties of Cheyennes and Sioux reached the camp, bringing much plunder—horses and goods taken from emigrants.

This was the general course of events at the Platte Bridge[1] as the Indians tell what they saw. The precise dates, however, and the sequence of events is given in a paper by Mr. S. H. Fairchild, of Alma, Kansas, entitled "The Eleventh Kansas Regiment at Platte Bridge."

From this paper a few paragraphs are extracted:

June 26, Lieut. W. Y. Drew of Company I with 25 men, while repairing the telegraph line had a hard scrimmage with some 300 warriors that pounced down upon them. On the 2d of July, the whole of Company I was attacked by several hundred Indians some twelve miles from the bridge. Major Anderson then ordered a detachment of troops from D, H, and K companies to report at headquarters at the bridge for duty, thus bringing up the number of enlisted men to 120 and two tipis of Snake Indians. This force was wholly inadequate to be stationed in the heart of the Indian country swarming with savages.

About the middle of July I went with a mail detail of twelve men from Platte Bridge a hundred miles down the line toward Fort Laramie. We were gone ten days, having to travel mostly in the night, as it was unsafe to travel by daylight in small bodies. While at Horse Shoe Station we learned that the Indians had appeared again along the North Platte and in our rear in large numbers, and were liable to give us serious trouble on our return. We arrived at Deer Creek, where our company was stationed, on the 24th of July. Another detail of twelve men under Corp. Henry Grimm relieved us and proceeded to Platte Bridge with the mail. There arrived there on the 25th also a small detachment of the Eleventh Ohio from Sweet Water Bridge. The Indians had been hanging around the bridge for several days and were bold and saucy, which indicated that they were there in force.

On the morning of July 25 an attempt was made to stampede the horses grazing below the bridge, but they were at last driven into the stockade by the soldiers. Reinforcements coming from the post, the Indians were driven back, but a little later they drove the troops back, and "recovered the body of their dead chief." This is presumably the occasion when High Backed Wolf was killed.

About nine o'clock on the morning of the 26th, a train of wagons from Sweet Water, escorted by twenty-five men under command of Sergt. Amos

[1] *Transactions of Kansas State Historical Society*, vol. VIII, p. 352. (Topeka, 1904.)

J. Custard, Company H, Eleventh Kansas, was seen coming over the hills some two or three miles away. The howitzers were fired to warn them of danger.

A detail of twenty-five men from I and K companies under Sergeant Hankammer, including the mail party under Corporal Grimm, was ordered to go to the relief of Sergt. Custard. Lieut. Caspar Collins, Eleventh Ohio, who had just arrived with Grimm's mail party volunteered to take command of the detachment. They crossed the bridge to the north side of the river and at full speed made their way toward the hills. They had proceeded about half a mile when from behind the hills and out of the ravines came swooping down upon them hundreds of Indians, yelling, whooping, shooting arrows and rifles and riding in circles about them like so many fiends, while a large body of them, coming down from the bluffs, attempted to get between them and the bridge. Capt. Greer, Company I, seeing the peril threatening the brave boys under Collins, charged, crossed the bridge with the balance of his company and poured a deadly fire into the howling savages, driving them back, and thus opening a way of retreat for Collins and his men, if they succeeded in making their way through the hundreds of savages that surrounded them. Collins, finding that more than half of his men were killed or wounded, gave command for everyone to make for the bridge. It was a race for life. Nehring, a private of Company K, Eleventh Kansas, not understanding the order, dismounted to fight from a deep washout in the road. Grimm looking around, yelled to him in German: "To the bridge." That was the last that was seen of poor Nehring. Camp, also of Company K, Eleventh Kansas, lost his horse and then ran for dear life, but when within a few rods of safety was overtaken and tomahawked. Sergeant Hankammer's horse was wounded, but carried him safely to the bridge and there dropped.

A wounded soldier fell from his horse and called out to his comrades: "Don't leave me; don't leave me." Collins turned and rode back to the man and thus lost all possibility of saving his own life. The brave lieutenant was mounted on a magnificent horse and might have escaped had he not gone back on this errand of mercy. . . . Our soldiers held the bridge and stockade, although the Indians crossed the river above and below the bridge and fought desperately, harassing our forces on every side throughout that day and a part of the next. On the evening of the 26th two men came out of the chaparral in a bend of the river on the south side, about one-half mile above the bridge. A party went out to rescue them. They proved to be Company D boys from Sergeant Custard's command. They said that when they heard the howitzers in the morning, Custard ordered a corporal to take five men and go forward to see what the firing meant. They had proceeded but a short distance when they were cut off from Custard's escort. Pursued by the Indians they struck for the river, but only three of them succeeded in crossing to the south bank and one of these was killed before the friendly shelter of the chaparral was reached. The nineteen men remaining with the train under Custard were also surrounded, but made a brave fight from ten in the forenoon until three in the afternoon. From that time there was an ominous silence, which to the troops at the bridge boded ill for Custard and his men.

The following day the Indians had apparently withdrawn, and troops were sent out to bury the dead.

Shortly after this the Eleventh Kansas was relieved by the Sixth Michigan, and was ordered to Fort Leavenworth to be mustered out.

XVIII

FORT PHIL KEARNY

1866

SEVENTY-NINE officers and men, and two civilians were killed December 21, 1866, near the recently established Fort Phil Kearny. Captain W. J. Fetterman, brevet lieutenant colonel, was in command of the troops, and the annihilation of the command was due to his disobedience of orders. For ten years after it took place this so-called Fetterman massacre was the Indian battle most talked of in the western country.

The Harney-Sanborn treaty of 1865 had guaranteed to the Indians of the northern country—Sioux, Cheyennes, and Arapahoes—the land which they occupied, and in which there was still abundant game. It was the territory lying between the Black Hills, the Rocky Mountains, and the Yellowstone River, generally known as the Powder River country, the great tract extending from the Little Missouri on the east to the foothills of the mountains on the west.

The discovery of gold in Idaho, in 1861, and somewhat later in Montana, had created much excitement east and west, and from all directions miners and prospectors set out for the gold-fields. The principal routes thither were the Missouri River, which was available only for a portion of the year, the trail up the Arkansas to Denver, and the Oregon trail through Nebraska and up the Platte and Sweetwater Rivers. After the discovery of the Montana mines, efforts were made to select a new road which should greatly shorten the distance to the mines. That chosen was the Bozeman trail, which passed directly through the country which had been conceded to the wild Indians.

In the latter part of 1865 and in 1866 the Government tried to make an agreement with these northern Indians for a right of way through this territory to Montana. A few of the Sioux assented to such an arrangement, but the Ogallalas and the Cheyennes declined to sign the treaty. Nevertheless, in the spring of 1866 General H. B. Carrington was ordered to proceed from Fort Kearny, Nebraska, via Fort Laramie, to the northwest, to garrison Camp Connor, established the year before by the Powder River expedition—afterward Fort Reno—and to build two new forts near the Bozeman road.

General Carrington reached Fort Laramie in June with about seven hundred men of the Twenty-seventh Infantry, of whom five hundred are said to have been raw recruits. They were armed for the most part with old-fashioned muzzle-loading Springfield muskets, though the band had Spencer breech-loading carbines. The amount of ammunition carried by the command was wholly insufficient. General Carrington was a man of great ability and of varied pursuits, but he knew nothing of Indians and their ways and so was ill fitted to command an expedition sent out into the heart of a country where there was certain to be fighting. Carrington reached Fort Reno late in June, set to work repairing it, left a garrison there, and marched on. On the 13th of July, 1866, he made camp on the banks of Big Piney Creek, a tributary of Powder River, and there began preparations for building the new post, which was called Fort Phil Kearny.

The troops had already been warned by the Indians that they must leave the country and that no new forts must be built. No attention was paid to the warning, and the troops had scarcely settled themselves on the site where the fort was to be built when their horses were taken by the Indians, and the party that followed them was attacked and several were killed and wounded. The same day a French trader and his outfit were killed, and from that time on constant watchfulness was required. Early in August General Carrington located Fort C. F. Smith about ninety miles northwest of Phil Kearny, sending two companies to that point to build the post. Meantime timber was being brought in to be sawed; a stockade was put up, and quarters, stables, shops, and a corral were built. Fort Phil Kearny was to be, and afterward was, a very complete establishment.

The trains sent out to bring timber into the Government sawmill were constantly harassed by small parties of Indians, and these attacks resulted in the killing of a number of the troops. Vedettes were stationed on some high hills—Sullivant Hills—to watch for the approach of enemies, and when a gathering of Indians was seen within range, howitzers, loaded with explosive shells, were fired at them, and always dispersed them. A little southwest of the post was a high, steep ridge, called Lodge Trail Ridge, which divides the waters of Powder River from those of Tongue River.

The officers and men of General Carrington's command were ignorant of Indians and Indian fighting. Service on the battle-fields of the South many of them had seen, but Indians on the naked prairie, or in the rough mountains, were to all an unknown quantity. Some of the officers seemed to regard the Indians as a sort of game to be hunted for sport. The books quote them as expressing a keen desire to "take a scalp," or to "get Red Cloud's scalp."

Early in December Colonel Fetterman with forty men, sent out to protect a wood-train, pursued the Indians into a situation where the troops were almost surrounded. In an effort to inter-cept the Indians, however, General Carrington led out twenty additional men, and coming up at the critical moment rescued the command, with a loss of two or three of the party. This experience taught General Carrington a lesson, as is shown by the orders he gave Fetterman later.

On the 21st of December the picket on Sullivant Hills sig-nalled that the wood-train was being attacked, and a relief party of seventy-six men—forty-nine from the Eighteenth Infantry and twenty-seven from the Second Cavalry—was ordered out. General Carrington gave the command to Captain Powell, Lieu-tenant Grummond commanding the cavalry, but just as they were about to start Colonel Fetterman begged for the command of the expedition, pleading his seniority in justification. His re-quest was granted. Captain Fred H. Brown volunteered to ac-company the troops, and two frontiersmen, Wheatley and Fisher, went with them.

Before the command left the stockade General Carrington gave orders to Colonel Fetterman, twice repeated, to relieve the wood-train and drive back the Indians, but on no account to pursue the Indians beyond the Lodge Trail Ridge. The force set out, but instead of proceeding directly toward the corralled wood-train it passed back of the Sullivant Hills on the southwestern slope of the Lodge Trail Ridge, perhaps with the purpose of cutting off the Indians who were attacking the train. As the troops approached the train the Indians dispersed, and at the same time a number appeared close to the fort. The cannon was fired, and the shell exploded near them. It was now discovered that no surgeon had gone with the relief party, and Doctor Hines with one man was sent toward the wood-train with instructions to join Fetterman. The wood-train was free from attack at the moment and Hines started after Fetterman, but saw many Indians in the country before him and returned to the post. Firing began to be heard from the other side of Lodge Trail Ridge, continuing for some time, but gradually becoming less and less. General Carrington despatched Captain Ten Eyck and a force to help Fetterman, giving him all his available men. By this time the firing had ceased. In the post hours of anxious waiting ensued.

When the relief party looked down from the top of Lodge Trail Ridge no soldiers were to be seen, but all over the valley, and above all on the ridge running down toward Clear Creek, were excited Indians riding about and shouting their war cries, evidently celebrating a triumph.

Captain Ten Eyck sent a messenger to the fort to report the situation, and presently the relief party descended to the battleground, for the Indians, satisfied with what they had done, began to withdraw and soon disappeared. Wagons were sent for, and late in the evening Ten Eyck's relief party came to the post with the bodies of forty-nine men. The next day General Carrington with eighty men returned to the battle-ground and found the remaining bodies, which were brought in for burial. No white man lived to tell the tale of the fight and for what happened on the field we must depend on Indian witnesses.

The Indians engaged in the fight were very numerous. They were chiefly Sioux, with some Cheyennes and Arapahoes; and they practised the simple strategy—so often and so effectively used among the plains tribes—of sending out a few men on swift horses to induce the enemy to pursue them into an ambuscade where a large force was concealed. The Cheyennes and Arapahoes took part in this fight merely as a matter of friendship for the Sioux, although the fact that a few days before some

Cheyennes had been fired on by the troops at the fort may have made the tribe more willing to take part in this battle.

In the printed accounts and on the tablet which marks the monument on this field it is stated that the Indians were led by Red Cloud,[1] the Ogallala chief, who, however, according to all Indian testimony, was not present—at least under this name. They say that the principal chiefs of the Sioux were named Black Leg and Black Shield.[2] The important Cheyenne men were Dull Knife, Walking Rabbit, Wolf Lying Down, Black Moccasin (or Iron), Painted Thunder, Walking White Man, and Wild Hog.

I have talked of this fight with a number of the Cheyennes who took part in it, and from several of these have had the detailed story. One of them—White Elk—accompanied me over the battle-ground and pointed out the route of the troops, the hiding-places of the Indians, and the spots where different groups of the soldiers fell.

This is the history of the events of that day as White Elk saw them, and as he recalls them forty-eight years after the event. He was then a young man sixteen or eighteen years of age:

It was at the beginning of cold weather. The Cheyennes were camped on Muddy Creek, and Crazy Mule was exhibiting to them his power. Different people were shooting at him, but the bullets and the arrows did not enter his flesh.

Soon after these ceremonies were over White Elk, Plenty Camps, and Rolling Bull began to talk together about making an excursion to war, and at last determined to go, and set out toward the mountains. After leaving the camp they began to discuss the route they should follow to reach the country of the Shoshoni. They determined to go in below Fort Phil Kearny to the head of Powder River.

As they were marching along, just getting out of Tongue River Canyon, they met four Cheyennes returning to the camp, who asked: "Where are you going?" The young men said they were going to war against the Shoshoni. The four men warned them, saying: "Be careful how you go about the fort. Up to

---

[1] At this time chief of a small band—Bad Face—of Ogallala.
[2] Mentioned *Tenth Annual Report Bureau Ethnology*, p. 751.

this time we have always been friendly with those people, but now they have been shooting at us. They are on the watch; so be careful." The three kept on their way and stopped at Big Springs on Tongue River. After they had reached camp, Rolling Bull asked: "What do you think of this that has been said to us? Shall we go back?" Plenty Camps said: "Let us go on a little farther and see what will happen." Both these men were older than White Elk. The message given by the four Cheyennes, of course, threatened some danger from the post, and besides this to be warned in this way just as they were starting out on a journey was a bad omen.

Plenty Camps, who seemed to be thinking, at length spoke, saying: "I believe that those four men we passed must have done some mischief up there by the fort. Let us stay here overnight and to-morrow return to the camp."

At Fort Phil Kearny something like this had perhaps happened: The Sioux had been attacking the wood-trains and already had killed some people. They had thus shown their hostility. The four Cheyennes may have ventured near the fort, been recognized as Indians, and so have been fired on by the troops. To these soldiers an Indian was an Indian and so an enemy.

Next morning the three young men remained in this camp till late in the day, when Plenty Camps said: "We will not go in to-night; let us sleep here again." Next morning early Rolling Bull said to White Elk: "Friend, get up and go down to the river and get some water." White Elk got the water, and had come half-way back to the camp when he thought he heard some one utter a yelp, and stopped to listen. As he listened closely he heard far off a number of people singing. He carried his water to their shelter and said to the others: "I think I heard a number of people singing." As they stood there listening on a sudden four Sioux rode in sight. They rode up to the camp and spoke to Rolling Bull, who could talk their language. He turned and said to his companions: "These men tell me that many people are coming, some on foot and some on horseback. Women are coming with the men. They are coming up Tongue River on their way to the Cheyenne camp."

The Sioux told them that this was a war party brought together for the sole purpose of fighting the soldiers who were at

Fort Phil Kearny. The Indians had laid a plan to try to get the soldiers into the open. They intended to send a small party to make an attack on the post to see if they could not induce the soldiers to come out from the fort. "If we cannot get the soldiers to come out as we want them to," they said, "then we will attack the post."

The four Sioux stayed there talking with the Cheyennes, and presently the whole Sioux party came in sight. Some of the older Sioux shook hands with the Cheyennes and asked them to return with the Sioux to the Cheyenne camp. The Cheyennes went with them and that night they camped at the Big Springs near the head of the canyon.

At dark an old crier went about the circle of the camp and called to all the companies of soldiers to get together, for a council was to be held. The Sioux men formed in a big circle about the camp and the chiefs and the soldier chiefs gathered in the centre, where the Cheyennes too were taken. There was much talking, all of it in Sioux and so comprehended only by Rolling Bull.

After they had finished talking the Sioux came over to the Cheyennes and said to them: "Now to-night we have made our plans as to what we shall do, and we intend to ask the Cheyennes to join us. We have chosen four men to go on ahead and notify the Cheyenne and Arapaho camp of our plans." These two camps were close together. The four men selected had got their horses and saddled them and now rode up, and the Sioux chief spoke to them and at length they rode off.

The next day near sundown the four Sioux messengers returned to the war party and told the chiefs that they had reported to the Cheyennes just what the chiefs had ordered, but that the Cheyennes had said that they must have time to get ready. Nevertheless, the Cheyennes must have left their camp in the night and come part way toward the Sioux camp, for the next morning—not very early—the Cheyennes and Arapahoes charged the Sioux camp—a friendly act. Then, after the charge, the Cheyenne chiefs gathered by themselves and told their young men that the Sioux had sent for them to help fight the soldiers. They must not weaken, but every man must stand his ground and do his best. After that all the Cheyennes fell in single file and rode all around the Sioux camp and stopped on the river below the camp and dismounted. They remained there overnight.

Next morning they went as far as Crow Standing Off Creek— Prairie Dog Creek—and camped. After leaving this camp they went up Crow Standing Off Creek beyond where it forks, keeping up the right-hand fork. Soon they came to a flat prairie and the Sioux were directed to form a line with a wide front— abreast. There were many of them. A Cheyenne chief called out to his people, saying: "Men, do not fall in line with the Sioux. We are not carrying on this war party." The Arapahoes did not form abreast like the Sioux, but stood to one side.

Soon a person, half man and half woman[1]—Hē ē mǎn ěh″— with a black cloth over his head, riding a sorrel horse, pushed out from among the Sioux and passed over a hill, zigzagging one way and another as he went. He had a whistle, and as he rode off he kept sounding it. While he was riding over the hill some of the Cheyennes were told by the Sioux that he was looking for the enemy—soldiers. Presently he rode back, and came to where the chiefs were gathered and said: "I have ten men, five in each hand; do you want them?" The Sioux chiefs said to him: "No, we do not wish them. Look at all these people here. Do you think ten men are enough to go around?" The Hē ē mǎn ěh″ turned his horse and rode away again, riding in the same way as before. Soon he came back, riding a little faster than before and swaying from one side to the other on his horse. Now he said: "I have ten men in each hand, twenty in all. Do you wish them?" The same man replied: saying, "No, I do not wish them; there are too many people here and too few enemies." Without a word the half-man-half-woman turned his horse and rode off. The third time he returned he said: "I have twenty in one hand and thirty in the other. The thirty are in the hand on the side toward which I am leaning."

"No," said the Sioux, "there are too many people here. It is not worth while to go on for so small a number." The Hē ē mǎn ěh″ rode away.

On the fourth return he rode up fast and as his horse stopped he fell off and both hands struck the ground. "Answer me

[1] A man dressed as a woman, a "berdash," supposed sometimes to be a hermaphrodite.

quickly," he said, "I have a hundred or more," and when the Sioux and Cheyennes heard this they all yelled. This was what they wanted. While he was on the ground some men struck the ground near his hands, counting the coup. Then they all went back and camped on Tongue River, at the mouth of the little creek they were going to follow up.

That night the names of ten young men were called out, and those called were ordered to start that night and to be ready the next morning to attack the post. There were two Cheyennes, two Arapahoes, and two from each of the three tribes of Sioux who were present. The two Cheyennes were Little Wolf and Wolf Left Hand. After he had been chosen Little Wolf rode over to the fire at which his brother, Big Nose, was sitting. A few days before the two brothers had quarrelled with one another. Little Wolf said to his brother: "Brother, I have been called to go and attack the post; take my horse and do you go." Big Nose was still angry and said: "Take back your horse; I do not want him." Bull Hump, who wished to make the brothers friends again, said to Big Nose: "My friend, here are my moccasins and my war clothes. If you have any bad feeling you may have those clothes to lie in" (i. e., to be killed in). Big Nose accepted the clothes and agreed to go. Little Wolf and his brother Big Nose were both good men in a fight—one as good as the other.

Some time after the young men sent to the fort had gone—just as day was about to break—all the men were called and ordered to saddle their horses, and when this had been done they moved out. They followed the stream up to the forks and there stopped. The Cheyennes kept by themselves and did not mingle with the Sioux. At the forks they stopped and a Sioux cried out, haranguing the Cheyennes, and asking them to choose which side of the ridge they wished to be on, the upper or the lower side. The Indians hoped to draw the soldiers down this ridge between their two forces hidden on either side.

One of the Cheyenne chiefs said that his people would take the upper side of the ridge, and presently the order was cried out for the Cheyennes and Arapahoes to take the upper—west— side. In going up to the place selected, the people who were on foot stopped near the lower end of the ridge, not far from the stream, while those on horseback, who had the longest distance to go, went on up above. All the Cheyennes and Arapahoes were mounted. Some Sioux women who were along stayed below with the Sioux men who were on foot.

After the different parties had gone to their places and hidden themselves everyone kept very still. All were waiting, listening for what might be heard. After a little time a single shot was heard. Later it was said that when the young men who had been sent to the fort had charged the post they had killed a sentry. This was the shot. A long period of silence followed, during which they waited and listened; then a number of shots were heard, but the firing lasted for a few minutes only. It was afterward said that some troops came out from the fort as if to attack the decoy Indians and then turned back and went into the fort and that someone who was with the soldiers made motions to the young Indians to go away, that the soldiers were going to eat. This was the Indian understanding of the signs, whatever they may have been.

The Sioux signed back to them that to-day they would get a full stomach of fighting. The soldiers re-entered the post and the young Indians remained in sight riding about.

After a time a number of bugle-calls were heard and soon after a troop of cavalry marched out of the post toward these young men, and after them a company of infantry. At a bugle-call the cavalry charged and fired at the Indians who, of course, ran away. This was the distant shooting heard.

It was some time before the watchers heard any more shooting. The cavalry after firing had stopped, and would follow no longer, and the Indians were obliged to return and attack again, be shot at, and followed a little farther. In this way the infantry kept well closed up with the cavalry, which was perhaps the reason the cavalry followed slowly.

After the third and fourth volleys the shooting came closer, and before long some of the Indians came riding down the ridge and a little later another man, Big Nose, the Cheyenne, mounted on a black horse, was seen riding back and forth across the ridge before the soldiers, seeming to fight them and they were shooting at him as hard as they could. It looked as if Big Nose was trying to fight and hold back the soldiers in order to help someone ahead

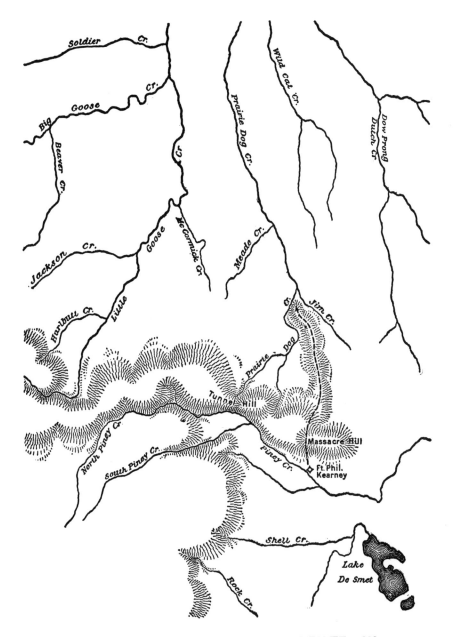

SCENE OF THE FORT PHIL KEARNY FIGHT, 1866.

The town of Sheridan, Wyoming, is about at the juncture of Big Goose Creek and Little Goose Creek, about 25 miles north of Fort Phil Kearny.

of him to get away. From the place where the Indians were waiting Big Nose seemed almost against the soldiers. The great body of Indians hidden along the ridge kept themselves well concealed. Not a move was made nor a sound heard.

After Big Nose, followed slowly by the soldiers, had come down off the steep ridge the troops stopped, and Big Nose charged back and seemed to go in among the soldiers so that he was lost to sight. He went into the troop from the right and came out on the left, wheeled his horse, rode into them again and came out, and turned as if to go back.

The troops kept following, coming down the old Bozeman Road which runs down the crest of the ridge. The Sioux on foot were hidden in the grass on the flat beyond the end of the ridge, perhaps one and a half miles distant from the place where the troops came to it at its upper end. The mounted Sioux were hidden behind two rocky ridges on the east side of this ridge, while the Cheyennes were on the west side of it. It had been announced that a certain Cheyenne, Little Horse, who was a Contrary, should give his people the word to charge, and when the proper time came this word was to be passed on from one to another until all were notified and then all should spring up and charge.

The cavalry, who had been following the ridge down nearly to the flat by the stream, were now pretty close to the Sioux footmen, and the infantry were well within the Indians' lines. When the decoys had forded the stream beyond the end of the ridge and the cavalry had nearly come to it the decoys separated into two parties, riding away from each other, and then, turning, came back and crossed each other. This was very likely a signal, and the Indians charged. Little Horse, following the law of the Contraries, held his contrary lance in his left hand. The Cheyennes watched him, and when they saw him pass his left hand behind his neck and grasp the contrary lance with his right hand they knew that he was about to charge, and all sprang up.

When the charge was made the sound of many hoofs made a noise like thunder and the soldiers began to fall back. On the ridge near the place where it leaves the hill are many large loose flat stones. The infantry took a position behind these. The cavalry moved back up the hill and stopped.

On the infantry hidden among the rocks a Sioux came charging down the old road and the infantry stood up in sight as if about to leave the shelter. They did not do so, but let the Sioux pass through them and after he had passed fired at and killed him. Soon after this another man came down the road on foot and began to shoot at the infantry and when they rose up to shoot at him the other Indians shot at them. This young man was killed.

White Elk—at that time named Wandering Buffalo Bull—was with those fighting the infantry. Soon after the second Sioux was killed the cry was given to charge and the Sioux and Cheyennes charged and got to the infantry about the same time, and for a little while Indians and soldiers were mixed up together in hand-to-hand fighting. Just before and in this charge a Sioux was killed and another wounded by arrows shot by their own people. The one killed was struck in the forehead just over the root of the nose, and the arrow-point pierced his brain. The arrow was shot from the other side of the ridge and had passed through or over the crowd of troops.

The cavalry, who had followed the decoying party of Indians down nearly to the level of the river bottom, when they saw the Sioux charging them from the northeast turned and retreated up to the top of a high hill toward the end of the ridge. There they halted and waited in line until the infantry were all killed at the rocks about a hundred yards north of the line of cavalry. Then the cavalry began to fall back, but slowly and in order. Some were even on foot leading their horses.

After the infantrymen had been killed the Indians rushed up toward the cavalry, but the ground was slippery with ice and snow and in many places the hill was too steep for them to charge up it. Still many people crept up toward the place, and Little Horse is reported to have approached behind the rocks within forty feet of the soldiers, and fought there, yet he was not hurt in the fight. While this was going on White Elk was a little behind, where he could see the Indians shooting at the cavalry with arrows, and the arrows flew so thickly above the troops that to him they seemed like a lot of grasshoppers flying across each other. On the hill an officer was killed and when he fell the troops seemed to give way and to begin to fight their way up the ridge. The weather now grew very cold, so that blood running from wounds soon froze. After the soldiers had reached the end of the ridge they began to let go their horses and the Indians, eager to capture the horses, began to lessen their shooting.

Up to this time Big Nose had not been hurt. Someone called out: "There are two good horses left there." Big Nose charged up toward the horses, struck them with his whip, thus taking possession of them, and then rode back and turned again, but here his horse stopped, exhausted. He could not get it to move, and here Big Nose was shot off his horse. This was the only wound he had and his horse was untouched.

White Elk went to where his friend lay. He spoke to White Elk and said: "Lift my head up the hill and place me where I can breathe the fresh air." This was all he said. He breathed for a day or two after this. Big Nose was killed on the ridge in the first sag northwest of the monument, near some large rocks west of the crest of the ridge. His horse stopped as he was crossing the ridge and began to back toward the soldiers, who were west of where the monument is. While White Elk was helping Big Nose the soldiers were shooting at them constantly.

The cavalry kept moving back to some great rocks, perhaps four hundred yards from where the infantry had been killed. On the other side of the rocks there was a flat with no cover behind which the Indians could approach, and they could not get near to the soldiers. The Indians kept calling to one another to keep hidden, but to continue to creep up. They did so, and every now and then an Indian would show himself and seem to be about to charge, and when the soldiers rose to their feet to shoot all the Indians would shoot. In this way they killed some of the soldiers. They kept calling to each other: "Be ready. Are you ready?" And others would call back: "We are ready." They were preparing for the charge—a hand-to-hand fight.

When at last the order was given to charge they rushed in among the soldiers and a number of Sioux were killed among the soldiers. Here they killed every one. After all were dead a dog was seen running away, barking, and someone called out: "All are dead but the dog; let him carry the news to the fort," but someone else cried out: "No, do not let even a dog get away"; and a young man shot at it with his arrow and killed it. The last of the cavalry was killed just where the monument now stands.

The fight began when the sun was quite high in the heavens and ended about noon. Little Horse led the Cheyennes in the charge which had been ordered. All watched him and when he went forward they followed. Only two Cheyennes were killed. The Sioux were laid out side by side and made two long rows, perhaps fifty or sixty men. The number of Indians was very great. Of Arapahoes and Cheyennes there were a good many hundred, and there were three times as many Sioux. White Elk believes that in the Fetterman fight there were more men than in the Custer fight. Most of the Indians were armed with bows. The few who had guns had old smooth-bore flintlocks. Only six of the eighty-one white men bore gunshot wounds, and of these Colonel Fetterman and Captain Brown are supposed to have killed themselves with their own revolvers.

The so-called Fetterman Massacre caused much excitement in the East, and accusations were freely made against the commanding officer, General Carrington, who in turn complained that reinforcements and ammunition often asked for from General P. St. George Cooke had been refused him. As a matter of fact, neither reinforcements nor ammunition would have prevented the disaster which, as already stated, was brought about by the recklessness of the officer in command of the force. In those days, and the same might be said of many other days, most army officers understood little or nothing of the character and methods of warfare of the plains Indians.

The destruction of the force under Fetterman led to a long investigation which was ordered by the President, with the result that troops were withdrawn from the Powder River country in accordance with the treaties then in existence. Fort Phil Kearny stood on what is now the ranch of George Geier. The fort buildings were later burned by Old Little Wolf.

XIX

HANCOCK CAMPAIGN

1867

IN the spring of 1865, while General Connor was preparing to move on the Indians north of the Platte, Colonel Ford was assembling on the upper Arkansas a very strong force,[1] with the purpose of attacking the tribes south of that river—Black Kettle's Cheyennes, the Southern Arapahoes, the Kiowas, Comanches, and Apaches. General Dodge, commanding the Department of the Missouri, was eager to see these tribes punished, but Agent Leavenworth declared the Indians were friendly, and after great exertions he at length succeeded in stopping the march of Ford's troops and in arranging a council to be held with all the tribes in early fall.[2] In October a commission, which included General Harney, General Sanborn, William Bent, and Kit Carson, met the tribes in council on the Little Arkansas, and here treaties of peace were signed and lands were set aside for all of the tribes in the region south of the Arkansas. At this time most of the Southern Cheyennes were on Powder River, but when they returned south in late December, 1865, most of them accepted the treaty as binding. The Dog Soldiers, however, refused to accept the treaty, as it ceded their lands on the Republican and Smoky Hill. The Government was anxious to secure the relin-

---

[1] General Dodge reports Ford's force as seven thousand men, the largest body of troops ever assembled in one place to operate against Indians, as far as I know. *Official Records*, vol. 102, p. 335.

[2] Leavenworth and Dodge fought this out all spring and summer. Dodge said the Indians were hostile, Leavenworth that they were friendly. Except part of the Kiowas, they probably were friendly. Leavenworth appealed to the Interior Department, and secured Stanton's order stopping Ford's march; then Dodge appealed to General Pope and Pope appealed to Stanton, who reversed his decision. Dodge at once ordered Ford to move, but Leavenworth got hold of Senator Doolittle, and he wired to Stanton and stopped Ford again, and so on all summer. *Official Records*, vol. 102, p. 137.

quishment of these lands, as the Kansas Pacific Railroad was to be built through that region at once. Two attempts were made to induce the Dog Soldier chiefs to agree to give up the Republican and Smoky Hill country but without result.[1] The mere fact that this band declined to leave the lands which they had never ceded to the Government was taken by many men in Kansas, and some army officers, as an indication that the Dog Soldiers were planning a war.

The year 1866 was an unusually quiet one on the Kansas frontier, only minor Indian troubles being reported. The Kiowas made some raids into Texas and a young Cheyenne killed a Mexican trader near Fort Zarah during a drunken quarrel.[2] This year the old quarrel between the Indian agents and the army officers was bitter, however, and the frontiersmen and Kansas State officials took the side of the army and united in accusations against the agents and the Indians under their control. An examination of the record seems to show that there was very little to complain of. Most of the stories put in circulation were without any basis of truth.[3]

During the winter of 1866–7 there was so much talk in Kansas of raids said to have been made by the Indians that it was commonly reported that all Indians threatened to begin war as soon as the grass was up in the spring. Congress was induced to appropriate $150,000 for a military expedition into Kansas.

In his report for 1867 Major Wynkoop, agent for the Cheyennes and Arapahoes, said that he was very nearly discouraged, but at last he got matters into working order and issued goods to

[1] Wynkoop attempted to induce the Dog Soldiers to accept the treaty of 1865, which ceded these lands, in February, 1866, but failed. A second attempt was made at Fort Ellsworth late in fall, and also failed.

[2] Fox Tail, son of Rock Forehead, killed this Mexican, while drunk.

[3] Governor Crawford says the Cheyennes made a raid on the Republican in May, 1866, but gives no details. Fox Tail's drunken attack on the Mexican was another charge against the tribe. Major Douglas, at Fort Dodge, was carrying on a quarrel with the agents, and secured an affidavit from Jones, a squaw-man, and one Captain Asbury, charging the Kiowas with making trouble on the Arkansas, and also some charges against the Cheyennes. This was sent to General Hancock. Soon after Tappan, a trader, and Major Page went to Douglas and swore to another affidavit, denying all the statements of Jones and Asbury. This second affidavit Major Douglas does not appear to have sent to Hancock. See Stanley, vol. I, chapter on "Hancock at Fort Dodge, May, 1867."

his tribes, and they were all off hunting quietly. No one was making any complaints about their conduct when Hancock's expedition arrived and brought on another war.

Lieutenant-General Sherman was in command of the Military Division of the Missouri. It was divided into several departments, of which the Department of the Missouri was under Major-General Hancock. General Hancock was given command of the Kansas Expedition and in April marched from Fort Riley with about one thousand four hundred men—cavalry, artillery, some infantry, and a pontoon train. So large a force had never before been sent against the Indians of this region.

Hancock moved by Fort Harker and Fort Zarah to Fort Larned, which he reached early in April. Meantime, he had sent word to the Indian agents to assemble their tribes to meet him in council. Wynkoop reports, September 15, 1867, that Hancock in his report to Grant charges him, Wynkoop, with representing his Indians as friendly when they were hostile. Wynkoop insists that the Indians were friendly and that Hancock drove them to war. "His whole course in reference to the Indians of my agency was a mistake."[1] Leavenworth, the Kiowa and Comanche agent, denounces Hancock even more bitterly than Wynkoop.

In his orders issued at the beginning of the march and printed in full by Stanley, Hancock says: "It is uncertain whether war will be the result of the expedition or not; it will depend upon the temper and behavior of the Indians with whom we come in contact. We are prepared for war and will make it if proper occasion presents. We shall have war if the Indians are not properly disposed toward us. If they are for peace and no sufficient ground is presented for chastisement we are restricted from punishing them for past grievances which are recorded against them; these matters have been left to the Indian Department for adjustment. No insolence will be tolerated from any bands of Indians whom we may encounter. We wish to show them that the Government is ready and able to punish them if they are hostile, although it may not be disposed to invite war."[2]

---

[1] *Report of Secretary of the Interior for* 1867–8, p. 310; also *Report of Commissioner of Indian Affairs for* 1867, p. 310.

[2] Stanley, vol. I, p. 10.

The tone of this order clearly shows Hancock's ignorance of things relating to these Indians; that he marched with infantry and a pontoon train in pursuit of mounted Indians shows how little qualified he was for the command of such an expedition. His men were all fresh from the battle-fields of the South and new to the plains.

There can be no doubt that the Cheyennes were friendly, but at Fort Zarah a rumor was received that five hundred lodges had gathered with hostile intentions and Hancock seems to have acted on the assumption that this was true and to have distrusted the Indians and their agents before he met them.

Wynkoop quotes a letter addressed to him by Hancock which says: "I request that you will inform them, the Indians, in such a manner as you may think proper, that I expect shortly to visit their neighborhood, and that I will be glad to have an interview with their chiefs; and tell them also, if you please, that I go fully prepared for peace or war, and that hereafter I will insist on their keeping off the main lines of travel, where their presence is calculated to bring about collisions with the whites. If you prevail upon the Indians of your agency to abandon their habit of infesting the country travelled by our over-land routes, threatening, robbing, and intimidating travelers, we will defer that matter to you. If not, I would be pleased by your presence with me when I visit the locality of your tribes, to show that the officers of the government are acting in harmony."

In compliance with this request Wynkoop called together the principal chiefs of the Dog Soldiers and of the Cheyennes at Fort Larned, to have a talk with Hancock. The chiefs answered the call at once, coming thirty-five miles to the post, although the snow was deep and their horses were miserably thin and scarcely able to travel. Hancock talked with these chiefs in his camp at night, an unexampled proceeding, for friendly councils with Indians are always held during the day. This talk at night made the Indians suspicious and Hancock's statement that he intended to visit the village made them more so. Hancock gave Wynkoop no opportunity to speak to the Indians, although in his letter the general had stated that he would defer the whole matter to the agent so long as the Indians kept off the road. Stanley[1]

[1] Stanley, vol. I, pp. 29, 30.

and Custer[1] give accounts of the council and Stanley gives Hancock's speech. Hancock spoke to these Cheyennes about white prisoners which he implied they had taken, but as a matter of fact these prisoners were taken in Texas and by the Kiowas. The Cheyennes had nothing to do with them and very likely knew nothing about them. Nevertheless Hancock held them responsible. Wynkoop[2] in his report says that he protested against the march to the Cheyenne village but Hancock insisted.

It was understood that the village was on Pawnee Fork, about thirty-five miles west of Fort Larned. Really it was about ten miles farther off. Hancock, leaving the Santa Fé Road, which his expedition had been sent to keep open, started directly away from the road to march to this village. He was thus unintentionally doing everything that he could to stir up a war. He took with him his whole body of troops and moved up the Pawnee Fork, the chiefs riding with the column in all friendliness, but very much worried as to what effect the appearance of the troops might have on their people. It may be imagined that after their experience in November, 1864, the Cheyennes were very much afraid of the approach to their village of a large body of troops and it is not strange that a considerable proportion of the Indians in this camp imagined that a second Sand Creek massacre was impending.[3]

The troops marched twenty or twenty-five miles from the fort and then encamped, the chiefs remaining with the soldiers. Hancock now sent word to the village asking more chiefs to visit him, naming among them Roman Nose, whom he in common with many other people insisted on considering the principal chief, although he was not a chief at all. The Indians did not arrive at the time set next morning, because their camp was ten miles farther away than Hancock had supposed and thus not enough time had been allowed them for reaching Hancock. Hancock now declared that he believed the Indians felt guilty and would not come, so he broke camp and ordered an advance.[4]

The column marched six miles and then met about three

---

[1] Custer's *My Life on the Plains*, p. 24.
[2] *Report of the Secretary of the Interior*, p. 311.
[3] *Ibid.*, p. 311.
[4] *Ibid.*, p. 312.

hundred Indians who were on their way to meet Hancock at his camp in response to his summons. Hancock at once deployed his men in line of battle, and Wynkoop says they had all the appearance of troops going into action, the cavalry coming into line at a gallop with sabres drawn.

Wynkoop asked permission to ride forward and reassure the Indians, and General Hancock told him he might go. Wynkoop rode forward to the Indian line and talked with Roman Nose and some of the chiefs and took them forward, and Hancock and others met them midway. Custer and Stanley do not mention that Wynkoop rode forward alone but say that the general and other officers rode forward, seeming to imply that to ride out and meet such hostile Indians was an evidence of courage. Wynkoop says that Hancock told the chiefs that it was too windy to talk there; that he would talk at his camp that night. Bent states that Roman Nose had just told Bull Bear that he intended to kill Hancock at the head of his troops, but Bull Bear begged him not to do this as it would endanger the women and children. The Indians seemed to have been prepared for any event, for they had their bows strung and spare arrows in their hands. They had very few guns. A magazine article printed in 1868 describes Roman Nose as heavily armed, with Spencer carbine, four heavy revolvers in his belt, while carrying in his left hand a bow and a number of arrows. Obviously, if Roman Nose was so well provided with firearms as said, he had no ammunition for them, or else he would have carried a firearm in his hands. Guerrier subsequently told George Bent that Roman Nose told him that he intended to kill General Hancock. Guerrier says that Roman Nose sat on his horse near the general and looked him straight in the eyes for a long time. Hancock asked sharply if the Indians wished war and Roman Nose replied sarcastically that if they had wanted war they would not have been likely to come out in the open and face such a force or have come so close to the big guns. Hancock then asked why Roman Nose had not come to the council and Roman Nose explained that his horses were too weak to travel, while everyone who came to him told a different story about Hancock's intentions.

When the troops had formed in line of battle a considerable number of Indians, who had been following the mounted men on foot, ran away, and during this talk a number of Indians slipped off.[1] As soon as the principal men returned to the line of Indians they wheeled and the Indians rode off rapidly toward their villages, while the troops resumed their march. Bull Bear again asked Hancock, through Guerrier, not to camp near the village lest the women and children, already frightened, should run away. Hancock replied that he intended to camp close to the village. Davis in the article[2] already referred to says that Hancock's purpose was to camp at some distance from the village, but because the Indians had burned the grass to keep him away there was no grazing for the horses except near their own camp. This burning of the prairie is not mentioned in other accounts. Soon after the troops had made camp some of the chiefs came in and reported that the women and children had run away. The substance of the talk is no doubt given in Guerrier's statement to be quoted later. Hancock asked why they had gone. Roman Nose said that they were frightened, and asked Hancock if he had not heard of Sand Creek, when the troops had come to the Indian village under appearances very similar to those of that day. Hancock declared that he regarded the flight of the women and children an act of treachery and demanded that they be brought back. According to Wynkoop, three chiefs said they would go and try to persuade them to come back; Guerrier says two chiefs offered to go. Hancock loaned them horses, their own being too weak to travel. Wynkoop says they returned about midnight reporting the women and children too far scattered over the prairie to be brought back. That the horses were returned is shown by the testimony of Wynkoop[3] and by that of Guerrier, who led the horses back to the camp and reported to General Hancock. Nevertheless it was claimed that the chiefs did not come back; did not return the horses, and that they took the horses and went on this trip without any intention of returning, acting treacherously throughout.[4]

---

[1] *Report of Secretary of Interior*, pp. 311, 312; see also Stanley, p. 37, and Custer's account in *My Life on the Plains*.

[2] "A Summer on the Plains," by T. R. Davis, *Harper's Magazine* for 1868, vol. 36.

[3] *Report of Secretary of the Interior*, p. 312.

[4] Custer, however, in his letters to his wife, makes no such charge. In a letter dated Pawnee Fork, April 15, 20 minutes to 3 A. M. (evidently written

About the time the command left Fort Larned, Edmond Guerrier was engaged by Hancock as interpreter. In 1908 he gave me his recollection of the approach to the Cheyenne village, saying:

Shortly after I was engaged as interpreter we had a visit from Bull Bear, the chief, and Tall Bull and White Horse, chiefs of the Dog Soldiers. They asked Gen. Hancock not to come near their camp. They feared that he had a purpose to harm them and thought that if his visit was a peaceful one he would not have brought such a great body of soldiers with him. That night Gen. Hancock said that he was going to where their village was, and he started for it. It took some time to get there, for they marched slowly and the troops had pontoon bridges which they put down over Pawnee Fork.

Some time before we got near the village some of the Cheyennes came out to meet us, Roman Nose, Tall Bull, White Horse, and Bull Bear. They talked and again asked Gen. Hancock not to come up near to the village. They said: "Because of what you told us last night, we have not been able to hold our women and children: they are all frightened and have run away and they will not come back: they fear the soldiers."

General Hancock said: "You must get them back, and I expect you to do so."

He marched up and camped quite close to the village. The Indians had told him that it would be impossible for them to overtake those who had run away, because it was early in the spring and all their horses were thin and weak and unable to travel.

Then General Hancock offered to give them a couple of horses that they could use in sending out runners, and he did so.

After camp had been made, in the evening he sent for me and said: "Geary, are you afraid to go up to the camp there and talk to these Indians and to stay there all night?" I said that I was not and expressed my willingness to go, and then Gen. Hancock said: "If those Indians run away I shall hold you responsible." Then I said I did not want to go on those terms; that I could not keep the Indians from running away, but could only report that they had run away.

"Well," said Gen. Hancock, "go up there anyway and if they run away come and let me know."

I went up to the camp and talked with the principal men. They were frightened and yet for some time said nothing definite as to what they in-

the night the Indians ran away, but misdated), he tells how a half-breed guide notified Hancock, about sunset, that the Indians were saddling up, and how he, Custer, surrounded the camp at midnight, but found the Indians gone. He says: "They feared us; feared another massacre like Chivington's. . . . I am to pursue them. . . . I do not anticipate war, or even difficulty, as the Indians are frightened to death, and only ran away from fear."—Quoted from *Tenting on the Plains*, pp. 560–1, by Mrs. E. B. Custer, New York, 1887.

tended to do. Then they left me in the lodge with the young men and went out and consulted among themselves and then came back and told me that they had decided not to stay, but to run away with their women and children. They returned to me the two horses that had been given them to use in sending messengers to the women and children and I mounted my own horse and leading the two others returned to camp and reported to Gen. Hancock that the Indians had decided to run away.

When Hancock learned that the Indians had gone or were going he ordered the cavalry to surround the camp. When it was captured no one was found in it except an old Sioux with a broken leg, his wife, and a little girl. Various tales are told about the treatment of this child, who was feeble-minded.[1]

Wynkoop says that General Hancock declared that same night that he would burn the village. Hancock, however, claims that he did not reach this decision until after he had learned from Custer that the Indians had begun raiding on the Smoky Hill River. Custer's report, however, was not received until April 16 at the very earliest and Wynkoop[2] made a written protest against the burning of the village on April 13. Stanley[3] said that Hancock had determined to burn the village April 14.

Guerrier was sent to guide Custer in following the Indians. He says that the trail was hard to follow because in order to travel faster the Indians had discarded their travois and packed their property on their horses' backs, and then soon after leaving the village had scattered out. However, they were followed to the Smoky Hill River, where it was found that they had attacked a stage station—Fossil Station—where they killed two men on the night of the 14th–15th. Custer sent two troops of cavalry after the small party, thought to be the Sioux, who made this raid, and with three troops followed the main body of Indians toward Beaver Creek, but failed to overtake them.

Hancock had threatened to chastise these Indians most severely if they made any trouble, but having now driven them to hostilities he found it impossible to strike them at all, as they moved much more rapidly than his troops. The only Indians killed were some friendly Cheyennes of Black Kettle's camp, six of whom

[1] Stanley, vol. I, pp. 39, 40.
[2] *Report of Secretary of Interior*, 1867–8, p. 313.
[3] Stanley, vol. I, p. 40.

had gone up to visit the Dog Soldiers just before Hancock came to the camp. They had gone on foot to the Dog Soldiers' village from the south. Their names were: One Bear,[1] Burnt All Over,[2] Wolf in the Middle,[3] Plenty of Horses,[4] Pawnee Man,[5] and Eagle's Nest.[6]

When General Hancock came and made camp close to the village and the Indians got frightened and ran away, scattering and leaving their lodges standing, these young men set out to return south to their camp. As they were starting One Bear said to them: "Well, now, come on; let us travel fast. I know where there is a stage station on the Arkansas; we will go back there as quickly as we can and perhaps there we may be able to take some horses and we shall have something to ride home." This ranch was at the Cimarron Crossing, above Fort Larned.

They travelled fast all through the night and at last, just about daylight, they reached the point of a hill, and looking over it could see the stage station. One Bear said to the others: "Now, friends, you stay here and I will go ahead and take a look, and see if any loose animals are wandering around near the station."

He went off and presently came back and said to the others: "There are soldiers there and a number of them are coming this way." Just then they all heard a bugle-call.

Plenty of Horses said to the others: "Well, what are we going to do? Here is a level prairie and these soldiers are coming."

"Well," said Burnt All Over, "there is a little hollow at the head of a ravine that we passed; let us go back there and hide."

They began to drop the things that they were carrying and started back, but just as they started they saw coming over the hill from the other way another party of soldiers. They were to be attacked on both sides.[7]

The Cheyennes stopped and stood there for a moment or two, and the soldiers stopped, too, and sat on their horses and looked at them.

---

[1] Nāhk'-nŭ-kā, One Bear.

[2] Māhĭm-hkā-heh", Burnt All Over.

[3] Hō-nĭ'-ōs-tsō-ĭnst, Wolf in the Middle.

[4] Mō-ĭn'-ō-hŭm-kā'-ĭst-kwĭst, Plenty of Horses.

[5] Ōn'-ō-hĭt, Pawnee Man.   [6] Nĭt-sĭv'-hŏ-ĭtsts, Eagle's Nest.

[7] Stanley, vol. I, p. 50.

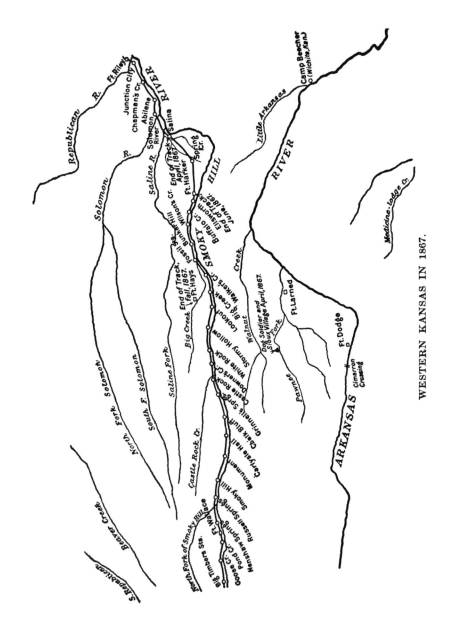

WESTERN KANSAS IN 1867.

WESTERN KANSAS IN 1867.

At this time the Kansas Pacific R. R. was being built up the Smoky Hill Road to Denver. The old Smoky Hill stage line ran from the end of track.

Distances:

    Leavenworth to Fort Riley, 116 miles.
    Junction City, 119 miles.
    Chapman's Creek, 131 miles.
    Abilene, 143 miles.
    Solomon River, 153 miles.
    Salina, 166 miles, end of track, April, 1867.
    Spring Creek, 181 miles.
    Ellsworth, 195 miles.
    Buffalo Creek, 205 miles.
    Wilson's Creek, 214 miles.
    Bunker Hill, 222 miles.
    Fossil Creek, 230 miles.
    Walker's Creek, 240 miles.
    Hays City, about 256 miles, end of track, fall, 1867.
    Big Creek, 252 miles.
    Lookout, 261 miles.
    Stormy Hollow, 273 miles.
    White Rock, 284 miles.
    Downer's Creek, 294 miles.
    Castle Rock, 305 miles.
    Grinnell Springs, 313 miles.
    Chalk Bluff, 316 miles.
    Carlysle Hall, 334 miles.
    Monument, 344 miles.
    Smoky Hill Springs, 356 miles.
    Russell Springs, 366 miles.
    Henshaw Springs, 380 miles.
    Pond Creek, 391 miles.
    Goose Creek, 402 miles.
    Big Timbers, 412 miles.
    The next station, Cheyenne Wells, is in Colorado. The road struck off thence to Sand Creek and northwest to Denver.

One Bear called out: "Let us make for the river, but strike it above the stage station, going around the soldiers on their right hand."

The soldiers followed them, but the Cheyennes got first to the river and crossed to a little island, and there got in the brush and began to throw up breastworks. When the soldiers reached the river bank they got off and tied their horses and started to attack them on foot. Just before the Indians were going into the river they passed through some high rushes that grew on the edge of the water, and here Pawnee Man and Wolf in the Middle turned off to one side, and lay down in the high rushes, while the other four went on over to the island.

Some of the soldiers tied their horses right close to where these two men were hiding, and Pawnee Man said to Wolf in the Middle: "Now, let us get up and take a couple of these horses and get away. The soldiers are not thinking of us now and we can get a good start"; but Wolf in the Middle said: "No, let us crawl farther down the stream and still hide. We may choose poor horses and they will catch us at once," so they crept farther down the stream and remained hidden in the grass until night.

Meantime the soldiers on the north side of the island began to shoot at the men who were hidden there, and after they had been doing this for some time One Bear made up his mind that the place was too dangerous, and he said to the others: "Let us get away from here." The four got up out of their hiding-places and started to run across the river. One Bear had crossed and was just climbing up the bank when a ball struck and killed him. As soon as he fell Plenty of Horses, who was close to him, ran back to One Bear and got his quiver so that he might have more arrows. Burnt All Over stopped, and while Plenty of Horses was taking the quiver was shot in the shoulder. Meantime Eagle's Nest had started off over the prairie, making for the sand hills a mile and a half away. The soldiers were coming and followed Eagle's Nest.

Burnt All Over and Plenty of Horses turned up the creek and, running in the valley, were not followed. The soldiers pursued Eagle's Nest and did not overtake him until he had reached the sand hills, where they killed him. Burnt All Over and Plenty of Horses went up into the sand hills, and just as they disappeared the soldiers took a shot at them. Among the sand hills they found a sand blowout and, creeping in there, hid until night.

These two young men, One Bear and Eagle's Nest, were the only Indians killed by Hancock's one thousand four hundred men during the spring campaign. Custer's pursuit was fruitless and he returned with his regiment to Fort Hays and went into camp. Hancock, after burning the Dog Soldier and Sioux village on Pawnee Fork, marched to Fort Dodge,[1] on the Arkansas and held talks with the Kiowas and Arapahoes, who had remained quiet and taken no part in the war. On hearing of the trouble on Pawnee Fork, the two tribes had fled from the Arkansas, but the chiefs came in to talk with Hancock. Hancock now marched to Fort Hays, where he found Custer in camp, and on May 9 he left for Fort Leavenworth and his campaign was over, but the trouble which Hancock had stirred up was not over. In May and June the Indians, whose village had been destroyed, repeatedly raided the Platte road.[2]

At this time the Union Pacific Railroad had been constructed as far as North Platte at the forks of the Platte, and the Kansas Pacific up the Smoky Hill as far as Fort Harker. The old stage line ran from the end of the track at Fort Harker west to Denver. Along this road the Indians were very troublesome, burning stations and attacking coaches, from June to September.[3]

---

[1] Fort Dodge, established 1865, above Fort Larned and below Cimarron Crossing.

[2] Stanley, pp. 110–3; also p. 119.

[3] June, 1867. Governor Crawford, in his *Kansas in the Sixties*, gives accounts of many raids on the Smoky Hill line in June, July, August, and September, pp. 255 *et seq.* These attacks were mostly on the railroad builders operating west of Fort Harker, and on the stage line that ran from Fort Harker west.

June 24, J. D. Perry, President of the Kansas Pacific Railroad, writes to Crawford that the Indians have been making raids and have stampeded one thousand laborers who had come in to Fort Harker, and refuse to go out and work because of danger from Indian attacks—p. 255. Same day report from Bunker Hill, two more men killed.

June 27, railroad engineer-camp attacked near Fort Harker, one man killed, etc. An attack was made almost every day, a man or two killed, and some stock run off in each attack.

When the Indians drove all the laborers off the railroad line west of Harker, June 24, Governor Crawford began to urge Sheridan and Sherman to permit him to recruit a regiment of Kansas volunteers "to protect the railroad workmen." Sherman at length authorized this on July 1, and the Nineteenth

To punish these raiders, General Custer was sent into the field with the Seventh Cavalry to try to strike the villages of the Indians.   He moved from Fort Hays on the Smoky Hill in May, and rode over much of the country north of this, as far as the Platte, but found no Indians.   His command camped at Jack Morrow's old ranch, near Fort McPherson, on the Platte.   This post had been built on the site of old Fort Cottonwood, at Cottonwood Springs, Nebraska, about midway between Fort Kearny and Julesburg.   Here the Sioux chief Pawnee Killer and other chiefs came in and had a talk with Custer.   They declared themselves friendly, were given some supplies, and went away. General Sherman reached the camp and told Custer that he doubted these peaceful intentions, ordering him to go after them and bring them in, but they were already beyond his reach.

After supplying his command, Custer set out again, marching southward from the Platte toward the Republican.   The country was rough and the hills steep.   On June 24 the command was attacked by Indians who endeavored to drive off the animals.[1] They were discovered in time, and secured nothing except the carbine and ammunition of a sentry.   Custer's own account is distorted and exaggerated.   He says several Indians were shot. After this the main body of the Indians drew off to a hill about a mile from camp, where they formed a line and, signalling with mirrors, were soon joined by other parties of Indians, who seemed to come from every direction.   One of Custer's scouts, named Gay, was ordered to ride out toward the Indians and try to induce them to come in.   He first rode toward them in a zigzag course, intimating friendship, and then called them to him by riding in a circle.   A few Indians rode toward Gay and told him that they would talk if the white chief would bring with him only a few of his officers.   Gay replied that in that case only as many

Kansas Cavalry was raised and sent out to Fort Harker.   But instead of protecting the line, the troops at once set out to chase Indians.   Two companies of this regiment found a trail and followed it toward the Republican.   They met one troop of the Tenth U. S. negro cavalry and went on, but on August 21 they were surprised by Indians near the Republican.   Next day the Indians attacked in force, killing three men, whose bodies fell into the Indians' hands, and wounding thirty-five others.   The troops fell back hastily toward Fort Harker.   Crawford, p. 261.

[1] Custer's *My Life on the Plains*, p. 57.

Indians should come as there were white men who came toward them. Returning to the command, he reported to Custer that Pawnee Killer and some other Sioux chiefs were anxious to talk. A small number of officers went out to meet the Indians, who were twice as many as they were, and besides that small bodies of Indians were constantly approaching nearer and nearer to the place of conference. The talk amounted to nothing; the Indians asked for food and ammunition, while General Custer, after trying to learn from Pawnee Killer something about the situation of his village, told the Sioux chief that he purposed to follow him. He returned to camp and moved off after the Indians, but without success. A little later a small party of the Indians showed themselves near the command, and Captain L. Hamilton was ordered to take twenty men and follow them. He pursued them for eight or ten miles, when the small band of Indians suddenly increased to several hundred, and in a short time surrounded Hamilton's little party, which, however, kept off the Indians with the loss of only one horse.

The wagon-train of the command was attacked and followed for fifteen miles, the wagons moving steadily along during the fight. These all appeared to be Sioux. The same day that the wagons were attacked, there was a fight at Fort Wallace between the Indians and a company of the Seventh Cavalry under Captain Barnit. Here the Indians imitated the white man's mode of fighting, abandoning the usual custom of riding in a circle, but forming a line and charging after the manner of a squadron of cavalry. This made the fighting desperate, for it was largely at very close quarters. Some of the bravest and most efficient non-commissioned officers of the Seventh Cavalry were killed. When an Indian was shot and fell from his horse two companions would ride up to him, pick up the body, and carry it to a place of safety. The Indians gave wonderful exhibitions of riding on this occasion. It is a high honor for a young man to expose himself by dashing into the battle and assisting in carrying off a dead or wounded tribesman. This was one of the hard fights of the year.

While Custer was on the Republican, Lieutenant Kidder with ten men of the Second Cavalry was sent by General Sheridan from Fort Sedgwick on the Platte with despatches to Custer. Red Bead, a Sioux from Powder River, guided the party. Kidder never reached Custer, but when Custer moved south toward Fort Wallace a scout struck a trail running along the high divide near Beaver Creek. The tracks showed cavalry horses moving at a walk. Suddenly the trail turned off the divide, but tracks showed the horses now moving at a gallop. The scouts followed the trail for about a mile from the ridge, and in a little hollow near the stream found the bodies of Lieutenant Kidder, Red Bead, and ten soldiers dead, stripped and shot full of arrows. No one ever knew just how these men came to their death, as the Indians have always been afraid to tell the story. It has often been written and speculated about, but recently Good Bear, a Dog Soldier, who took part in the fight, told the story to George Bent. He said that in June of that year he and a few other Dog Soldiers were camped with the Brulé Sioux hunting buffalo on Beaver Creek, a tributary of the Republican. The lodges of the Dog Soldiers were together, and at a little distance from the Sioux camp. One day some Sioux, who had been out after buffalo, came rushing by the Dog Soldiers' camp calling out that soldiers with pack-mules were coming toward the creek, and would be there in a few minutes. The hunters rode on to the Sioux camp and made the same report, and all the warriors began to prepare for a fight.

The Cheyennes, who happened to have their ponies tied up close by their lodges, were the first to get mounted, and at once rode off in search of the soldiers, whom they presently discovered in a little hollow near the stream, dismounted and ready for a fight. One of the Dog Soldiers, named Tobacco,[1] began riding around the soldiers and shooting, and the others did the same. Presently the Sioux rode up and jumped off their horses, preferring to fight on foot. They began to crawl through the grass on Kidder's party, while the Dog Soldiers kept circling about them and firing as they rode. Good Bear[2] had his horse shot under him, and Tobacco, the Cheyenne leader, also had his pony killed. All through the fight Red Bead, the Sioux who was with Kidder, kept calling to the attacking party of Sioux to let him out, but the Sioux would not listen to him, and kept creeping in closer and closer, until at last all the soldiers were killed. In this fight the Sioux lost two men, one of them Yellow Horse, who had been made a chief just before the engagement.

[1] Tsĭ-nĭm'-o, Tobacco.   [2] Nāhk'o-wū-ĭt-a, Good Bear.

There were only twelve Cheyennes in the fight, of whom were Tobacco, Big Head, and Howling Wolf. The Sioux were under Pawnee Killer, who only a few days before had had a peace talk with Custer on the Republican, and Bear Making Trouble.

This covers the principal fighting in 1867, except the wreck of the railroad train. General Hancock's command, while he was in the field and later, in four months of active campaigning had killed four Indians. Two of these were Cheyennes, at the Cimarron Crossing, as already explained, and two Sioux in the Kidder Fight.

XX

MEDICINE LODGE TREATY

1867

In the late summer of 1867, some Cheyennes succeeded in what was perhaps the only attempt to disable a railroad ever made by Indians. General Custer's summer campaign on the Republican and Smoky Hill Rivers had proved futile. The Indians continued to raid unchecked in Kansas and Nebraska, and on the South Platte, in Colorado. In the early days of August a camp of Cheyenne Indians under Turkey Leg,[1] came to the Union Pacific Railroad, near Plum Creek, and by interfering with the rails threw a hand-car off the track, and subsequently ditched a freight train. A number of men were killed, and one, William Thompson, was scalped alive, recovered, and as recently as 1912 was still living, in England.

The printed accounts state that the Indians took out a culvert and broke the track in that way, but the narrative of Porcupine, then a young man in the Cheyenne camp, gives the facts about it.

Hancock and Custer, by camping close to the Cheyenne village thirty or forty miles west from Fort Larned, on Pawnee Fork, in Kansas, had so frightened the Indians that they all ran away. They had travelled north or northwest and very likely had crossed the North Platte west of Ogallala, in what is now Nebraska.

Custer, sent in pursuit of the Indians—to bring them back—expected soon to overtake them, but, of course, did not do so. He followed them at a good rate, but as he more nearly approached them the Indians, pursuing their usual tactics, separated into little groups, and what had been a broad plain trail soon became very difficult to follow. Custer says[2] that the trails led north,

[1] Turkey Leg was a Northern Cheyenne whose camp was part of the time north of the Platte and part of the time on the Republican River. The actual leader of the party that ditched the train was Spotted Wolf.

[2] *My Life on the Plains*, p. 36.

and would have crossed the heads of the Smoky Hill and Republican Rivers. This would have brought them to the Platte River west of the forks, so that they would not have seen the track of the Union Pacific Railroad, which was then built west only as far as North Platte, Nebraska.

Porcupine's description of the country shows that the Indians approached the railroad from the north.

The story of the train wreck is told at length by Stanley.[1] The men he interviewed were perhaps not in a position to make very careful observations of what happened at the time, and we may prefer the story told by Porcupine. Stanley, however, quotes the story of Thompson, who was one of five men who started up the track on a hand-car to repair telegraph lines. When the hand-car was thrown from the track by the obstruction, the men ran. Thompson was shot through the arm, knocked down and partially stunned by an Indian, who jumped from his horse, scalped him, and remounted to ride off. Thompson saw the scalp slip from the Indian's belt and regained it, and later set out for Omaha, carrying his scalp in a pail of water, in the hope that it might be reattached to his head. He was treated by Doctor R. C. Moore, of Omaha. The operation was not successful, and Thompson finally went to England, and later sent back to Doctor Moore the scalp, which had been tanned. The scalp, preserved in alcohol, is now in the Omaha Public Library Museum.

Porcupine's story is the only one ever told by an eye-witness of the train wreck. We may imagine that the plundering of the train, and the acquiring of what to the Indians must have seemed an inexhaustible supply of extraordinary and valuable plunder made a wild scene. It is related that young men tied to their ponies' tails the ends of bolts of calico and muslin, and amused themselves by careering over the prairie with long streamers waving behind them, each boy trying to ride over, tread upon, and so tear off the adornment of one of his fellows.

After plundering the train, the Cheyennes went away to their camp, but almost at once came back, just in time to meet the Pawnee scouts who had come down to the railroad to look for them.

As soon as the news of the occurrence reached Omaha, Major

[1] Stanley, *Early Travels and Adventures*, vol. I, p. 154.

North, who was in command of four companies of Pawnee scouts then used in patrol duty along the line of the Union Pacific Railroad, was telegraphed to for help. He was at the end of track, and was asked to bring down a company of his Pawnees to follow the Indians who had wrecked the train. The nearest company that he could spare was stationed twelve miles west of the end of track, but he telegraphed for cars to be in readiness at the end of track, and with Captain James Murie went to Plum Creek and thence to the scene of the train wreck.

The Cheyennes were just returning for another load of plunder, and Murie attacked and chased them. A running fight ensued, during which a young girl, Mănăh'—Island Woman—a lad, her brother, and two other women, one named Ho wa heh', meaning Nothing, and the other named Wūn haī', meaning Burns, were captured. From this event the boy received the name he bears to-day—Pawnee. Island Woman escaped, and is still living. An old man was killed. It is said that thirty head of horses were captured. If so, these were old, slow horses.

Porcupine's account, with some interpolations, is as follows:

We had had a fight with the soldiers on (near) Ash Creek,[1] which flows into the Arkansas. There were Sioux and Cheyennes in the fight, and the troops had defeated us and taken everything that we had, and had made us poor. We were feeling angry.

Not long after that we saw the first train of cars that any of us had seen. We looked at it from a high ridge. Far off it was very small, but it kept coming and growing larger all the time, puffing out smoke and steam, and as it came on we said to each other that it looked like a white man's pipe when he was smoking.

The soldiers had beaten us in the fight and we thought that perhaps it was because of the way in which they rode and carried themselves, and we determined that we would try to imitate the soldiers, so we rode two by two in double file. One of the men had a bugle and from time to time he blew it in imitation of the bugle-call of the troops.

After we had seen this train and watched it come near us and grow large and pass by and then disappear in the distance, we went down from the ridge where we had been, to look at the ground where the train had passed, to see what sort of trail it made. When we came near to the track we could see

---

[1] So Porcupine, but perhaps he means near Ash Creek. All the printed accounts agree that the village was on the Pawnee Fork, which is just south of Walnut Creek, which the Cheyennes call Ash Creek, Mōtō shē', where ash trees grow thick.

white people going up and down by it, riding in light wagons. We were riding two by two and when we had come near to the track the man with the bugle sounded it, and the Indians spread out and formed a line and for a little way marched with extended front, and then again formed by twos. The white people paid no attention to us. Perhaps they thought that we were soldiers.

We crossed the track, looking carefully at it as we passed, and then went on and crossed the river.

Not long after this, as we talked of our troubles, we said among ourselves: "Now the white people have taken all we had and have made us poor and we ought to do something. In these big wagons that go on this metal road, there must be things that are valuable—perhaps clothing. If we could throw these wagons off the iron they run on and break them open, we should find out what was in them and could take whatever might be useful to us."

Red Wolf and I tried to do this. We got a big stick, and just before sundown one day tied it to the rails and sat down to watch and see what would happen. Close by the track we built a big fire. Quite a long time after it got dark we heard a rumbling sound, at first very faint, but constantly growing louder. We said to each other: "It is coming." Presently the sound grew loud, and through the darkness we could see a small thing coming with something on it that moved up and down.

It was a hand-car with two men working it.

When the men on the car saw the fire and the Indians, they worked harder so as to run by them quickly, but when the car struck the stick it jumped high into the air. The men on it got up from where they had fallen and ran away, but were soon overtaken and killed.

On the hand-car were two guns, and in handling them the Indians pulled something and the guns broke in two in the middle and the barrels fell down. The Indians said: "It is a pity that these are broken; if they had not been, we should have had two good guns."

These were Spencer carbines, the first breech-loaders these Cheyennes had seen.

After their success in ditching the hand-car they thought they would do more. They took levers, and after pulling out the spikes at the end of a rail, they bent the rail up a foot or two in the air. The next train came from the side of the bent-up rail. Porcupine said that the weight of the train ought to have bent back the rail in place; but in raising it they must have given it a sidewise twist, so that when the rail came down on the ties, the ends of the two rails did not meet, and the train jumped the track.

Looking east over the long level plain, we saw a small light close to the horizon, and some one said: "The morning star is rising." "No," said another, "that is one of those things that we have seen." "No," said a third man, "the first one has gone out and another one is rising."

It was learned afterward that they had seen the headlights of two trains that were coming, one following behind the other.

They sent men on the best horses they had eastward along the track to find out what these lights were and to come and report, telling them also to yell and shoot, in the hope that they might frighten it. The men went, and as soon as they saw that the first light was on a train, they started to return, riding as hard as they could, but before they had reached the place the train overtook and passed them. Some of them fired at the train and one tried to throw a rope over the engine, but when they got close, the horses were frightened and ran away. When they fired, the train made a loud noise—puffing—and threw up sparks into the air, going faster and faster, until it reached the break, and the locomotive jumped into the air and the cars all came together.

After the train was wrecked, a man with a lantern was seen coming running along the track, swearing in a loud tone of voice. He was the only one on the train left alive. They killed him. The other train stopped somewhere far off and whistled. Four or five men came walking along the track toward the wrecked train. The Cheyennes did not attack them. The second train then backed away.

Next morning they plundered and burned the wrecked train and scattered the contents of the cars all over the prairie. They tied bolts of calico to their horses' tails, and galloped about and had much amusement.

As they were going away with their plunder, another train came up from the west and many soldiers got off it, but they did not attack the Cheyennes. Later some of the Cheyennes went back for more plunder and were attacked by the Pawnees and driven away. An old man was killed and a woman and a boy, Pawnee, and a girl, Island Woman, were captured.

After Murie and his Pawnees had chased the Indians pretty well out of the country, they returned to Plum Creek, where they remained in camp for a couple of months. At the end of this time Turkey Leg sent a runner to North Platte, saying that the little boy who had been captured was his nephew, and that for the boy and the young women in the hands of the Pawnees Turkey Leg would exchange six white prisoners that he had. The Pawnees were consulted, and agreed that this should be done.

The message to Major North appears to have come through some of the Indians who had already begun to gather at North

Platte, for a council to be held between the Sioux and Cheyennes, and the members of the peace commission, who later made the treaty of Medicine Lodge.

It was agreed between Major North and Turkey Leg that the white prisoners should be brought in to North Platte, and that on the same day the two Cheyenne prisoners should be exchanged— the exchange to be made in the railroad eating-house. This was done. The white prisoners thus rescued were three young girls, two of them nineteen and one seventeen years old, a pair of twin boys six years of age, and a baby.

At the council there were present Spotted Tail of the Brulés, Man Afraid of His Horses, Man that Walks Under the Ground, Pawnee Killer, Standing Elk, Spotted Bear, Black Deer, Turkey Leg, Cut Nose, Whistler, Big Mouth, Cold Feet, Cold Face, Crazy Lodge, and several others.

The commissioners were Generals Sherman, Harney, Terry, Augur, and Sanborn, Honorable N. G. Taylor, Commissioner of Indian Affairs, Colonel Tappan, and Senator Henderson.

The chief subject discussed by the Indians was the abandonment of the roads running through their country. They urged this on the ground that the railroads drove off the wild game and so deprived them of their subsistence. The Indians, of course, asked for many things, but the main point they made was that they could not readily adapt themselves to the settled life which the commissioners recommended. Stanley quotes one man as saying: "Ever since I have been born I have eaten wild meat. My father and grandfather ate wild meat before me; we cannot give up quickly the customs of our fathers." This was a brief and telling summary of the Indians' point of view.

This council was preliminary to the one to be held near Fort Larned in October, and when it adjourned it was with the purpose of meeting there.

In October, 1867, at a camp on Medicine Lodge Creek, in southern Kansas, was signed the treaty of peace known as the treaty of Medicine Lodge. The Indian tribes who took part were the Cheyennes, Arapahoes, Kiowas, Apaches, and Comanches. The members of the peace commission were Generals Terry, Harney, Sanborn, and Augur, Senator John B. Henderson, Commissioner N. G. Taylor, and Colonel Tappan. There were present also Governor Crawford, Ex-Lieutenant Governor Root, and Senator Ross. The secretary was A. S. H. White. The occasion was one of importance. The commission was escorted to the place of meeting by three troops of the Seventh Cavalry, and a battery of gatling guns. A number of newspaper correspondents were present, among them H. M. Stanley, then correspondent of the New York *Herald,* and afterward famous as the African explorer.[1]

The events leading up to the council at which this treaty was signed were these:

During the spring of 1867 Indians had been doing more or less raiding on the Arkansas, and Colonel Leavenworth, then agent for the Kiowas and Comanches, had been ordered by the Commissioner of Indian Affairs to try to bring together all the tribes that had been hostile, and to make a peace with them. In order to do this, Colonel Leavenworth wrote to George Bent, asking him to do what he could to persuade some of the head men among the Indians to come in, and meet Leavenworth at the mouth of the Little Arkansas River, where the Wichitas were then living. Bent was then (June, 1867) camped with all the Southern Cheyennes in Texas, on a stream known to the Cheyennes as Bitter Water,[2] but called by the whites Sweet Water. The messenger from Leavenworth to Bent was a Mexican, named Sylvestro, who for a long time had been living with different tribes of Indians—Wichitas, Kiowas, Comanches, and Cheyennes.

When Black Kettle, chief of the Cheyennes, was consulted about the matter, he expressed his willingness to go, and he, Sylvestro, and Bent, with two or three other men and women, started to go to the mouth of the Little Arkansas. There they found Colonel Leavenworth, and camped with him were Ten Bears and Long Hat, chiefs of the Comanches, Wolf Sleeve, of the Apaches, and Black Eagle, a young chief of the Kiowas, with two or three of his people. Three Arapahoes came in the same day that Bent and Black Kettle reached there. One of these was a subchief, named Yellow Horse.

The day after these people got in, Colonel Leavenworth met

---

[1] The witnesses to the treaty were Thomas Murphy, Major Douglas, H. M. Stanley, John Smith, and George Bent. Lieutenant, now Major-General, E. S. Godfrey was attached to the escort.

[2] Wĭ ŭhk′ĭ măp.

the chiefs and explained to them that he had been ordered by
the Commissioner of Indian Affairs to meet some of the chiefs of
the different tribes, and discuss the question of peace, and to ask
them to select a place where they would meet commissioners
who were to come out from Washington to talk matters over, and
make a peace, if this could be arranged. Colonel Leavenworth
asked them to choose a place not too far from Fort Larned, because presents were to be sent out to them, and as there were no
roads in the country, and the goods would have to be hauled by
teams, they wished to deliver them as near the point of supply
as possible.

All the chiefs present seemed to agree that it was desirable
to be on friendly terms with the white people, and Black Kettle
declared that he would return to his camp, consult with his
people, and ask them to select a meeting place. He added that
the other tribes must be consulted, and all would have to agree
on the place of meeting. Ten Bears, of the Comanches, without
any hesitation expressed the opinion that some place on Medicine
Lodge Creek would be more convenient than any other. The
country from Fort Larned down to that stream was level, and
wagons would have no difficulty in reaching it.

To Black Kettle and Yellow Horse he said: "Tell your people
what I say, and tell them that this is the best place for us to
meet."

After their talk with Colonel Leavenworth, the chiefs dispersed to their various camps.

At this time the only people who were raiding on the Arkansas
were the Cheyennes, who had been running off stock, and killing
white men. As soon as Black Kettle had returned to his camp,
this raiding ceased. The chiefs stopped it, insisting that the
young men should no longer commit depredations on the whites.

Colonel Leavenworth now returned to Fort Larned for further
instructions, and asked Bent to remain at the mouth of the Little
Arkansas, until further orders. Leavenworth was gone for about
a month. William Griffenstein, a trader who had married into
the Cheyenne tribe, was camped near the Wichita, and Bent
stayed with him.

On Colonel Leavenworth's return he read Bent a letter announcing that Thomas Murphy, the Superintendent of Indian

Affairs for the District, was already at Fort Larned, and that great quantities of goods were being shipped in there for distribution to the Indians.

"Now," said Colonel Leavenworth, "I wish you to go out and gather up these Indians, and get them to come in to whatever point they have selected, and from time to time to send me a runner telling me where it is to be; then come back and meet me at Chisholm's ranch, at Council Grove, on the north fork of the Canadian."

Accordingly, with a companion Bent started out to look for the Indians. The first village they came to was that of the Arapahoes, all of whom were camped on the Cimarron. Bent delivered Colonel Leavenworth's message to the Arapahoes, who said that they would move in toward the Medicine Lodge, and soon started. He learned from the Arapahoes that the Cheyenne camp was on Beaver Creek, a little below where Wolf Creek runs into it, and after resting their horses for two days, they went thither, and found a large village of Cheyennes, in which were all the Dog Soldiers, who had recently moved south from the Republican River and joined the main village.

The Cheyennes agreed to go to the meeting place, and Black Kettle and a few men went over to the camp of the Kiowas and Comanches, who also agreed to meet at this place, whither the Apaches—at that time living with the Arapahoes—had already gone with the Arapahoes. Black Kettle asked Bent, when he returned, to take with him a part of Black Kettle's family, and leave them at the Arapaho camp. After leaving Black Kettle's people with the Arapahoes, Bent went on to Council Grove.

Colonel Leavenworth had not reached there, but Griffenstein had a letter saying that Colonel Leavenworth had been ordered back to Larned, and that Bent should go there, and on his way should get the chiefs of the various tribes, and bring them into the post to meet the superintendent. Griffenstein and Bent started for Larned, stopping on their way at a village of the Comanches. Ten Bears and Long Hat said that they were moving over to Medicine Lodge, and after telling Bent where the Arapaho and Cheyenne villages would be found, requested him to ask the chiefs of those tribes to await their arrival, so that all the chiefs might go together to Larned.

The Cheyenne and Arapaho chiefs waited as requested, and four or five days after Bent's arrival at the Cheyenne camp, the Kiowa and Comanche chiefs arrived, and these head men—perhaps sixty or seventy in all—started for Larned, about seventy miles distant. On the way they camped at Rattlesnake Creek, and starting very early in the morning reached Larned early in the day. Runners had been sent ahead to notify Colonel Leavenworth that they were coming, and when they reached the post they found that tents for their use had already been put up. The Indians had a talk with Superintendent Murphy, at which John Smith did the interpreting for the Cheyennes and Arapahoes, Bent declaring himself weary after the long rides he had made in the effort to get the Indians together.

At the council which was to be held, old Jesse Chisholm, a half-breed Cherokee who had a ranch not far from where Oklahoma City now is, on the north fork of the Canadian River, was to interpret for the Kiowas and Comanches, and Bent for the Cheyennes and Arapahoes. Yellow Horse, the Arapaho, talked good Cheyenne.

A few days after this, Murphy moved out to Medicine Lodge Creek, and selected a spot for the council ground. It was a wide, level flat on the north side of the stream, with timber above and below, and good camping places.

Black Kettle's camp of Cheyennes—only about twenty-five lodges—was on the south side of the stream, and at some distance below him was the camp of the Comanches, and below that the camp of the Kiowas. The Arapaho camp was on the north side of the stream, above Black Kettle's, and the camp of the Apaches was also on the north side, nearly opposite the Comanches. The main Cheyenne camp was over on the Cimarron, about twenty miles distant, and south of Black Kettle's camp on Medicine Lodge Creek.

Superintendent Murphy was camped here for about a month before the commissioners came, and during all this time six-mule teams were busy hauling out goods and presents from Fort Larned. Among the things sent out were a herd of beef cattle, much coffee, sugar and flour, and dried fruits, and a vast quantity of blankets and clothing, material made up for the use of troops during the Civil War, and at its close left over in the hands of the War Department. The War Department had turned this clothing over to the Interior Department for issue to the Indians. The beef was strange food to the Cheyennes and Arapahoes, who had been accustomed to live solely on buffalo, but the Kiowas and Comanches, who had been in Texas, ate it readily. In the region about the council ground buffalo were abundant, and the Cheyennes had no difficulty in procuring their accustomed food.

The peace commission left Fort Larned October 13, 1867, for the camp on Medicine Lodge. Word had been received from Thomas Murphy that he already had four hundred and thirty-one lodges of people on the ground, and expected about as many more. He believed that there would be five thousand Indians at the council. Besides the commissioners, the Indian Department was represented by Superintendent Murphy, Colonel Leavenworth, Major Wynkoop, Colonel Rankin, and John Smith, interpreter. General Augur reached the camp a little later. He had been ordered to join the commission, to take the place of General Sherman, who had been recalled to Washington.

Stanley gives the Indians present at the council at the time when the commission reached the camp as 100 lodges of Comanches, 150 lodges of Kiowas, 171 lodges of Arapahoes, 85 lodges of Kiowas-Apaches, and 250 lodges of Cheyennes.

When the commissioners arrived, their escort camped in a line some distance north of Medicine Lodge Creek. In front of the escort were lined up the wagons which had hauled out the supplies, and in front of these wagons was a line of tents occupied by the commissioners, a council tent, some tents containing stores, and at the east end of the line a guard tent. The council was held on the flat, between the commissioners' camp and the stream.

The commissioners sat in a row in front of the great council tent, in which their clerks and stenographers did their writing. The Cheyenne and Arapaho chiefs sat to the right or west, while the chiefs of the Kiowas and Comanches sat to the left or east. Behind the chiefs, in a wide circle, sat all the old and middle-aged men of the various tribes, and off toward the stream, sitting on their horses, or lying on the ground and holding them, a great throng of young men and boys viewed the proceedings from a distance, for in those days it was not permitted for youths to be present at important meetings.

At the first talk—an informal one between the members of the commission, and about twenty-five men from the different tribes—there seems to have been much difference of opinion among the Indians as to when the main talk should be held. The principal council, however, seems to have been October 19, when many speeches were made.

Senator Henderson proposed to the Kiowas that the Cheyennes and Arapahoes should be moved south of the Arkansas River; that the Kiowas should settle on the Red River, and around the Wichita Mountains, and made various promises to feed and clothe them, and to give them other presents. It was believed by Stanley that the Kiowas would sign the treaty on the following day, and, in fact, ten Kiowa and ten Comanche chiefs did sign it.

The Cheyennes took their time about coming in. It seems that they were making a medicine lodge, and, according to Little Robe, could not be there for five or six days. The commissioners agreed to wait four days, and apparently the Cheyennes did come in and sign, though definite information as to this is lacking.

After the treaty had been agreed upon and signed by the chiefs, the commissioners announced that they must return, and that now the presents would be issued to the people. The chiefs of the various tribes touched the pen to receipt for these goods, which were at once hauled out and deposited on the ground in three great piles; the one to the east was for the Kiowas and Comanches; that in the middle for the Cheyennes, and that to the west for the Arapahoes and Apaches. The chiefs selected a few men from the different bands of soldiers, and directed them to distribute the goods to the women and children. The quantity of material given out was very great—so great, in fact, that the Indians could by no means carry it all away, but left piles of clothing, blankets, and other things lying on the ground. When the tribes separated to go to their respective camps, almost all the people were on foot, for all the horses were packed with food, blankets, and other things, and so heavily loaded that the marches were very short. Many of the travois were full of nests of camp kettles, and axes, and other hardware. The packs were continually coming off, the travois breaking down, and the abundance of their property made much trouble for the women.

Later this same peace commission went north, and was supposed to have made a treaty of peace with the Brulé and Ogallala Sioux, and Northern Cheyennes, and with the Crows. On the other hand, General Pope had already opened the Powder River or Bozeman Road to Montana through the last hunting ground of Cheyennes, Arapahoes, and Sioux, and along it had been built—in the face of the protests of the Indians—Forts Reno, Phil Kearny, and C. F. Smith. As Stanley points out, by this means war had been brought about, and had raged along the Platte and along the line of this military road. The giving of a few presents and the signing of treaties by a few chiefs would not appease the Indians, whose livelihood, the buffalo, was being destroyed and driven away.

XXI

BEECHER ISLAND FIGHT

1868

In considering the old wars on the plains, certain conditions now forgotten must be remembered. The Indians were well supplied with horses, and were absolutely at home on the prairie. It was always difficult for the troops to overtake them. A party followed by enemies usually left behind a man or two on swift horses, who from the top of some high hill watched the back trail, so that the escaping people might have timely notice of the approach of pursuers. If the enemy drew too close, the Indians gradually separated, turning off by ones and twos from the main party—choosing places where the ground was hard and hoof-prints of the horses were not easily to be seen—until the pursued were reduced to a very few, who finally changed their direction, and the trail was lost. For the most part regular troops had little skill in prairie craft. They depended on citizen guides, who were supposed to be prairie men, to know the country, and to be good trailers.

In the summer of 1868, Major George A. Forsyth, brevet colonel on General Sheridan's staff, suggested the enrolment of a body of scouts enlisted from among the frontiersmen living on the border, who might fight the Indians somewhat in their own way. General Sheridan authorized Colonel Forsyth to employ fifty first-class frontiersmen, to be commanded by himself, with Lieutenant Fred Beecher as second in command. Like Forsyth, Beecher had served through the Civil War. Doctor J. H. Mooers, of the Medical Department of the Army, was the surgeon.

Fifty-one men were enrolled, armed with Spencer repeating rifles, carrying six cartridges in the magazine and one in the barrel, and Colt's army revolvers.

The little command moved out from Fort Hays August 29, and after some scouting struck the trail of a small war party of

Indians, which was followed until it disappeared. The scouts kept on north toward the Republican River, and its tributary streams, where buffalo were plenty. Here were favorite camping places of the Indians.

The scouts finally came on a broad and beaten trail, where a large village of Indians had passed. They followed this.

On the night of September 16, they camped on what they supposed to be Delaware Creek, the tributary of the Republican where in 1844 the Cheyennes had the battle[1] with Shawnee or Delaware trappers. The camp was actually on the Arickaree Fork of the Republican River. The stream bed was a wide, dry sand flat with here and there a water-hole, and on its south side, separated from the mainland by a narrow sandy channel, was the low island, or sand-bar, later called Beecher Island. It had not been overflowed for some time, for on it grew willows, rushes, and even a cottonwood tree of some size.

Here took place the Beecher Island fight, the tradition of which for many years was a vivid and thrilling story on the western plains. That story endured as an oft-told tale, until settlements became numerous and other matters, nearer in time, and so more important, occupied the attention of those who lived near the scene of the battle. As a new population came in, the memory of the occurrence grew dim, and its heroes were forgotten.

Twenty-five years after it took place, General Forsyth wrote an account of it, and later another writer took Forsyth's story, and enlarged on it. General Forsyth's story of the fight, written from a popular point of view, is misleading. That of the man who followed him is laboriously worked up to be still more exciting. Both stories—like most of those written about Indian fights—are full of error.

General Forsyth reported thirty-five Indians killed and believed that many more had been carried away on their horses, to which they were tied. He seems to make it appear that great numbers of Indians were killed in an early charge—before two o'clock. He tells of volleys fired by his men, of falling Indians and horses, and of the killing of Roman Nose.

The Cheyenne story is quite different. They give many de-

[1] P. 73.

tails of the fight, among them the names of the six Cheyennes and one Arapaho who were killed, the names of the two Sioux being unknown. Roman Nose was killed late in the day.

The diary of one of the scouts who fought on Beecher Island was recently published. It is a straightforward narrative of what he saw. The battle is described in temperate language, and the astounding events set down in earlier published accounts are not mentioned. The greatest hardship of the unwounded—apart from anxiety—was lack of food.

The scout whose diary[1] has been published was Chauncey B. Whitney, a good prairie man and Indian fighter, who was killed in August, 1873. His narrative is simple, and his figures of the loss by the Indians are as reasonable as could be expected from one who was guessing.

From August 29 to September 16, inclusive, the entries are brief, and without special interest:

(Sept.) 17.—About daylight this morning was aroused by the cry of Indians. Eight tried to stampede the stock, got seven horses. In a few moments the bottoms were completely filled with red devils. Went across the river on to an island, when the fight commenced. About 500 attacked us on all sides, with their unearthly yells. The balls flew thick and fast. The Colonel was the first man wounded. Lieutenant Beecher was wounded twice, as was also the Colonel. In a few moments eight or ten were hurt, some fatally. The ground on which our little squad was fighting was sandy. We commenced to scoop out the sand with our hands to make intrenchments for ourselves. In a few moments I was joined by two others, who helped me. With a butcher knife and our hands we soon had a trench which completely covered us from the enemy. Behind the works we fought the red devils all day till dark. Only two men were hurt after we intrenched ourselves. Culver was killed and McCall wounded. William Wilson was also killed early in the morning.

18th.—This morning the Indians made a slight charge on us, but were speedily repulsed. They were after three of their dead who lay about twenty yards from us. About fifty of the red devils were killed and wounded. They kept firing from the hills and ravines all day. No one hurt to-day. Two men started to Wallace.

19th.—The Indians made another attack this morning, but were easily driven off. About ten o'clock this evening myself and A. J. Pliley were requested by the Colonel to go to Fort Wallace. We started, but a few rods from the battle ground we found the Indians had surrounded the camp,

[1] *Kansas Historical Collections*, 1911–12, vol. XII, p. 296.

and forced us to return. Was awake all night. It rained all night steady, and everybody was wet and cold. Am very lame with rheumatism to-day.

20th.—Sunday, and all is quiet. No attack this morning. Last night I slept for the first time in three nights. Our surgeon, Doctor Mooers, died this morning about daylight. He was shot in the head. He did not speak from the time he was shot until he died. We had twenty men killed and wounded; four dead.

21st.—No Indians seen to-day; all dined and supped on horse meat.

22d.—No Indians to-day. Killed a coyote this morning; it was very good. Most of the horse meat gone. Found some prickly pears which were very good. Are looking anxiously for succor from the fort.

23d.—Still looking anxiously for relief. Starvation is staring us in the face. Nothing but horse meat.

24th.—All fresh horse meat gone. Tried to kill some wolves last night, but failed. The boys began to cut putrid horse meat. Made some soup to-night from putrified horse meat. "My God! have you deserted us?"

The following day the first rescue party appeared, and from that time on there was plenty to eat.

Their imagination colored the stories told by the whites. They were fighting for their lives against tremendous odds, and were excited, anxious, doubtful. The Indians' viewpoint was quite different. For years war had been their almost constant occupation, and the work of carrying it on had become commonplace. Fights such as this—not so large to be sure, but essentially similar—were of frequent occurrence. Sometimes they were successful; sometimes they lost men, were beaten and ran away. Whatever the event, they manifested neither special triumph in success, nor mortification at failure. The old-time Indian was a far better observer than most white men. He saw more clearly what was happening, and usually reported facts more accurately. On the other hand, he was weak in reasoning from what he saw.

As the Indians report the Forsyth fight, there was no such great loss as the whites claim. Their killed would have been fewer, but for the fact that two or three of the white scouts were hidden in rifle-pits, in the long grass, at a little distance from the main command, and the Indians, ignorant of this ambuscade, often rode close to it, and three were killed there.

A number of Indians who took part in this fight have told me what they saw of it. Some of these live in Oklahoma, and others in Montana. In the main incidents all the stories agree. All give the same names and numbers for the killed, and describe what took place in matter-of-fact fashion, and with no apparent thought of making much of it. It was a hard fight, but one of the everyday happenings of the time. They do not know whether they killed any of the white scouts or not.

About twelve miles down the river from the scouts' camp of September 16 were two large villages of Sioux, under Pawnee Killer, and one of Cheyennes, with a few Northern Arapahoes. The Cheyennes were chiefly Dog Soldiers, and among them were such well-known men as White Horse and Tall Bull, chiefs of the Dog Soldiers, but not chiefs of the tribe, and Roman Nose, a man of great courage, a splendid fighter, and looked up to by the whole tribe. He was a brave, possessed great influence, and was an acknowledged leader in war. He was not a chief.

These three Indian villages knew nothing of the presence of white men in the vicinity. A war party of Cheyennes returning from the South had reached the Cheyenne camp only three days before the whites were seen, and, a day or two before Forsyth reached the camp where he was attacked, a war party of Sioux had started south from this camp. Some of the young men of this war party left it and turned back, and were returning to the Sioux villages when they discovered Forsyth's command on the march. They recognized these as white men, and a fighting force, and did not show themselves, but went around, keeping out of sight, and when they reached their village announced that "soldiers" were coming. This news was shouted out to the camp, and caused much uneasiness, and some of the Sioux rode up to the Cheyenne camp, and told them what had been reported.

The Indian camps were now buzzing with excitement, and young men and boys were running about, driving in the horses from the prairie. All wanted their war horses. An old crier began to harangue the Cheyennes, urging them to make ready, and get into the fight as soon as possible. Roman Nose asked the crier to direct the Cheyennes to go on to the fight, and not to wait for Roman Nose. When he was ready he would come.

The report was received early in the day, and it was the middle of the morning—nine or ten o'clock—when they began to get ready to fight. Each man must first catch and tie up his favorite war horse, and then paint himself and dress for the fight. If there was time, each man put on his finest war costume before going into battle. Meantime, White Horse and Tall Bull had gone down to the Sioux camp, and had advised the Sioux to make ready, so that the Indians might attack in one body.

Failure to organize—in war as in most other things—has always been the weakness of Indians. Small groups of men were likely to steal off from the war party, and make independent attacks in the hope that they might accomplish some great thing, which would gain the applause of their fellows. Many of the Dog Soldiers, however, were opposed to these independent attacks; and besides giving advice to the Sioux, they sent word to the Arapahoes asking them to wait so that all might go together. At length, when all were ready, they started in a body to meet the enemy. There were many Indians, and all prepared for the fight. The warriors had war bonnets, shields, and lances, and all their protective medicines. Notwithstanding the statements made by white writers, they had few guns, and all of these were old muzzle-loaders.

The Indians supposed that the soldiers, as they called them, were on the way to attack the village, and they moved slowly in the direction where they supposed the troops to be, awaiting the attack. But Forsyth had gone up above on the river, and did not know that this camp was below him. He was marching directly away from it. On the other hand, the Indians had lost Forsyth's command, and did not know where he was. By this time it was late in the day, and when night fell and it grew dark the chiefs determined to stop where they were, until they could learn the situation of the soldiers.

In the middle of the night, eight young men, eager to perform some creditable act, mounted their horses and set out to look for the enemy, thinking that they might capture some of their horses. Two of these—Starving Elk and Little Hawk—were Cheyennes, and six were Sioux, and of the six Sioux one had been of the war party who had brought to the village the news that white men were coming. He gave his fellows the general direction in which he supposed the white men must have gone, but they could find no sign of them. They rode from hill to hill, stopped to listen, and often dismounted and held their ears close to the ground, but could hear nothing. Just before daybreak, however, they saw, far off, the light of fires being kindled. They rode toward them quietly, until they could see the horses and mules scattered about, and then, making all the noise they could and waving robes and blankets, they charged through the herd, to stampede it. A few horses broke loose from their picket-pins, but they secured only seven. This gave the first alarm the scouts had, and was their first knowledge that Indians were about.

Just as day began to show in the morning, the main party of the Indians rose, and started off to the northwest. As they passed over the next hill, those in the lead saw the distant fires. Forsyth's animals were now nearly packed, ready to start. Men who had gone ahead to make sure that the fires were those of the soldiers returned and called out: "It is the soldiers." Then, although the chiefs tried to restrain the Indians, they formed a line with a broad front, and charged.

It was just then that the scouts saw the Indians. Forsyth's men hurried over to the island, and took the loads off their animals, piling up the packs for breastworks.

When the Indians began their charge they must have been two or three miles from the troops, so that Forsyth's men had some time to heap up breastworks. The Indians charged up the valley and the dry stream bed, and when they came to the island divided, a part going on one side, and a part on the other. The island was only about a hundred yards long, and not very wide. The channel was broad on one side of it, but on the other narrow. The troops began shooting just as soon as the Indians were within range.

The charging Indians had intended to ride over the white men, but when they had come close to the island their hearts failed them, and they passed around on either side. One man, Bad Heart—died 1875—did ride over the island and through the scouts, and was not hit by the bullets, nor was his horse hit. He completed the first charge, and rode up on the hill beyond, and, after a little, turned about, and again charged back over the island and through the scouts, and came out unwounded. No Indians were killed in this first charge.

After the first charge, the Indians circled around the island, and while doing this, the first Indian was killed. It was Dry Throat[1]. During a part of this time many of Forsyth's men were

---

[1] Ŏ'ĕ ĭs tŏ'ŏv, Dry Throat.

outside the breastworks, some standing up and others in plain
sight, but soon the Indians came so close around them that all
jumped behind the breastworks into the rifle-pits. The older
Indians had stopped on the hill to look on, while the younger
men kept riding toward and about the island from all directions.
Soon after this Cloud Chief's[1] horse was killed, and near it they
also shot the horse ridden by Two Crows.[2]

Two or three of Forsyth's men were not on the island behind
the breastworks, but were by themselves on the mainland. It is
said that they had been sent down to hold the lower, or east, end
of the island, and that on the way there, instead of going to the
east end of the island, they crossed the narrow channel, and dug
rifle-pits in the sand in some high grass under a low sand bluff
on the east side of the stream. One of these men was Stillwell.
There were at least two men in this position, but for some time
the Indians did not know that they were there.

The second man killed was White Weasel Bear.[3] Some interpreters call him White Bear, or Ermine Bear, and one of his boy
names was Scalp. He was killed by the scouts on the bank.
Weasel Bear was on his horse, charging toward the island, and
shaking his shield over his head, when he rode almost over the
scouts' rifle-pit, and they shot him, the ball striking the hip, passing up through the body and coming out at the top of the back.

Weasel Bear had a nephew, White Thunder,[4] or Old Lodge
Skins.[5] He saw his uncle fall from his horse, but did not know
whence the shot had come that hit him. He supposed his uncle
had been shot from the island, and went down to see if he was
dead. When he was about ten feet from the scouts, as he was
stooping down in the high grass, they shot him through the
shoulder, and the ball came out just above the waist. White
Thunder was a young man of nineteen or twenty, the son of
White Horse.

The Indians continued to ride about the island, and to shoot
at the men behind the breastworks. Two Crows's horse having

---

[1] Wŏ'ē vī'hiŭ, Cloud Chief.   [2] Ōk'sĭa nĭs'sĭs, Two Crows.

[3] Hvā'hē nāh'ku, White Weasel Bear.

[4] Wŏh'k pē nŭ nūm'a, White Thunder, also translated Gray Thunder or
Painted Thunder.

[5] Mŏhk sē'ă nĭs, Old Lodge Skins.

been killed, he was now out of the fight and was sitting down looking on. White Horse[1] now rode up to his brother, Two Crows, and said to him: "Your nephew, White Thunder, has been killed. You will do well to get his horse and go into the fight." Two Crows got the horse and mounted, and soon the Indians got together and made another charge toward the island. This time they did not go as close as before, but kept farther away. The balls were flying worse than ever.

After the charge Two Crows went over the hill, and soon one of the chiefs called out: "All you men get back and tie up your horses and then go forward on foot."

All dismounted and soon went forward on foot, approaching as near the island as they dared. The prairie was level, but just south of the island grew a few little red willow twigs which made a sort of cover. Three Indians crept through these and then rushed up close to the breastworks and dug holes in the sand to hide in. When they approached the island they ran openly over the sand until they had come close to the white men, and fell on their bellies and began to dig away the sand and heap up little shelters for themselves, so that they should be hidden from the men who were shooting at them only a few yards off. After they had made their hiding-places, as they raised their heads to shoot two of these men were shot in the head. One of them was Prairie Bear,[2] another was a Northern Arapaho named Little Man. The third, Good Bear,[3] got up and ran away, dodging and running from side to side.

Roman Nose[4] had not yet got to the fight. Runners had gone to the camp and told Roman Nose that there was fighting, and a good many Indians were being killed. Then Roman Nose got on his horse and rode up to the battle-field, and when he got there one of the old chiefs cried out that Roman Nose had come. The Indians were still all about the island, but the fighting had stopped and everyone was standing back, waiting to see what Roman Nose would do.

Roman Nose stopped on the top of the hill. Tangle Hair (died 1911) overtook him at this place and they sat down together, and two or three other men came up and dismounted.

[1] Wŏhk'pŏ ăm, White Horse.   [2] Tŭk tŭ ē nāh'ku, Prairie Bear.
[3] Nāh'kū wū'hī tăh, Good Bear.   [4] Wŏ ŏ hkĭ nĭh", Roman Nose.

Roman Nose spoke to the others and said: "At the Sioux camp the other day something was done that I was told must not be done. The bread I ate was taken out of the frying-pan with something made of iron. I have been told not to eat anything so treated. This is what keeps me from making a charge. If I go into this fight I shall certainly be killed."

While they sat there White Contrary rode up and said: "Well, here is Roman Nose, the man that we depend on, sitting behind this hill. He is the man that makes it easy for his men in any fight." Then, addressing Roman Nose, he went on: "You do not see your men falling out there? Two fell just as I came up." Roman Nose laughed and replied: "What the old man says is true." White Contrary went on: "All those people fighting out there feel that they belong to you, and they will do all that you tell them, and here you are behind this hill."

Roman Nose said: "I have done something that I was told not to do. My food was lifted with an iron tool. I know that I shall be killed to-day." Then he went off to one side and painted himself and got out his war bonnet, and began to shake it and to make ready to put it on.

This war bonnet had been made long ago by White Bull—also known as Ice—a Northern Cheyenne. It had always protected Roman Nose in battle.

There were certain taboos which were a part of the medicine of this war bonnet and which, if disregarded, took away its protective power. One of these was that the man who wore it might not eat food that had been taken out of a dish with an iron instrument. The food for the owner of this bonnet must be taken from the pot or other dish by means of a sharpened stick. If this law was not complied with the owner of the war bonnet would be hit by bullet or arrow in his next battle. An elaborate ceremony of purification might restore the protective power of the war bonnet, but this ceremony was long and required much time.

Shortly before Forsyth's command had been discovered, Roman Nose had been invited to a feast by a certain Sioux, and the woman who was preparing the food for the feasters used a fork to take from the frying-pan the bread she was cooking. This was not known when the food was served to the feasters, and Roman Nose ate the bread instead of abstaining, as he would have done if aware of the circumstances. Afterward Eight Horns, one of the Dog Soldiers, noticed that the woman, who was continuing her cooking, was using a fork and pointed out to Roman Nose what she was doing. Then Roman Nose said: "That breaks my medicine."

Tall Bull, who heard of the matter, advised Roman Nose to go through the ceremony of purification at once, but almost immediately afterward and before Roman Nose had done anything Forsyth's scouts were discovered, and there was then no time for the ceremonies.

After he had prepared himself for battle, Roman Nose mounted his horse, and rode fast up toward where the scouts were, and behind him followed many Indians. He rode almost over the scouts hidden in the high grass—the men who had shot Weasel Bear and White Thunder—and they shot Roman Nose in the back just above the hips. He fell off his horse at the edge of the grass, but a little later had strength to creep up from the sand to the bank, and before long some young men came down and carried him off. He lived for a little time, and died about sundown.

The Indians continued to charge toward and around the breastworks and to shoot at the soldiers, but with what result they did not know, because their enemies were out of sight behind the breastworks.

During the day Two Crows and some other Cheyennes went down toward the river, creeping through the grass to try to recover the bodies of Weasel Bear and White Thunder, and when they got part way down there, they came on three other Cheyennes who had gone down for the same purpose. These men said to them: "Be very careful how you creep through the grass, because whenever the soldiers see the grass move they shoot at us, and two or three times they have come near hitting us." The Indians still did not know that Stillwell and his party were hidden in the grass just at the place to which they were going.

Two Crows and his party went forward slowly and cautiously, so that they should not make the grass move much. As they were creeping along, scattered out and going very slowly, two shots came from the grass right in front of them. This was their first knowledge that Stillwell and his party were there.

A man named Bear Feathers[1] was cut across the right shoulder by one of these balls. It made only a flesh wound.

Black Moon[2] told Bear Feathers to go back, because he thought he was badly wounded, but Bear Feathers said: "No, it is only a flesh wound." The shots sounded very close to them, and they knew that they were but a short distance from the white men. Nevertheless, Two Crows, Black Moon, and Cloud Chief continued to creep up toward the bodies. They were as slow and cautious as possible, but presently two more shots came from the rifle-pit, close in front of them. Two Crows' shield was tied on his back, and one of the balls hit the shield, and almost turned Two Crows over. The other bullet made a flesh wound in Black Moon's shoulder. Cloud Chief and Two Crows were now the only two men who were not wounded. Two Crows and Cloud Chief advised Black Moon to go back, because of his wound. The men who had started with Two Crows had stopped when they had overtaken Black Moon and Bear Feathers.

Weasel Bear and White Thunder had been killed in the grass very close to the rifle-pit, and to one another, and by this time Two Crows and Cloud Chief were only ten feet from the dead men.

Spotted Wolf and Star, who had been left behind, now crept up cautiously through the grass. Two Crows and Cloud Chief lay still. They dared not move, for fear that they might stir the grass. Cloud Chief was lying about six feet from Two Crows. The men who were coming up from behind must have moved the grass, for presently two more shots came from in front, and one of the balls cut Cloud Chief in the arm, making a flesh wound. Star came up behind and caught Two Crows by the feet and said: "How much further ahead are they?" meaning the men they were trying to drag away. Two Crows said very softly: "They are right over there ahead of us, only a little way." Presently they all crawled up fast through the grass, and the white men

[1] Nāhk'wū tūn ĭvt', Bear Feathers.
[2] Ĭsh'ĭ mŏhk tă'văs, commonly translated Black Moon, but really Black Sun and meaning a total eclipse of the sun from an eclipse once seen by a war party on its travels. The war party, of course, turned back.

shot twice again, but the balls went over them. Cloud Chief, being wounded, did not go up to the bodies.

Weasel Bear and White Thunder were lying almost side by side, White Thunder just behind Ermine Bear. When they reached White Thunder they turned him over on his back. He was dead and already stiff. Other Indians were creeping up behind, and the white scouts shot at them, but they did not shoot any more at the men nearest to them.

When they began to pull White Thunder along, crawling on their bellies, they could not drag him fast nor easily, but they started back on the trail that they had made in coming, and so did not move the grass much, and the white scouts did not seem to see them. At all events, they did not shoot at them, but shot at the men behind them.

Before they started with White Thunder, Star said: "Look at Weasel Bear; he is not dead. I can see his body move; he is still breathing." Two Crows said: "Are you still alive, Weasel Bear?" "Yes," replied Weasel Bear: "I am badly wounded; I cannot move." Then Two Crows said to him: "Wait, we are trying to get your nephew away from here, and when we get him away we will come back and try to get you."

Weasel Bear asked: "Is that my brother-in-law?" and Two Crows said "Yes." "I feel all right," said Weasel Bear: "Except that I am badly wounded through the hips and cannot move."

Star said: "We cannot move White Thunder; I will creep quietly back and have them get a rope. In that way we can all get hold and pull him away."

These men were lying in a line, one behind another, along the trail in the grass which they had made in creeping up to this place, and when they got the rope they threw it from one to another, and in that way it was soon passed up to the front. When the rope got up to where Two Crows and Spotted Wolf[1] were lying, they passed the noose around the two feet of White Thunder and pulled it tight. All the different men who were lying there and who could reach it got a hold on the rope and pulled on it, and dragged White Thunder away. His body was pulled away by the other men, but Two Crows and Spotted Wolf

[1] Ōh nǐ″ŏ wŏ wŏ′hăs, Spotted Wolf.

just moved to one side, so as to let the body pass between them, and they remained there, near Weasel Bear.

The scouts, seeing the grass move where the body of White Thunder was being dragged, fired a good many shots, but did not hit anyone. Two Crows and Spotted Wolf moved back a little.

When White Thunder had been taken out of range of the white men's guns, they carried him away over the hill. Two Crows then took the rope, and with eight or nine others went to get Weasel Bear. They went very carefully along the trail that had been beaten down in dragging out the other body, and did not move the grass, and the white men did not shoot at them at all. When Two Crows got up to Weasel Bear he said: "My brother-in-law, we have come for you now."

Weasel Bear said: "That is good. I am glad of it. I feel all right except that my legs are paralyzed. I cannot move."

Two Crows looped the rope about Weasel Bear's feet, and they dragged him away as the other man had been dragged.

The last man killed in this fight was Killed by a Bull. He was a Cheyenne Dog Soldier, and the Indians say he was shot on the hill at a considerable distance from the breastworks while helping to carry the body of Dry Throat. General Forsyth describes this death in detail, and says that on being hit the Indian sprang into the air with a yell "of surprise and anguish and rolled over stone-dead." This yell must have been heard at a distance of two-thirds of a mile—a long way.

Killed by a Bull was buried in the lodge found by the troops that came to rescue Forsyth, and on him much imagination and many adjectives were expended, under the impression that he was Roman Nose.

Roman Nose was buried on a scaffold. Medicine Woman, still living, and now the wife of Porcupine Bull, helped the wife of Roman Nose to bring up her lodge-poles to raise the scaffold for his burial.

The night after the first day's fight, Colonel Forsyth sent out two men, Trudeau and Stillwell, to Fort Wallace, asking for help. These men got through without much trouble, reached Fort Wallace and delivered their despatches. A party set out from Wallace, guided by Stillwell; and a courier was sent to Colonel L. H. Carpenter, who was scouting toward Denver. On receiving the news, Carpenter turned north, and was the first to reach the beleaguered men, whom he brought back to the post. The wounded all recovered.

The day after Roman Nose was killed, the Indians returned and charged up to the command and fought there all day, and again on the third day some of the Cheyennes went back to see whether the soldiers had gone away or were still there. On this day also they had a little fight.

There were many Indians in this fight, probably six hundred. There were killed in all nine Indians—six Cheyennes, one Arapaho, and two Sioux. Roman Nose and Prairie Bear were Northern Cheyennes. Dry Throat, White Thunder—or Old Lodge Skins—Weasel Bear, and Killed by a Bull were Dog Soldiers. The Northern Arapaho was Little Man. He was a chief. The names of the two Sioux killed are not known. The Indians agree that all that saved Forsyth and his command was that he got on the island and remained there. If he had gone out on the prairie there were so many Indians that the whole command would have been destroyed.

As the most famous of the Northern Cheyennes, Roman Nose was regarded as the hero of this fight on the Indian side, yet it is clear that no one in Forsyth's command knew Roman Nose. General Forsyth states that the scout Grover identified Roman Nose, but while Grover had had some intercourse with the Sioux he did not know the Northern Cheyennes. In the accounts of the fight, a description of Roman Nose by General Fry is often quoted. The Indian is described as wearing a white buffalo-robe—a bit of fanciful description, like one in another sentence which says: "The muscles under the bronze of his skin stood out like twisted wires." Indians are notable for their smooth, rounded, small, and symmetrical limbs. They are never muscled like a blacksmith or a prize-fighter—though painters sometimes represent them so.

Roman Nose is said to have been a chief, to have led the early charge in the first day's fighting, to have worn a war bonnet with two bull's horns, to have worn a white buffalo-robe, and to have been buried in a lodge. None of this is true.

Roman Nose never wore a white buffalo-robe. To the Cheyennes the white buffalo was a sacred object, which might not be handled or used by anyone. The flesh might not be eaten, nor the hide tanned by a woman of the tribe. The flesh was left on the prairie, and the skin was presented as a votive offering to the powers above.

It is said that back of the mounted warriors the bluff was covered with women and children watching the progress of the fight, and that from the camp were heard dismal wailings, the women mourning over their dead. The Indians declare that the only women who appeared near the battle-field were those who came with travois to carry away the dead. It would have been impossible to hear at the island the sounds of the camp twelve miles away.

The scouts made a brave fight against tremendous odds and came off with comparatively slight loss. Colonel Forsyth's good judgment kept the command from being annihilated.

The Carpenter Fight

Soon after the fight at Beecher Island the two villages of Sioux moved up the Republican River and the Northern Arapahoes also went away. There remained only the Cheyenne Dog Soldiers, with a few Northern and a few Southern Cheyennes, and half a dozen lodges of Sioux.

Not long after the return from the rescue of Forsyth's scouts, about the middle of October, Captain L. H. Carpenter, with three troops of the Tenth Cavalry, was marching up the Beaver River on the north side of the stream. Some Indians, who were starting out to hunt buffalo, saw the troops and, returning to the village, announced that soldiers were coming. At this report the Cheyennes got up their horses and painted and dressed themselves for war.

A Northern Cheyenne, named as a boy Wān hāi yū ĭv and later Bullet Proof,[1] had just devised a special medicine which should render the soldiers' guns ineffective and make it possible for the Cheyennes to ride up close to them and kill them without danger. In order to exhibit this power to the people he had chosen a number of young men whom he had instructed how to dress and act. Of these two wore each a sash made of the hide from the head, shoulders, and fore legs of a four-year-old buffalo

[1] Hō hō'ĭ tū'ĭ, Bullet Proof.

bull which hung over the right shoulder and, passing across breast and back, met under the left arm. The horns left on the bull's head rested on the man's shoulder, one in front and the other behind. The other young men wore similar sashes of deerskin with the hair on, and to each end of each sash was attached a tiny mirror.

The men chosen for this work were: Feathered Bear,[1] Little Hawk,[2] White Man's Ladder,[3] Bobtailed Porcupine,[4] Breaks the Arrow (by stepping on it),[5] Big Head,[6] and Wolf Friend.[7] There were thus to have been eight men including Bullet Proof, who, however, was not to take any part in the fight, but merely to stand apart and direct operations. The whole camp had faith in Bullet Proof's power, because at the fight at Beecher Island he had been shot in the breast and the ball appeared to go through him and come out at his back. When he found that he had been wounded Bullet Proof dismounted, put his hand on the ground and rubbed the hand over the wounds in front and behind. By this means he closed both wounds so that they did not bleed. From that time he was well. He declared to the Cheyennes that he would so instruct these young men that they might ride around the troops untouched by the bullets, and that finally the guns used against them would not go off at all. "At last," he said, "you will see the balls coming out of the muzzles of the guns and will see them fall to the ground."

Bullet Proof told the young men that they must ride around the troops four times and that at the end of the fourth circle, if none of them had been killed or wounded then, any one of them might charge in among the troops and kill them without danger.

After the Cheyennes had learned that the troops were near and had made their preparations, they set out in a body, riding very fast. The seven special men who were to prove Bullet Proof's power rode apart, on the right side of the main party.

---

[1] Näh'kū wūt ŭn'ĭvt, Feathered Bear, as it is commonly called, but better translated as Bear Wearing a Plume of Eagle Feathers—Näh'kū = bear + wū tŭn = Eagle Tail Feathers + ĭv = suffix of possession of quality.

[2] Ain'hūs, Young Hawk.

[3] Vi'hĭo ē ĕ wōn hä, White Man's Ladder.

[4] Ĕs cū'ăts ē'wa ho, Bobtailed Porcupine.

[5] Mä āi'ō sĭ ĕh ĭ hō, Breaks the Arrow (by stepping on it).

[6] Mähk sĭ ah', Big Head.   [7] Onĭ'h ŏ mă hăn', Wolf Friend.

At last from the top of a hill they saw the troops and wagons climbing another hill. The Indians at once charged down toward them, and when the troops saw them coming they turned north toward the head of a little creek and made a corral of their wagons, putting the horses inside. When the Indians reached this corral of wagons they divided, one party going by on either side, and rode down into the little stream valley to wait and see the special men fight the soldiers. As the Indians passed, the soldiers opened fire on them and shot fast, but when they reached the stream beyond the soldiers the Indians dismounted and stopped there. Before they made the charge Bullet Proof had said to them: "After you have passed the soldiers and are on the other side, stop there and watch us. We are going to ride around them and let them shoot at us."

Bullet Proof sent off his young men one by one. First came Feathered Bear, riding a fine spotted horse. This young man was already noted for his bravery. It was his father's practise before his son went into a fight always to tie on the son's head an upright plume made of the tail feathers of a sage hen. Feathered Bear had never been hit in battle, and when he heard of Bullet Proof's power he determined to take part in this attempt, thinking that it might add to his reputation.

Next after Feathered Bear came Little Hawk, who rode a buckskin horse, long-winded and fast—one of the best horses in the tribe.

White Man's Ladder came third. He rode a light sorrel horse painted with a black disk on either shoulder, and with black zig-zag lines running down his legs.

During the ride from the camp to where the troops were found the horses of Big Head and Wolf Friend had become tired out and could not run, so that they took no part in the charge.

The fourth to start was one of the bull robes, Bobtailed Porcupine; and after him followed the fifth and last man, the other bull robe, Breaks the Arrow.

Bullet Proof took no part in the charge, but stood off at a distance and looked on.

The young men rode hard, but did not get very far. Feathered Bear almost completed the circle, and then his horse was shot through the shoulders and fell, and Feathered Bear walked away. Little Hawk's horse had his left leg broken at the point of the shoulder; was shot below the right eye and in the neck close to the body. The horse fell and Little Hawk, jumping off, struck the ground on his feet, running hard. He had forgotten the rope, which was tied to his belt and to his horse—as was usual in going into battle—and when he reached the end of the rope it jerked him back and he almost fell. He cut the rope, however, and ran on unwounded. The horse ridden by White Man's Ladder was shot in the black spot painted on its shoulder, in the paunch and also in the rump, three wounds. It did not fall, however, and the rider, seeing the animal's condition, turned out of the ring. Before the circle had been completed Breaks the Arrow and Bobtailed Porcupine were both killed. The latter was shot over the right eyebrow, and his relation, Breaks the Arrow, in the backbone. Each had only a single wound, a wonderful thing when it is considered that the troops were shooting as fast as they could and the bullets were flying thick.

After this result of Bullet Proof's medicine the Indians who were looking on mounted their horses and went away, and this was the end of the fight. It was, as a matter of fact, not a fight at all but the testing of Bullet Proof's power. Nevertheless, the military reports declare that ten Indians were killed and intimate that there was a battle, but the Indians did not charge on the troops.

The soldiers walked up to where the dead men lay and looked at the one who was dead and the one who was wounded, and shortly after straightened out their wagons and went away, just before dark.

The soldiers cut off parts of the scalps of the dead Indians. The one who was not dead was killed, the soldiers afterward said, by opening a vein in the neck. The Indians saw that he had a small cut in the neck. General Carr speaks of talking to the wounded Indian through a scout, Grover, familiar enough with the Sioux tongue, but unable to speak Cheyenne. He might, however, have talked by signs.

The negro soldiers who came into the post after the occurrence said that they could not tell how many Indians had been killed, but that they knew of two. They also expressed surprise that the Indians showed so little fight.

Bullet Proof explained the failure of his medicine by saying that the young men had not followed out his instructions, but had gone too close to the troops at the beginning. He declared that he had told them to begin riding around the troops at a considerable distance and to draw nearer and nearer to them only gradually.

After the troops had gone on, the Cheyennes took the two men who had been killed, laid them across horses, and brought them to the camp, where everyone came to see them. They were placed on a bed in a lodge.

Bullet Proof, who was related to the two—one being a cousin and one his uncle—stood on his feet and said: "You people blame me for this, but it is not my fault; they did not do as I told them. Of course, if you want to you can blame me, but they did not do as I instructed."

An old man, the father of one of the boys killed, stood up and said to Bullet Proof: "Friend, it is well. It is better for a man to be killed in battle than to die a natural death. We all must die. Do not let the killing of these young men make you feel badly."

Others said: "Let Bullet Proof not feel badly. We do not blame him for what has happened."

Bullet Proof now tried to show his power by bringing to life the two men who had been killed. He walked around the bodies and grunted like a buffalo bull. Then he puffed out his breath toward them, imitating the snorting of a bull, and afterward a bull's moaning. He ran toward them and stopped and stamped his foot. While he was doing these things Bobtailed Porcupine raised his hand over his head and drew up his leg a little, but nothing else happened. Bullet Proof then spoke to the people and said he could not make his medicine work as he wished and gave up all hope. The young men were afterward buried on one scaffold in a large lodge.

This was the Carpenter fight about which much has been said. It was a mere skirmish of no consequence, undertaken to enable Bullet Proof to show his power.

XXII

THE BATTLE OF THE WASHITA
1868

THE peace commission appointed by Congress in July, 1867, made its report January 7, 1868. An interesting conclusion which it reached was that in all cases investigated by the commission of difficulties which existed with Indians at the date of the commission's creation, and for some years previous, the cause of the difficulty was traced to the acts of white men—either civilians or soldiers.

The treaties made at Medicine Lodge Creek were not ratified by the Senate until July, 1868, and were not proclaimed by the President until August, 1868—the treaty with the Sioux not until February, 1869. The delay in ratifying these treaties put it out of the power of the authorities to do anything to locate the Indians on the lands arranged for them to occupy under the treaty stipulations. Besides, the Cheyennes and Arapahoes objected to settling down on the reservation selected for them because of the bitter water of many of the streams, it being in the gypsum belt between the southern line of Kansas and the Cimarron River. It did not help the Indians—and they did not know of it—that by the Act of July 20, 1868, Congress appropriated $500,000 to be expended under the direction of General Sherman in carrying out treaty stipulations; that is, in preparing homes, furnishing provisions, tools and farming utensils, and subsistence for those tribes with which treaties had been made and not yet ratified. General Sherman assigned Generals Harney and Hazen to the two military districts which he had established, the latter being given control of the Cheyennes, Arapahoes, Kiowas, and Comanches, and perhaps other bands. To the use of General Hazen $50,000 was allotted.

Meantime there was some disorder on the plains, and some raiding by young men who had started north on the war-path against the Pawnees and had committed some outrages on the Saline River.

The invasion of the country by white people had driven off the buffalo, and, according to Colonel Wynkoop, the Indians were starving. At this time the massacre of the Cheyennes and Arapahoes at Sand Creek was less than four years distant, and was still fresh in their minds, while the attack on the village on Pawnee Fork and its destruction by Hancock was only a year old. General Sherman and General Sheridan, neither of whom had been enough in contact with Indians of the plains to know anything about them or their methods of thought, seem to have determined that they must be punished. This was a common feeling in those days, the military officers seeming to forget that before Indians could be punished they must be caught, and that before they could be caught they would have every opportunity to commit enormous injuries in the way of killing people and destroying property.

About the middle of October, General Sheridan was authorized to go ahead with his proposed work of punishing the Indians, and about the 6th of November, 1868, he left Fort Hays to join his forces at Bear Creek. It was reported that a million rations had been provided for the troops, and a large supply of extra horses taken along. At that time a large number of Indians, all of them at the time peaceful, were camped on the Washita River, not very far from old Fort Cobb.[1] The village of Black Kettle—about seventy-five lodges—was the farthest west of these camps on the Washita. Below him was a large village of Cheyennes and Arapahoes, and below them the Kiowas and Comanches. Before this the governor of the State of Kansas had declared that Kansas would do her part in punishing the Indians, and the militia regiment, known as the Nineteenth Kansas, had been enlisted for this purpose.[2]

[1] Hazen says the Indians were encamped on the Washita eighty miles above Fort Cobb. Black Kettle and other chiefs came in to see him and to ask what they ought to do, but it was the same old story of divided authority, and Hazen had to tell them he had no power to offer them protection. He says Custer attacked them the very next day after they reached their camps, following this talk with him. *Report Secretary of Interior*, 1869–70, pp. 830 *et seq.*

[2] The Nineteenth Kansas Cavalry was commanded by Governor Crawford in person. He says he resigned the governorship to take part in this campaign. Delayed by severe snow storms he did not reach Camp Supply with his command until November 26. Crawford, *Kansas in the Sixties*, pp. 322–4.

At Camp Supply, which Sheridan reached November 21, he found General Sully engaged on the work of the post, but the Kansas militia had not made its appearance. The weather was tempestuous, very cold and snowy, but the horses of the Seventh Cavalry were in good condition, and that regiment was ready for service. On the morning of November 23, General Sheridan ordered General Custer to set out, with the idea of looking for Indians. A few days later took place the Battle of the Washita—commonly spoken of as a great victory.

The story from the point of view of the troops is told in General Custer's report to Sheridan, which has been printed many times.[1] It is claimed that one hundred and three warriors were killed and fifty-three women and children captured.[2] As usual, there were many women and children killed. An Indian was an Indian and always good to shoot at. The village was captured and burned. The troops lost Major Elliot, Captain Hamilton, and nineteen enlisted men killed, three officers and eleven enlisted men wounded. The Indians from the lower camps came up toward Black Kettle's village, perhaps to fight, perhaps with the purpose of saving the women and children, but Custer scarcely waited for them, and withdrew without a collision with this larger force. Ben Clark, who was in the fight, stated that when the first people appeared from the lower villages General Custer ordered Major Elliot to take a few men, and disperse those Indians. Elliot set out to do this, but found the Indians too many to disperse, and was soon driven up a side ravine. Here his force was surrounded, and the men turned loose their horses, and got into a hollow where they lay in tall grass so that the Indians could see only the smoke from their carbines. Before long they were all killed.

The Indians say that from Camp Supply, whence Custer's command started, it went up Wolf Creek to a point about eighteen

---

[1] *Record of Engagements with Hostile Indians*, p. 15.

[2] In April, 1869, several Cheyennes, including Red Moon, Little Robe, Minimic (Eagle Head), and Grey Eyes, had a talk with Special Agent Colyer and General Grierson at Camp Wichita and stated that the Cheyenne loss was 13 men, 16 women, and 9 children. *Report of Secretary of Interior, for 1869–70*, p. 525. Hazen in his report says (p. 823) the Arapahoes had had two men killed, the Comanches one. He does not say the Kiowas had any killed.

miles above Supply. From Wolf Creek Custer crossed over by
way of the Antelope Hills to the South Canadian River, following
the trail made by a war party that had been raiding on the Smoky
Hill River. The snow was nearly two feet deep and the trail was
easily followed from the point where the Osage scouts had found
it on Wolf Creek. As the soldiers travelled along, they found
buffalo along the South Canadian, and some were killed for the
uses of the command.

The Indians whose trail Custer was following had passed along
only the day before. Some of the Cheyennes were going to Black
Kettle's village on the Washita, and some to other Cheyenne
villages which were down below. When they reached the Canadian one party crossed, and went on south by the Antelope Hills,
while the other party kept on down the river, each group wishing
to go directly to the village where each belonged.

Bear Shield and his party, who had gone down the river,
camped five or six miles below the Antelope Hills, and the next
morning when about to start on they heard shooting up the river.
One of the party, named Wood, said: "One of you men had
better go up on that hill and look back and see what you can see.
To me those guns sound like the guns of soldiers." "No," said
Red Nose, "it must be that other party. They have stopped
somewhere, and have found buffalo, and are killing some." So
the Indians did not take the trouble to go up on the hill to look
back to see who was doing the shooting. Bear Shield and his
party went on, and that night reached the village on the Washita
below Black Kettle's village.

The party with which Crow Neck was went on over toward
Black Kettle's village. They struck the Washita about fifteen
miles above the village, and seeing where the camp had just
moved down the river, followed the trail, and reached home that
night. At the point where they reached the Washita, Crow Neck
left a worn-out horse, and the next afternoon, thinking that by
this time the animal would be rested, he went back to get it.
When he had come almost to the place where he had left the
horse, he saw something coming over the hills, a long line of
people or animals, and being afraid that these were soldiers he
turned back to the village without getting his horse. When he
reached the camp he said to Bad Man, in whose lodge he was

stopping: "I believe I saw soldiers going over the hill to the river when I went to get my horse. They were either soldiers or buffalo; at all events, I was frightened and did not get my horse. You will do well to get in your horses this afternoon, and to-morrow morning to move away. I am afraid that perhaps soldiers are coming." Bad Man got in his horses, as advised.

What Crow Neck had seen was Custer's command marching over from the Canadian to the Washita. It was during that night that Custer made the march through the snow and cold, and the next morning he attacked the village.

When the firing began many of the women and children rushed out of the village and down into the bed of the stream, and tried to hide there. Black Kettle and his wife were killed close together in the village. The Indians who could do so hurried down the stream or crossed it, and sought refuge in the hills. Most of those killed were shot in the valley of the stream, close to it, and practically all the women and children who were killed were shot while hiding in the brush or trying to run away through it. Many women and children ran into the river, and waded down through the water, waist or breast deep, and by keeping close under the banks escaped the shots of the soldiers, who were riding along the bluffs, and on the bank above them. The weather was bitterly cold, and the people half froze, but in view of the greater danger of the soldiers, they thought little of that discomfort. Perhaps two miles below Black Kettle's village was a horseshoe bend of the Washita, about which the water was deep for the whole width of the stream, and it was impossible for a person to walk, even close under the banks. The Indians knew about this and warned the women and children of it, telling them, when they got to the beginning of this bend, to leave the river, and cut across the point, and then re-enter the water below. This they did.

Among those who waded down the river was a large party of women and children behind whom followed three men ready to fight, a Kiowa and two Cheyennes named Packer (Stō ko' wo) and Little Rock (Hō hăn ĭ no o'). When these people emerged from the water they were seen by Custer's command, and these may have been the Indians that Major Elliot is said to have been ordered to attack and disperse. Elliot went down toward them with his force of fourteen or fifteen men. Farther down the river a number of Indians were gathered on the south side of the stream, and the orders may have referred to them. When Elliot got near to these women and children, the three men who were with them stopped behind to fight.

About the middle of this cut-off across the point, Little Rock, who had a rifle and powder-horn, stopped and fired back at the soldiers and killed a horse under one of them. Almost at the same moment he himself was killed. The Kiowa jumped back to his body, snatched from him his rifle and powder-horn, and as he retreated began to load and fire. Packer and the Kiowa escaped and are alive to-day.

A little farther along Buffalo Woman (Wo' ïsta) with three children became exhausted and stopped and sat down. When the soldiers came up, Elliot detailed the man who had been dismounted to take these prisoners back to the command. As they were going back toward the command a number of Indians were beginning to come in from the south. The woman saw them, and said to the soldier: "Wait a moment; these children's feet are pretty nearly frozen; let me wrap some rags about them, to protect them." Of course, it is not to be supposed that the soldier knew what she was saying, but he saw her tear pieces from her dress and bind up the feet of the children. While she was doing this, the Indians who were coming in had time to creep around and get between her and the command. Then, when she and the soldier started on, the Indians, who had recognized her, charged on them, and killed the soldier and took the woman away. Little Chief, of the Arapahoes, counted coup on the soldier with a hatchet.

When the party of women and children, and the two men with them, had reached the bank of the river they climbed down and continued to wade through the water under the high bank. From time to time, as the Kiowa finished loading his gun, he crept up the bank and fired a shot at the soldiers. Once while he was doing this he saw a great crowd of Indians coming toward him from down the river, and a moment after saw Elliot's men turn off from the stream and ride up toward the hills. The Kiowa called to Packer, who also crept up on the bank, and just then they saw a crowd of Indians coming down the stream—Little

Chief and his party who had cut off the soldier and rescued the woman and the three children. Then the Kiowa called out to the women and children and said: "They are charging from both sides. You can come up on the bank now."

Meantime the Indians had surrounded Elliot's party. His men let their horses go and all lay down in the high grass to fight. Those who were looking on from a distance could see nothing but smoke and confusion. The shooting by the soldiers was constant. The Indians who had surrounded them crept closer and closer, and presently they could see that the soldiers were apparently not taking any aim, but were holding their carbines up over the grass and shooting wildly. Meantime Packer, the Kiowa, and many of the women and children hurried to the place where the fight was taking place, but when they reached it the shooting was all over and the soldiers were dead. The fight must have been short.

Among the Indians there was a difference of opinion as to who it was that counted the first coup on Elliot's men. Some people declare that it was Roman Nose Thunder, a Cheyenne, who rushed in among the troops and was shot in the arm, and others that it was an Arapaho, who also rushed in and was killed. Opinion seems to favor the Arapaho, who was the only man killed by Elliot's force in the final battle. His name was Tobacco. He was the owner of a flat war club similar to the one owned by the Arapaho who was killed in the big fight with the Kiowas in 1838. A man who carries one of these war clubs feels obliged to perform some great feat. Another Arapaho, Single Coyote, was mortally wounded here and died some time after.

The Indians all say that the soldiers lay flat on the ground and did not rise up above the grass to take any aim. They seemed to depend for safety on concealment rather than on defense; and while they fired many shots these shots were not directed toward their enemies. Roman Nose Thunder, who rode close to and around them, could see them in the grass and shooting, but to him they appeared to be shooting upward and not toward the Indians. The Arapaho, who with many has credit for counting the first coup, rode immediately over them and was shot in the breast by an upward-directed ball.

A number of the older and more prudent Indians thought that

they would crawl up the ravine and get close shots at Elliot's men and began to do this. They moved slowly, on hands and knees, and before they had come near the troops the Indians made a charge and almost ran over them.

In the killing of Elliot's men Cheyennes, Arapahoes, Kiowas, and Apaches took part, so there was a great counting of coups, each tribe being at liberty to count the coups allowed by its own customs. In that way twelve coups might have been counted on each one of Elliot's men.

It has been stated on supposed Indian authority that Elliot held the Indians off for two days, but this is clearly a misunderstanding of what the Indians said, for the fight was very short, probably much less than an hour.

The people of Black Kettle's village who survived went down to the other villages below, in many cases being taken there by friends who came up with horses for their transportation. Custer very prudently made no move to attack the villages below, and the Indians thought that if he had done so his whole command would have been wiped out. It was not until about two weeks after the battle that Custer's command returned to the scene to look after the remains of Elliot and his party, who were found close together at the place where they were killed.

After the Washita fight the tribes which had been camped together there withdrew to the Red River, and most of them camped on the north fork of the Red River.[1] The captured women and children were taken to Fort Hays, Kansas, but before long an old woman named Red Hair was sent out to find the Cheyennes. About this time Little Robe, a Cheyenne, and Black Eagle, a Kiowa, went into Fort Cobb to see what terms they could get if their people surrendered and to procure news of the Cheyenne prisoners. They saw General Hazen, who talked with them and advised them to wait for the coming of General Sheridan, who reached there a few days later. Sheridan told the Indians that

[1] Hazen says that immediately after the battle the Indians fled down the Washita toward Fort Cobb, alarming the whites there, who feared an attack. But before nearing the post the Cheyennes and Arapahoes turned off toward the south. The Kiowas, Apaches, and part of the Comanches came down and camped near the fort for protection. Later, when the troops came to Fort Cobb, the Kiowas became alarmed and ran away, but the troops seized their chiefs and compelled the Indians to return.

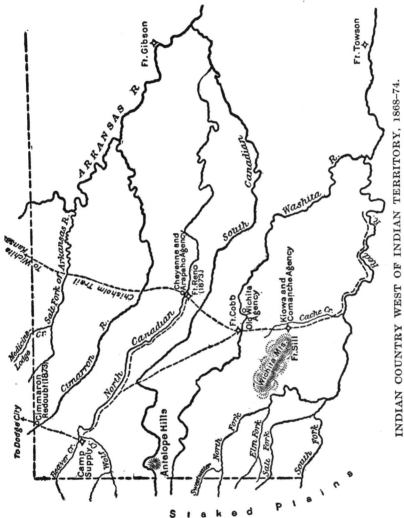

INDIAN COUNTRY WEST OF INDIAN TERRITORY, 1868–74.

Fort Sill was called "Camp Wichita" when it was established. It was still known under that name in the spring of 1869. It was on Cache Creek, 22 miles south of the Old Wichita Agency, on Washita River.

they must give up the white prisoners they had; that he would send Custer to the Cheyenne camp for the prisoners, and that the chiefs must go back and warn their people that Custer was coming, so that the Indians would not fight him. He told them that the Cheyenne prisoners would be given up in the summer at Fort Supply, and advised the Cheyennes and Arapahoes to go in there and surrender.

Custer's story is somewhat different. He says the Indian woman and an Apache chief named Iron Shirt were sent to the Cheyennes; that Iron Shirt[1] returned alone and said that two chiefs would soon be in to talk. A few days later Little Robe and Yellow Bear,[1] "second chief of the Arapahoes," came into Fort Cobb and said their people were talking of coming in and would send a runner with the news of their purpose in a few days. Custer says he waited but no messengers came, so, with forty men, he and the two chiefs set out. They went to the Arapaho village and persuaded that tribe to come in, but the Cheyennes did not come. In March Custer, with eleven troops of the Seventh Cavalry and ten of the Nineteenth Kansas Cavalry, set out to look for the Cheyennes. He moved from the neighborhood of Fort Cobb, where the troops had been nearly all winter, toward the Red River, and striking a trail followed it to the north fork of the Red River, where in the middle of March he found the Cheyennes on a timbered stream. Custer rode out ahead of his command with an orderly and was met by some chiefs, including Medicine Arrow.[2] The Indians say that Custer was brought into the camp and to the medicine arrow lodge, where he sat down under the medicine arrows, and the keeper of the arrows lit a pipe and held it while Custer smoked, and while Custer was smoking Medicine Arrow told him in Cheyenne that he was a treacherous man and that if he came there with a bad purpose—to do harm to the people—he would be killed with all his men. Then the arrow keeper with a pipe stick loosened the ashes in the pipe and poured them out on the toes of Custer's boots, to give him bad luck.

The Indian was not far wrong as to Custer's intention, for

---

[1] Both these men signed the treaty of Medicine Lodge.

[2] So called by the whites. His Cheyenne name was Hŏ hŏ nĕ vĭ ŭhk tăn uh", Rock Forehead.

Custer says that while he was smoking this pipe he was planning how to surround the camp and attack or capture it. However, he now learned that there were two white women in the camp, so he did not dare attack until he could secure them. Custer says that when his troops approached the Indians fled from their village and made toward Little Robe's camp, which was some distance off. He says that he caused to be seized Big Head and Dull Knife, Dog Soldier chiefs, and two other men, whom he held as hostages. He then sent word to the Indians to return and take away their lodges if they chose, and many did so. After waiting here a few days for the delivery of the white prisoners, he told them that if the prisoners were not given up on the following day, he would hang the Cheyennes he held. The following afternoon the women were given up.

Bent says that while the Indians were making a friendly visit to Custer's camp they heard the officer give a loud command, and the soldiers all seized their guns and attempted to surround the Indians. All got away except three, whom Custer held and sent to Fort Hays, where they were imprisoned with the Cheyenne women. Afterward two of these men, Slim Face, eighty years old, and Curly Hair, fifty, were killed by the guards. There seems to be some confusion about the men who were captured.[1] They are the three who were photographed and whose picture has been printed in a multitude of books on the early West, with a great many captions. The names are differently given by different people. Ē hyōph'stā says they were Younger Bear, Chief Comes in Sight, and Island. Bent gives the name of the man Island as Lean Man, and old Two Moon, of the Northern Cheyennes, identifies the picture as that of the brother of his mother.

Ē hyōph'stā tells the same story as that given by Bent. These three men, she says, went in to make peace. They were surrounded by the soldiers, captured, and their pictures were taken. Afterward they were killed.[2]

[1] For another account see *Report of Secretary of Interior*, 1869–70, pp. 524, 525, where the men arrested are said to have been young men. They were middle-aged or old men.

[2] Ē hyōph'stā says that Island was her uncle. She believed, in 1912, that she was eighty years old. She died in August, 1914, while on a visit to the Southern Cheyennes at Oklahoma. The picture above referred to was taken at Fort Dodge, Kansas, March 13, 1869.

Custer, with the two rescued white women and the "three chiefs" he had captured, marched back to Camp Supply. Soon after this the Cheyennes came in and settled down at Supply. In the South there was no more fighting between the Cheyennes and the whites, until 1874.

In Black Kettle, White Antelope, and Yellow Wolf, all old men, who were killed by the whites, we have three examples of high patriotism. These men were constant workers among the Indians in behalf of peace with the white people. They did this not because they loved the white people, from whom they had received nothing good, but because they loved their own tribe, and wished to guide it in paths that would be for the tribe's greatest advantage. White Antelope and Yellow Wolf were killed at Sand Creek, and Black Kettle four years later, when Custer attacked his village on the Washita. Black Kettle was a frank, good man, who did not hesitate to expose himself to any danger if he thought that his tribe might be benefited thereby. Notwithstanding the attacks made on different parties of Cheyennes by troops in Colorado, Black Kettle was quite willing to visit Governor Evans in Denver. Before and after Sand Creek he consistently talked and acted for peace, and his last words in this behalf were spoken to General Hazen only a few days before he was killed in the village on the Washita. He was the first of the Cheyenne chiefs to dare to attend the meetings of the peace commission at the treaty of Medicine Lodge, in 1867. Taught by past experience—at Sand Creek and on Pawnee Fork —the other Cheyennes feared to present themselves at a place where there was a large number of troops and where they might be attacked without warning.

Black Kettle was a striking example of a consistently friendly Indian, who, because he was friendly and so because his whereabouts was usually known, was punished for the acts of people whom it was supposed he could control.

XXIII

BATTLE OF SUMMIT SPRINGS

1869

As so often said, the upper waters of the Republican River, near where the states of Kansas, Colorado, and Nebraska come together, had always been a great buffalo country. For this reason they were a favorite camping-ground for the plains Indians, of whom, between 1860 and 1870, some bands of Cheyennes, Arapahoes, and Sioux were hostile.

In the early summer of 1869 General Eugene A. Carr set out from Fort McPherson, Nebraska, with the Fifth Cavalry, accompanied by a battalion of Pawnee scouts, for the Republican River. During the first days of July General Carr's command was camped on what the Cheyennes call Cherry Creek, which flows into the Republican from the northwest. At the same time the Cheyenne Dog Soldiers with some Sioux were camped on the head of the same stream. The Cheyennes learned of the presence of the troops and attacked them in the night, trying to drive off their horses. Owing to the readiness and keenness of the Pawnees this attack was not successful. During the Cheyenne charge on Carr's camp the horse ridden by Yellow Nose fell with him, and Yellow Nose was thrown and lost his horse. No one noticed the occurrence, but a little later, as the Cheyennes were returning to their camp, they found with them a loose horse. Yellow Nose was out for two nights and then came into the camp. That same day the Cheyenne village—Dog Soldiers under Tall Bull, and a number of Sioux—moved over toward what was later called Summit Springs, under the White Butte.[1] The stream which runs southeastwardly from Summit Springs is called White Butte Creek.

It was at this place that in 1864 Big Wolf and his family had been killed by Dunn's soldiers.

[1] Wōhk pō ōm′ĭn ō ĭ nōs, White Butte.

The first night the Indians camped among the sand hills on the divide, and the next morning moved over to Summit Springs. They purposed to cross the South Platte that day, but the chief, Tall Bull, told them that the streams were up, and that it would be just as well to wait there for a couple of days, so that the water might fall and their horses might rest. Tall Bull said: "We will stop here for two days; then we will rush across the South Platte and go up to the rock where we starved the Pawnees." This is Court House Rock.

Tall Bull sent six young men to the river to learn about the crossing. When they reached it they stripped themselves and their horses and rode into the water, expecting to find it very deep, but the water was not so high as they had expected. It ran only up to about the middle of the horses' shoulders. After the young men had crossed, some remained on the north side while others went back to search for the ford which was most shallow. Those who stayed on the north side cut willow poles, and when the ford had been selected they went across the river, sticking up these poles in the sand in order to mark the crossing, so that when the women should come the next morning they would be able to cross more easily. When they returned to the camp they reported that the river was not high.

It was shortly after the last attack on the troops that Captain North with some Pawnees discovered a group of Indian buffalo hunters returning to their village. The camp's exact location was not seen, but it was evidently near. When the troops took the trail, among the tracks was seen the print of a woman's shoe, evidence that the Indians had a white captive. The troops travelled faster than the Indians, and the afternoon of the second day camped where the Indians had spent the previous night, fresh antelope heads showing that the camp had been abandoned for not more than twelve or fifteen hours. Here General Carr determined to take some of his best mounted men and pursue the Indians, leaving his wagon-train to follow.

On Sunday, July 11, the command started about four o'clock, and at eight came to a point where the trail split into three forks. General Carr took the left-hand trail, to the northwest, and with him were sent a white sergeant of the Pawnee battalion and ten Pawnees. Colonel Royal took the right-hand trail, with William

Cody. Major Frank North and his brother, Captain Luther North, with twenty-five of the best mounted Pawnees, took the middle trail. They rode faster than the others, and got some distance ahead of them. The Pawnee scouts with General Carr found the Indian village, and one of them was sent to overtake the party on the middle trail. He reached them a little after noon, and they started across the hills at a gallop and joined General Carr's command, where he was waiting behind a ridge of hills. The Pawnee scouts said the Indian camp was not in sight, but that they could see horses on the hills. After resting their horses for a few minutes, General Carr ordered the charge. The Pawnees were fairly well mounted, and took the lead. When they reached the hill overlooking the camp, Major North was fifty yards in advance of his brother, who was three hundred yards ahead of the main body of the scouts. At the top of the hill they saw some Indians, who ran back into a ravine, and then shot at Captain North. The Pawnees charged down into the village and the cavalry came galloping past, turned to the left and rode on past the village, perhaps with the idea of surrounding it. The Indians of the village were running in all directions. They were completely surprised, and before they fully took in the situation the troops were in the village. The day was warm and pleasant, and the Indians were sitting about in the shade of the lodges. At the appearance of the troops they rushed to get their horses, and on foot and on horseback scattered like birds in every direction.

So far as known, the first man who saw the troops was Little Hawk, but he was far away from the camp hunting antelope, and was riding a slow horse and could not get to the camp in time to warn the Indians. In fact, the troops reached the village before he could do so, and when he met a number of escaping Cheyennes he joined them.

Two Crows was sitting in the lodge talking when he heard someone outside exclaim: "People are coming." He paid no attention to the call, but continued his conversation, and presently, without any warning, shooting began to sound close to the camp. All rushed out of the lodge and saw the Pawnees charging up and down on the nearby hillside, and firing into the camp. At first some of the people thought that these Indians were the advance messengers of a Sioux war party that had been out and were returning with scalps, but in a moment or two the soldiers began to pour over the hill. Many of the Indians had their horses tied up in camp and in a few moments a number of them had mounted. These took women and children on behind them and started to run away. The troops appeared on the east side of the village, and on the west side, and presently began to come over the hill from the north. Only the south side was open for the Cheyennes to get away. Meantime there was the confusion that always exists in a surprise attack on an Indian village. Horses were running in every direction; people were trying to catch their horses, and were springing on their backs, and many others were running away on foot, some toward the south and others to hiding-places in the bluffs.

Two Crows started on foot, running as hard as he could. As he started he picked up a rope, a bridle, and pistol, and his medicine war club, which he afterward threw away. As he ran he heard hoof-beats behind him, and looking back saw coming a herd of loose horses, followed by a Cheyenne, named Plenty of Bull Meat. Two Crows called to him, saying: "Turn the horses toward me," and as they came up to him Two Crows saw in the lead a fine black horse belonging to Tall Bull, which he knew as a good and gentle horse. As it ran by him, Two Crows ran fast by its side and made a cast with his rope, which by good luck fell over the horse's head. He had just time to slip the bridle on the horse, when close behind came a party of charging Pawnees. By this time two more Cheyennes had joined them.

Presently they overtook four women riding double, on two horses, and an old man, and immediately behind them were five Pawnees shooting at them. The Pawnee horses were tired out, and they could barely gallop. The old man with these women called out: "Young men, turn about and come behind these women, and whip up their horses and help them to get along." Two Crows and Plenty of Bull Meat turned and rode behind the women and whipped up their horses, which then ran much faster. The women were so frightened that they seemed not to have thought of urging their horses forward.

They drove the women forward, and with them the old man. He had a gun, which he did not use, expecting if his horse gave out to get off and fight on foot. Presently they overtook an old

woman on foot leading a horse. When they overtook this woman,
they recognized her as a very old woman who ordinarily wore the
old-fashioned Suhtai woman's dress. They tried to help her up
on her horse, but they could not do it and the Pawnees were
so close behind them that they did not dare to dismount to lift
her. For a little while they tried to fight for her, but when the
Pawnees got quite close they left her and rode on. A little farther
along they came upon two Sioux women running on foot, but they
were obliged to go on, and the Pawnees killed them.

Still farther along they came to a Cheyenne woman with two
little children, a boy and a girl, running hard, and there they did a
bad thing. They stopped and fought for a time, trying to turn
the Pawnees, but could do nothing, and rode on, and the Pawnees
killed the three. They ought at least to have picked up the little
children and carried them away with them and saved them.

They went on farther, but after this they saw no people on
foot. An old Sioux woman's horse fell with her, and she was
thrown off and killed by the Pawnees.

At this time about twenty-five or thirty more Pawnees came
up and a little later Two Crows and Plenty of Bull Meat, Lone
Bear and Pile of Bones, who had good horses and were fixed for
fighting, saw down below them a woman on a horse going very
slowly. Lone Bear called out to the others: "Now, we must stop
here and fight for this woman. You two must do your best.
Go down there and help her. We will stay behind and fight
these people off."

Three Pawnees who had been following the woman were quite
close to her, shooting at her. Two Crows and Plenty of Bull Meat
rode down to her and whipped her horse and turned it up into the
hills, while the three Pawnees rode back toward their fellows.
Then Two Crows and Plenty of Bull Meat rode back toward Lone
Bear, but before they got to him the Pawnees had shot him and
Pile of Bones, and they had fallen off their horses. The Pawnees
had dismounted and were scalping the two men. They were
also throwing up into the air the war bonnets that the men had
worn. The Pawnees did not attempt to follow Two Crows and
Plenty of Bull Meat. These two said: "It is useless for us to
stay here any longer," and they rode away as fast as they could.
They were riding off when on a sudden they met Bad Heart with

six other men, and told him what had happened to Lone Bear and Pile of Bones; that they were lying over there where they could see the Pawnees standing.

Bad Heart said to them: "Come on, now; let us ride back and see our friends." The nine men started toward the Pawnees, who by this time had turned and were riding back to the troops. When the Cheyennes got near the Pawnees they charged them, but the Pawnees' horses were exhausted and could do no more than walk, and presently two of the Pawnees jumped off their horses and started to run. Two Crows tried to ride around the abandoned ponies and drive them off, but one of them kicked up behind and struck him in the shin and kicked his horse in the neck. The Cheyennes rode up to where Lone Bear and Pile of Bones were lying and saw that they had been scalped and cut to pieces.

Red Cherries, a Northern Cheyenne, was in the camp with his wife and his little baby. Some Cheyennes who had been to war in the South and had captured a lot of mules had come to the camp and told them that soldiers were on their trail, and that with the soldiers were some Pawnees. After two or three moves, when they had camped at Summit Springs, Red Cherries said to his wife: "We will do well to go north again. These people seem to be dodging about from place to place all the time." He and his wife had saddled up and started, but met the approaching soldiers and soon after the camp was attacked. The young people, both Sioux and Cheyennes, left the camp and ran away over the prairie, but the old people ran to a deep ravine to hide there. Among them were Tall Bull, the chief, Black Sun, and Heavy Furred Wolf. Black Sun had been wounded through the body in a fight, but was now up and able to be about. Red Cherries went to the outer edge of the camp, and stopped there and dismounted and turned his saddle-horse loose. The Pawnees were already in the camp. A number of young men who rode by him asked him to get on behind them and escape, but to each one he said: "No, my friend, I shall stop here in this camp." It was a pretty hard place, for Pawnees and soldiers charged through the camp, following the people. Red Cherries walked around the edge of the camp, and the bullets struck all about him, close to his body. Presently Tall Sioux rode up to him and said: "Jump on behind me and come away; take pity on your little baby; do not leave it fatherless."

"No, my friend," said Red Cherries, "I shall stay here."

When Tall Sioux received this answer he rode off. The soldiers were in line on two sides of the camp shooting. Presently Tall Sioux again rode up to him and said: "Friend, take pity on your wife and child; listen to what I say."

As Tall Sioux rode up to him it seemed that all the guns went off at once, opening and firing. The sound was continual.

Then Red Cherries said: "My friend, you have come for me twice and I will listen to you." He jumped on behind his friend, and they rode off over the hill.

After they had got beyond the ridge they stopped, and fought and then retreated, and presently the firing stopped. A little later from far off in the distance they saw five Pawnees come in sight over the hill. The two Cheyennes supposed that these Pawnees were alone and charged down on them, when suddenly coming over the hill were seen more Pawnees, and a line of soldiers. A good deal farther on Red Cherries found a place where some women and children had come together. His wife and child were there. Afterward his wife was killed and his mother-in-law, and her two little children. All of the camp that was left later crossed the Platte,[1] and did not stop travelling until they had reached the Sioux camp on White River.

Major North and his brother Captain Luther H. North, with a party of Pawnees and a few soldiers, had surrounded the ravine into which a number of people, and a woman and child had fled. One of the men was Tall Bull. He had run to his horse, and putting his wife and child on it had mounted behind them and sought this shelter. When he reached the ravine he found a place for the wife and child where they would not be exposed to fire, and returning to the mouth of the ravine stabbed the horse behind the fore leg. This was where he intended to die.

The mouth of the ravine was narrow and its banks almost perpendicular. The Cheyennes cut hand and foot holds in these sides so that they could climb up to the top, and discharge their guns, and in this way for some time they kept the attacking party at bay.

[1] They crossed the Platte August 7—a month after the fight.

Some of Major North's Pawnees had crept up within about twenty paces of the ravine on one side, and were thus in a position to fire at the Indians climbing up the opposite bank.

While this was going on an Indian climbed the bank nearest to the soldiers, and showing only his head and shoulders fired a shot at Major North and his brother, who were galloping toward the bank. The Indian then lowered his head. Major North marked the spot where the Indian's head had disappeared, dismounted and handed his bridle-rein to his brother, telling him to ride away. He believed that at the sound of the galloping hoofs the Indian might raise his head again to learn the result of his shot. Major North dropped on his knee and taking a knee rest aimed the rifle at the spot where the head had been. A moment later he saw the Indian's rifle appear over the edge of the bank, and then the head rise as the man prepared to fire. Major North pulled the trigger, and the Indian fell back without discharging his gun, leaving the rifle cocked and ready for shooting on top of the bank. The ball had entered his forehead. Later in the day the dead chief Tall Bull was found in the ravine directly under this spot.

Shortly after this another head appeared at the same spot— the head of a woman. She reached the top of the bank, pulled her little six-year-old girl after her, and making signs that she wished to talk, walked to Major North, and passed her hands over him, asking him for pity. Major North sent her to the rear, where she would be safe. She proved to be the wife of Tall Bull. She told him that there were still seven Indians alive in the ravine. These were afterward killed, thirteen having already been killed at the head of the ravine.

The two captive white women in Tall Bull's camp were said to have been shot by Tall Bull at the time of the attack. One of them was killed. They were Germans and could not speak English.

The reports tell of the capture of the village, the killing of fifty-two Indians, and the capture of eighteen women and children, with something like four hundred horses and mules. Nothing is said about how many of the fifty-two killed were women and children.

The day after the fight all the Indian lodges, robes, camp

equipage, clothing, and dried meat were brought together and burned.

Among the plunder found in the village were many articles obtained from white settlers on the Saline, and a considerable amount of gold and silver money, together with some jewelry. These things passed into the hands of the soldiers and scouts, and during the march toward Fort McPherson an effort was made to collect all the money captured in the village in order to give it to Mrs. Weichel, the rescued captive. The Pawnees cheerfully gave up $600 in $20 gold pieces, that they had taken, while from the soldiers only about $300 were collected. About $600 besides this had been found in the village, which the white soldiers concealed.

XXIV

FIGHT AT ADOBE WALLS

1874

Up to within a few years there was on the south fork of the Canadian River, in Hutchinson County, Texas, an adobe ruin long known as Adobe Walls. In 1864, it was the scene of a fight with Kiowas, Comanches, and Apaches by New Mexican troops under Kit Carson, and again, in 1874, a group of southern Indians attacked a large party of white buffalo hunters who had established themselves near this point.

The history of Adobe Walls has never been written, but it has been conjectured to have been an old trading-post, perhaps built by the traders Bent and St. Vrain.

Within a few years this supposition has been confirmed by George Bent, son of Colonel William Bent, who has given me the following account of this matter:

Between 1864 and 1868 at different times Kit Carson and old John Smith told him that many years before William Bent sent a party from Bent's Fort down to the southeast to build a trading-post on the head of the South Canadian River for the purpose of trading with the Kiowas, Comanches, and Apaches. Just when this took place is not known, but it seems altogether probable that it was before the year 1840—perhaps before 1837, as suggested in an earlier chapter. Up to that time the Kiowas, Comanches, and Apaches had been at bitter war with the Cheyennes and Arapahoes, some of whom were almost always about Bent's Old Fort, and the likelihood of meeting their enemies would naturally have prevented these more southern tribes from going there to trade.

The post was built and some of Colonel Bent's best men were sent down there with goods, to start a trade. The men chosen were Carson, Smith, Murray, Maxwell, Fisher, and two Mexicans, a cook and a herder.

John Smith stated that they were directed to trade chiefly for horses and mules. The party remained there for some time trading with Kiowas and Comanches, and got together quite a herd of horses and mules, which they corralled every night inside the fort. One day, however, while the horses were at pasture on the prairie, some Indians came down and ran them off, killing the Mexican herder. The men had only two or three mules left, and it was impossible to remain there without horses. They cached—buried—most of their goods; packed their ammunition and most valuable things on the animals, and at night started on foot for Bent's Fort.

They had a hard and difficult march. It was dark, and the country was little known to them so that they were obliged to travel by direction, and their way led through great beds of cactus. All were shod with moccasins, and the thorns of the cactus penetrated the buckskin and caused them torture, so that Smith said that they suffered from fever from the inflammation of their feet.

They had gone some distance, and daylight was just beginning to appear when Indians were seen coming. Murray, who was in charge, and had ordered during the night that no one should smoke, said: "Here they come, boys; bunch up those mules and the rest of you scatter out."

The Mexican held the ropes of the mules, and the others got around them. An Indian carrying a lance charged up boldly, and when close to them Murray and Fisher both fired, and the Indian fell. Two more Indians were killed and three or four horses. Murray had told the men not to fire unless they had quite sure shots. "If we make good work of it," he said, "they will leave us."

It turned out as he had said, and presently the Indians drew off out of rifle-shot, and had evidently had enough. Murray stepped out in front of the animals, in plain sight, and made signs to the Indians inviting them to come on, but they declined to do so. Murray went out and scalped the nearest Indian, and the others went away.

Old Tohausen (Little Mountain), the Kiowa chief, afterward told the white men that the people who took the horses were Mountain (Jicarilla) Apaches, and that those who attacked the men on the retreat were Comanches. On the other hand, George Bent heard from Anadarko in 1912 that the Indians who made the early morning attack were Kiowas.

The Comanches were much irritated by the pushing southward of the hide hunters from the neighborhood of Fort Dodge, for it was well understood in 1873 and 1874 that no hunting should be done south of the Arkansas River. That was regarded as the Indian country, and the terms of the Medicine Lodge treaty provided that white hunters should not cross that stream, which was patrolled at intervals by troops. So long as buffalo were plenty north of the Arkansas the hunters respected this feeling, but after buffalo got scarce the dead-line, in their estimation, was moved down to the Cimarron, where buffalo were found abundant, and when the great beasts were killed off there, they followed them still farther south.

The Indians strongly objected to the farther movement south of the white hunters, realizing, of course, that the extermination of the buffalo meant starvation for themselves.

In the spring of 1874 a Comanche medicine man announced that he had a power which would enable the Indians to overcome the whites. This man was generally believed in by all the southern tribes, including not a few of the Southern Cheyennes. Among the Cheyennes who believed in him were Medicine Water and Iron Shirt—brothers of Alights on the Cloud, who was killed in 1852—Gray Beard and many others. Little Robe, on the other hand, so soon as he heard of the threatened trouble moved his whole camp into the agency, and many other Cheyennes would have moved in had it not been that they were held in the outside camp by the soldiers of the various bands, chiefly the Bow String soldiers.

That spring the Cheyennes had been greatly troubled by white horse thieves, who had come down and run off many of their horses, taking them to the settlements where they sold them. In one of these cases the thieves were followed by some Indians under a son of Little Robe, but when they reached Dodge City they received no satisfaction, and starting back to their camp angry took some horses from some white men, got into a fight, and one was wounded. At this time there were a great many rough white men in the country peddling whiskey, wolfing, and hunting buffalo, and many of them, if they had the opportunity, would not hesitate to run off horses belonging to anyone, red or white.

White hunters killing buffalo for their hides had moved south to the South Canadian River and there established a settlement with a store, saloon, and blacksmith shop, a little west of Adobe Walls.

The fight with the buffalo hunters at Adobe Walls took place June 27, 1874, or almost exactly two years before the Custer fight on the Little Big Horn. Of the twenty-eight men and one woman at that time in the settlement, Billy Dixon was one, and in the account of his life, published in 1914, he tells the story of the fight as he saw it.

The Indians supposed that it was their charge which awoke the buffalo hunters, but, as a matter of fact, a considerable number of them had been aroused by the cracking of the ridge-pole in Hanrahan's saloon, and worked until morning propping it up. By the time the work was finished the sky was beginning to grow red in the east, and to Dixon and some of his companions it seemed hardly worth while to go to bed, so they prepared to make an early start. It was during the preparations for this start that the Indians were seen at a distance charging in line.

Most of the white men were still in the buildings when the Indians made their charge. Two freighters, the Shadler brothers, who had come in late the night before, were still asleep in their wagons and were killed. William Tyler was also killed early in the fight. Dixon says that with the Indians was a man who used a bugle, and that the Indians charged at the sound of the bugle. The white men, Dixon says, soon came to understand these signals and whenever the bugle sounded prepared for the charge.

About the middle of the day the Indians grew discouraged and drew off out of shot. Within the next two or three days small parties came back once or twice to look over the hill at the settlement, but no further attack was made. However, the battle put an end for the time to the buffalo hunting in that section, and thus—though at a considerable loss to themselves—accomplished the purpose of the Indians.

A story of the fight told by Cheyennes who were present gives the Indian view:

In the spring of 1874 a Comanche named Ĭ sǎ tai′ announced
that he had a medicine which would make useless the guns of
the white people, and proposed that they should be exterminated.
A Comanche carried the pipe to the Cheyennes, Arapahoes,
Kiowas, and Apaches, and asked them to go with the Comanches
and destroy the buffalo hunters who were gathering to hunt on
the South Canadian and were making a settlement there.

The Comanche reached the Cheyenne camp on the head of the
Washita River, where the Cheyennes were then holding a medicine-
lodge, made by Crazy Mule. The Comanche gave a great feast
to the Cheyenne chiefs and chiefs of the soldier bands, and asked
them to help him. Ĭ sǎ tai′ prophesied, saying: "Those men
shall not fire a shot; we shall kill them all." The Cheyennes
accepted the pipe offered them by the Comanche.

After the medicine-lodge was over, a large war party of
Kiowas and Comanches came to the Cheyenne camp. They
charged up to the camp circle and rode all about the circle, outside and inside. Four men led the war party, and with these
four men rode the medicine man, Ĭ sǎ tai′, who was to make the
guns of the hunters useless. Four other brave men brought up
the rear. The soldiers of each society were singing their own
songs. In the charging line were some Arapahoes.

After the Kiowas, Comanches, and Apaches had made this
charge the Cheyenne soldiers made a similar charge, and that
evening all the soldiers of the different societies of each tribe,
including the Cheyennes, danced around the camp circle. There
was much excitement. Next morning the great war party set out
for the Adobe Walls. The leaders went ahead early in the morning, and at noon stopped for the others to overtake them, and
they spent the night at that place. The next day they went on
and all through the day men kept overtaking the party. The
evening of the third day they began to paint themselves and their
horses and to prepare their shields and all their war medicine
so as to be ready the next morning to charge the buffalo hunters.
Their camp was five or six miles from the Adobe Walls.

Next morning the Indians all formed in line. The Comanche
medicine man stood on a hill and to the right of the line. He was
naked except for a cap or bonnet made of sage stems. Just about
daylight he called on them to charge and all started. The noise

of the horses' hoofs was like thunder—so great that it awoke the
buffalo hunters, who soon began to shoot through the windows.
At this time and place they shot three of the attacking party, one
Comanche and two Cheyennes. Stone Calf's son rode seventy-
five yards before he fell from his horse. The other Cheyenne
was named Horse Chief. The Comanche fell from his horse
close to the door of the building.

The buffalo hunters knocked holes in the walls of the houses
to shoot through. The Indians charged about for some time and
then got behind the stables and behind the stacks of buffalo-hides.
After a time they realized that they could do nothing and about
two o'clock they left the hunters. Six Cheyennes were killed:
Horse Chief (Mō in'ă ăm mī vih″), Stone Calf's son (Wōhk pōs'-
ĭts), Stone Teeth (Hō hō nē'wōh nĭn'), Coyote (Ō'kōhm), Spots
on the Feathers (Hōhs'tāi wūt'), Walking on the Ground (Hō
ĭv'stā mĭsts ts). Three Comanches were killed, no Apaches and
no Arapahoes, nine in all. After the fight a Cheyenne named
Hippy seized the bridle of the Comanche medicine man and was
going to quirt him, but the other Cheyennes said: "Let him go."
He was disgraced.

It was reported in July, 1912, that Ĭ să tai' was still living
at Fort Sill. He declared that his medicine would have been
effective and the buffalo hunters would have been destroyed as
promised except for the fact that that morning after they had
started out to make the attack some Cheyenne killed a skunk,
and in that way broke his medicine.

Following their defeat by the buffalo hunters, and seeking revenge for their losses, a party of Cheyennes under Medicine Water
started on the war-path to the northeast, and on the Smoky Hill
River massacred a party of emigrants—the Germaine family.
They killed five of the nine members of the family, and captured
four girls from sixteen years of age down to four or five. These
girls were later all rescued, the two older ones being brought into
the agency and given up by Stone Calf and the chiefs of his band
in the spring of 1875.

In September Colonel R. S. Mackenzie with seven troops of
the Fourth Cavalry captured the villages of the Kiowas, Comanches, and Southern Cheyennes in a canyon near the Red River
of Texas. The troops came down into the canyon at the very

end of the camp, near where the Kiowa village was, and the Cheyennes being at the upper end of the camp had time to jump on their horses and escape. A great many Kiowa and Comanche horses were captured, but the loss in horses by the Cheyennes was slight. At this time the Indians had been talking of going in and surrendering, but alarmed by this attack they turned about again and returned to the Staked Plains.

Toward the end of the year there were various other small skirmishes, none of them of importance. Two of the smallest Germaine girls were with Gray Beard's band, and the smaller of the two being unable to ride a horse they were both left behind in charge of a young Indian. He took them up on a hillside and placed them on the ground on a buffalo-robe and left them, and when the troops came along they were recognized as children through the field-glasses and were rescued. Some of the military reports seem to infer that these children were captured from the Indians after a battle, but, as a matter of fact, they were set free. Billy Dixon in his *Life*[1] speaks of this. The rescue seems to have taken place November 8, 1874.

That autumn some war parties of young men who had been out came into the camps of Whirlwind and Little Robe at Darlington, Indian Territory, now Oklahoma. These Indians were in charge of Agent John D. Miles, who had been appointed in 1872. They were quiet and peaceable, living at the agency and having rations issued to them. Colonel Neal, with several companies of troops, was also camped near Darlington.

Early in 1875 White Horse, with the Dog Soldiers, came in and surrendered to the military, and a little later Stone Calf appeared with his village and also surrendered. These villages of Indians were sent up on the north fork of the Canadian River, about three miles above Darlington, and Captain Bennet, with his company of infantry, camped near them to act as a guard. The troops built dugouts and remained there through the winter, and the two villages of Indians were held as prisoners of war and rations were issued to them by the military.

It was in early spring that Colonel Neal, on information given him by certain Mexicans, had all the male Indians drawn up in

---

[1] *Life and Adventures of "Billy" Dixon of Adobe Walls, Texas Panhandle, Guthrie, Oklahoma,* 1914, p. 294.

line, and passing along the line arrested certain men whom the Mexicans pointed out and put them in the guard-house. There were about twenty-five of these, who were afterward sent to Florida and held there as prisoners.

A few days after the arrest one of the Indians was brought out of the guard-house to be shackled with a ball and chain, but while the blacksmith was preparing to iron him he broke away from those who were holding him and ran for the camp. The soldiers shot at him and the balls went into the camp, striking the lodges and frightening the Indians there, who at once rushed out from the camp on the other side, crossed the river and ran into the sand hills, where they threw up breastworks and prepared to fight. This occurred about ten o'clock in the morning.

There was considerable shooting through the day, part of it with a Gatling gun. Two of the Indians were killed outside the breastworks. The one who had broken away had been wounded. Two soldiers were also killed. Toward evening the firing ceased, but a guard was stationed around the sand hills to keep the Indians from getting away during the night. Nevertheless, all the Indians slipped out and all went down to the camps of Little Robe and Whirlwind and remained there for some days. No attempt was made by the military to get them back, and after a little while the women in small parties went up and took down their lodges and transported their property down to the camps below, where they remained unmolested.

Shortly afterward they were turned over to the Interior Department, and became a part of Agent Miles's Indians. A day or two after the fight the prisoners still held in the guard-house were sent off at night to Fort Sill, and from there, with some Comanches and Kiowas, were sent to Florida, where they were held for five years. On the way, while passing through Mississippi, Gray Bear was killed by one of the guards. A number of the Indians died in Florida. Finally the survivors were returned to their home in the Indian Territory. Some of the younger men were persuaded by Captain Pratt to go to the Carlisle School, where they gained some knowledge of the English language before their return to the West.

XXV

CROOK'S FIGHT ON THE ROSEBUD

1876

In 1874 General Custer led an expedition to the Black Hills of Dakota and prospectors who accompanied him discovered gold. The announcement of this find caused much excitement, and parties of prospectors at once began to lay plans for invading the hills. That region was then one of the few untouched hunting grounds left to the northern Indians, and certain species of game, as deer and bears, were very abundant there.

During the year 1875 the Sioux Indians made active objection to the incursions of miners into the Black Hills. Many parties were attacked, and not a few people were killed. The Government endeavored to purchase the Black Hills from the Indians and a number of groups of Sioux agreed to sell, but others refused.

In the spring of 1876 the War Department determined to punish and reduce the hostile Indians who were living in Montana, Wyoming, and North Dakota, and Generals Terry and Crook set on foot operations looking to this end. General Terry was to ascend the Missouri and Yellowstone Rivers and from some favorable point there to work south, while General Crook was to operate from the south north and to cover the headwaters of the Powder, Tongue, Rosebud, and Big Horn Rivers.

On May 29, with a strong column of about fifteen troops of cavalry and five companies of infantry, General Crook left Fort Fetterman for Goose Creek. On June 9, on Tongue River, the command was attacked by Indians and two men were wounded. The Indians, however, were easily driven off. Captain Bourke credits this attack to Crazy Horse, but, as a matter of fact, these Indians were Northern Cheyennes from the camp on the Rosebud, at the mouth of the Muddy. Led by Little Hawk, they had rushed over to Tongue River in the hope of driving off a lot of horses. The Cheyennes say that the soldiers met them with a long rain of bullets, and they gave up the attempt and returned to their camp.

On June 17, at the bend of the Rosebud, an important engagement took place. It is commonly spoken of as Crook's fight on the Rosebud, and was in fact a victory for the Indians. The *Record of Engagements* declares that Crook had less than one thousand men, and that the Indians were driven several miles in confusion, while a great many were killed and wounded in the retreat. The troops lost nine men killed and eighteen wounded, one of whom was Captain Guy V. Henry, who happily recovered.

The official documents[1] state that the scene of the attack was at the mouth of a deep and rocky canyon with steep timbered sides, and it is intimated that this was the reason for General Crook's retiring to his main supply camp to await reinforcements and supplies.

I am familiar with the ground and have been over it more than once. The lay of the land scarcely bears out the description the reports give. The fight took place in a wide, more or less level valley, with high bluffs on either side. It is true that two or three miles below the battle-field the river bends sharp to the left and the valley becomes narrower, with high more or less wooded bluffs on either side, but, though varying somewhat, the width of the valley is for the most part a mile or two, and is nowhere, I think, less than half a mile. There is no "dangerous defile" such as is told of. There was no effort by the Indians to lead the troops into a trap. The ground was not suitable.

It has long been well understood by those familiar with this fight that General Crook was thoroughly well beaten by the Indians, and that he got away as soon as he could. Considering the number of men engaged the losses were not heavy on either side. At the same time it was a hard battle. The story as told from the military point of view can be found in the *Record of Engagements*, in Captain Bourke's *On the Border with Crook*, and in Finerty's *Warpath and Bivouac*. In the account given by the Cheyennes who fought in this engagement will be recognized a number of incidents spoken of by Bourke.

The Indian narrative comes from several men, well known to me for many years, who took part in it.

[1] *Record of Engagements*, p. 52.

The man who discovered the presence of the soldiers on the Rosebud was Little Hawk, the son of old Gentle Horse, who sixty or seventy years ago was one of the most famous of Cheyenne warriors. From the fact of this discovery it has been the duty of Little Hawk of late years, whenever the ceremony of the medicine-lodge has been held among the Northern Cheyennes, to go out and choose the centre pole for the medicine-lodge.

The Cheyennes were camped on the stream now known as Reno Creek. In the early summer Little Hawk, then a leading warrior, called four young men, Yellow Eagle, Crooked Nose, Little Shield, and White Bird, and said to them: "Let us go out and see if we cannot get some horses from the white people." They started that night, passing through the Wolf Mountains, and then stopping to wait for daylight.

When morning came they went on through the hills, and about midday reached the big bend of the Rosebud. As they went down into the Rosebud they saw a great herd of buffalo bulls, and Little Hawk said: "Now let us kill a bull and stop here and roast some meat." He killed one close to the stream and nearby found a nice spring of water. One of them started a fire, and they began to skin the buffalo. Before the meat was cooked a large herd of cows came in sight. The young men said to Crooked Nose: "You stay here and roast this meat, while we go up to those cows and see if we cannot find a fatter animal." They went toward the cows, and after they had gone part way one of them happened to look back to where Crooked Nose was cooking, and saw that he was making motions to them from side to side, calling to them to come back. They thought no more about killing a fat cow, but turned their horses and rode down to him.

When they reached him Crooked Nose said to them: "On that hill, by those red buttes, I saw two men looking over, and after looking a little while they rode up in plain sight, each one leading a horse. They rode out of sight coming toward us. I think they are coming in our direction—right toward us."

Little Hawk said: "Saddle up quick. I think those men coming are Sioux; now we will have some fun with them"; for he thought that they could creep around and pretend to attack them, and so frighten them. The Sioux were their friends and allies.

They saddled their horses and rode up a little gulch, and when they had gone a short distance Little Hawk got off his horse and crept up to the top of the hill and looked over. As he raised his head it seemed to him as if the whole earth were black with soldiers. He said to his friends: "They are soldiers"; but he said it in a very low voice, for the soldiers were so near to them that he was afraid they would hear him speak. He crept down the hill and got on his horse, and Little Shield said: "The best thing we can do is to go back to where we were roasting meat. There is timber on the creek, and we can make a stand there." Little Shield spoke in a low tone of voice, and Little Hawk did not hear him say this, but started down the gulch as hard as he could go, and the others after him. As he was riding at headlong speed he lost his field-glasses, but he did not stop. He went down to the Rosebud and rode into the brush, and through it, up the stream. He left a good many locks of his hair in the bushes. While they were going up the creek they did not simply gallop; they just raced their horses as fast as they could go. Keeping on up the Rosebud in the timber and so out of sight of the troops, who had not yet reached the river, they came to a high butte about three miles above the soldiers. They had not yet been discovered. Here they stopped and looked back. They could see the soldiers still coming down the valley. If the Cheyennes had not killed the buffalo they would have kept on their way and would have ridden right into the soldiers. The buffalo bull saved their lives.

When they left this round butte they rode on over the mountains toward the Little Big Horn River. After they had crossed the mountains, they passed along the foothills of the Wolf Mountains, and just as day began to break came to the camp, which had moved only a little way down Reno Creek. When they were near the camp they began to howl like wolves, to notify the people that something had been seen. They reached camp just at good daylight.

The people in the camp on Reno Creek had suspected that there were soldiers in the country, and some of the young men of the village had spent the night riding around the camp as if they were guards. Nothing had happened during the night, but now early in the morning they heard someone howling like a wolf, and when they heard this they knew that some discovery had been made.   Young Two Moon—son of Beaver Claws and nephew of the chief Two Moon—rode toward the howling as soon as he heard the sound and met the scouts coming in.

Little Hawk said to the people: "Near the head of the Rosebud, where it bends to turn down into the hills, we saw soldiers as we were roasting meat. I think there are many Indians with them, too. They may come right down the Rosebud. Get ready all the young men, and let us set out."

All the men began to catch their horses and painted themselves, put on their war bonnets, and then paraded about the camp, and then set out to meet the soldiers, going straight through the hills.

Little Hawk led a party of men who went straight across through the Wolf Mountains. With young Two Moon's party were about two hundred men—Sioux and Cheyennes—and one woman, the sister of Chief Comes in Sight. When this party reached the mouth of Trail Creek, on the Rosebud, they were stopped by the Cheyenne soldiers, who had formed a line and would not let them go on up the stream, because Little Hawk had expressed the opinion that the soldiers were coming down the Rosebud River.

On the west side of the Rosebud, near where William Rowland's place now is, is a high hill which commands a wide view, and to the top of this high hill four Indians, who were serving as scouts for the troops, had gone to look over the country to see if any Indians could be seen.   From young Two Moon's party four men, two Sioux and two Cheyennes, were sent forward to this same hill to see if they could discover the troops, and were told if they found them to come back at once.   Some time after these four scouts had started the main party moved on after them.

The scouts sent out by the troops reached the top of this hill before the scouts sent by the Indians had passed out of the bottom. They saw the approaching Sioux and Cheyenne scouts, and began to fire at them.   When the Sioux and Cheyennes who were farther down the Rosebud heard the shooting they rushed up the valley, and the scouts from the troops retreated over the high land, while the Indian scouts, having signalled their people that they had seen something, followed them toward the soldiers. The soldiers, hearing the firing, formed in line and prepared to fight. The rifles began to sound more to the right, and the Indians, leaving the bottom, cut across the hills toward the river above.

When they reached the top of the hill, looking down into the valley of the Rosebud, they could see the soldiers following some Indians back into the hills. The soldiers were pretty strong and were fighting hard. The horses of the Indians were being wounded and falling as they climbed the hill. When the Sioux and Cheyennes saw this they did not stop long on the high divide, but charged down on the soldiers, who stopped pursuing the other group of Indians and fell back. Little Hawk, with his party, who had been running away, then turned and charged back so that now there was a large body of Indians charging down on the soldiers. The sister of Chief Comes in Sight charged with the men.

At first the Sioux and Cheyennes had seen only one body of troops, and supposed that all the soldiers were there together, but later, after the soldiers began to withdraw up the creek, they learned that more troops were up above. The Cheyennes believe that the Indian scouts from the troops intended to lead the pursuing Indians down between the two groups of soldiers, but made a mistake and went down the wrong ridge. These scouts were supposed to be Pawnees and Snakes; really they were Crows and Snakes. They killed a Snake who wore a spotted war bonnet.

On the side from which the Indians charged a little ridge ran down toward the stream, and when they reached this ridge they all dismounted and stopped there out of sight of the troops. Beyond was a smooth, level piece of ground. They did not stay there long, but started on toward the hills. Those who were out on the level ground were obliged to fight there, though there was little cover.

After the Indians had got back out of sight of the soldiers Two Moon looked over the ridge and saw four cavalry horses starting toward a hill. With Black Coyote he set out to capture them, and behind him followed two Cheyennes and then two Sioux. When they came in sight, charging down the hill, the soldiers came to meet them and drive them back. They began to shoot at the Indians and came near overtaking them. They almost caught them but at last gave up the pursuit and rode back. The six men who had charged, when they saw that they could accomplish nothing, turned to join another body of Indians that was coming in above them. These were chiefly Cheyennes. Here two brave men, White Shield and a Sioux, charged on the troops and all the Indians followed them. When the charge was made the troopers were on foot, but as the Indians approached they all mounted and retreated toward the main body of the troops. They did not run far, but wheeled, fell in line, fired a volley and then mounted and ran back. Here White Shield killed a man and ran over and counted coup on him. The Sioux did the same.

On a little ridge the soldiers again dismounted, trying to hold the Indians back, but the body coming against them was large; an officer was shot, and the troops retreated. Among them was a soldier who could not mount his horse. White Shield rode between him and his horse, to knock the reins out of his hands and free the horse. He did not get the horse, but counted coup on the man, who carried a bugle.

When the Indians left the ridge from which the troops had been driven, they had to cross a steep gulch to get on the next flat. On the flat a soldier fell off his horse, perhaps wounded, and lost his horse. A Cheyenne named Scabby Eyelid rode up to the soldier and tried to strike him with his whip. The soldier caught the whip and pulled the Indian off his horse. They struggled together, but separated without serious hurt to either. Now the Indian scouts of the troops made a charge and the Sioux and Cheyennes ran, and retreated over the deep gulch which they had just crossed. After crossing this they wheeled and fired once and then again turned and ran. The number of soldiers behind them was large.

The soldiers made a strong charge, but the Indians divided, some going down the ridge and some up. Young Two Moon left the ridge and when he reached the flat his horse began to get tired, and close behind him and coming fast were the soldiers. Those Cheyennes who were up above could see there alone a person whose horse had given out. Two Moon thought that this was his last day. He was obliged to dismount, leave his horse and run off on foot. The bullets were flying pretty thick and were knocking up the dust all about him. He saw before him, coming, a man who was riding on a buckskin horse and thought that he was going to have help, but the bullets flew so thick that the man who was coming turned and rode away. Again he saw a man coming toward him, riding a spotted horse. He recognized the person, Young Black Bird—now White Shield. White Shield rode up to his side and told him to jump on behind. In that way White Shield saved his life that day.

They had not gone very far, but farther than he could have gone on foot, when this horse too began to lose its wind and to get tired. Soon they saw another man coming, leading a horse that he had captured from the Indian scouts who were with the troops. It was Contrary Belly. Meantime two Sioux had dashed up to the two men, but when they got close one of them said: "They are Cheyennes," and they rode away. Then Contrary Belly came up and Two Moon jumped on the led horse and rode off. When they reached the main body of Indians the soldiers were still coming up, but there were so many Indians that they could not drive them. Here the fight stopped. The Cheyennes and Sioux remained there for a little while and then went away and left the soldiers. Many men had been wounded and many horses killed and wounded, so that many of the Indians were on foot.

They left four men to watch the troops to see what they did. These four men were: Lost Leg, Howling Wolf, and two others. They saw the soldiers gather up the dead and bring them down near the creek not far from their camp.

For this fight White Elk was given by his uncle, Mŏhk sta′eĭ āī′nō, his medicine, which was that of the swallow that has a forked tail—a barn-swallow. On his war bonnet, low down on the tail of the bonnet, was tied the skin of a swallow, while the brow piece was painted with many butterflies and dragonflies, and on the side of the tail-piece of the war bonnet were eagle-down feathers four or five inches apart, and between each two feathers a tiny leaden bullet.

Among the Cheyennes in this battle was Chief Comes in Sight, a brave man and a good fighter. His sister had followed him out to the battle. At the beginning of the fight he had charged the soldiers many times, and when they were fighting the upper group of soldiers, as he was riding up and down in front of the line, his horse was killed under him. White Elk was also riding up and down the line, but was going in the opposite direction from Chief Comes in Sight, and it was just after they had passed each other that Chief Comes in Sight was dismounted. Suddenly White Elk saw a person riding down from where the Indians were toward the soldiers, pass by Chief Comes in Sight, turn the horse and ride up by him, when Comes in Sight jumped on behind and they rode off. This was the sister of Chief Comes in Sight, Buffalo Calf Road Woman (Mūts ĭ mī′ŭ nă′).

The Cheyennes have always spoken of this battle by this name:

"Where the girl saved her brother—
Ksē ē′   sē wō ĭs tăn′ĭ wē   ĭ tăt′ăn ē."
Young girl   saved his life   brother.

Comes in Sight is still living in Oklahoma, about sixty-six years old. It was near where Comes in Sight was unhorsed that the Shoshoni with a spotted war bonnet was killed.

White Elk expresses the opinion that in this fight there were perhaps ninety Cheyennes. He does not know how many Sioux may have been there. In the place where the hottest fighting occurred there were more Indians than soldiers, but this does not count the troops who were on the other side of the stream—about three troops of cavalry.

The account of what White Shield saw and did in this battle is interesting, because it gives so well the Indian point of view and explains to some extent the Cheyenne belief in the help received from animals. White Shield's name at that time was Young Black Bird. He is the son of Spotted Wolf, one of the bravest of the old-time warriors of the Cheyennes, who has been dead for about twenty years. White Shield says:

Spotted Wolf, when he heard the news that the soldiers were coming, said: "My son, you had better tie up your horse. Do not let him fill himself with grass. If a horse's stomach is not full he can run a long way; if his stomach is full he soon gets tired. I wish to see you take the lead on this war trip."

His father had been taught by the kingfisher bird and understood it.

Spotted Wolf said further: "Son, go out and from one of the springs that come out of the hillside get me some blue clay." After it had been brought to him he painted on the shoulders and hips of the horse the figure of a kingfisher with its head toward the front. "Now," he said, "your horse will not get out of wind. Take him down to the stream and give him plenty of water; all he will drink."

When White Shield brought the horse back, his father said: "When you are ready to start I will go with you, and before you make the charge I will put some medicine on you."

Just before they left camp Spotted Wolf said: "Now, drink plenty of water and let this be your last drink until the fight is over."

They started from camp after the sun was down and travelled all night, stopping from time to time. At daylight they were on the Rosebud at the mouth of Trail Creek. Above this they stopped and decided that as they were getting near to the enemy they would dress (paint) themselves here. His father dressed him, painting his whole body with yellow earth paint. Spotted Wolf had a bundle containing the war clothing that he himself was accustomed to wear in fights. From this bundle he took a scalp and, placing the horse so that it faced toward the south, he tied the scalp to its lower jaw. He then put his own war shirt on White Shield, took his kingfisher (the stuffed skin of a kingfisher) and held it up to the sun and sang a song.

"My son," he said, "this is the song sung to me when the spirits took pity on me. If the kingfisher dives into the water for a fish he never misses his prey. To-day I wish you to do the same thing. You shall count the first coup in this fight."

After he had finished speaking he tied the kingfisher to his son's scalp-lock. Held in the bill of the kingfisher were some kingfisher's feathers, dyed red. These feathers represented the flash of a gun. Then he hung about his son's neck a whistle made of the bone from an eagle's wing. He said: "If anyone runs up to you to shoot you, make this noise" (imitating the cry of the kingfisher) "and the bullet will not hurt you." He took in his mouth a little medicine and a little earth and raised the right fore foot of the horse and blew a little of this on the sole of the hoof, and did the same thing on the right hind foot, the left hind foot, and the left fore foot. Then he blew the medicine on the horse between the ears, on the withers, at the end of the mane, and at the root and the end of the tail. "Putting this on the soles of his hoofs," said Spotted Wolf, "will make him carry himself lightly and not fall. When you come within sight of the enemy and are going to charge, put the whistle in your mouth and whistle. That is what the kingfisher does when he catches the fish. You shall catch one of the enemy. When you see the enemy they may frighten you so that you will lose your mind a little, but I do not think this will happen. You will frighten your enemies before they frighten you. I have dressed you fully for war. There are some women with the party; you must not ride by the side of any of them. Give me your quirt, son."

He took some horse medicine and rubbed it over the quirt and said: "If you see anyone ahead of you and whirl your quirt about your head the man's horse may fall. When you charge try to keep on the right-hand side of everyone. Take pity on everyone. If you see some man in a hard place, from which he cannot escape, help him if you can. If you yourself get in a bad place, do not get excited, but try to shoot and defend yourself. That is the way to become great. If you should be killed, the enemy when they go back will say that they fought a man who was very brave; that they had a hard time to kill him."

Such were the instructions given White Shield by his father.

Before this was finished some of the Cheyennes had already gone forward and a little later he heard shots—those fired by their own scouts who had met some Crow scouts. When the shots were heard the Sioux and Cheyennes all charged, riding across the hills to where they heard the shooting, running up one hill and down another. They did not follow the stream valley.

When they reached the place the Indian scouts had retreated to the soldiers, who sat there on their horses. Old Red War Bonnet, Walks Last, Feathered Sun, White Shield, and White Bird were among the first to reach this point. The Sioux and Cheyennes were beginning to come toward the soldiers from all directions. At the top of the hill they stopped about six hundred yards from the soldiers. Suddenly to the right a man appeared charging toward the soldiers. He was followed by a little boy twelve or thirteen years old. They recognized Chief Comes in Sight, and the boy was a little Sioux boy. The five Cheyennes just mentioned charged down, following the two, and about fifty yards behind them. Neither the soldiers nor Indian scouts fired, but they kept moving about. When the Cheyennes were quite near to the soldiers, Chief Comes in Sight turned his horse to the left and the boy to the right. Chief Comes in Sight fired two shots from a pistol and all the soldiers shouted and fired and charged. They began to overtake Chief Comes in Sight, who now joined the five Cheyennes, and all had to run. The Indian scouts chased the little boy and overtook him, taking him from his horse and killing him. As the six Cheyennes went back to the hill they had been on, the soldiers almost overtook them. When the soldiers were within fifty yards of them Feathered Sun said: "Let us dismount; they are pushing us too closely." Feathered Sun and White Shield dismounted and the troops stopped, all except one scout, thought to be a Crow. He carried a long lance and, lying down on his horse's back so that he could not be seen, charged straight toward the two. White Shield and the other man were some distance apart and the Crow was coming straight for White Shield. He was obliged to shoot at the horse, aiming at its breast. When he fired the horse turned a somersault, turning clear over. The Crow dropped his lance and White Shield rushed to his own horse, and as he mounted it was like a wave of water coming over the hill behind him—the Cheyennes. They seemed to come from all the foothills and now the soldiers fell back. When the Cheyennes and Sioux charged down they were less than fifty yards from the troops. White Shield turned his horse and rode along in front of the Indian scouts, who were all on foot and shooting. A little off to one side the soldiers were fighting the Cheyennes and Sioux. As he rode along he saw a man who had been shot and who was wearing a large war bonnet. The Cheyennes tried to count coup on the body, but the scouts fought for it. Here a Sioux had his leg smashed and a Cheyenne's horse was killed. White Shield got to within three or four yards of the body, but he was obliged to turn his horse. As he looked down he saw a troop of cavalry galloping toward them, but not yet shooting.

When they had come pretty near, the soldiers began to fire and the Cheyennes and Sioux retreated to the hills. The Indian scouts and the soldiers made a strong charge, and were right behind the Cheyennes and Sioux, who were forced to whip their horses on both sides to get away. It was a close race. The soldiers were shooting fast. Some men called out: "Stop, stop, some horses have been killed; let us save these men and stand off the soldiers." They did not stop, but they succeeded in saving all the dismounted men. The troops chased the Indians to a steep ravine which the horses could not cross. Those who reached it first dismounted. When they reached here two more companies of soldiers came up.

Before they came to the ravine, the ground dropped off a little, making a ridge behind which the Sioux and Cheyennes stopped and all dismounted. This made them feel good, for here was something to fight behind. They were about two hundred men. At this time three separate fights were going on, of which this was the one in the middle. At this place they shot down the horse of one of the scouts, and when this horse fell the soldiers and scouts turned back and the Cheyennes and Sioux mounted and charged them. They followed them back to the place where they had fought for the man with the war bonnet. On the way back they overtook a scout on a wounded horse. He was a Shoshoni. He threw himself off his horse, and ran ahead on foot. Two Sioux were close behind him and White Shield was off to one side. One Sioux carried a long lance, and as the Shoshoni turned to fire he struck him with his lance, and afterward with the body of his horse he knocked him down. As the Shoshoni was getting up the second Sioux ran over him with his horse, and then White Shield came up and shot him, but counted no coup. The soldiers and scouts charged back on them, and followed them back to the place where they had been before, at the edge of the ravine. All this time the firing was heavy on both sides.

When the Cheyennes and Sioux had run behind the ridge again, they stood with about half the body exposed, shooting over it. A Cheyenne standing by White Shield was shot through the body, but did not die until they got him to camp. For a long time, on a little flat a quarter of a mile wide, they fought there, each side alternately retreating and advancing. Far off to the right they could hear shooting which sounded as if it were going up into the hills.

After a time White Shield left this fight, and rode off to one side to get into this other fight. When he rode his horse up on the hill he could see the fight; one company of soldiers following up some Indians. The soldiers had left their horses, and were advancing on foot. Their horses were a quarter of a mile behind them. Riding up and down before the soldiers, he saw a young man whom he at length recognized as Goose Feather, a son of the chief, Dull Knife. White Shield rode on until he met Goose Feather, who had gone behind a little knoll. He said to Goose Feather: "Hold my horse for a moment," and he stepped over the hill in sight. As he did this all the soldiers threw themselves on the ground and began firing, but he managed to jump behind a rock so as to be out of sight. Then the soldiers turned their guns and began to shoot in another direction at the Indians on the hill. White Shield shot at the nearest soldier, who was about forty yards off, but shot under him, throwing the dirt over his body. The soldiers now all rose to their feet to go back to their horses, and the nearest soldier, having partly turned, ran, and White Shield shot at him and he fell. White Shield ran back to get his horse, but Goose Feather had let it go so that he might run down and count coup on the soldier. White Shield caught his horse, but Goose Feather reached the soldier first, and counted coup on him with a lance, while White Shield counted the second coup with his whip. The third man to count coup took the soldier's arms and belt. The soldiers kept on running toward their horses.

White Shield and Goose Feather went on after the soldiers. Just as the soldiers reached their horses an officer called out giving an order, and all the soldiers faced about to meet the charge of a great crowd of Cheyennes who were following. White Shield turned off to the right, and got behind a little knoll. Every Cheyenne and Sioux dodged behind the knoll and now both sides were shooting as hard as they could, only about thirty yards apart. All at once the soldiers ceased firing, but the Indians kept on shooting. White Shield crept over the hill to look and see why the soldiers had stopped. The horses were all in line and the soldiers had one foot in the stirrup. Off to one side a man was seated on a roan horse, who gave an order and then turned to look back. White Shield shot just as he turned his head, and when they found the man he was shot just over the eyebrow. The soldiers started to retreat, and as they did so they scattered. A man on foot, holding his horse with one hand and a six-shooter in the other, was trying to mount his horse. White Shield made a charge to count coup on him. The man shot as White Shield was coming up, but the horse pulled him and he missed his aim. White Shield rode his horse between the man and the horse he was holding, and knocked the man down with his gun. The next man behind White Shield rode over the soldier. White Shield turned his horse and rode back to the officer he had killed, and as he was going he saw some guns. When he came back the guns were gone, but the officer still had a six-shooter and a belt full of pistol cartridges. White Shield took the six-shooter.

As he looked back he saw the soldier that he had knocked down creeping about on his hands and knees and went back and killed him. He took his belt and cartridges, but his six-shooter was gone.

At this place White Shield stopped and got off his horse, and led it up and down. At a distance he could see the people fighting. The soldiers had separated and were split up in twos and threes. Far off he could see a great many soldiers and the scouts. As he kept looking presently he saw a person riding toward the soldiers and then he saw his horse fall, catching the man under its body. He seemed to be trying to get out, but the scouts rode up and shot him. After the man was shot, all the Indians ran and the soldiers followed them back to the place from which the Indians had driven the soldiers, and now the Indians had to scatter out by twos and threes. White Shield did not move from the place where he was until the Indians got up to him. Then he mounted. Some of those who came up to him were riding double—men whose horses had been shot or had given out. Still he waited, thinking he would have a chance to get in some more shots. He fired a shot or two and then looking down to one side he saw a man on foot and soldiers following and overtaking him. When he tried to open his gun after firing, he could not open it. He had put in a captured cartridge, too small for the gun, and it had swelled and stuck in the chamber. He was unarmed. By this time the people had all passed and the only man between him and the soldiers was the one on foot. He rode down to this man, and found him almost exhausted. It was young Two Moon. White Shield called out to him: "My friend, come and get on behind me." The remainder of the Indians were a long way ahead of them. He said to Two Moon: "I can no longer shoot; I have a shell fast in my gun."

Many Indians ahead of them were now on foot, and many horses were constantly being shot and wounded or were giving out and stopping. Here Feathered Sun's horse was shot, and its rider jumped up and ran along on foot. The soldiers were close behind—only about thirty yards. Another man on foot was running along behind Feathered Sun, and just as he reached Feathered Sun's horse which had been knocked down, it got up on its feet, and he jumped on it and it ran off as well as ever. It had only been creased. Down the line a man was seen coming, and when he got near they saw it was Contrary Belly. He was leading a roan horse and as he overtook them he said: "Here is a horse for you to ride"; and Two Moon took it.

As White Shield rode on, he saw in front of him a Sioux on horseback and another Sioux on foot carrying a stick in his hand. He rode up to the man on foot and saw that he was carrying a ramrod, for he had been using a muzzle-loader, and with this ramrod White Shield knocked the shell out of his gun. Meantime, the soldiers and the Indian scouts behind them were seeing how much noise they could make with guns and cries, and the Cheyennes and Sioux in front were running and stopping and firing and running. The Sioux on horseback had on a war bonnet and shield. As he rode, his horse's leg was broken. He would not leave his horse, but stopped to fight, and then turned and ran to some timber. The soldiers and scouts all seemed to follow him and this gave the other Indians a chance to get away. The soldiers killed the Sioux and then all turned back. The Cheyennes and Sioux watched them a long time from the hills, and then went to their camps.

When White Shield's gun was made useless by the shell, he never once thought of the six-shooter he had captured. He might have been killed wearing this without attempting to defend himself.

When they got down on the Little Big Horn River they began to have war dances. They took out the buffalo hat and hung it up and then danced, tying a scalp to it. For four nights of this dance his mother carried the gun that he had used.

At the Big Bend of the Rosebud, where the lower group of soldiers was, is now the farm of Thomas Benson. The battle-ground on the river above his ranch includes the farms of J. L. Davis, A. L. Young, and Charles Young. On a little stream running into the Rosebud below where the fight with the upper group of soldiers took place is Mrs. Colmar's, and on the south prong of the Rosebud lives M. T. Price. Ranches and cultivated fields occupy the ground fought over by the white troops and Indians in 1876. The camp of the soldiers was on land now belonging to Mr. Benson. There the dead were buried. It was on the ground between the Big Bend and the Young places that the fighting took place. It was all on the open prairie above, or in the wide open valley. There was no chance for ambushment or approach under cover. In the hot fighting and the fierce charges made much courage was displayed by Indians and whites alike.

XXVI

THE CUSTER BATTLE

1876

The defeat of General Custer and the Seventh Cavalry on June 25, 1876, with a loss of two hundred and sixty-five men killed and fifty-two wounded, was the most sensational battle of the Western Indian wars. Under orders from General Alfred H. Terry, the Commander of the Department of Dakota, General Custer had been sent from the mouth of the Rosebud River, in Montana, on a scout to find the Indians believed to be camped somewhere to the south—perhaps on the Little Big Horn River. The trail of these Indians, leading up the Rosebud River, had been discovered some days before, and June 22 practically the whole Seventh Cavalry, about seven hundred men and twenty-eight officers, had ridden out from the camp to follow that trail.

The story, told so many times, need not be repeated in detail here. From a lookout on the divide between the Rosebud and the Little Big Horn General Custer learned from his scouts the location of the Indian village, and at a point on Reno Creek near the Little Big Horn divided his forces into three battalions, sending Major Reno with three troops of cavalry and some scouts to a point on the Little Big Horn River above the uppermost village, and Captain Benteen with three troops to scout a little to the left in a southerly direction toward the Little Big Horn. Benteen's orders were if he saw any Indians to attack them. Custer himself went around to attack the village farther down the stream. His scouts had warned him that the village was very large and that the issue would be doubtful.

Near the point where Custer and Reno separated, Reno crossed the river and soon after attacked the upper village. Seeing the size of the camp and being afraid to continue the attack, he retreated to a body of timber, where he remained but a short time and then, panic-stricken, left the timber, crossed the Little Big

Horn River and took refuge on the high bluffs on the north side of the river, where he afterward intrenched himself. A little later Benteen joined him, as did Captain McDougall with the pack-train. Meantime Custer went around, came within sight of the lower part of the great camp where the Cheyennes, Brulés, and Ogallalas had their lodges, and then, instead of crossing the stream and charging through the village, halted and took a position on a long, high ridge; and after a fight which lasted not more than two or three hours his whole command was killed.

General E. S. Godfrey, retired, at that time lieutenant in the Seventh Cavalry, was with Benteen and Reno and in 1892, in the *Century Magazine*, gave by far the most complete account we have had of the matter.

There were no white survivors of the Custer battle, and such information about it as we have comes from Indian accounts. What is told here comes altogether from the Northern Cheyennes. Many of the informants are still living. These accounts consist of a number of individual observations, from which it is not easy to get any general idea of the fight.

In 1875, Sitting Bull took part in a medicine lodge held on Tongue River. White Bull, who was present, has told me what took place. Sitting Bull professed to have a vision, after which he announced to the people that the Great Power had told him that his enemies would be delivered into his hands. He did not profess to know who these enemies were, but explained that perhaps they might be soldiers.

In the spring of 1876 the Sioux and Northern Cheyennes came together near the mouth of the Rosebud River, near the Yellowstone, where a large camp gathered. While there it was reported that white soldiers were in the country somewhere, but just where nobody seemed to know. In March, in bitter cold weather, General Reynolds[1] attacked and captured a camp on Powder River occupied by Sioux and Cheyennes. No Indians appear to have been killed, but the troops lost some men. The whole Indian herd was taken. Suddenly without apparent reason the troops retreated, and the Indians followed them and recaptured most of the horses.

[1] *Record of Engagements*, pp. 50, 51.

From the mouth of the Rosebud the Indians moved up that stream, and then over to the head of Reno Creek, always keeping scouts out to look for enemies.

After the men had left the camp on the head of Reno Creek to go to fight Crook the villages moved a short distance down Reno Creek toward the Little Big Horn River, and after two nights there they moved to the mouth of Reno Creek and camped there for five or six days. While in this camp seven Arapahoes came to the camp. The Cheyennes and Sioux believed that these men were scouts from some camp of soldiers and seized them, took their arms and horses, and a part of their clothing, and were inclined to kill them. Two of the Cheyennes, Black Wolf and Last Bull, took their part and advised the people not to act hastily but to wait. The Arapahoes were taken to old Two Moon's lodge, which was closely surrounded. While they were there many Sioux came up with cocked guns, and, pointing them at the Arapahoes, said that they must be killed. Women whose relations had been killed asked for the death of the Arapahoes. Nevertheless most people said: "This is Two Moon's lodge; we must wait until he comes; he shall decide." They sent out a young man to look for Two Moon, who at last was found in one of the Sioux camps. In the meantime they had taken the Arapaho chief into the lodge. After a time Two Moon with five or six Sioux chiefs came to his lodge and called in all the Arapahoes. These chiefs were to decide what should be done with the prisoners.

After some conversation Two Moon called out: "These Arapahoes are all right. They have come here to help us fight the soldiers. Do not harm them, but give them back their property." The Sioux chiefs said the same thing, and then their horses, arms, and clothing were returned to the Arapahoes. Some old people then advised that these strangers should be invited to go to different lodges and be fed.

The day before Custer's attack the Indians moved again and camped in the great bottom of the Little Big Horn, at the place where the battle was fought. There seems to have been a general impression that they were to be attacked, but no specific information was at hand. The very morning of the fight two young men went fishing on the Little Big Horn River. From time to time a little lad, who accompanied them, was sent up to the higher land away from the river to catch grasshoppers to use in the fishing, and the last time he returned he said to his uncle, White Shield: "I saw a person wearing a war bonnet go by just now. They must be looking for someone." White Shield rode up on the hill to look and heard distant shooting and saw people running about. This told him that the camp had been attacked, and he hurried to it.

We have definite accounts of the Seventh Cavalry until the time of the division of the command, when Custer sent Reno to charge the upper end of the camp and himself went about to come in below. Cheyenne and Sioux scouts left to watch the troops under Crook had seen that command march south, and while returning to their own camp saw Custer's command marching up the Rosebud River. Not long after the man who made this discovery reached the camp four or five lodges of Sioux hurried in. They had set out to go to Red Cloud agency, had discovered Custer's people close to them, and turned back frightened. Their report caused much alarm.

At a point on Reno Creek two men, wounded in the Crook fight on the Rosebud, had died and been left there in lodges. The troops discovered these lodges and charged them, but found no one there alive. It was known in the camp that the troops had separated on Reno Creek, and an old man harangued that the soldiers were about to charge from the upper end and also from the lower end. When this was called out men began to prepare for the fight and to mount their horses, but many of the horses had been sent out on herd and most of the men were on foot. Reno's party was seen approaching the upper Indian camp, and most of the men went up there to meet him. He charged down on the flat where there was timber and near to the upper end of the Sioux village. Then the troops stopped and seemed to become very much excited and retreated to the timber.

After a short stop in the timber the troops rushed out and began to retreat, their commander apparently leading the way. The Indians say they acted as if they were drunk, which perhaps means that they were very much excited—probably panic-stricken. At all events, they bolted out of the timber and charged back through the Indians, to cross the stream and reach the higher ground on the other side. They did not cross where they had come over before, but jumped over a bank. All the Cheyenne evidence shows that they made no attempt to defend themselves but thought only of getting away. The Indians rode up close to them and knocked some of them from their horses as they were running while some fell off while crossing the river. "It was like chasing buffalo—a great chase."

"We could never understand why the soldiers left the timber, for if they had stayed there the Indians could not have killed them."

The troops crossed the river and got up on the hill. Just about that time the Indians saw the large pack-train of mules, which went directly to Reno. At the river all the Indians stopped. They did not follow the troops across the stream, but turned back to look over the dead to see who of their own people were killed, and to plunder. While doing this they heard shooting and calling down the river—a man shouting out that troops were attacking the lower end of the village. They all rushed down below and saw Custer coming down the hill and almost at the river.

Before this the women and children down at the lower villages heard the shooting up above and becoming frightened set out to cross the river to the north side and so to get farther from the Reno fight. While some were crossing the river and some who had already crossed were going up the hill they discovered more troops coming—Custer's party. The women ran back and out the other side of the village and toward the bluffs to the southeast of the river. By this time the men who were fighting Reno had learned that more soldiers were coming, and all the men rushed down the creek to the lower camps. By that time—according to Brave Wolf—a part of Custer's troops had got down toward the mouth of the little, dry creek and were near the level of the bottom. There they began fighting, and for quite a long time fought near the river, neither party giving back.

When White Shield, hurrying back from his fishing, reached the camp his mother had already secured his horse and was waiting for him. He began to dress, and while doing this he saw Custer's troops in seven groups approaching the river. Some Sioux and Cheyennes had already seen them, and some men who

were in the camp had crossed the river at the ford to meet Custer.
White Shield overtook a group of four Cheyennes, among whom
were Roan Bear, Bobtail Horse, and Calf. Mad Wolf—probably
Mad Hearted Wolf, often called Rabid Wolf, but actually meaning
Wolf that has no sense—was riding with White Shield. He
was one of the bravest and wisest men in the tribe. As they
rode along he said to White Shield: "No one must charge on the
soldiers now; they are too many." As the Cheyennes rode out of
the river toward the troops, who were still at a distance, they saw
that the soldiers were following five Sioux who were running from
them. They gradually circled away from in front of the soldiers
and the troops did not follow them, but kept on toward the river.
The troops were headed straight for the ford—about half a mile
above the battle-field—and White Shield and the other Cheyennes believed that Custer was about to cross the river and get
into the camp. The troops were getting near them, but suddenly
before the troops reached the river the gray-horse company halted
and dismounted, and all who were following them, as far as could
be seen, also stopped and dismounted.

White Shield rode off to the left and down the river, while
Bobtail Horse, Calf, and the two or three who were with them
stopped close to the river, and under cover of a low ridge began
to shoot at the soldiers. The five Sioux whom the troops had at
first seemed to be pursuing now joined Calf and Bobtail Horse,
and the ten Indians were shooting at the soldiers as fast as they
could. About the time the soldiers halted one was killed. Now
more Sioux and Cheyennes began to gather, the Indians crossing
the river and stringing up the gulch like ants rushing out of a
hill, and the two troops of cavalry that had come up nearest to
Bobtail Horse and his party fell back to the side of a little knoll
and stopped there. Yellow Nose charged close up to them alone.
The two troops remained there only a few moments. Crowded
back, they crossed a deep gulch and climbed the hill on the other
side, going toward where the monument now stands, where by
this time the gray-horse company had stopped. Some of the soldiers were killed on the way, but the gray-horse company opened
so heavy a fire that the Indians fell back.

Certain brave Cheyennes—Yellow Nose, Contrary Belly, and
Chief Comes in Sight—had been charging up close to the sol-

diers, and these charges seemed greatly to frighten the troop-horses held behind the line, so that they were struggling and circling about the men who held them.

Now the call went along the Indian line ordering them to dismount, and the Cheyennes began to shoot fast. A long way off to the southeast two men, followed by many Indians, made a charge, and Yellow Nose snatched from the ground where it stood a company guidon, carrying it away, and as he went counting coup on a soldier. After this charge the frightened horses of this company broke away from those who were holding them and stampeded. Some Indians cried: "The soldiers are running," but this was not true.

By this time all the soldiers had moved back from the river except the gray-horse company, which stood its ground on the place where the monument now is. The different groups of soldiers moved about a little on the higher ground, some going toward the river and some away from it, and when the Indians charged from all sides the soldiers drew a little together. By this time three of the troops had lost their horses, but four still had theirs. One company that had lost its horses was near where the road goes now, and the men, all on foot, were trying to work their way toward the gray-horse company on the hill half a mile from them. About half the men were without guns. They fought with six-shooters, close fighting—almost hand to hand—as they went up the hill.

They did not reach the top of the hill. Every ravine running down from the northwest side of the ridge, every little bunch of brush, was occupied by Indians, who kept up a constant and galling fire, and the Indians were so many that the destruction among the troops was very great. By this time the Indians were to some extent provided with improved arms. In the Crook fight they had captured a number of carbines from the troops, and to-day were constantly acquiring new arms while they found that the saddle-bags of the captured horses were full of ammunition. White Bull says: "If it had not been for this they could not have killed them so quickly." When the fight began about half the Indians had guns and the remainder bows, for which, however, they had many arrows. The guns were of many sorts—muzzle-loaders, Spencer carbines, old-fashioned Henry rifles, and old Sharps military rifles.[1] The Sharps were probably the best guns they had, except those recently captured from the soldiers.

White Shield says that the gray-horse company held their horses to the last, and that almost all these horses were killed. On the other hand, Bobtail Horse declares that some of their horses got away from the soldiers and charged down through the Indians, knocking them down and running over them. Bobtail Horse caught two of these horses and took them across the river to the camp, to which the women had now returned.

Brave Wolf, who was the fighting chief of the Cheyennes, had been in the fight with Reno until the shooting was heard down the river, when all the Indians went down there. He told me: "When I got to the Cheyenne camp the fighting had been going on for some time. The soldiers (Custer's) were right down close to the stream, but none were on the side of the camp. Just as I got there the soldiers began to retreat up the narrow gulch. They were all drawn up in line of battle, shooting well and fighting hard, but there were so many people around them that they could not help being killed. They still held their line of battle, and kept fighting and falling from their horses—fighting and falling, all the way up nearly to where the monument now stands. I think all their horses had been killed before they got to the top of the hill. None got there on horseback, and only a few on foot. A part of those who had reached the top of the hill went on over and tried to go to the river, but they killed them all going down the hill, before any of them got to the creek.

"It was hard fighting; very hard all the time. I have been in many hard fights, but I never saw such brave men."

[1] American Horse has told me that the emigrants passing up the South Platte River to the mines between 1858 and 1865 were largely armed with the Sharps military rifles, and the Indians secured many of them in trade from these travellers. They were useful arms. The Indians also had some old-fashioned cap six-shooters, and during the year 1875 there was a good deal of trading done for improved rifles.

The method by which the Indians kept themselves supplied with ammunition for firearms, not only loose ammunition but also fixed, has always been more or less mysterious, but they explain that in those war days they were constantly purchasing powder, lead, primers, and also outfits for reloading cartridges. They carried with them as part of their most prized possessions sacks of balls they had moulded and cans of powder. So far as possible, they saved all the metal cartridge shells they used or found, and no doubt became expert reloaders of shells.

Just after the three companies had reached the gray-horse company, a man riding a sorrel horse broke away from the soldiers, and rode back up the river and toward the hills, in the direction from which the soldiers had come. Some Indians followed him, but his horse was fast and long-winded, and at last only three men were left in pursuit. A Sioux, and two Cheyennes, Old Bear and Kills in the Night, both living in 1915, kept on, trying to overtake him. The Sioux fired at the man, but missed him; then Old Bear fired, and a little later the man fell from his horse and when they got to him they found that he had been shot in the back, between the shoulders. It is believed that Old Bear killed him. It is conjectured that this was Lieutenant Harrington, whose body was never identified.

A man supposed by some of the Indians to be General Custer was on the outer edge of the gray-horse company, toward the river. White Shield saw this man while he was being stripped. He was clad in a buckskin shirt, fringed on the breast, with buckskin trousers; wore fine, high boots, and had a knife stuck in a scabbard in his boot. A large red handkerchief was tied about his neck. He was armed with a six-shooter and a long knife. He died with his pistol in his hand. He had a mustache, but no other hair on his face, and had blue marks pricked into the skin on the arms above the wrist. This was probably Tom Custer.

The Indians state positively that they did not kill the troops by charging into them, but kept shooting them from behind the hills. The final charge was not made until all the troops in the main body had fallen, though, of course, many soldiers were still on foot scattered down toward the river. When all the troops on the hill had fallen, the Indians gave a loud shout and charged up the ridge. The soldiers toward the river backed away, and after that the fight did not last long enough to light a pipe.

After the fight was over the women and children went up to the battle-ground, and as usual there was mutilation of the dead. Spotted Hawk, who was then seven years old, relates that he went up with a group of children a little older than he, and they began to take what they wished from the slain. Among other things they tried to take off the clothing, cutting loose the waistbands of the soldiers to remove their trousers. While engaged in this work a child happened to rip up a waistband and noticed in it pieces of green paper, some small and some large—the small no doubt fractional currency and the larger pieces bills. The children thought these things pretty, and looking further found that almost every waistband contained some money. They did not know what this was, but, since it was hidden, they assumed that it must be precious, and took it back to camp. Spotted Hawk says that after this, while playing at making mud images, as the children did, he made a clay horse for a clay rider, and used a folded bill for a saddle blanket for the horseman to sit on.

After the Custer command had been wiped out, the fighting men returned up the river to attack Reno's command, with which were Captain Benteen's men and the pack-train. The subsequent operations here have been detailed by General Godfrey in his article in the *Century Magazine*, which still remains the best account of the fight. During the afternoon thirteen of Reno's men—twelve soldiers and one civilian scout—who had been in the timber rejoined the command. George Herendeen was one of these.

Lieutenant De Rudio and Tom O'Neal, an enlisted man, together with William Jackson and Fred Girard had remained in the timber and were now concealed there. The Indians knew that there were people in the timber, but devoted their attention chiefly to the troops intrenched on top of the hill, and kept shooting at them.

The morning after the Custer fight the Indians were still watching Reno's troops. By this time the besieged had begun to suffer for water. The Indians say that a soldier stripped to his underclothing ran down the hill to the river, and the Indians began to shoot at him. In one hand he held a quart cup, and in the other a canteen. When he reached the river he threw himself down in the water, filling his vessels and drinking at the same time. Half the time they could not see him because of the water splashed up by the bullets. After two or three moments he rose and ran up the hill again, entering the breastworks unhurt, though they had been firing at him all the time.

The Indians stayed here all day long and made several charges, but at length their scouts brought word of the approach of Terry, and they determined that they must go. The criers went about shouting out orders that the camp should move, and the women began to pack up and were soon on their way.

Among the scouts killed with Reno was Bloody Knife, a well-known Ree, who had been brought up among the Sioux, for during some period of peace his father had married a Ree woman. By the time that Bloody Knife was a well-grown boy in the Sioux camp his mother was seized with a great wish to see her own people, and her husband consented that she should return to the Ree village on the Missouri River. Bloody Knife went with her and after that lived with the Rees, and was considered a Ree. In 1874 he accompanied the Custer expedition to the Black Hills of Dakota and was a good scout.

During the flight of Reno's troops across the Little Big Horn River, Bloody Knife was killed. Later among the women who came down from the Sioux and Cheyenne camp to get trophies to take back to their camp were two young women, daughters of Bloody Knife's sister, a Sioux woman. They found an Indian, and seeing from his clothing that he was a scout for the soldiers, cut off his head, put it on a pole, and returned to camp. They showed the trophy in triumph to the people, and among others to their mother, who recognized it as the head of her brother, Bloody Knife.

Some years ago Major De Rudio wrote for *Harper's Weekly* an account of the adventures of the four men who were left in the timber after Reno had fled across the Little Big Horn River to the hill. They became separated; Major De Rudio and O'Neal stayed together, and Jackson and Girard. The two former unexpectedly met some Indians who were travelling through the timber and killed two or three of them. All four finally reached Reno's command on the hill.

The community of Indians attacked here by the Custer command was a large one—how large no one knows. Young Two Moon has declared to me that there were two hundred lodges in the Cheyenne village and six villages of Sioux, each one larger than the Cheyenne. Even if the Sioux villages were no larger than the Cheyenne this would make one thousand four hundred lodges, and beside the people occupying the lodges there were a multitude of strangers—Indians from different reservations— whose number cannot be estimated. That spring the Sioux and the Cheyennes sent out runners to Red Cloud, Spotted Tail, Standing Rock, and other Sioux reservations to call warriors to join the camp, and the response to this invitation was large. There were also in the camp some Southern Cheyennes, some Yankton Sioux, and some Arapahoes. Many of these people were guests in the lodges, and many others camped under shelters outside of the lodges. Cheyennes have told me that they believed there were more than one thousand five hundred lodges, and perhaps three or four fighting men to a lodge, a total therefore of from four thousand five hundred to six thousand men.

Eastman's account[1] is quite different, and his numbers much smaller. He gives only a little more than nine hundred lodges, and perhaps one thousand four hundred warriors. Yet perhaps this is as much too small as the other estimate is too large. Northern Cheyenne testimony agrees that there were two hundred lodges of Cheyennes, while Eastman gives only fifty-five. His enumeration of the Sioux may be closer. Of one thing we may be sure, that if Reno and Custer had kept on and charged through the village from opposite ends the Indians would have scattered, and there would have been no disaster.

For many years past the Northern Cheyennes whenever the Custer fight has been under discussion have expressed the opinion that if Reno had remained in the timber the Indians could have done nothing with him. They agree further that if Custer had continued his charge and gone to and through the villages the Indians would have fled, and he would have killed many of them. "If the soldiers had not stopped, they would have killed lots of Indians," said one of their most famous warriors. Anyone familiar with Indian ways, mode of thought, and war customs knows very well that as a rule the Indian avoids coming to close quarters with his enemy. If the enemy charges, the Indian runs away, but as soon as the vigor of the charge lessens or the enemy stops the Indian becomes encouraged, turns about and himself charges. This was characteristic of the old intertribal wars which consisted largely of charges backward and forward by the two opposing forces.

Examinations of the battle-ground have been made by many people without clearing up the events of the fight. It seems,

[1] *Chautauquan*, July, 1900.

however, that a part of Custer's command did come nearly down to the ford, and if the two companies that reached that point—with whom I suppose were Lieutenants Crittenden and Calhoun—had kept on and crossed the river they would no doubt have been followed by the rest of the command, and a great victory might have followed. It is clear that Custer's purpose was to charge the camp from both ends. The plan was a good one, but required that the two charges should be made about the same time and should be led by men who were without fear. Either Reno charged too soon, or else it took Custer far longer than expected to get round to his position. The distance Reno had to go was but three miles, while Custer had six or seven, or even ten to ride. Reno had been defeated and was on his hill before Custer drew near the river. It is possible that Custer stopped on the hill to look for Reno, and that this gave the Indians time to get together, and that then Custer supposed that the force he had to meet was too strong. Yet the Cheyennes say that at first only ten Indians were present at the ford to oppose any charge that might have been made. The hill on which the monument stands seems well enough chosen for defense, but the borders of the ridge are cut by many little ravines and draws, which provided effective shelter for the Indians' approach.

Assuming that for whatever reason Custer could not or would not cross the river and charge through the camp, a plan of defense better than the one he adopted would have been to get down on the flat of the river bottom, where a steady body of men fighting coolly under competent officers could have worn out the Indians, who would have left them after a day of fighting. If Custer had kept moving and either crossed the river at the ford at the mouth of the dry gulch toward which Crittenden and Calhoun seem to have been going when killed, or had gone down the river, crossed there, and come up the flat, I have no doubt that the Indians would have run. If Crittenden and Calhoun's companies had crossed the ford and shown Custer the way he would no doubt have followed them, and the day would have turned out differently.

XXVII

CAPTURE OF DULL KNIFE'S VILLAGE

1876

AFTER the Custer battle the hostile Indians engaged in it separated and scattered in different camps. During the month of August various small fights took place in the northern country. In September the camp of American Horse—Sioux—was captured at Slim Buttes, in South Dakota. General Crook, after long and fruitless marches in Wyoming and Montana, returned to the Black Hills and remained there for a time. In October a body of troops, escorting a wagon-train from Glendive to the cantonment at Tongue River, was attacked by Indians under the leadership of Sitting Bull. A little later in October Red Cloud's camp was surrounded and captured, and his horses were taken. Of the Cheyennes Two Moon's band remained in the general vicinity of the Tongue River and the Rosebud and, avoiding the soldiers, occupied themselves in killing buffalo and preparing food for the winter. Dull Knife's large village, which for some time was on Powder River, at length disappeared and it was not known what had become of it.

General Crook had determined on a winter campaign, and in the autumn preparations were made to send out a military expedition under General Ranald S. Mackenzie into the country of the Indians to look up hostile camps. The troops chosen consisted of eleven companies of cavalry from the Second, Third and Fifth Regiments, four companies of the Fourth Artillery, dismounted, and eleven companies of infantry from the Fourth, Ninth, Fourteenth and Twenty-fifth Regiments, under Colonel R. I. Dodge, together with about four hundred Indian scouts—Pawnees, Sioux, Arapahoes, Shoshoni, Bannocks, and a few Cheyennes. Two hundred Crow scouts were expected, but did not join the expedition until after the fighting was over. A train of one hundred and sixty-eight wagons and seven ambulances transported the supplies, and there was a pack-train of four hundred mules. The drivers and their assistants and the packers numbered about two hundred and eighty-five men. In all, therefore, this was a force of something over two thousand people.

The different scouts, divided according to their tribes, were commanded by Lieutenant W. P. Clark, Second Cavalry; Lieutenant W. S. Schuyler, Fifth Cavalry; Hayden Delaney, Ninth Infantry; Major Frank North, of the Pawnee scouts; while the few Cheyenne scouts were in charge of William Rowland, who had married into the tribe in 1850 and been associated with them ever since.

Preparations for the expedition went forward rather deliberately, but were about completed by the middle of October. The first operation was the capture of Red Cloud's village at Pine Ridge Agency, near Fort Robinson. During the summer of 1876 Red Cloud had been at peace, but General Crook did not trust the young men of the camp and deemed it safer to set them all afoot than to give them the opportunity to go off to join the hostile camps. Red Cloud's camp was located in the hills near Chadron Creek, about forty miles from Pine Ridge Agency. He had been ordered by the Indian agent to move in close to the agency, but had not done so and the agent feared that he would break out into hostility, and finally applied to General Crook for force to compel him to move in. General Mackenzie started from Camp Robinson with six companies of the Fourth and two of the Fifth Cavalry, and Indian scouts were needed. Major Frank North, who, with his Pawnee scouts, was on his way to Camp Robinson, received October 22 an order to present himself that day at the department headquarters in the field.

The horses furnished the Pawnee scouts were not in good condition, but Major North selected forty-eight men, and that same night overtook General Mackenzie. Twenty miles beyond where they met, the trails forked, one branch leading to Red Cloud's camp, the other to that of Swift Bear. General Mackenzie, with four companies of cavalry and twenty-four Pawnee scouts under Major North, took the left-hand trail to Red Cloud's camp, while Major Gordon, with the same number of Pawnee scouts under Captain North, and four companies of cavalry, set out for Swift Bear's camp.   General Mackenzie proceeded through the darkness until the crowing of a rooster notified his scouts that people were near. Todd Randall, a scout with a Sioux wife, declared that they must be close to Red Cloud's camp, since Red Cloud had a lot of chickens. The camp was surrounded without alarming the Indians, and it was not until after daylight that Randall, sent out by General Mackenzie, announced to the still sleeping village that they were surrounded and must surrender. No men came out of their lodges, but the women and children made a rush for the brush, to hide there. There was no resistance, and no shots were fired. The Pawnees charged through the village and rounded up the horses, which were driven to the rear. A Sioux boy showed great courage in trying to run off a bunch of ponies, but left them after a few shots had been fired at him.

The women, when they had been gathered together, were directed to go to the bunch of horses and select enough of them to pack their camp equipage and utensils, and then to set out for Camp Robinson. The women, however, would do nothing, and finally General Mackenzie told them that if they did not move he would burn the village. They still remained obstinate and would not stir until the soldiers began to set fire to the lodges. Then they swiftly set to work.

Swift Bear's village had been captured in essentially the same way. The two columns came together; the captives being one hundred and twenty men and their families, together with arms and ammunition, and more than three hundred horses.[1] The captured Indians were held under guard at Camp Robinson, and the horses a little later were sent on, in charge of the Pawnees, to Fort Laramie.

The Big Horn expedition started from Fort Fetterman, November 14, 1876. It was to march north, thoroughly scouting the country for signs of Indians, and if a trail of any considerable body was found, to follow the trail and locate the village. This work would naturally fall on the cavalry under General Mackenzie with the pack-train, which, if necessary, could fall back on the column of infantry and the wagon-train for supplies.

The North Platte River was crossed through floating ice, and

---

[1] *Record of Engagements* says four hundred warriors and seven hundred horses.

the march was taken for old Fort Reno, which had long before been abandoned. This point was made in four days, a distance of ninety miles. The country was thoroughly examined by the Indian scouts, who travelled with their usual caution, keeping their own movements concealed, but letting nothing escape them. The weather was very cold and from time to time snow fell. At old Fort Reno the command was joined by the Shoshoni scouts under Tom Cosgrove, an old frontiersman.

On November 20, a party of scouts came in with a young Cheyenne Indian[1] whom they had captured. He said that he was one of a small party camped on upper Powder River, and that Crazy Horse, the Sioux, was camped on the Rosebud River, near the big bend, where General Crook had had his fight with the Sioux and Cheyennes on June 17.

On November 22, the command moved to Crazy Woman's fork of Powder River, and established a camp, parking their wagons, to be left there with a strong guard under Major Furey, the quartermaster. Ten days' rations were laid out, and ammunition issued, and preparations made to set out for the village of Crazy Horse.

Early next morning a Cheyenne Indian from Red Cloud Agency came in and reported that the camp to which young Beaver Dam belonged had started to join Crazy Horse, and also that there was a large Cheyenne village hidden in the Big Horn Mountains near the head of the very stream the command was on. General Mackenzie was ordered to take the Indian scouts and all the cavalry, and to start out to find this village. His force consisted of about 1100 officers and men, of whom one-third were Indian scouts. The infantry and one company of cavalry were left behind with the wagons. Presumably it was here that Cheyenne scouts discovered the troops, as told further on, in young Two Moon's narrative.

The fighting force set out early in the morning—November 24—marched twelve miles up Crazy Woman, and camped in a spot well hidden among the foothills of the mountains. Captain Lawton,[2] Fourth Cavalry, General Mackenzie's field quartermaster, was sent twelve hours ahead of the command to prepare

[1] Beaver Dam, by name.
[2] General Lawton, killed in the Philippines.

stream crossings and ravines. With him went John B. Sharp, his wagon-master, a man of remarkable efficiency. They did a great amount of work in frozen ground to smooth the way for the command, but even so the next day's journey was difficult. The ground was much cut up by steep-sided ravines, and progress was slow. By this time the Arapaho scouts had discovered the Indian village. It was not far off. Toward evening the command halted, waiting for dark and the rising of the moon; and as soon as it became light enough to travel set out again, and moved on through the night over trails sometimes exceedingly rough, sometimes so narrow that only one horse could pass along. Every precaution was taken that no noise should be made. Orders were given that no one should smoke, and no one should light a match, but these orders were not obeyed, and there was considerable smoking. The intention, of course, was to surprise the village, which, however, had for days been aware of the proximity of the troops, and but for the obstinacy of the chief of the Fox Soldier band would have packed up and gone that day.

As the command drew nearer to the village, the Indian scouts, with senses keener and better trained than those of the white men, could hear the distant sounds of the drum, and sometimes the wind bore faintly to their ears the sound of dance songs. During the frequent halts made to permit the troops to close up, some of the men, tired by the hard night march, stretched themselves on the ground, with the bridle-reins of their horses twisted about their wrists, and slumbered quietly, notwithstanding the bitter cold. Then would come the word to advance and, led by the Indian scouts, the column moved on again.

Gradually from up the valley the sounds of the village became distinct to all. The camp was close now. From the front came more plainly the sound of drumming and singing, while from the rear was heard the low murmur of horses' hoofs as the column, stretched out for a mile or two, slowly closed up and each man took his place. The Indian scouts were looking and listening, eagerly searching for any sign that the hostiles were alarmed. The younger soldiers were excited, impatient, and anxious to push on, the old ones self-contained and waiting for orders. The moment for the attack was at hand.

On the left of the valley rode the Shoshoni and Bannocks, led by Tom Cosgrove and Lieutenant Schuyler. On the right rode Major Frank North and his brother Luther, followed by the Pawnees. Up the centre came the Cheyennes, Arapahoes, and Sioux, under William Rowland, Lieutenants Clark and Delaney.

The gray dawn of November 26 was just breaking when the order was given to charge, and the column rushed out into the wider valley, where were seen standing the white lodges of the Cheyennes. Soon the thunder of many hoofs and the loud war songs of some of the Indian scouts, which their officers could not check, reached the ears of the people in the camp, many of whom had just gone to bed. Warning cries were heard, and as the shooting began men, women, and children rushed from the lodges.

The Pawnees had been ordered to keep up the left bank of the stream until they had passed the village, and then to swing across the stream and meet the cavalry that was coming up the right bank, thus surrounding the village. Just before they reached the lodges, an English-speaking Pawnee, Ralph Weeks, who was with General Mackenzie, shouted across the creek to the Pawnees to cross over to the right bank, as there was no trail up the side the Pawnees were on. Major North at once turned down the bank into the stream and crossed, and the Pawnees moved along abreast of the Shoshoni, who at length turned to the left, and went up on the mountainside that overlooked the village. The Pawnees kept on into the village.

The first lodges at the end of the village were near the mouth of a dry creek full of underbrush and small trees. Just before the Pawnees entered the village, a blanketed form sprang from this underbrush almost in front of Captain Luther North, threw a gun to the shoulder and fired. At the same instant Captain North swung around in the saddle to the right and shot at this form. The two rifles sounded almost together, and the Cheyenne boy, a son of Dull Knife, fell, and the passing Pawnees counted coup on his body.

Many of the Cheyennes had not time to save anything except their lives. Some of them rushed naked from their beds, carrrying cartridge belts in one hand, and rifles in the other, and hurried their women and children up the ravines on to the bluffs and among the rocks behind the village. Elk River, more thoughtful of his family than of fighting, cut a long slit through the back of his lodge with his knife, drove out the women and the little ones, helped them to cover, and then returned to try to save the horses, usually the first things looked after by the Indians.

A group of Cheyennes had taken possession of a ravine, and were dimly seen hurrying through the mist, and trying to get in front of and to hold back the troops. Lieutenant McKinney, with his company of the Fourth Cavalry, was sent to this place to dislodge them. He set out, but presently, before reaching a ravine with cut banks which could not be crossed and which he could not yet see, the Indians fired upon him and his command, killing McKinney, wounding a number of men and killing several horses. Lieutenant McKinney received seven wounds, four of which were fatal. The troops dismounted, and, charging into the ravine, killed all the Cheyennes who were still there. Some of these were Tall Bull, Walking Whirlwind, Burns Red (in the Sun), Walking Calf, Hawks Visit, and Four Spirits. Scabby was badly wounded and died in two days. Curly was badly wounded but lived. Two Bulls, who was wounded, is still living. White Shield, Yellow Eagle, and Bull Hump, had been with this party, but had gone before the soldiers charged.

Meantime, the troops of Captain Wirt Davis of the Fourth Cavalry, and Captain Hamilton, Fifth Cavalry, were hotly engaged, and might have suffered severely but that Lieutenant Schuyler took his Shoshoni scouts up among the rocks above the Cheyennes, and by a hot fire drove them away. Captain Hamilton showed great bravery and even sabred one or more of the Indians.

By this time the Cheyennes had all retreated to the mountainside above the camp, and the fighting was confined to long-range shooting. The Pawnees charged through the village to the south end, and then crossed back to the west side, and Major North and his brother there left their horses and climbed up on a knoll where there were perhaps twenty or thirty soldiers. Other soldiers were in groups farther to the west. Major North sent fifteen Pawnees on foot up the low swale to the west, and told them to try and climb up the mountain and get around behind the Cheyennes. The Pawnees started, but when they had gone part way up they came out in sight of the troops that were over to the right, and the soldiers, supposing them to be Cheyennes, began to shoot at them, so that the scouts had to get under cover behind the rocks and then to creep back to the village.

About two o'clock Major North and the Pawnees were ordered to go into the village and camp there, and destroy it. The lodges were pulled down, the lodge-poles heaped together, and clothing, weapons, dried meat, robes—all were piled together ready for burning.

In the village were many articles which had belonged to the Seventh Cavalry or its members, for Dull Knife's village had taken active part in the Custer fight. One of the most interesting of these was a roster book of a first sergeant of the Seventh Cavalry, giving many details about the troop. The book had been captured by an Indian who had filled it with his drawings. It came into the possession of Colonel Homer W. Wheeler, and was deposited in the Museum of the Military Service Institution at Governor's Island, New York. Years later it passed to a dealer, from whom it was purchased by John Jay White, of New York, and finally was given to me to take out to the Cheyenne reservation to see whether I could identify the artist who had illustrated it. Bull Hump, the son of Dull Knife, and Old Bear, both of whom had been in Dull Knife's village, instantly recognized the book as the property of High Bear, who had drawn the pictures.

When the Pawnees kindled their fires for cooking supper the Cheyennes from the hillsides began to shoot at them at long range, and to drop bullets close to the fire. One Cheyenne had a heavy gun, and at intervals of about ten minutes would fire a shot at the Pawnee cook-fire. While Major North and his brother were sitting on a log near the fire a shot killed a mule about twenty feet in front of them. More than once dirt knocked up by the bullets flew into the frying-pan, and a bullet knocked a tin cup off a log on the other side of the fire. At length Major North had the Pawnees build a breastwork of bundles of captured dried meat on the other side of the fire, and behind this shelter they ate their food in quietness. That night the village was fired, and from the hills the Cheyennes saw their property being destroyed. In the dead of winter, without food or shelter of any sort, they sat or stood on the mountainside and saw all that they owned—their subsistence and their homes—disappear.

In the first charge that morning many Cheyenne horses had been captured, but they had not got them all. Some of the Indians had saved their horses, but others grazing out in the hills had not been reached either by the Cheyennes or by the troops. Lieutenant Wheeler and some of his men had saved about fifty that the Indians were trying to run off.

Between the border of the village and the long rocky ridge behind which a considerable number of Cheyennes were hidden, a band of about one hundred Cheyenne horses were feeding within two hundred or three hundred yards of the Cheyenne breastworks, and three-fourths of a mile from the Pawnee camp. By keeping among the bushes in the bed of the stream it was possible to approach within two hundred yards of them. The Indian scouts with the troops made two or three efforts to get them. A Sioux scout, Three Bears, with two or three companions rode up through the bushes and made a dash for the horses, but the Indians behind the ridge opened such a hot fire on them that Three Bears and his party turned and galloped back. A little later another party of scouts tried to get them and failed. Both these attempts were witnessed from the Pawnee camp, and the failures to get the horses made them seem all the more desirable. Captain North asked permission of his brother to take one of their scouts and try to bring these horses in, and after some hesitation he assented.

When the two men left the bushes they lay well down on the necks of their horses and urged them at full speed toward the Cheyenne herd. Each carried a blanket over his arm, and as soon as they were between the horses and the ridge they began to shake the blankets and yell. The horses were not disposed to move, but by running back and forth behind them they were finally started and driven at full speed down to the camp. During all this time the Indians behind the ridge were firing at the scouts as fast as they could load, but though four horses were killed and several others wounded, the men came in without a scratch and with nearly one hundred head of Cheyenne horses.

The morning after the destruction of the village no enemies were to be seen, and Indian scouts sent out found that the Cheyennes had gone away to a distance of six miles. On November 27, therefore, the troops moved away carrying, under the special charge of Lieutenant Wheeler, their dead on the backs of pack mules, and their wounded on travois made of lodge-poles taken from the village. Two or three days later they reached the main camp. On the way back they met two parties of miners headed for the Big Horn Mountains. The miners were advised not to go on until the Cheyennes had left the country, but, laughing, they said confidently that they believed they would take their chances. One of the parties was attacked by five Sioux, who killed one of the men and took everything they possessed. All the members of the other party were killed.

The Crow scouts, seventy-six in number, under command of Major Randall, reached the camp about Christmas time, and a little later the command marched to Fort Laramie. The narratives of this fight by Cheyennes who were in the village, to be given later, explain their views of the battle and tell also of the route followed by the people on their way to Crazy Horse's camp. They are of peculiar interest when compared with the story given by Captain John Bourke, by far the best narrative that we have of this fight, but written wholly from the military point of view.

I have pointed out that the troops that attacked Dull Knife's village supposed that they had surprised it, but the Cheyenne account of the fight and the events immediately preceding it show that the proximity of the troops was known to the Indians days in advance of the attack. They might readily have escaped and undoubtedly would have done so except for the obstinacy and arrogance of Last Bull—at that time chief of the Fox Soldiers— who seems to have cowed not only the chiefs of the tribes but also the owners of the two great medicines of the Cheyennes and the chiefs of the other soldier bands.

In this village Dull Knife and Wild Hog were the principal chiefs. Two Moon was there, and the two keepers of the great mysteries of the Cheyennes, Black Hairy Dog, keeper of the medicine arrows, and Coal Bear, of the sacred hat.

I have received the story of the fight from many of the people who were in the village, among them young Two Moon, nephew of old Two Moon; Little Hawk, a son of old Gentle Horse, a famous Cheyenne of the old war times; other men, and some women.

The camp had been over on the west side of the Big Horn Mountains on the head of the Big Horn River. After a time it moved over to Powder River, and they camped near the mouth of the little Striped Stick Creek.[1] Some young men, who had been out hunting antelope and deer and had gone some distance down Powder River, told the people when they reached camp at night that they had seen the tracks of many horses travelling down the river on the divide south of Powder River.

Next morning the head men called a meeting and decided to send out four men to learn what the tracks meant—by whom they were made. They directed two chiefs to go out and bring in certain men for this duty. The two chiefs went to the lodge of Hail,[2] took him by both arms and brought him to the meeting. They then went to get Crow Necklace,[3] and brought him. Then they brought young Two Moon,[4] then High Wolf.[5] These four men were set in line and the chiefs spoke to them.

"We have chosen you four men," they said, "because we can depend on you to go out and follow this trail. When you find it, stick to it; do not leave it. It may be that it will join the trail made by some other party. We depend on you to find out about this and to return and let us know. Now go and saddle up, and after you have saddled your horses ride back here to this meeting."

After they had returned to the chiefs, an old man cried through the camp, saying: "Here are four men for whom we shall look, and for whose words we shall listen. They are going out to look for this party and to bring back news of it."

The four scouts started, and camped the first night on Elk Mountain Creek. There was a little snow on the ground and it was cold. Next morning they started and travelled southeast, and that night camped on Visiting Creek. The next day they travelled to War Bonnet Ridge—so called from three trees which at a distance look like a war bonnet—and went on beyond to House Ridge—from rocks that look like a house. They did not

---

[1] Tsĭns kăh′nĭ kă măk′.   [2] Au′tsĭt ĕ.
[3] Ōhk′tsē wōh′tān āh.   [4] Ish′ĭ ēyo nĭs′sĭ.
[5] Hōhnĭ′ō hkā hĭ yo.

keep close together, but rode at a distance one from another looking for trails and closely watching the country. They travelled slowly, and at every ridge stopped and looked for a long time.

From this place they struck north toward Powder River, and came down the ridge until they reached a wagon-road which went to Powder River. It was now night and snowing. Hail, the oldest man of the party, said: "We can take this road and follow it down, crossing Powder River and going to those buttes over there, and can stay there until morning. From there we can see much country." When they reached this hill they went around behind it and stopped there, for Hail said: "It is useless to climb up there until near daylight." When it began to grow light Hail said: "Now let us climb this hill, and when day comes be ready to look over the ridge up and down Powder River Valley."

As soon as they reached the top of the hill they could see smoke rising in a bend on the river below them, and as the light grew tents were seen standing there in a long line and looking like one big tent. As they watched they saw the soldiers and scouts turn loose their horses. One herd came straight to the foot of the hill the Cheyennes were on and stopped there. The Indian scouts took their horses across Powder River to the southeast side. Two of the guards with the horses near the Cheyennes rode a couple of hundred yards away from the horses and up on a high point, and remained there watching the horses. It was hard for the Cheyennes to keep out of sight of these men. They did so only by lying flat on the ground.

Crow Necklace proposed to charge down on the horses and drive them away, but Hail would not consent. Crow Necklace insisted, but Hail still refused, saying: "Look at the snow that fell last night; it is deep. There are many people here. They might easily enough overtake and catch us. Look at the distance to the foot of the mountains before we could get into the breaks. It is a long, level road, and they would surely overtake us before we got there." Finally Crow Necklace ceased urging this. The Cheyennes could not get away from this place without being seen, and all day long they remained there waiting and watching. In the afternoon, not long before the sun set, the soldiers began to move the horses toward camp. After the sun had gone down and it was dark the Cheyennes came down from the hill and rode to within half a mile of the soldiers' camp. By that time the horses of the troops were all tied to a long picket-line. The four Cheyennes dismounted and tied their horses, intending to approach the camp on foot. After they had tied the horses, however, Two Moon suggested that two should go to the camp and two remain with the horses. Two Moon was chosen to go to the camp and asked: "Who will go with me?" Crow Necklace said: "I will go." Two Moon said: "We may have an opportunity to get a change of saddle-horses down there."

The two went down the stream toward the camp. When they reached the soldier camp, they walked straight on, thinking that in this way there was less likelihood that they would be suspected than if they tried to hide. Just at the edge of the camp, they found a large fire built, and about it Indian scouts playing "hands." These were Shoshoni and Arapaho scouts. They recognized two Cheyennes standing by the fire singing, Crow and Wolf Satchel (i. e., possibly Sack), and they thought that there must be more Cheyennes with the troops.

After a little while they left this place and went around below the camp, and there found the camp of the Pawnees. They stayed around the camp for a long time, until the fires died down and the only lights seen were those in the tents. The Indian scouts were not in tents, but were living in shelters built of bent willows covered with canvas, and some had built war lodges of poles.

At the place where the Pawnees were camped, they cut loose three horses and led them back around the outside of the camp to where they had come from. When they came around to the Arapaho camp, they could see there a man who was frying cakes and had quite a pile of them. Two Moon said: "We had better go in here and get something to eat." They were hungry. They turned loose the horses to go into the Arapaho lodge. The scouts in the camp were singing, and as the two Cheyennes were about to go into the camp two soldiers rode up and spoke to the Arapahoes, and then someone called out: "Stop singing, and keep a good lookout." The singing stopped, and all the Arapahoes went into their lodges. As the last man went in, Two Moon and Crow Necklace stepped up and cut loose three horses, Two Moon taking two and Crow Necklace taking one, and led them off.

When they got to where they had left Hail and High Wolf, they found these two sound asleep and all four horses gone. The two men had let their horses go, so that they might feed, and they had wandered off while the men were asleep. When they awoke and found their horses gone, one of them jumped on behind Two Moon and they set out after their own horses, which at last they overtook travelling back toward the Cheyenne camp.

While these four scouts had been gone, the camp had moved over the divide to another little creek. The sun had risen only a little way when they came in sight of the camp, and when they were seen coming the people began to gather in the middle of the camp, and the scouts rode on to the centre of the village and stopped there. There they reported that they had found many soldiers down on the main Powder River. "There were four different languages spoken in the camp," they said: "Pawnee, Shoshoni, Arapaho, and Cheyenne." Two Moon said: "If they reach this camp I think it will be a big fight."

When the chiefs learned that the soldiers were near, Black Hairy Dog wished to move camp along the foot of the mountains, to join the large Sioux camp which was not far off, but Last Bull, one of the soldier chiefs, said: "No, we will stay here and fight." On the fourth night after the scouts had got in, they learned that the soldiers were close to them. That evening the chiefs had again said: "Let us go up on the mountainside and throw up breastworks behind which the women and children can stay. There are so many of them that we cannot carry them all away if we are attacked." "No," said Last Bull. "We will stay here." He was determined to do this. He said also: "We will dance here all night." Before sundown they built a "skunk"; that is, a pile of wood for a fire to dance by, and after dark they set this on fire and began to have a dance. During the evening a man named Sits in the Night[1] took his horses down below the camp, and later went down to look at them to see if they were safe. Before he reached the horses, but when near enough to see them, he saw someone driving the horses away. He turned about and came back to the camp without the horses. After he had returned, an old man cried about the camp: "Sits in the Night has some news to tell. He went down to look for his horses, and

[1] Tāĭ ĭv′hkŏk.

found someone driving them away. Go to his lodge and hear the news." The people began to run from all directions, to hear what was to be told. Sits in the Night spoke and said: "I reached my horses in time to see people driving them off, and whipping them. I was so near that I could hear the blows as they struck them. I think the soldiers are there, for further down the stream I heard a rumbling noise." An old crier called out through the camp: "They have already taken Sits in the Night's horses; we had better look about for a place to build breast-works."

Crow Split Nose, chief of the Crooked Lances (Hǐm′ ō wē yŭhk ǐs), spoke to the people, and had an old man come to his side and call it out, saying: "I think it would be a good idea for the women and children to tear down the lodges, and take them up to that cut bank where there is a good place to throw up breastworks. They should do this at once." The old man re-peated this, and in a short time those of the people whose horses were nearby packed them and were ready to move. Mean-time, however, Last Bull, chief of the Fox Soldiers, had called to his old crier and ordered him to call in the Fox Soldiers. When the Fox Soldiers had come together, he ordered them to permit no one to leave the camp. Many people had already started for the place advised by Crow Split Nose, but were turned back by the Fox Soldiers, and told to return to the camp and unpack. Last Bull said: "No one shall leave the camp to-night." He said also: "We will stay up all night and dance." A little later Crow Split Nose and Last Bull met, and Last Bull said to the other: "You will not be the only man killed if we are attacked by the white soldiers; what are you afraid of?"

Crow Split Nose replied: "I do not care for myself; I am thinking of the women and children. I want to get them up there where they will be safe, so that only we men will be left in the camp ready to fight."

"You will know in the morning what is to happen; wait till the morning."

Young Two Moon danced all night, and toward daylight went to his lodge, which was close to the mountains, and awoke all his people, telling them that they had better get up; that day-light was coming and something might happen. These were his father and his father's two wives. They jumped up, dressed, and began to pack. It was not yet light.

Very early in the morning Black Hairy Dog untied all his horses, and took them up on the hill. Little Hawk had gone to his lodge and was lying on his back, half awake, looking up through the smoke hole of the lodge. It was just beginning to show a little light. He heard someone call—it seemed a long way off— "Get your guns. The camp is charged. They are coming." It was Black Hairy Dog who cried. At the same time there was the flash of shots and the sound of guns down the valley.

When the soldiers charged, the Cheyennes at the lower end of the camp were nearly all on foot, but most of those at the upper end were on their horses, and got away on horseback. The Indian scouts charged the camp on the south side, and some soldiers came on the north side. They were shooting all the time. The first enemies who got into the camp were the Indian scouts.

At the first sound of the fighting, young Two Moon mounted his horse and rode down through the middle of the camp. The shooting was quick; he did not quite get to where his friend Crow Necklace was, but saw him wearing a war bonnet and riding a spotted horse. Crow Necklace rode around on the south side of the camp, and Two Moon turned and went on the north side. He was wearing a war bonnet whose tails reached the ground. When Two Moon made his charge, four troops of soldiers were coming up in line. He charged across the camp to the south side, and as he reached it he saw his friend, Crow Necklace, and a moment afterward saw him fall from his horse. When he reached the gulch where most of the people had gone up, he saw none of them. He was ahead of the soldiers, who were coming toward the camp. From the camp a deep gulch ran into the mountains, with high cliffs on either side. Some of the people ran up this gulch, and some ran up another gulch, until they reached the forks of the creek. Little Hawk was with these. Just as they reached a place where they were going to build up their breastworks, two companies of cavalry on gray horses dashed up to within thirty yards of them and stopped. Yellow Eagle fired the first shot, and knocked an officer out of his saddle, and the troops backed their horses down the slope out of sight. Three men rushed forward to count coup on this officer; Yellow Eagle counted the first coup and got the officer's gun; Two Bulls counted the second, and Bull Hump the third. Little Wolf had gone up the big gulch leading a number of people, and had lost some men, but he stood out there in the open to let the others get out of sight—most of them women and children—and many bullets were fired at him.

Young Two Moon kept on his way up the side gulch, and at a little round knoll overtook three men, Stump, Red Winged Woodpecker, and Split Eye, and presently another man, Brave Bear, overtook them. They dismounted here. Brave Bear said: "Some of our friends are up this deep gulch. I think they are in a bad place." Some distance behind them the soldiers had now fallen in line, the gray-horse company in the middle, and were charging toward the camp at a lope. Another company was marching toward the knoll where these five men were, and firing at them. The gray-horse company came to the mouth of the gulch up which the people had gone, and the Cheyennes who were in it fired at them, and a soldier fell from his horse. Two Cheyennes jumped out from the gulch and took his gun and belt. The soldiers fell back and dismounted and began to fire into the gulch as fast as they could. The deep gulch ran up into the hills and opened out into a wide flat. The gray-horse company stood at the mouth of the gulch, while the black-horse troop watched the flat above. Two Moon thought to himself: "My friends are in a very bad place; I fear they will all be killed."

In the gulch Yellow Nose was the only man on horseback. He rode around and came out through the flat, and came back to just above where these five men were, and when he reached the top of the hill three of them joined him. Young Two Moon and Brave Bear charged down toward the soldiers, who turned and faced them. They had intended to go into the Cheyenne camp, but before reaching it they saw that the Indian scouts were in it. They turned back to the hills and there separated. Brave Bear's horse was killed, and he got away on foot. Two Moon went to the breastworks, where the women and children were. Nine men were killed in the gulch at the mouth of which the officer had been killed. Those who were saved ran across one by one to another gulch.

At the breastworks Two Moon changed horses and rode off east. Some distance away was a man coming down from a high hill, and before the man was very close to him he saw that it was Beaver Dam. He was mounted on a cream-colored horse with a white mane and tail, which was one of those taken from Sits in the Night the night before. The two men rode up on a little ridge, and when the Cheyennes saw them and recognized the horse they charged down on them. Gypsum, all of whose sons had been killed in the gulch, tried to kill Beaver Dam, thinking that he was with the soldiers, but Beaver Dam said: "I am not a scout for the soldiers. I left Sitting Bull's camp to come home, and on my way was captured by the Arapahoes and taken into their camp. I was in the soldier camp the night you took those three horses." Gypsum would not believe what he said, but Beaver Dam kept repeating: "We were quite a party coming home, and I was sent on foot to find out who some people were that we had seen. I saw that they were Indians, and went up to them and found out that they were the scouts of these soldiers. I do not know where my party is; they may have gone back to Sitting Bull's camp. White Bull is there now." The Cheyennes were still holding Gypsum back to keep him from harming Beaver Dam, who kept on talking. "I came near being killed by the scouts, and now I get back home I am going to be killed here. I only escaped because the Arapahoes let me go, and gave me this horse to ride away on. Until to-day I have been travelling on foot. When the Arapahoes turned me loose, they told me to choose any horse I liked. I knew this horse to be a good running horse, and I chose it."

Left Handed Wolf said to Gypsum: "This man has told his story and it is not long since he left us. Let him alone."

"No," replied Gypsum, "I shall kill him. My sons are dead." About this they quarrelled, and almost fought among themselves. Left Handed Wolf said: "This man did not kill your sons. You hear those people shooting. They have not ceased since we have been here. They killed your sons. Fight them. If you do not let this man alone I will lay my whip on you." He rode up to where they were holding Gypsum and lashed him over the head with his quirt. They put Beaver Dam with the women. All along the foothills people were fighting.

When Beaver Dam had been sent to the women the men started back to the fight. They could see a gray-horse troop of soldiers on foot marching toward a little ridge and started down toward them. Beyond this little ridge there were five Cheyennes.

When they reached the third ridge from the soldiers they had to cross an open space in order to get to the second ridge. The soldiers had ascended the ridge that they were on so far that the Cheyennes could see the tops of their heads when they rose up to fire. The Cheyennes could not reach the place where the five men were. They had to stop at the second ridge. From where the Cheyennes were they tried to do what they could to save the five men, who had no way of escape from the soldiers. They kept firing, hoping to keep the soldiers back—to keep them from coming over the ridge. Presently they looked behind them and saw coming a man riding on a pacing horse. It would pace a little while and then lope. Soon they saw that it was White Shield. His horse had been shot through the body. He rode up close to Yellow Nose and said to him: "If I were a noted man in the tribe as you are I would never be standing behind any hill. Look at the clothing you wear; you are all dressed up. Why do you not do something? Look at your friends over there. We ought to save them." Yellow Nose replied: "What my friend says is true. If those soldiers reach the top of the hill they will kill those men who are lying behind it. We must protect them. Now, mount your horses; form a line along this ridge." Yellow Nose was below—the main force was up on the hill. By this time a good number of Cheyennes, perhaps twenty or more, had gathered there. They cried: "Charge," and dashed toward the upper—right-hand—end of the gray-horse company. Every one of the twenty wore a war bonnet. When they made the charge some of the soldiers began to shoot at them from one side and turned them. They did not quite reach the gray-horse company. This was the closest that they got to the soldiers. The five men behind the ridge had got together in a circle and were hugging the ground. Young Two Moon recognized one of them as Long Jaw. The Cheyennes who had charged now turned back over the hill and dismounted and again began to shoot. Young Two Moon said to his fellows: "Now do you stay here and keep shooting, and I will charge over to those five men and find out who they are." He rode over, reached them, and dismounted and turned loose his horse which went back over the hill to the point he had come from. The men were: Long Jaw, Little Horse, White Horse, Braided Locks, and another. While they were fighting these soldiers some Cheyennes must have gone around behind the soldiers and begun to fire at them, and now the gray-horse troop and another troop moved off to the east and the six Cheyennes behind the ridge were able to get away and save themselves.

When Lieutenant McKinney fell and the coup was counted on him his horse fell also, and Bull Hump, after counting his coup, cut away one of the saddle-bags on the horse and started to run back. He had only made one or two jumps when he saw on the ground before him a six-shooter and near it another. He picked up both and thrust them in his belt, and kept on running, but his long infantry rifle, his two six-shooters, and the bag of ammunition made a heavy load, and soon he got out of breath and was so tired that he could hardly use his legs. He felt that he must either drop his load or stop running. He would not give up the things that he had captured, and so he had to walk and take the bullets. Luckily none of them hit him.

Yellow Eagle started up a gulch to find a place which some women and children could reach and be out of danger. He found one place but it was too open. All would have been killed had they stopped there. Then he found another place where their lives might be saved, but it was hard to reach. Yellow Eagle said: "I will go first to lead the way." He was obliged to jump into sight of the troops and to run thirty yards before he was out of sight. Only one person could go at a time. The soldiers were lined up in front of this place where the people had to run, and every time a person stepped in sight the guns going off all together sounded like a bank caving in. But all crossed in safety —perhaps twenty-five or thirty people.

Little Wolf's group suffered, and six were killed. In Yellow Eagle's group four men were wounded. In another place, where twelve stayed behind to fight while the women and children were helped to safety, Bull Hump, White Frog, Two Bulls, and Bald Faced Bull were wounded.

From near the black-horse troop of cavalry a Cheyenne scout

rode out northeast to a knoll not far from where a group of Cheyennes were gathered. He had some ammunition and called across to those whom he was fighting—of his own tribe: "I am obliged to fight against you, but I am leaving on this hill a lot of ammunition." Later, when the Cheyennes got to the place, they found there a pile of cartridges.

Ē hyōph'stă, the sister of Bald Faced Bull, and Buffalo Wallow Woman were camped at the lower end of the camp at the mouth of the gulch where the soldiers charged. Many people ran out of their lodges without their robes and reached the breastworks without any covering whatever. Ē hyōph'stă had only a little piece of robe. After they were in the breastworks the women stood in line there and sang strong heart songs to encourage the fighting men. From this point they could see some of their people fighting a group of soldiers. The soldiers on foot charged the Cheyennes who retreated. Then the Cheyennes charged, and the soldiers retreated to their horses, and then charged again. In this way they fought almost all day in the same place. During the day Yellow Nose, wounded through the breast from the right side to the left, came to the breastworks. They had nothing with which to bind up his wound except a strip cut from a buffalo-robe. They put this around him, the hair next to the skin. After a time White Antelope came to the breastworks and said to Buffalo Wallow Woman: "I think your brother, Bald Faced Bull, is killed. I saw him fall from his horse over there." Ē hyōph'stă said: "I will go to my brother," and was about to start when Bird Bear rode up. When he had heard what White Antelope had told, he said: "I will go over and look." The two men went and Ē hyōph'stă followed them, but when she had gone part way White Antelope sent her back. Bald Faced Bull was found wounded, but was able to get to the breastworks.

In this battle many men did brave things. White Shield and Medicine Bear and Long Jaw and Big Crow showed much bravery. It was odd in this fight to see the way in which the loose horses ran. When the shooting began they heard the bullets strike the lodges beyond them and turned and ran away from this sound and the lodges, and so toward the shooting.

Only one wounded man was taken off the battle-field. This was Crawling; who was carried away by two men on foot. He was shot in the leg, and Braided Locks, wearing a war bonnet, and Hairy Hand rushed in on foot and carried him away. They ran with him until they were out of breath and then threw themselves down on the ground and waited until they had recovered breath. At length they reached the stream and waded up it until they reached the breastworks.

The camp had been burned, but about ten lodges on the other side of the creek from the main camp were left unburned. That night Two Moon went to these ten lodges and found two robes and then a third. He put these on his horse, and just as he did so he heard someone down the stream utter a yell and fire a shot and, as if this had been a signal, firing began from all directions. He and his party rode back to the breastworks. That night the Cheyennes with what horses they had set out up the mountains.

When they got on top of the ridge, they built big fires and slept a little, and before day came arose and began to pack. They had no food, and nothing to cook in. Some had robes, and some none.

The next morning young Two Moon, Yellow Eagle, and Turtle's Road were sent on far ahead. They had not gone very far before they saw a large herd of Cheyenne horses coming toward them, and driving these horses were five Pawnees going in the wrong direction; that is, away from the soldiers. The Cheyennes think they must have got lost. The three Cheyennes charged on the Pawnees. The hill down which they charged was very steep. The Pawnees left the horses and ran, and other Cheyennes came after and chased them over two or three ridges. The horse of one of the Pawnees gave out, but he jumped on behind one of his companions and all got away. The Cheyennes got his horse, a gray with a government saddle. Here they got seventy-five or eighty horses. The Cheyennes kept on down the backbone of the Big Horn Mountains.

After two camps, six or seven young men started on the back trail to go to the old camp to look about for horses, for some of the people thought that some horses might have escaped and come back to the camp. In this party were Big Head and Walks Last. When they reached the camp they found there a good number of horses that had been left. The horses must have followed up the only trail that led up into the big deep canyon by the breastworks into which the people had run.

In all this time the people had nothing to eat except a few horses that they killed. They had no kettles to cook food in, and in cooking the horses' meat they built great heaped-up fires of ash or box-elder or cottonwood, and when this had burned down to coals they threw the meat on it, and kept turning it until it was cooked.

Major North, Captain Bourke, and other white authorities say that the Cheyennes went down Powder River and joined Crazy Horse on that stream. Those who made the march, however, tell a different story. The Cheyennes followed the ridge of the Big Horn Mountains down until they reached the head of Clear Creek—Lodge Pole Creek of the Cheyennes—and followed it down by the big lake.[1] Then they crossed over to the head of Prairie Dog Creek—Cheyenne, Crow Standing Creek—followed that down to Tongue River and down Tongue River to just above the mouth of Otter Creek. One of their camps was on the east side of Tongue River, just opposite where White Elk now lives. From Tongue River, above the mouth of Otter Creek, they made a cut-off to Otter Creek, followed that up to its east fork and crossed over to Beaver Creek—Box Elder Creek of the Cheyennes—where Crazy Horse was camped. The Sioux treated them very kindly and supplied most of their wants.

[1] Lake De Smet.

XXVIII

SURRENDER OF TWO MOON'S BAND

1877

AFTER the Custer fight all the Indians moved up Little Sheep River and then over on to Pole Creek—Clear Creek—a tributary of Powder River. There they separated. The Sioux went west to Tongue River and the Rosebud and with them about ten lodges of Cheyennes. These were the lodges of Black Moccasin, and his son White Bull, Limber Lance, Left Handed Shooter, his son, Shadow That Comes in Sight, Walks on Crutches, Wooden Leg's father, Bull Head, White Whiskers, and Black Hawk. This was late in the fall.

The other Cheyennes moved toward the Big Horn Mountains, and then to the head of Powder River where General Mackenzie found them.

One day some Sioux of Crazy Horse's camp who were on the top of a high hill below where Saint Labre's Mission now is, but on the other side of Tongue River, with their glasses saw far up the river many people coming. One of them ran to the camp and notified it that many people were coming down Tongue River and perhaps they might be soldiers.

The Sioux watched the people coming, and at length saw that they were Indians, and presently learned that they were Cheyennes, who when they came up told of the fight with General Mackenzie and that the people were very poor; that they had no horses, no robes, no blankets, nothing to eat. The Sioux treated them well, and gave them many things that they needed.

When the Sioux and Cheyennes met they all moved south and struck Tongue River about the mouth of Hanging Woman Creek. From the camp on Hanging Woman the Sioux and some of the Cheyennes went up Hanging Woman Creek, but White Bull and Two Moon went up Tongue River. General Miles was following up Tongue River.

Old Wool Woman went up Hanging Woman with the Sioux,

but after a while with some women she turned back to come and overtake White Bull and Two Moon. Wool Woman and the widow of Walking White Man, afterward Little Chief's wife, were coming along down the stream. General Miles, from his camp at the mouth of Hanging Woman, had his Crow scouts out looking over the country. They saw the two women and four children coming down the stream and hid, and when the women came up captured them. A man and boy who had been with them had killed a buffalo and stopped behind to skin it, and so escaped capture. The young men who got away overtook White Bull and Two Moon and told them what had taken place. The Cheyennes came back to rescue the women, and had a little fight with the soldiers.

After the fight the soldiers went on down Tongue River with their captives, and the Cheyennes went over to the mouth of Rotten Grass. Buffalo were plenty and they stayed there a long time. A few of Crazy Horse's band moved in and camped with them.

Toward spring, Wool Woman, who had been captured, came to the Cheyenne camp with an interpreter, bringing tobacco and presents. She brought a message from General Miles asking them to go down to Fort Keogh and surrender. The Cheyennes decided to do so.

The next morning Two Moon, White Bull, Sleeping Rabbit, Iron Shirt, Crazy Mule, Black Bear, Little Creek, White Thunder, Crazy Head, and a few other young men set out for the soldier camp to surrender. A few women went with them, but most of the women and children remained in the camp. With them went some Sioux with Hump as leader. Bruyere,[1] the interpreter, left them on Tongue River and went in a day ahead of them, saying that when they appeared at Keogh he would come out and meet them. Before they got in he came back with another scout, and met them not far from the fort. He brought from General Miles a message telling them not to fear anything, but to come right in to the post. As the Indians came to the edge of the parade-ground the white soldiers all fell in line. White Bull said to Two Moon as they rode on: "Make up your mind now; have courage, for here we are to be killed."

[1] This name is spelled in many different ways.

When they reached the parade-ground General Miles, wearing a short bearskin coat and on a gray horse, rode up in front of the line of Indians. He shook hands with Two Moon and White Bull, calling them by name. White Bull, though frightened when he first rode in, soon learned that they had nothing to fear. The officers shook hands with them, and had tents put up for them. The post consisted altogether of tents, except a few little log houses, in one of which General Miles lived, and to this they were called.

When they had come in, General Miles said to them: "Here you are in my house and I want to talk to you. In some ways I am a mean man. In other ways I am a good man. I want you people to come here and surrender to me; to give up your arms and your horses, and turn them over to me. If you do as I tell you I will be a good man to you, but if you do not do this I will be mean to you."

Two Moon replied: "It is well; we will go back to our camp, and move right in to the post and surrender to you."

After he had made this promise, Miles asked him for one man to stay here while all the rest should go back. Two Moon asked his men for a young man who should stay behind, but no one seemed to wish to stay; they all wanted to go back. Then the council broke up. That night Two Moon talked to the young men and also the next morning, but none would volunteer to remain behind as a hostage. Finally White Bull said to Two Moon: "You tell General Miles that I will stay. I don't know what he wants to do to me, but I will stay."

Next morning all the Indians mounted and fell in line in front of General Miles's quarters. They still retained their arms intending to keep them until the camp had moved in. Two Moon said: "Here we are, all ready to go back. You ask for one man from my party to stay with you, and I am going to give you one who will remain here until we return."

"Who is the man?" asked General Miles.

"It is this man, White Bull," replied Two Moon.

General Miles said to White Bull: "Come in to my house," and he put a chair for him to sit on.

Then he spoke to Two Moon and said: "I will do no harm to this man whom you are leaving with me, but I shall enlist him now as a scout." This was so that White Bull could begin to draw pay at once.

Two Moon said: "That will be good. I do not wish to have him killed or hanged. I would rather have him shot than hanged. When I return I will move my camp right down through the middle of this post and camp above it."

"If you will move down through the middle of this post," said Miles, "it will be a good thing. You will help yourself. If you do that I will help you. Now, perhaps you had better move back to your tents, and I will give you food that you can live on while you are going back," but General Miles kept White Bull in the house with him. It took a long time to give out the rations, and they told Two Moon he had better wait there overnight and start early the next morning.

While they were drawing rations White Bull was enlisted as a scout. He held up his hand to the sky and promised that he would serve faithfully. They gave him a uniform. After he was dressed in his uniform Captain Ewers, who was to command the scouts, and White Bull walked over to the tents where the Cheyennes were, so that the others could see him in his uniform. White Bull spoke up to the others and said: "My friends, I have enlisted as scout and I think it will be a good thing if you come in and surrender as soon as you can. Tell my father and my family what I have done and ask them to come in."

Some of the Cheyennes remained at the post with White Bull, for when they saw that he had enlisted they thought there was no danger and that they would be well treated, and they preferred to remain rather than to ride back to the camp and immediately return.

The next morning when Two Moon and his party were ready to start, Two Moon turned his horse and rode to headquarters to shake hands with General Miles, and the interpreter went with him.

Two Moon said to General Miles: "You see that trail up Tongue River? That is the trail I shall return by. I have picked out a place to camp in that thick timber above the post. I shall not make a crook in my trail returning, but shall come straight."

When the camp moved back Wool Woman rode in ahead and

told White Bull that the people were coming. White Bull told General Miles about it, and he ordered eighteen head of cattle sent out for food for the camp. White Bull drove them out. After he had started two sergeants overtook him to help to drive the cattle. They went part way with him until they saw people coming. Then White Bull told them that they would better go back—he would hold the cattle. The interpreter came out from the post and overtook White Bull just before he met the people. He helped hold the cattle.

When the Cheyennes came to where the cattle were they camped. The men killed the cattle and divided them while the women were putting up the lodges and gathering wood. That night White Bull remained with the camp and the next morning early set out and rode fast to Fort Keogh. He got in early and reported that the Cheyennes would be in some time during the day.

When General Miles heard they were coming he gave orders to have tents put up in the timber near the river. The Indians moved straight through the parade-ground as Two Moon had said and went down to where the tents were. The horses were all thrown into one bunch and driven into the fort. The men gave up all their arms.

A few days later thirty of the men were enlisted as scouts. White Bull was the first of the Cheyennes to be enlisted and Brave Wolf the next.

THE LAME DEER FIGHT

The day after the camp had come in—probably April 30— General Miles sent for White Bull, saying: "My people have reported to me that somebody is chasing buffalo at the mouth of the Rosebud. I think they may be Sioux. We will go and find out."

White Bull went to Brave Wolf and said: "I am going out. Enlist as scout and go with me." Brave Wolf did so. They went out with General Miles and his orderly, the troops having moved on the day before, and went three days' march up Tongue River, as far as the bend of the Rosebud, and camped on Tongue River.

Next morning General Miles sent an interpreter with White

Bull and Brave Wolf on a scout. They went out to look for a trail. They crossed the Rosebud and after going some distance struck a trail. The same day the troops moved over to the Rosebud. White Bull and his companions followed the trail to the Sioux camp, where they found fresh meat that had not had time to spoil. They followed the trail a little way until it turned back to the Rosebud and reached it below the mouth of the Lame Deer, below the Painted Rocks. Here they saw the soldiers coming, and waited until they came up. General Miles sent White Bull on to follow the trail until he should see something, saying that the troops would wait here until his return. White Bull and the interpreter set out on the trail, which crossed the Rosebud at the mouth of the Lame Deer. When they got to the Lame Deer it was still light but the sun was low. They went up on a high point south of the Lame Deer to look up the Rosebud, and when they looked up there they saw a long string of Indians coming in from the buffalo chase with loaded horses crossing over the trail where the wagon-road now goes. When they saw the Indians they pulled back their horses to hide in the ravines until they should have got out of sight. When the people had disappeared White Bull and the interpreter went up through the hills and crossed the trail of the buffalo hunters, where the road now runs and where there used to be water. When they got there they drank, and then rode up on the hills a little way and got off their horses.

White Bull said to the interpreter: "We cannot both leave the horses; one must stay and hold them while the other climbs that hill to look. If we leave the horses someone may take them away."

The interpreter said: "You go up there and see what you can see and I will stay here with the horses."

The interpreter gave White Bull a little book and a pencil and said to him: "Take this and every time you see a lodge make a mark and when you get back I will count them up for you."

White Bull climbed the hill and looked over and saw the camp. He counted the lodges up to ten, then made a mark in the book. He counted all the lodges he could see and when he got back the interpreter counted them and made thirty-eight lodges. It was springtime but the grass was well up.

Now White Bull and the interpreter started back to the troops. By the time they had reached the mouth of the Lame Deer it was quite dark. They could see nothing, but they knew where they had left the troops at the Painted Rocks. When they came close to the troops the interpreter took out a little whistle and blew it. This was an understood signal, and when a sentry heard it he knew who blew it and called out to them.

When they got into the camp they reported to General Miles where the Sioux camp was situated and how far off. The interpreter had made notes of the position of the camp. General Miles asked: "White Bull, what do you think about our starting to-night? Did you get the lay of the land and see where we can get the troops in?"

"Yes," said White Bull, "right up that creek is a red point.[1] I think that would be a good place to post the troops to-night. It is near the camp." They started and stopped for the night at this red point.

Just before daylight White Bull went to the top of a hill and saw light in some of the lodges. The women had already begun to build their fires. He returned and reported to General Miles. No noise was made, but word was passed among the soldiers and all got ready. There was some cavalry and some infantry. A cavalry horse was led up to White Bull and given to him and his pony, which he had now been riding for two days, was led back. He spoke to the interpreter and said: "Tell General Miles I have another idea in my head and I think we can work it so that before they know anything about us we will be all around them. Yesterday when I was on the hill I saw two little creeks coming in, one at the camp and one just below it. On the hill on the other side of the camp there are some pine trees. I can take the cavalry up to the first creek I saw and take them up that and over the divide and down on to the other creek, and on the other side of that I can take the cavalry up the hill and get above the camp, and the infantry can follow up the main valley here."

"No," said the interpreter, "let us give these people a chance to get away."

"But," said White Bull, "if we surround them they will have

---

[1] This red point is nearly a mile below the present agency at Lame Deer.

to surrender and we shall get them all," but the interpreter said "no" and did not speak to General Miles.

The troops started. They had got nearly up to where the agency now stands when they saw a man on horseback. White Bull said to the interpreter: "There is a person who has seen us," and the interpreter told General Miles.

The Sioux must have ridden fast back to the camp, but it seems that he did not alarm it. All remained quiet. The interpreter, after speaking to General Miles, ran on to a little point near where the trader's store now is, and looked up the creek. Then began the charge as far as the first ravine below the camp, where some of the troops stopped. Most of the cavalry did not stop but charged through the camp and got above it on the creek. As they charged up the trail the first soldier was killed just where Cooley's house is now. By this time it was full daylight but the sun was not yet up. When they stopped above where the round-house now is[1] the soldiers began to fire. Three men charged them from Lame Deer's camp. Then they could see the women and children run out of the lodges and race for the hills.

In a bend of the Lame Deer is a bank about six feet high and three hundred yards east of this is a high knoll, on which General Miles and White Bull stood. Bob Jackson was interpreter after Bruyere had gone on with the leading soldiers. Jackson said: "This is Lame Deer's camp and I bet that is Lame Deer over there now," pointing to a Sioux man in the distance. Then Hump, who was back with the infantry, rode up to the three on the knoll and said: "I will call down to these men and see what they say."

The man Jackson had said was Lame Deer had a white rag in his hand and raised it, and when he did so all the shooting stopped. Then Hump called down to them, asking them to surrender. The man was Lame Deer and with him were his son and another man. Hump rode down to Lame Deer. His son was not quiet for a minute. After speaking to Lame Deer, Hump rode back to the commanding officer. He said: "That is Lame Deer, and he wants to see General Miles."

General Miles had a white cloth tied around his head. He took off the white cloth and gave it to his orderly, who took a

---

[1] The present fair grounds at Lame Deer.

white hat out of his saddle-pockets and gave it to General Miles. He handed his gun to the orderly, but kept his pistol. Then they rode down toward Lame Deer, eight persons in all.

The approaching party were Lame Deer, his son, and another Sioux, and a fourth Sioux leading Lame Deer's horse. When they came together Lame Deer and General Miles shook hands and General Miles took off his hat. The son did not keep still. He walked up and down. The Sioux leading the horse led it off toward the creek. General Miles said to the interpreter: "Tell Lame Deer to put his gun down."

Lame Deer put his gun on the ground with the muzzle toward General Miles, and as he put the gun down he cocked it. The other Sioux did not put down his gun. The son walked up and down like a sentry on post. The only thing he said was: "I am a soldier walking on my own land. I will give up my gun to no man. They have already killed my grandmother." He kept repeating this. An old woman had been killed.

General Miles did not notice that Lame Deer's gun was at full cock and White Bull rode around close to General Miles, touched his leg with his foot, and when Miles looked around at him he made a motion with his mouth at the gun and signed that it was at full cock. This was to put General Miles on his guard about the gun in case it should be picked up by Lame Deer.

As they sat there on their horses the interpreter rode to White Bull and said to him: "Do you ride over to Lame Deer's son and tell him to surrender. Tell him to look at all the women and children running to the hills. Let him remember no one will be hurt and we will get in all the horses and bring them to the fort."

White Bull turned his horse and as he turned the interpreter said: "That captain will help you." The captain and White Bull rode up to the son and White Bull spoke to him. The young man replied: "I have told you once that I am a soldier on my own ground," and he raised his gun and struck White Bull on the arm. White Bull spurred his horse close to the young man and caught the gun by the muzzle and the captain caught the young man by the arm. They struggled for a moment and White Bull pulled away the gun, which went off in the scuffle and the ball passed through White Bull's overcoat. Lame Deer exclaimed in

excuse for his nephew: "My friend is young." Then Lame Deer
picked up his gun and fired at General Miles. General Miles
bent to one side on his horse and the ball tore a hole in his coat.
Then every one began to shoot. White Bull let go the young
man and as he turned he saw a sergeant, Sharp, draw his pistol
and ride up to Lame Deer and shoot. Then Lame Deer's son ran
toward the sergeant who shot at him, and the son shot, too, and hit
the sergeant in the breast. White Bull thinks that the sergeant's
shot killed the Sioux who was with the two. General Miles drew
his pistol and fired at Lame Deer who started to walk away.
Soon all of them began to fire at Lame Deer and now the infantry
came up on a charge. The Sioux kept moving, walking toward
the hills where the women and children had gone. Lame Deer
said to his son: "Turn and fight." But the son was too weak.
He was using his gun for a crutch or was dragging it. They
crossed the Lame Deer and went up a little gulch. White Bull
and the interpreter were close to them and the soldiers and
scouts were firing all the time. Lame Deer walked up to his
son and took him by the shoulder and just as he did so Lame
Deer fell. The son turned and faced the soldiers and then he too
fell and sat there bracing himself with his two hands. Then he
tried to load his gun and succeeded in doing so, but had not
strength to raise it to his shoulder. As he sat there the interpreter, Jackson, knelt down and fired, and the ball struck the
young man in the middle of the forehead, just cutting the lower
edge of the brow-band of the war bonnet.

This was a brave young man to walk so far with such bad
wounds as he had and not to give up his gun. He died with his
gun in his hands. After the fight was over White Bull scalped
Lame Deer and his son. The son was not Lame Deer's son but
his nephew, the son of his brother. He was called Big Ankle,
which is said to have been also the name of the boy's father.

While they were fighting here some young Sioux must have
slipped around behind. Brave Eagle and some others charged
a pack-train of six mules which had been left behind, killed one
of the packers, and captured two mules and the ammunition.

That night after the fight White Bull was called in to General
Miles's tent. General Miles said to him: "Do you remember
what I told you when you enlisted? Now, these horses that we

have taken you may have, and I want you always to keep this gun that you have been shooting with against the Sioux."

White Bull kept it until the summer of 1905, when it was burned up in a fire which destroyed his house. General Miles asked White Bull what he could do for him for what he had done. White Bull said he wished for nothing except to be helped to continue to live in this country where he belonged. White Bull had offered Ankle's scalp to General Miles, but he declined to take it.

At this time the Lame Deer River was called Muddy Creek. Five Sioux men were killed in this fight and one woman. Others may have been killed. Two soldiers were killed and one person—soldier or citizen—with the pack-train. Troops about the village had destroyed and ruined everything in it. They took what they wanted. They got a lot of food. The people in this village were chiefly Sioux of Lame Deer's band, but there were some Cheyennes. Among them was White Hawk. The Cheyennes were camped some little distance above the Sioux and had time to escape without loss of lives or horses.

Supplementary to the account of this fight given by White Bull is the narrative of Colonel David L. Brainard, at that time of the Second U. S. Cavalry, who was in the fight. It is evident from Colonel Brainard's account that White Bull has lost track of several days of the time which elapsed between the departure of the troops from Cantonment at the mouth of Tongue River on the Yellowstone. Colonel Brainard's account is as follows:

Four troops (F, G, H, and L) of the Second Cavalry, under command of Captain Ball, were ordered to report to General Miles early in May, 1877. We had been stationed at Fort Ellis, Montana, and marched down the Yellowstone River in April, arriving at Tongue River on the 27th of that month.

On May 1st we broke camp at the Cantonment and marched up Tongue River for a distance of about fifteen miles.

The command consisted of four troops of Second Cavalry, two companies of the Fifth Infantry, four of the Twenty-second Infantry, and a company of mounted scouts under the command of Lieutenant Ned Casey.

After marching three days, the wagons were abandoned and pack mules were taken, the Cavalry pushing ahead, leaving the Infantry to follow. From this time on we marched day and night, stopping now and then for a few hours' sleep, to allow the horses to graze, and for refreshments for the men.

On the afternoon of the 6th we halted about 6 o'clock, and word was passed that the command would move forward at 1 o'clock in the morning, with a view of making an attack on the hostile camp about daylight. The command started somewhat later than 1 o'clock, and first moved at a walk, then at a trot, and before daylight we were moving at a fast gallop. The Indian scouts, headed by Bob Jackson, had returned about 12 o'clock, reporting that the Indian camp was much farther away than it was originally supposed to be, and that it would be necessary to travel very rapidly to reach it by daylight.

Just as the sun was coming up we rounded a point and saw the camp above us, probably a mile away; the smoke was curling lazily upward from a few tepees, and a few Indians were moving about the camp. H troop, commanded by Lieutenant L. H. Jerome, was in advance, and charged directly through the left side of the village and on beyond, where it surrounded and captured the pony herd, consisting of about five hundred ponies. G troop coming next, charged through the village about the same place as H troop, wheeled to the right, dismounted, and pursued the Indians up the hill, men, women and children having left the camp and passed up the steep hillside to the right. L troop, to which I belonged, came next; we wheeled directly through the village, dismounted, and charged up the hill on foot. F troop, under Captain Tyler, also wheeled to the right and charged up the hill on our right; the troops now facing the hill were ranged in the order from right to left, F under Tyler, L under Norwood and Hamilton, and G under Wheelan.

Just before entering the village, I saw General Miles riding toward two Indians, who were standing alone, one of them wearing a long war bonnet which hung to his heels. Near him, but to his rear, was another Indian. Miles was followed by an orderly. The Indian wearing the war bonnet advanced toward Miles at a rapid walk, extending his hand as though to grasp Miles' hand. When within a few feet of Miles, the other Indian called to him sharply, and he turned and ran for his gun, seized it and fired directly at Miles. Miles wheeled his horse sharply, at the same time ducking his head, the bullet passing over him, and striking his orderly, who was immediately in the rear, in the breast, and he fell from his horse dead. The Indians then ran up the hill.

About this moment the troop to which I was attached dismounted, and we followed the Indians up the precipitous hills. The head-dress made a very conspicuous target, and many shots were fired at the Indian wearing it. Finally he was seen to totter, and the other Indian, presumably his son—Iron Star, placed his hand about the other's waist and supported him up the hill; Lame Deer was seen to take a pistol from his belt and fire backward in our direction. As he was just able to totter along, being weakened from many wounds, this was regarded by us as an act of defiance. The shots were probably fired without any expectation of striking us. When the old man fell, Iron Star escaped over the hill through our left, and ran into the face of G troop under Wheelan, and was shot by Wheelan, who used a pistol.

After driving the Indians to the top of the hill, the horses were brought up, we mounted, and pursued them for some distance, but the most of them had disappeared. The command then returned to the Indian camp, which was destroyed, the tepees being torn down, piled one on another, and tons of dried buffalo meat, hundreds of beautiful buffalo-robes, saddles, arms, bridles, and equipment of all kinds were burned with the tepees.   We camped on this ground that night, and the following day retraced our steps toward the Rosebud.   Two companies of the Fifth Infantry entered our camp very soon after the fight, but they were too late to participate in the action.

I do not recall that Miles halted that morning from our bivouac to Lame Deer camp.   It is possible that he may have started out some distance in advance of the column, which would have given him an opportunity of stopping, but I am sure that the command did not stop from the time we started until we reached Lame Deer camp.

It is true that the Indians circled about in the rear of us and captured several of our pack animals—loaded with ammunition, and true that one of the men with the pack train was killed, and another had his horse shot, but instead of fighting his way up the creek to camp, he intrenched himself on a little hill and fought the Indians until the Fifth Infantry came up to relieve him.

Bob Jackson's horse gave out as we reached the scene of the fight, but he knew too well the danger of being left in the rear of the command, and he caught the tail of one of the Cavalry horses and held on until the command was in the village.

I believe there were sixty-three lodges, instead of thirty-eight of these Indians.

No doubt the identification of Lame Deer and his son is as given by White Bull, who personally knew Lame Deer, and who unquestionably discussed the fight, and all its circumstances with Hump, the Sioux who was acting as scout for Miles.   The fact that the younger man wore a war bonnet undoubtedly gave the impression that he was the important man of the two.   It is not conceivable that White Bull should have been mistaken in a matter of this kind, and besides, he was close to the men who were killed, while Colonel Brainard was at a distance.

The coulée where Lame Deer fell is just below what is known as the Cooley House.   Fifty or sixty yards above the little wash, or waterway, in that narrow valley—southeast of it—is a little red knoll and not far beyond that, to the south and southeast, is a higher knoll, or point, strewn with black rocks and with small trees growing on it.   On this higher knoll Lame Deer was buried, and here twenty years later I saw his daughter mourn for him with wailings as keen and as touching as if he had been buried only yesterday.

Forty yards still beyond this—up the ravine—is a still higher point with bigger trees.   Lame Deer fell just as he got to the wash, south of it, across a small pine sapling.

Brave Wolf was with the troops that charged up the Lame Deer, on the east side where the road now runs. He got up beyond the camp and then turned back.

Lieutenant Edward Casey, Twenty-second Infantry, took twenty mounted scouts, and led this charge up the valley, Brave Wolf riding by his side until they crossed the stream, when Casey went ahead.

In the fight three soldiers were killed and six Sioux. The Sioux were Lame Deer, his son, a man named Hump, a young man whose name is not known, and an old man and an old woman. Brave Wolf thinks that Lame Deer's son was named Flying. A Sioux named George Flying By, said to be a nephew of Lame Deer, resided a few years since at Standing Rock Agency.

XXIX

LITTLE WOLF AND DULL KNIFE

1876–1879

THE winter of 1876–1877 was spent by Dull Knife's camp of Northern Cheyennes with the Sioux of Crazy Horse's village on Powder River. In the spring of 1877, Dull Knife and his people surrendered to the troops. Most of them were sent south to the Indian Territory, with the understanding that they were to remain there with their relatives—the Southern Cheyennes.

There they at once found themselves facing new conditions.

They had come from the high dry country of Montana and North Dakota to the hot and humid Indian Territory. They had come from a country where buffalo and other game were still plenty to a country where the game had been exterminated. Immediately on their arrival they were attacked by fever and ague, a disease wholly new to them. Food was scanty, and they began to starve. The agent testified before a committee of the Senate[1] that he never received supplies to subsist the Indians for more than nine months of each fiscal year. These people were meat eaters, but the beef furnished them by the Government inspector was no more than skin and bone. The agent in describing their sufferings said: "They have lived and that is about all."

The Indians endured this for about a year, and then their patience gave out. They left the agency to which they had been sent and started north. Though troops were camped close to them, they attempted no concealment of their purpose. Instead, they announced that they intended to return to their own country.

We have heard much in past years of the Nez Percés' march under Chief Joseph, but little is remembered of the Dull Knife outbreak, and the march to the north, led by Little Wolf. This march was over an open country, where there was no opportunity

---

[1] *Senate Report* No. 708, 46th Congress, 2d Session, p. 64.

to avoid pursuers or to hide from them so as to get a little rest and respite. The story of the journey has not been told, but in the traditions of the old army this campaign was notable, and men who were stationed on the plains forty years ago are likely to tell you—if you ask them—that there never was such another journey since the Greeks marched to the sea.

Troops sent after them from Fort Reno overtook the little band before it had gone a hundred miles. The Indians were ordered to return to the agency. They refused to do so, and a fight took place. The troops left them and the Indians went on. The fugitives pressed constantly northward, while orders were flying over the wires and special trains were carrying men and horses, cavalry and infantry, to cut them off at all probable points on the different railway lines they must cross. Of the three hundred Indians sixty or seventy were fighting men. The rest were old men, children, women, and boys. An army officer once told me that thirteen thousand troops were hurrying over the country to capture or kill these few people who had left the fever-stricken south, and in the face of every obstacle were steadily marching northward.

The War Department set in operation against them all its resources, but they kept on. If troops attacked them, they stopped and fought until they had driven off the soldiers, and then started north again. Sometimes they did not even stop, but marched along, fighting as they marched. For the most part they tried—and with success—to avoid conflicts and had but four real hard fights, in which they lost half a dozen men killed, and about as many wounded.

During the winter following the capture of Dull Knife's village, in November, 1876, General Mackenzie learned where the Cheyennes were, and sent out a runner asking them to come in and surrender. The runner returned with the message that they had assented and had already started in. They reached Fort Robinson early in April, surrendered, and made peace. The Indian Bureau wished to bring all the Cheyennes together on one reservation in the Indian Territory, which for the past forty years or more had been the range of the Southern Cheyennes. Orders were given, therefore, that these surrendered people should be sent to the Indian Territory, but they were much opposed to going there. From time to time many of them had visited the southern country, but scarcely any of them had ever lived there.

They felt so strongly about this that General Crook and General Mackenzie had a council with them to decide what should be done. General Crook spoke kindly to them, and told them that they might choose one of three courses; either to go south, or to the agency of the Shoshoni and Arapahoes at Fort Washaki, or to stay at Fort Robinson for a year, at the end of which time the authorities would decide what should be done with them. All the Cheyennes wished to remain at Fort Robinson, but they had appointed Standing Elk to speak for them, and presently he stood up and declared that they were willing to go south. When he said this the Indians were all so much astonished and confused that no one objected, and at length they accepted what he said and agreed to go. This decision pleased the army officers, and they urged that the Indians should start at once, and so by mingling threats and persuasions the Cheyennes were half forced and half persuaded to leave their country.

They started south about May 1, and for one day's march had an escort of troops, who then left them. Lieutenant—afterward General—Lawton, Fourth Cavalry, was in charge of the camp. There were some wagons and a small pack-train to help transport their supplies and to carry the sick and poor. Five soldiers acted as packers and stood guard over the wagons. William Rowland was interpreter.

All through the trip things went pleasantly and smoothly. They travelled south for seventy days, and then reached their destination, Fort Reno and Darlington—the Cheyenne and Arapaho agency, in what is now Oklahoma.

Almost as soon as they arrived, when they had been in camp but a very few days, they began to be stricken with fever and ague. Of nine hundred and ninety-nine in the camp nearly two-thirds sickened within two months after their arrival. Every lodge held one or more sick people. During that winter forty-one died of sickness.

There was an agency physician at this agency, and there were five thousand Indians scattered over a considerable area and all dependent on this one man. Malarial diseases were prevalent among all these Indians. The Northern Cheyennes, fresh from the high dry plains of Montana, were peculiarly susceptible to such diseases.

Though there was a physician here, the Indian Bureau had furnished him with no medicines. Medical supplies, which that year should have been ready for use in the summer, were not received until the following January. Besides this, the Indians were ill-fed, receiving only about three-quarter rations, food of such a character that it was greatly complained of. Even the agent, who would be likely to take a cheerful view of the supplies he was issuing, could say nothing better about the meat than that "it was not grossly bad."[1]

It is not strange, then, that before the Northern Cheyennes had been a year in the Indian Territory they became greatly disheartened and discontented. They saw themselves sick, starving and dying and were much alarmed. They wished that they had never come to this southern country; they longed to be back again in their old dry country, and they began to ask to be taken back.

All shared the feeling expressed by Little Chief—who died in 1906—when he said of that time before the congressional committee: "A great many have been sick; some have died. I have been sick a great deal of the time since I have been down here—homesick and heartsick and sick in every way. I have been thinking of my native country and the good home I had up there where I was never hungry, but when I wanted anything to eat could go out and hunt buffalo. It makes me feel sick when I think about that, and I cannot help thinking about that."

About the middle of the summer, somewhere near the Fourth of July, Little Wolf, the leader of a section of the tribe, gathered together all his men and went to the agent and said to him: "These people were raised far up in the north among the pines and the mountains. In that country we were always healthy. There was no sickness and very few of us died. Now, since we have been in this country, we are dying every day. This is not a good country for us, and we wish to return to our home in the mountains. If you have not the power to give us permission to

[1] *Senate Report* No. 708, 46th Congress, 2d Session, p. 76.

go back there, let some of us go on to Washington, and tell them there how it is, or do you write to Washington and get permission for us to go back north." The agent's answer was: "I cannot do this now. Stay here for one more year and then we will see what we can do for you."

"No," replied Little Wolf, "we cannot stay another year; we want to go now. Before another year has passed we may all be dead and there will be none of us left to travel north."

The agent said to him: "I am told that some of your people have gone off already."

"I do not know that any have gone," replied Little Wolf.

They talked a little longer without result and the Cheyennes went back to their camp and continued to discuss the matter, trying to decide whether they should wait another year or go now. Soon after this some of the Indian policemen came to the camp, saying that they had been sent by the agent, who declared that three of their young men had run away and that he believed they were all going. He had sent the policemen to stop them.

Little Wolf said to the policemen: "You go back and tell the agent that we intend to move a little way up the river to camp there, and that then we will come and see him again."

They moved camp as he said they would, but before they had had time to go in to see the agent some troops came up to the camp, bringing with them a howitzer and told the Indians that they must go back to the agency. The troops camped close by the Indians and they stayed there for four days longer, when a messenger came from the agency asking Little Wolf to go in and talk with the agent. He went, taking with him two men, Wild Hog and Crow.

When Little Wolf entered the agent's office he asked: "What do you want with me; why did you send for me?"

The agent said: "Three of your young men have run off, and now I want you to give me ten of your young men, to hold here as prisoners until I get back the three that have gone off. The soldiers will go after these three, and when they have brought them back I will give the ten men their liberty."

Little Wolf stood up and after he had shaken hands with the agent, and with some army officers who were there, he said: "I will not do what you ask. If you follow those three men, you cannot find them.   Three men who are travelling over the country can hide, so that they cannot be found.   You never could get back these three and you never would set my men free.   You would keep them always."

The agent said to him: "If you do not give me these ten men, I will give you no rations.   I will give you nothing to eat until I get them.   You shall starve until they are given to me.   So you must give me those men, and I want them at once."

Little Wolf answered again: "I cannot give you the ten men you wish, to be held for the three who have gone.   I will not give them.   I am a friend to the white people, and have been so for a long time.   I went to see my Great Father in Washington, and he told me that he did not wish any more blood spilled; that we ought to be friends and fight no more."   The agent's reply was that he must have these hostages and must have them quickly.

Then Little Wolf said to him: "You and I have always been friends, but to-day I cannot do for you what you ask.   I do not want any trouble, nor do I wish to have blood shed at this agency, but I cannot do what you ask."   For some little time they talked in this way, the agent insisting that he must have the men —that he would have them.

At last Little Wolf stood up and again shook hands with all present and said: "My friends, I am now going to my camp.   I do not wish the ground about this agency to be made bloody, but now listen to what I say to you.   I am going to leave here; I am going north to my own country.   I do not want to see blood spilt about this agency.   If you are going to send your soldiers after me, I wish that you would first let me get a little distance away from this agency.   Then if you want to fight, I will fight you and we can make the ground bloody at that place."

Little Wolf and his companions went back to the camp, about twenty miles above the agency on the Canadian River.   There were about three hundred people in this camp and the leading men were Dull Knife and Little Wolf; both brave and wise men, though Dull Knife's reputation had been won more in counsel than in war, while Little Wolf was above all things a brave man and a warrior.

The man who did the interpreting at these talks was Edmond Guerrier, who is still living in Oklahoma.   He was the one sent out by Agent J. D. Miles to ask them to come in, and during this last talk he tried to persuade the Indians from their threatened course and offered them some presents. He advised them not to go as they had announced they should, saying to them: "If you do you will have trouble." Little Wolf replied to him: "We do not want trouble. We are not looking for anything of that kind. All we want is to get back to where we came from." The temper of the Indians was such that one of Guerrier's relations in the camp advised him not to interpret for the Indians any more, saying that they might get angry at him and kill him.

The next morning the Cheyennes broke camp and started north to go to their old home. They travelled rapidly. On the evening of the second day, after they had camped and were eating, someone who was out watching on the hill made signs to them that many soldiers were coming. This was on Little Medicine Lodge River.

Little Wolf ran out of his lodge and called out to the young men: "Do not any of you shoot until the troops have fired. Let them shoot first. But do you all get your arms and horses and I will go out and meet the troops, and try to talk with them. If they kill any of us, I will be the first man killed. Then you can fight."

When they had come within sight of the camp the soldiers halted. With them were some Arapaho scouts and some Cheyenne policemen from the agency. The officers sent forward an Arapaho, whose name was Ghost Man, to talk to them. When he had come so near to the camp that his voice could be heard and quite close to Little Wolf, he called out the names of Dull Knife, Little Wolf, Wild Hog, and Tangle Hair. He said to Little Wolf: "The white men want you to go back. We are sent out to overtake you and bring you back. If you will surrender and return, they will give you your rations and will treat you well."

Little Wolf replied: "Tell them that we do not want to fight; that we will not go back. We are leaving this country. I have had no quarrel with anyone. I hold up my right hand that I do not wish to fight with the whites; but we are going to our old home to stay there."

Again the Arapaho called, repeating what he had said, and again Little Wolf answered: "No; we are going back to the country where we were born and brought up."

Presently the Arapaho went back, and Little Wolf rode toward the soldiers, wishing to talk further with them and perhaps hoping that they would go away and leave him, but before he was close enough to them to talk, a bugle sounded and the soldiers advanced and began to fire at Little Wolf. Then the Cheyennes charged out and met the troops, and for a time they fought there. So it happened that the soldiers did not get near to the Cheyenne camp. It was perhaps four o'clock when the fighting began, and they fought till dark. Then the fire of the soldiers slackened, and Little Wolf called to his young men to stop firing and go to their camp.

The soldiers remained there all night, and the Cheyennes stayed and watched them. They did not fight during the night, but now and then all through the darkness shots were exchanged. Early the next morning they began to fight, and fought until the sun began to go toward the west, when the troops all turned and went back down the river. After they had gone, Little Wolf went over to where the soldiers had been. Lying on the ground there were three dead men—a sergeant, a private soldier, and the Arapaho messenger. The troops had wounded five Cheyennes badly, but had killed none. That night they remained in camp and ate and rested, and then started on north.

After two nights more of travel other troops overtook them; a body of men mounted on gray horses. By this time they were close to the Cimarron River. The troops had either come from the north or had gone around them. At all events they charged the Indians from the north; perhaps they had come down from the Arkansas River. Of these troops there were not so many as of the others. It was in the daytime and the Cheyennes were moving when the troops were discovered. The soldiers formed a line and charged, but the Cheyennes drove them back in the direction of Dodge City, and kept on northward. The fight was a very short one, and the soldiers left them and the Indians camped not far from the scene of the fight.

The next day they went on, and about the middle of the day a large body of troops was seen coming toward them from the

Arkansas River, and with the soldiers were many citizens. There were more of these troops than in either of the other forces that had attacked them. As soon as the troops came in sight of the marching village, they charged it. There was a short fight, only a few shots, and then the bugle began to blow and the troops went away. It seemed as if they did not want to fight. Nevertheless the troops were the first to fire. In this fight they broke a Cheyenne's leg. Up to this time Little Wolf had held his men well in control, and had in most cases waited before fighting until the troops had begun to fire. He had also told his young men that he had no wish to fight with the citizens; that their fight was with the soldiers. Up to this time there had been nothing but straight up and down fighting and no depredations of any character, except the killing of some cattle and the taking of some horses, both of which might fairly enough be called military necessities.

After these last troops had gone over the hill out of sight, and the Cheyenne village had got together and begun to move on again, suddenly the troops came back, and it seemed as if there were more of them than there had been before. It was now late in the day, pretty well toward evening, and the Cheyennes went down into the little creek and made camp, and the troops went off in another direction and they too went into camp. There was no fighting. The people slept there all night.

Very early in the morning, someone went out on the high hill to watch the troops. They had broken camp and were moving toward the Cheyenne camp. It could now be seen that they had many wagons, perhaps thirty or forty, and the wagons made the force look like a large body of men. Now the Cheyennes got on their horses and fought there hard all day. It was hard fighting, not playing. They lost no men, for they did not charge. Where they had camped at first, one of the Cheyennes had said: "This is a very exposed place; let us move back into those broken hills, where we shall be better protected." They moved. After this the soldiers began to move in to get below them, and they drew up the wagons in a long line, side by side with the tail gates toward the Cheyennes. Close by the wagons the whites dismounted. They were in plain sight and all their movements could be seen. The soldiers began to advance on foot in a skir-

mish line, firing all the time. There were so many of the white
people that the Cheyennes began to get excited. But Little
Wolf spoke, saying: "Let no man fire a shot, and do not get
excited. They have plenty of ammunition; we have very little.
Lie hid and wait."

When the soldiers had come quite close to the Cheyennes,
Little Wolf ordered them to fire. They shot and killed a soldier,
and when he fell all the others fell, too. The soldiers remained
lying on the ground, but kept firing at the top of the hill constantly; only now and then receiving a shot in return.

As they looked over the hill, presently the Cheyennes saw
twenty men rise to their feet and walk away toward the wagons.
When they reached the wagons, they mounted their horses and
rode away, striking in below the wagons, so as to go around the
point of the hill the Cheyennes were on, and get behind them.
Then Little Wolf took some men around to meet the twenty
white men, and when he met them, he charged them and drove
them back to the wagons, killing one. When the soldiers saw
them coming back, they all jumped up and rushed for the wagons.
Then Dull Knife ordered the Cheyennes to charge from the top
of the hill. The soldiers all mounted and started away, and the
wagons started, the mules on a lope. As the Cheyennes were
following them, trying to overtake them, Little Wolf called out:
"Stop, stop; the grass is not very high and our horses are not
strong enough to stand a long run." All stopped and turned back.
Where the wagons had been, they found a box of cartridges which
the soldiers had not had time to put in the wagon after unload-
ing, and where the soldiers had been lying they found half a box
of cartridges. All the guns they had were forty-five calibre. They
took the ammunition and went to their camp. This was all done
quickly.

When the fight began, the women were frightened, but during
the day they built their fires, and cooked food, and fed the men
while they fought.

That evening Little Wolf said to his men: "My friends, there
are too many troops here for us to fight. We must run away.
We must move out this night and try to get away from here."
Soon after dark, therefore, they moved out. Early the next
morning, when they were near the Arkansas River, they came

upon a company of men who were killing buffalo—hide hunters. They rushed in on them and surrounded them and took eighteen buffalo cows they had killed. Little Wolf had ordered his people not to kill the men if they would give up their guns, and no one was harmed. They took all the ammunition they had, great long cartridges for these heavy guns, kegs of powder, lead, bullet moulds, and everything they had for reloading their cartridges.

After they had crossed the Arkansas River they came to a little creek and camped. Buffalo were plenty, and while the men were chasing buffalo the women were making breastworks on the knolls back from the creek, and when they had finished this they busied themselves cutting out and drying the meat. The point where they had crossed the Arkansas was a short distance above Fort Dodge.

After a time, some watchers who were out on the hills saw soldiers following their trail. The Cheyennes got together and crossed over to the little creek, camping where the breastworks had been made. The watchers told the camp everything that was happening, and the Cheyennes formed a line on the ridge where the breastworks were.

Close behind the soldiers followed their wagons. With the soldiers were some Indian scouts. When the soldiers had come close to them, the Cheyennes fired and then turned about and went to their breastworks. They saw three soldiers fall. The troops crossed the ridge the Cheyennes were on, passing over to the next creek and there corralled their wagons. They were in plain sight of the Cheyennes. When the soldiers dismounted, they marched toward the breastworks, constantly spreading out and almost encircling the camp. There were many of the troops. On the right an officer was swinging his sabre and leading on his men, and the soldiers followed him. Little Wolf said to his people, "Let them come on; lie quiet; do not fire a shot. Wait until I tell you."

The soldiers kept getting closer, walking ahead and firing as they came, but Little Wolf would not allow his men to shoot. While the soldiers were advancing and firing, the bullets were coming so thick that they were constantly knocking up the dirt about the Cheyennes, and covering them with dust. Little Wolf sat there smoking a pipe and calling out to his men, encouraging them. "Do not get excited," he said; "keep cool, and mind what I say to you." Tangle Hair, who sat next to him and watched him, said to me: "Little Wolf did not seem like a human being; he seemed like an animal—a bear. He seemed without fear."

At last the soldiers had come quite close, and some of them began to climb the hill. Then Little Wolf said: "Now men, get ready, but let every shot you fire count for a man." When the Cheyennes fired, some of the soldiers fell, and all moved back, some of them running hard. After they had moved away the fight continued until dark. Then the soldiers went back to the wagons.

That night Little Wolf again said to his people: "My friends, we must try to get through here without so much fighting, or we may all be killed. We must go faster."

That night they packed up and set out north again, moving as fast as they could and travelling two or three days without stopping, until they got to the White Man's Fork (Frenchman's Fork of the Republican in Southern Nebraska). There the troops came on them again, but there was no fight. The Cheyennes kept travelling. They did not stop at all. They went on from here without seeing any troops, sometimes travelling night and day, and sometimes travelling by night and camping during the day. They kept scouts out far behind and on either side, watching. At different places as they went along they captured fresh horses. They crossed the South Platte, about four miles west of Ogallala, then a railroad, and the North Platte. After they had crossed the North Platte River, near the mouth of White Clay Creek, they stopped to rest, and that day some soldiers came within sight of the camp, stopped and looked at them and went away.

After they had crossed the Platte River they separated, Little Wolf going on to the northern country, and Dull Knife turning west toward Fort Robinson. Just where the separation took place is not clear. Little Wolf told me that it was on the Running Water. From Tangle Hair's story I suppose it was soon after they crossed the Platte, while Big Beaver says that it was south of the South Platte River on a little stream which lies between that and Driven Creek—Punished Woman's Fork. Tangle Hair and Big Beaver remained with Dull Knife, while

Little Wolf kept on north. Little Wolf regretted the separation. He wished them all to keep together, and said to Dull Knife: "You can go that way if you wish, but I intend to work my way up to the Powder River country. I think it will be better for us all if the party is not divided." Dull Knife, however, felt that they had now got back to their own country, and that nothing bad would happen to them. Later his party surrendered to the troops without a fight. Dull Knife's following had split off from the main party, a few at a time, some by day and some by night. But before the troops captured them they had all come together again.

After the two parties had separated, Little Wolf followed down the Running Water to the Sand Hills, and there all winter they lived well on the deer, the antelope, and cattle, which were very plenty there. They kept a good lookout and sometimes saw white men—soldiers and others—but none of these ever discovered them. They left there in the early spring (March), and went on north, until they were near Powder River.

Meantime Lieutenant W. P. Clark had been sent out from Fort Keogh to try to intercept Little Wolf's party, which the troops had entirely lost. Clark was camped at the mouth of Powder River. He had with him a number of Indian scouts, Sioux and surrendered Cheyennes.

It was south of Charcoal Butte that two of Lieutenant Clark's Sioux scouts met Little Wolf. One was named Red War Bonnet; the other, a half-breed, George Farley.

Little Wolf saw that they were Government scouts, but asked them where they came from. They said: "We are from Canada, from Sitting Bull's camp;" but Little Wolf saw that they had soldier's guns, and clothing and horses, and was not deceived.

The next morning when they started to move camp, Red War Bonnet said: "I am going out to hunt antelope." He started, but as soon as he got out of rifle-shot, he ran his horse to get away. Then Little Wolf said to the half-breed: "I know you and everybody knows me. Go and tell the soldiers I am here." So George Farley rode off.

Red War Bonnet rode hard all day and all night, and reached the camp at the mouth of Powder River about noon. He reported that he had met Little Wolf, and the troops started that same day. Late that night Farley came into camp. Meantime Little Wolf had moved to a point north of the Charcoal Butte, on the west side of the Little Missouri River.

Lieutenant Clark that night called together all his scouts, and asked them what they thought he should do. He did not wish to fight with Little Wolf. Among the scouts were Two Moon and Brave Wolf, important men of the Northern Cheyennes. Brave Wolf was eager to fight, but after some talk Clark determined to send Young Spotted Wolf, White Horse, Little Horse, Hump, and Wolf Voice, the interpreter, to Little Wolf's camp with a message. He told them that when they found Little Wolf's camp, they should send back a man with the news. They started that same night.

The scouts camped in the mountains on the west side of the Little Missouri, and when they went on next morning they saw the soldiers only about six miles behind them. Before moving they climbed to the top of a high hill, to look for Little Wolf's camp. They saw nothing of it, but during the morning, as they went on, found horse tracks only a day old, and following these came to Little Wolf's camp of the night before. A short way beyond, the trail passed over hard ground, where the Indians had spread out, and here for several hours the scouts were puzzled, trying to find the tracks. At last they found the trail again, and a little later when they passed over a hill came upon some worn-out and abandoned horses. Just before dark they stopped, thinking that at night they might be able to see the fires. From here they sent back White Horse to tell Clark that the camp was close by.

They started on again, and presently Wolf Voice came upon two or three horses, and as he stood there looking at them, he saw a man wrapped in a white sheet walk by, only about thirty steps from him. Wolf Voice waited and presently when the man returned he followed him, and on a sudden found himself in the camp. The lodges were small and well hidden in the bushes. For a few moments he did not know what to do. Then he called out in a loud voice: "I am a Cheyenne," and immediately every one jumped up and began to run about to get in the horses.

In a short time Wolf Voice was taken to Little Wolf and told him that he was with the soldiers, but he did not say that they were coming and perhaps were close at hand. The next morning the Cheyennes started on, Little Wolf riding ahead, and soon two men were seen coming, and presently one called out: "I am White Hat"—Lieutenant W. P. Clark's Indian name. Behind Clark were soldiers all drawn up in line—two troops— and Clark with the interpreter sat on his horse in front of them. Little Wolf and his company moved toward the soldiers, and the packers were frightened and left their animals and hid in the brush.

Clark said: "I have prayed to God that I might find my friend Little Wolf, and now I have done so." The two shook hands, and then Clark moved into Little Wolf's camp, and that night they gave rations to the Cheyennes. Some of the Indians were very much afraid of the soldiers.

After they had camped together for three days Clark said to Little Wolf: "I come to you as a friend; I want you people to turn over your arms and to go with me to Fort Keogh." Because of his friendship for Clark, Little Wolf said: "It is well; we will go with you wherever you say."

There the Cheyennes gave up their arms and all started for Fort Keogh. They moved on all together, soldiers and Indians, as far as the mouth of Powder River, where there was a large camp of troops. The Cheyennes camped there with them, and not long afterward moved on up the Yellowstone to Fort Keogh.

Soon after they reached there General Miles came out to their camp and shook hands with Little Wolf and said to him: "You and I have been fighting each other for a long time" (meaning the Indians and the white men); "now, to-day, we meet and shake hands, and will always be friends. I want you to give me all your horses." Little Wolf told his people to drive in all their horses and turn them over to General Miles, and they did so, giving him every horse they had.

Soon after this General Miles sent for Little Wolf and said to him: "Now we have made a peace, and I should like to have you and your men enlist with me as soldiers, and help me to fight other tribes."

Little Wolf replied: "My friend, I have been travelling and fighting for a long time now, and I am tired. I do not like to do this at present."

"Well," said General Miles, "think the matter over and see how you feel about it."

Little Wolf did so and talked about it with his young men. A few days later General Miles again sent for him, and said to him: "Why do you not want to be a soldier? I have heard that you and your people are great fighting men. I have heard of your long journey up here; how you fought all the way through. Now I want you to enlist and help me whip the Sioux tribe, and take them and bring them all in here so that I may make with them a peace such as you have made."

Little Wolf yielded. He and all the young men that were with him enlisted.

During their march north the Cheyennes killed no citizens until after a cowboy had killed one of their young men who was off to one side. After that they killed some people, but against Little Wolf's order. His instructions from the first were that they were to fight only those who attacked them, and always to let the soldiers shoot first. Little Wolf said: "We tried to avoid the settlements as much as possible. We did not want to be seen or known of. I often harangued my young men, telling them not to kill citizens, but to let them alone. I told them that they should kill all the soldiers that they could, for these were trying to kill us, but not to trouble the citizens. I know they killed some citizens, but I think not many. They did not tell me much of what they did, because they knew I would not like it."

XXX

THE FORT ROBINSON OUTBREAK

1879

VERY different from the fortunes of Little Wolf and his party were those of Dull Knife.

After the escaping Cheyennes had crossed the Platte River, Dull Knife went about through the camp haranguing and saying: "Now we have again reached our own ground, and from this time forth we will no more fight or harm any white people." Dull Knife declared that he was going straight to Red Cloud Agency, where he believed he and his people would be permitted to remain. He did not know that Red Cloud Agency had been discontinued.

As they were marching toward where Red Cloud Agency had been, about half-way between White River and a little branch of the Running Water, as the Cheyennes were going over a hill October 23, 1878, they saw coming over another hill some soldiers who went down to the same stream that they intended to camp on. The meeting between the soldiers and the Indians was pure accident. When the troops were discovered Dull Knife spoke to his young men, reminding them of what he had said after they crossed the Platte River, and they kept on to a wide flat and camped. When the Indians came close to them the soldiers who were approaching fell in line, as if to fight, but Dull Knife told his head men to go toward the soldiers, and they met and shook hands. To the officer in command—Captain Johnson, Third Cavalry—Dull Knife said: "We have come back home to go back to our old agency; you can return at once. We shall go to the agency as soon as we can get there." The soldiers turned about and marched back, and the Cheyennes followed them. The Indians camped on the stream and the soldiers camped near its head.

At daylight next morning the Indians moved out and found that the soldiers had already gone. When they reached the soldiers' camp they found there two boxes of hard bread, left, as they supposed, for their use, and they opened the boxes and divided the food among the people. Following the trail made by the soldiers, they crossed over to Chadron Creek, and late that night camped near the soldiers in a bend of the stream pointed out by the officers. While they were unpacking their loads the soldiers, many of whom still had saddles on their horses, rounded up the Indian ponies and drove them off to one side. After these had been taken away, and while the women were putting up the lodges, some of the people were called over to the soldiers' camp and were given rations, including sugar and coffee. It was supposed by the Indians that the soldiers must have sent out runners calling for more troops, for all through the night they could hear soldiers marching in, and when day came they found that the soldiers were camping all about them. The troops had brought big guns which stood on the hill overlooking the camp. With the soldiers who had come in during the night were some Sioux, and some of them came over and talked with the Cheyennes and said to them: "Our agency used to be here, but now it is farther down the stream, but not far."

That morning after they had eaten, the soldiers asked them to give up their arms and they did so. The Indians brought their old guns and piled them together, but some guns and pistols were hidden under the blankets and in the women's clothing. Bows and butcher-knives were not taken from them. The men were searched, but not the women. The wife of Black Bear, who was one of the prisoners confined in the barracks at Fort Robinson, said to me: "I had a carbine hanging down my back."

For ten days they remained in that camp, and during this time there was much debate as to where the Indians should go. The officer in command wished to take them to Fort Robinson, while the Indians wished to go to the agency of which the Sioux had spoken to them. The Indians were beginning to get angry, and so were the soldiers. Neither side would yield. Nearly every night they could hear wagons coming in, and each morning there seemed to be more troops. The soldiers began to throw up breastworks and the Indians to dig rifle-pits. But they had only five guns. On the tenth day it looked as if there would be a fight.

During all this time one of the officers was talking to them. He kept saying: "We just want you to come into the post and surrender there. Then you shall have plenty of rations and we intend to send you down to the agency." This was said to them so often that at last they believed it.

After they had agreed to surrender, word must have been sent to the fort, for wagons came down and in them they put the women and children. The snow was quite deep. The wagons started and the men marched behind. After a time the men were told to get into the wagons, and they rode with the women and children. There were soldiers in front and soldiers behind, and two files of soldiers marched on either side of the wagon-train. They kept the wagons well closed up together.

Presently the train reached the old abandoned Red Cloud Agency and then crossed a little creek, in which the snow lay deep. As they were crossing the stream a body of the Sioux scouts overtook them and crowded in between the wagons and the soldiers who were following them. The snowdrifts were so deep that the soldiers could not cross the stream close to the wagons, and were obliged to swing out on either side. Big Beaver, sitting on the end of a wagon, saw Bull Hump's wife roll up in a ball, and as the wagon crossed the creek throw herself out of the wagon into the deep snow. The Sioux scouts at once got around her and took her off with them and did not report it; so she escaped. The Sioux moved off to one side of the road so that the soldiers who were following the wagons could pass.

It was about sundown when they reached Fort Robinson, and a long building was pointed out as the place where they were to remain. When they entered the building, they found that food was being cooked. The lamps were lighted, and they were counted. A list was made of those counted; and the names of the leading men were asked for and written down. These head men and chiefs were Dull Knife, Bull Hump, Wild Hog, Tangle Hair, and Strong Left Hand.

The next day after breakfast some officers came in and had a talk with them; and with the officers were some of the Sioux and Bull Hump's wife, now with her hair braided like a man, dressed and acting as a Sioux scout.

There was then no Cheyenne interpreter at Fort Robinson,

and all the talking had to be done through two interpreters. Tangle Hair talked both Sioux and Cheyenne. He told the interpreter in Sioux what the Cheyenne said, and the interpreter told it in English to the commanding officer.

The commanding officer said to Dull Knife: "Now, the fighting is over. We are friendly with one another. You must stay here for three months before the Government will decide whether to send you south or to send you to the Sioux. While you are here nothing bad will happen to you, but you must stay for three months. You will have the freedom of the post and may even go off into the mountains, but each night at supper time you must be here. If one man of you all deserts or runs away, you will not be treated like this any longer. You will all be held responsible for him."

Dull Knife rose to his feet and spoke to his people, telling them to do as they were told. He said: "We are back on our own ground, and have stopped fighting. We have found the place we started to come to."

Things went on in this way for some time, and the people seemed contented. They had a good time, plenty to eat and nothing to fear. Old people used to go down to the stream and gather red-willow bark, and young people would go up on the mountains, but all were back by supper time. They used to have dances in the barracks. Sometimes the soldiers would go to the store and buy food for the next dance, and sometimes they gave presents of money to the girls they used to dance with, so that the girls might buy ornaments. For about two months they had a fine time. No people could have been better treated than they were. They thought their troubles were over.

During this period some of the Cheyennes went out as scouts, and Tangle Hair told me that he was sometimes called out, given a horse, and sent to ride over the country looking for trails, to see if any people had passed by.

One day, at the end of two months, the cook found a cup too many. A man was gone. They looked about to see who was absent, and found it was Bull Hump. His wife was at the Pine Ridge Agency, and he had gone to join her. The cook did not report the absence of Bull Hump until he had been away over three meals. When he reported it, the officers investigated and found that he had gone. So they counted the people over again and took away their liberty and locked them up. During the time the people had their liberty, no guards had been set over them, but after Bull Hump went they were locked in and sentries were put about the building. Two or three days later Bull Hump was brought back.

About this time, James Rowland, who was living with his father, at Pine Ridge, went to Fort Robinson to do the interpreting for the Cheyennes.

Now the officers began to persuade the Indians to go back south, but Dull Knife, answering for his people, refused, always saying that they would not go south. "We will not go there to live. That is not a healthful country, and if we should stay there we would all die. We do not wish to go back there, and we will not go."

The officers continued to urge them to consent, but Dull Knife did not waver. He said: "No, I am here on my own ground, and I will never go back. You may kill me here; but you cannot make me go back."

For some days the commanding officer kept asking them to agree to go south, but when Captain Wessels found that they could not be moved, their rations were stopped, and they began literally to starve. In behalf of the commanding officer, it must be said that he tried to induce the women and children to come out of the barracks, leaving the men in there alone, but the young men would not consent to such separation. Wild Hog, Crow, and Strong Left Hand were induced to come out, and were taken into the guard-house, seized, and at least one of them put in irons. When the soldiers seized Wild Hog he drew his butcher-knife. It was said that he tried to kill the soldier and also that he tried to commit suicide. At all events, he cut himself and a man. While the soldiers were struggling with Wild Hog, Strong Left Hand ran out of the door and back to the barracks, and called out to those within: "They have got Wild Hog; they are going to handcuff him." All the young men in the barracks said: "Well, we must fight." They declared war that afternoon, and from that time forth they had no good answers to give to those who spoke to them. The young men ordered the wives of Wild Hog and Crow and their children and some of the old women out of the building, but Wild Hog's older son did not go out, and one of his daughters remained with her brother.

After the women were taken out, the soldiers gave them no food and no water and no fuel. It was winter and bitterly cold. After Captain Wessels had begun to starve them, Dull Knife still said: "You can starve us if you like, but you cannot make us go south." Some of the Indians say that for eight days they had neither food nor water, but others say that they had no food for five days, and no water for three days. During this time all that they had to eat was such scraps as had been left over from previous meals. The little children used to try to slip out by the sentries to get water or snow, but they were always turned back. They had scraped away all the snow that had collected on the window-ledges. A little later the commanding officer had another talk, telling them that they must go south, but Dull Knife was firm. "We will not go," he said. "The only way to get us there is to come in here with clubs and knock us on the head, and drag us out and take us down there dead. We have nothing to defend ourselves with, and if you want to you can come here with clubs and kill us like dogs."

The Indians were now sullen and desperate and walked up and down in their prison, waiting for death. During these days of starvation some of them acted like a lot of drunken people. A young man would say: "I want to jump out now and be killed." Then the others would hold him and not let him do it. Others used to stand up and make speeches, saying: "We might as well be killed outside as starve here in this house." The women were just as brave as the men.

They told the interpreter not to come in among them, and not to let any one else come in, for they would kill whoever came. A Cheyenne, then living at Pine Ridge, who went into the building to talk to them, was attacked and would have been killed except for the intervention of a special friend. They talked through the window to the interpreter, telling him that they expected to die there and they hoped soon. A special friend of the interpreter—a young man named Bird—talked with him, and Rowland tried to persuade him to come out and go to the commanding officer, for he thought that perhaps he could induce Captain Wessels to set Bird free. The young man said: "No, I will stay here and die with the tribe."

In the afternoon of January 9, 1879, Little Shield, a soldier chief, said to the others: "Now, dress up and put on your best clothing. We will all die together." They had been saying to each other: "We will never go out and give up to these people to be taken back to the country we ran away from. We have given up our horses and our arms, and everything that we have, and now they are starving us to death. We have been without food and fire for seven days; we may as well die here as be taken back south and die there." As they kept thinking about this, and talking to each other, they said: "It is true that we must die, but we will not die shut up here like dogs; we will die on the prairie; we will die fighting." They all painted their faces, and put on their best clothing and their fancy moccasins, taking little precaution against the cold, though they were without fire and the mercury stood at zero.

The five guns which they had saved had been hidden under the floor, and it is believed that they had eleven pistols with some ammunition. Most of these arms had been taken to pieces. The barrels and stocks of the rifles and the frames of the six-shooters, with the ammunition, had been hidden under the women's clothing, but the small parts of the arms were distributed among the children as ornaments. The little things wore, one a trigger, another a hammer, and another a screw or a spring tied to the wrist or about the neck or in the hair. Almost every child had such an ornament. These were noticed, of course, but no special attention was paid to them. After the people were shut up they put the arms together, took up a board in the floor under the heating stove and there concealed the weapons.

From their actions during this day it was suspected that before long the Cheyennes would do something desperate, and the commanding officer put a chain-guard about the building. The beats of these sentries crossed each other, that is to say, a sentry's beat did not end when he came to the end of the beat of the man next to him, but each one's beat overlapped those of the two on either side of him.

Toward sunset, after all the Indians had put on their best clothing, they went about and kissed each other for the last time. Then, after sundown, a young man stood at each window. Under the windows they piled up their saddles, parfleches, and other things, so that all could easily step out of the window. Little Shield sat in the north window and other men at the other windows, the purpose being to shoot the guards. Little Shield was the first man who fired. As he fired the shot he knocked out the window-sash, and the others did the same, and then the people all jumped out of the windows. The wife of Black Bear was one of the first to get out.

Five or six inches of snow covered the ground; there was not a cloud in the sky; the moon was full, and it was nearly as bright as day. The dwellers at the fort rushed to their doors to learn what was happening, saw the crowd of fugitives streaming across the post toward the creek, heard the shooting of the soldiers, and saw the people drop on the snow—here a child, there a man, then a woman. To the Indians looking back, the soldiers who rushed out of the barracks seemed all in white. Most of them had jumped out of bed, and were in their underclothes.

Before they left the barracks, the Indians had tied on their blankets so as to leave the hands free. A blanket was tied about the neck and another about the waist.

When the Indians jumped out of the windows they all rushed for the stream, and most of them on reaching it threw themselves down to drink. The bullets were flying fast. Many of them drank too much and afterward could hardly run. They all raced up the valley, cutting across the bends of the creek and crossing it, and frequently breaking through the ice, so that most of them were wet. The night was very cold but still. After they had gone a little way they were beginning to scatter; some were getting tired and falling behind, and some, longer-winded and with no babies to carry, were gaining on the others. It was hard to run in frozen clothing, and besides that they had starved so long that they had not much strength. The firing was continual; it did not stop. A woman said to me: "Some people who were ahead of me got to the top of the hill, but I got out of breath and stopped by a big tree with some other women. One of these was the wife of White Antelope. She was already wounded and White Antelope was carrying the baby. When the soldiers got up close, White Antelope rushed back on them with his knife and fought for a little while and was killed. When the soldiers had come up close, I was shot in the back and in the side of the head and knocked senseless, and knew nothing after that. Two other women were killed there."

Some of the Indians did not get very far. Old Sitting Man, who, during the march from the south, had been wounded in the leg, jumped from a window, and when he struck the ground the leg broke again and he had to sit there. A soldier ran up to him and put the muzzle of a rifle against his head and fired, and the top of his head flew off. Later he was seen lying there with the top of his skull beside him in one place, and all his brains on the snow in another place.

Enfeebled by starvation and encumbered by women and children, the Indians could not go fast, and the soldiers were soon close upon them. A man jumped on a horse and rode after the soldiers. The dead scattered on the snow—most of them the women and children who were least swift of foot—made a trail easy to follow. After fugitives and pursuers had turned up into the hills, this man came upon a group of five women lying under some pines, all apparently dead except Dull Knife's daughter, who with her back against a tree trunk was just drawing her last breath. He tried to talk to her, but she was too far gone to speak aloud. On her back she had a little child—not her own—shot, and lying about were two or three other children, all of them dead. These women had run, carrying their babies, until they were exhausted and had then sat down here to rest and get their breath, and had been overtaken by the soldiers and killed as they sat.

Between the time of the outbreak and daylight sixty-five captives, many of them wounded, were brought into the post. Next morning the commanding officer sent out a detail of soldiers with six mule teams to bring in the dead. They found about fifty, which were brought in and unloaded like logs. The soldiers got into the full wagons and standing on the bodies took the frozen corpses by heads and feet and tossed them to the ground. After a wagon was partly unloaded, men standing on the ground reached in, took the bodies by the feet or head, dragged them out and let them drop to the ground.

A boy thirteen or fourteen years old, who is still living, had the following experience:

One group of people was ahead of the main body and the soldiers who had saddled up, in going around on horseback, came in between the leading party and those behind them. I did not understand the words of the troop commander, but he kept calling out orders and the troops went by without firing a shot at us. They made a circle and came back in front of us and dismounted, and all the Indians dropped to the ground. Just as the people dropped the troops fired on them. A good many were killed here, but some young men jumped up and ran to and through the line of the soldiers who were standing ten or twelve feet apart and so escaped. I was not hit by bullets, but the powder from a close shot had burned me.

After running a hundred yards we came to some great sandstone bluffs, in which there were large holes, and into these holes we crept. We could hear the women and children crying and at last the shooting stopped. Some time after it stopped, wagons were heard coming. In the wagons they must have loaded up all who were left alive, for as they went back, women could be heard crying. After this we heard the wagons coming back, and again going away, taking the dead.

Next morning at daybreak we saw the soldiers marching in the direction of the people who had gone on beyond, but only about a mile farther. When the soldiers came up with them we could hear the guns and the yelling. They fought there until sundown, and at that time a troop of cavalry came to where we were hidden. There were five of us and we had one gun and one pistol. The troops began to shoot into the holes where we were and kept shooting, and presently all had been killed except me. When I looked about and saw that every one of my friends was dead, I did not know what to do. I waited and at length the soldiers stopped firing.

I thought then that I might as well go out and be killed as stay in there, and I walked out of the hole in which I had been hidden and went toward the soldiers. A white man called out something and no one fired at me. The officer rode toward me and drew his sabre, but did not strike me with it. When the officer had come close to me he reached out his hand and I stretched out my hand, and we shook hands. The officer called up his soldiers and they surrounded me. I was not tied up, but was helped up behind a soldier on his horse and taken into the post.

The day that the bodies were brought in, Captain Wessels went into the prison and said to the captives: "Now, will you go south?"

A girl who was badly wounded in the foot stood up, supporting herself against the wall, and said: "No, we will not go back; we will die rather. You have killed most of us, why do you not go ahead now and finish the work?"

A little company of fifteen, men, women and children, had gotten away together and were followed up by the troops and overtaken. They were in the Bad Lands and were caught up with and fought with about every other day. So long as they kept in the hills, it is said that they had no trouble in holding off the four troops of cavalry that pursued them, but they were weak and starving and wanted to get to Pine Ridge, where there were Indians who would feed and hide them, and they started down into the plains country to go there. The snow had disappeared but the weather had grown warm, so that the ground was soft and they could be trailed. They were followed. They did not know where the Pine Ridge Agency was, for it had been established after they had been sent south. They had sixty miles to go. On the plain they were overtaken and took refuge in an old buffalo wallow. Here the four troops of cavalry surrounded them, one at each angle of a square. The two troops which were nearly opposite each other kept up a continuous fire on the hole, while the two other troops at frequent intervals charged close up to it from opposite sides. The fire was so withering that a head could not be shown. The only way the Indians could shoot was to reach up a hand and fire gun or pistol without aim. The four troops of cavalry fought these people all day, and killed them all except three women, one of whom was wounded.

The first time the troops overtook these fifteen people, Captain Wessels wished to try to induce them to surrender. He asked Rowland, the interpreter, if he would go out with him and talk. Rowland said: "I don't much like to do this, captain. These people are desperate; they have not had anything to eat for a week, and if we get close enough to talk with them they are pretty sure to shoot us."

Captain Wessels said to him rather contemptuously: "Are you afraid?"

"Well, yes, I am afraid," said Rowland, "but if you want me to, I will go"; and go he did. He crept up as close as possible to the hole the Indians were hidden in, without showing himself, and Captain Wessels followed. Then Rowland stepped out on the hill and in plain sight, and called out to the Cheyennes that the commanding officer wanted them to give themselves up. Captain Wessels, who was behind Rowland, had just put his head up over the hill so that he could look by him, but had not exposed his body. The reply to Rowland's call was a bullet, which seemed to pass between the interpreter and the head of the commanding officer. Captain Wessels ducked down, lost his footing, rolled down the hill and ran off as fast as he could toward the troops. Rowland called out to him, asking if he did not want to talk any more. His reply was: "Come on," and the interpreter was glad to follow him.

At the time of the outbreak from the barracks an opportunity was given to Tangle Hair to come out. An officer told him that if he and his family wished to leave the barracks, they would put him for a time in another place and then send him to Pine Ridge Agency. He was then the chief of the Dog Soldiers, and on the way north had always led the march of the camp while the young men scattered out over the country.

When this suggestion was made, the young men threatened his life if Tangle Hair should attempt to leave the house. Little Shield, who did all the talking, said of him to the others: "This man cannot go out; he owns us and can do what he likes with us," referring, of course, to his chieftainship of this soldier band and to his being principal fighting man of the tribe.

The night they jumped out of the window Tangle Hair was the first to jump out of his window, and four men were behind him —among them Blacksmith and Noisy Walking. The five were armed, and stopped to fight off the soldiers until the women and children got started to run toward the hills. All five were soon shot down. Tangle Hair dragged himself to some soldiers' quarters, where the soldiers were sitting, and they took him in and sent for a doctor and had his wounds dressed. Before he had been there very long, wounded women began to be brought in.

Dull Knife,[1] his wife and son, and son's wife and child, together with Red Bird, turned off from the course the Indians were keeping before most of the Cheyennes turned up into the hills. They found a great hole in the rocks and hid there. The soldiers lost their trail and did not find them. They remained there for ten days and almost starved to death. Then Dull Knife and his family set out for Pine Ridge Agency and after eighteen days' wandering, travelling at night, eating their moccasins, and such roots as they could find, and some sinew which one of the women had, came to the house of William Rowland, the interpreter at Pine Ridge, and told the story of their suffering.

[1] Dull Knife—this name is the translation of his Sioux name; his Cheyenne name is Morning Star, Wŏ′hē hĭv′.

Red Bird, who was wounded, remained in the hole, but reached Pine Ridge Agency later. Though only a boy, he still carried on his back the ancient shield given him that night just before the outbreak by his uncle, who had received it many years before from his father.[1]

Of about one hundred and fifty Cheyennes who had been confined in the barracks up to this time, sixty-four were killed in the outbreak, about fifty-eight were sent to Pine Ridge, about twenty to the south, while eight or ten were never again heard of, and no doubt were killed or starved to death in the hills. Those who were left alive drifted up to Fort Keogh, or in later years were transferred to the Tongue River Indian Reservation, where some of them are living to-day. Among these are many cripples who bear the scars of wounds received at Fort Robinson.

Dull Knife died about 1883, and is buried on a high butte near the valley of the Rosebud River. Little Wolf lived on the Tongue River Indian Reservation in Montana for nearly thirty years. He grew old and blind and was poor and helpless, but he was a great man to the end.

[1] This shield afterward came into my possession, and is now on exhibition at the American Museum of Natural History in New York.

XXXI

SCOUTING FOR THE SOLDIERS

AFTER the surrender of the Northern Cheyennes to General Miles, practically all the young and middle-aged men enlisted as scouts. They were furnished with horses, arms, and ammunition, and rendered effective service not only in fighting the still hostile Sioux, but even in locating and fighting with those camps of their own people that had not yet surrendered. This was not the first time the Cheyennes had served as scouts for the troops, for in 1876 some of them had served under General Crook and taken part in the fight in which Dull Knife's village was destroyed.

The Cheyennes enjoyed the service, and made excellent scouts. Fully trusted and with absolute freedom to go and come, they were faithful to their duties. One of them once said to me: "My friend, I was a prisoner of war for four years, and all the time was fighting for the man who had captured me."

From 1877 to 1880 the northern country was still more or less overrun by Indians who were hostile, and carrying on war— killing white people or taking horses whenever the opportunity offered. These small groups were not large enough to fight with any body of troops, but they were well provided with horses, knew the country thoroughly, and were skilful in misleading the troops, or, when too closely followed up, in concealing their own trail.

The pursuit of such people was hard but fascinating work. Almost everyone enjoys hunting, but the hunting of men, when hunter and hunted are equally acute, watchful, and brave, possesses peculiar attractions.

Of the men who took part in such scouting some of the younger ones are still alive, and the memory of these chases and battles remains vivid. Told in simple Indian fashion, their stories possess a very great interest for people who knew something of the old wild days. Not long ago such a tale—of one of the little Indian fights in the northern country—was told me by Willis Rowland, who took part in it. He is an educated half-breed, and at the time was seventeen or eighteen years old.

On Beaver Creek, about thirty-five miles from Glendive, Montana, there was a camp of four companies of cavalry, commanded by Captain Bell. To this camp, in the summer of 1880, had been assigned three Cheyenne Indians—prisoners of war who were acting as scouts—Shell, Howling Wolf, Big-Footed Bull— and Willis Rowland, who acted as scout and interpreter. He was the only one who could speak English.

In August news was received that a stage-driver had been killed by Indians near the head of Cabin Creek, and Captain Bell sent out two or three parties to scout the country, and secure information about the affair. The news reached the camp a day or two after the driver had been killed, and for this reason it seemed unlikely that those who had made the attack would be found. Willis Rowland tells what happened to the scouting party that he was with:

With eight soldiers, we four scouts were sent out from Beaver Creek, and crossed over—sixty miles—to the head of Cabin Creek. A lieutenant with twenty men was to have gone up Cabin Creek from Glendive to meet us at the stage station, but did not reach there that night.

When we reached the mail station, we asked the keeper where it was that the stage-driver had been killed three or four days before. He told us to go on to the next station, and we went twenty miles along the stage road to another station, and there met two Sioux scouts and twelve soldiers. There was no officer with them. These men said that they had found the body of the stage-driver; but the Sioux who had killed him were gone, and they could not find the trail.

Howling Wolf said to me: "You tell our sergeant that these Sioux are lying. They are hiding the trail. We ought to keep on further, and ourselves try to find it and follow it up." The other party of soldiers went back, following the road we had just passed over, and we kept on our way about five miles, and then turned off to the right toward the head of a little ravine. Shell had said: "We had best turn off to those badlands there—at the edge of the Rattlesnake Butte. If any Indians have done mischief here, they are pretty sure to have gone toward those hills."

About a mile beyond where we left the road, Shell said to me: "Go back now and tell the sergeant to keep his men half a mile behind us, while we look for the trail."

I gave the message to the sergeant, who was about fifty yards behind us, and he said that he would keep back, but told me to notify him if any sign was found.

When I returned to Shell, he said to me: "You two young men go off to the left, and Howling Wolf to the right, and I will go straight ahead. When you reach that point half a mile further on and Howling Wolf gets to that other point, turn and cross each other and I will go straight ahead." Before us was a wide flat on which grew some sage-brush, but with wide, bare spots, where tracks could easily be seen.

"If you see a track," Shell went on, "do not call, but make a sign. We must watch one another."

We had gone only a quarter of a mile, when Howling Wolf stopped and began to ride in a circle to call us to him. We all went over to where he was.

He said: "I have found a track, but it is a mule track."

"That is good," said Shell, "it will be easy to follow." To me he said: "Go back and tell the sergeant that here, where we can see well and the trail is easy to follow, we shall go along on a lope." They waited until I came back, and then Shell had us spread out in a line abreast and about twenty-five yards apart, the two younger men on his left and Howling Wolf on his right.

"When I lose the track," he said, "I will stop and you boys then ride across and look for it."

We followed the trail at a lope and trot for ten miles, and lost it only once. Presently we came close to a big hill, and Shell said: "Let us stop here and take a look through the field-glasses from the top of this hill. Besides that our horses will have a chance to rest."

We rode nearly to the top of the hill and dismounted and sat down, and Howling Wolf went on foot to the top of the hill to look. Everywhere there were buffalo and all were quiet and unfrightened. This seemed a sure sign that no one had gone by lately. We had passed many scattered horse tracks —fifteen or sixteen animals—but these had not joined the mule tracks.

Just after we had turned off the mule trail to go to the top of the hill, we two boys thought we heard a shot far off, but the older men had not heard it and thought we were mistaken. On the hill, however, a shot was heard by all four, and Howling Wolf said: "The boys were right; yet the buffalo are all quiet."

We could see nothing from the hilltop and were thinking of going back to our horses, but before we started Howling Wolf took a last look. He looked for a long time, and then said: "I have discovered something. It looks like two people, and there seems to be something on the ground in front of them." He handed the glass to Shell, who, after he had looked, said: "To me it looks like two people butchering an animal." He gave the glasses to me. What I saw looked like two people on the ground with horses a few feet from them and the figures seemed to be bending over what was on the ground.

Shell said to me: "Go back and tell the sergeant what we have seen."

"Let us wait a little while," I replied. "If they are people, it will not take them long to cut up that animal, and when we see them ride away we shall know more."

Howling Wolf kept watching with the glasses, and presently said: "We must stay here and watch. I think they are camped down in this creek not far from us. Just now I saw some horses come up out of it on a little point."

We all crept up and could see the horses with the naked eye. It was now getting late in the afternoon. When the soldiers had reached the foot of the hill we were on, they stopped and dismounted.

Howling Wolf was watching all the time and reporting to us what he saw. He said: "Those two men have left the place; now they have gone up on the ridge; they are coming this way; now they have gone out of sight. They are going to the creek and will follow it down. When they do that we can go down from the hill."

We had been travelling south and the little creek spoken of runs into the Little Missouri River. After a time we left the hill and went down to the sergeant. By Shell's direction I told him that we must go up on a ridge half a mile to the east of where we were and there leave our packs and lighten up the loads on our saddles for the pursuit. The sergeant said: "Now you scouts must lay the plans how to get the Indians. I will follow and support you." Our horses were tired for we had come a long way that day.

We had to go about three miles before coming to the little creek which joined the one on which the enemy were camped. We struck it above where the Sioux were and followed down the stream at a run. We had not seen the Sioux nor anything to show us how many of them there were. Before we reached the mouth of the side creek Howling Wolf rode off a hundred yards to a little rise and looked over it. He made signs to us that he could see the two men going down into the creek, and as soon as they were out of sight he signed to us to go ahead. He pointed to a ridge three-quarters of a mile away, and said: "They have just gone over that ridge; we had best ride fast and get there." As we went, it seemed to me that the horses made an unusual amount of noise as they ran. When we reached the ridge we stopped, and Howling Wolf rode half-way up and dismounted and walked to the top. When he had looked over, he signed: "They are going up the hill—they have reached the top—they have gone over it." He came down to his horse and motioned us forward, and I heard him tell Shell what he had seen. There were four Sioux and they had a bunch of horses. Two of them seemed to have stopped on the creek and held the horses, while two had gone off to kill a buffalo.

We went over the hill and rode across a flat half a mile wide. At the next ridge, when Howling Wolf looked, he signed at once: "All dismount." We did so and rushed up to him. There were the four Sioux about two hundred and fifty or three hundred yards off. One was riding ahead on a little mule; following him came the horses and three Sioux rode behind.

We began to shoot at once. The first man hit was the one on the mule. His leg was broken and he fell off his animal. The other three ran about a hundred yards and passed over the hill and out of sight. Their horses stampeded.

We ran back to our horses and mounted to follow the three Sioux. Howling Wolf and Big-Footed Bull set out after the Sioux horses, while Shell and the soldiers and I went after the Sioux. We had gone half a mile when we saw a Sioux. He turned about and rode toward us. When I came to the top of the hill he was only about fifty yards off. At first I did not see him and Shell pulled me back. Nevertheless, I rode up on the hill and we all fired and knocked the man off his horse. A little farther on we came to another Sioux who was badly wounded, and we killed him. He had an old muzzle-loading rifle, not loaded. The Sioux had been shooting, and this man was perhaps too weak from his wounds to reload his gun. The fourth Sioux ran for a long way and we shot at him as far as we could see him. Presently he rode up on a point and sat looking at us and then turned and rode back toward us and around a point to where the first man killed lay, and then he rode off. He had perhaps come back to get the dead man's gun, a good Winchester rifle. We had dismounted and gone down into a ravine to kill the second Sioux and now had to run back to our horses, and before we had mounted the fourth man was nearly half a mile away. Just as we reached the first man killed, Howling Wolf returned to us with the horses. Four of them carried packs and in the packs were bundles of letters and of newspapers, showing that these were the men who had killed the stage-driver. We turned the mail over to the sergeant.

We now rode back to where our packs were, and when we reached them Shell said: "Let us leave these soldiers and go home and have a dance over our scalps."

It was about four o'clock when we started over toward Cabin Creek. There, near the stage station, we met the lieutenant and twenty soldiers, who had arranged to meet us there the day before. He scolded us for not waiting for him and called up the sergeant and severely reprimanded him.

That night the Cheyenne Indians went home, but said that they would wait half a day for me on Powder River. I spoke to the sergeant that night and he advised me to start early in the morning, because the lieutenant had threatened to make me walk the next day. I started early and followed the stage road to Keogh.

These scouts under General Miles did such excellent work that the idea occurred to Lieutenant E. W. Casey to get authority to enlist a company of scouts who should be subjected to the discipline of soldiers—drilled so that they might be effective not only as scouts, but also as a military body. The scouts enlisted by General Miles had not been under any special discipline. Lieutenant Casey enlisted such a company of scouts in the winter of 1889–90. Many of the young men were glad to serve as soldiers, for life on the reservation was monotonous, and the pay would be very welcome.

For a time the company lived in tents, and then began to get out logs in the mountains and build quarters for themselves not far from Fort Keogh. Lieutenant Casey was in command of the scouts, and Lieutenant Getty was his lieutenant. William

Rowland was the interpreter, and his son Willis was first sergeant of the company.

In the summer of 1890 I stopped at Fort Keogh to see Lieutenant Casey, who many years before had been my schoolmate. Unluckily, as he was up in the mountains getting out timber, I missed him, but I saw his scouts and was interested in the promise they gave of making an excellent body of soldiers. The same year Lieutenant—now Colonel—Homer W. Wheeler enlisted a company of soldiers from the Southern Cheyennes and Arapahoes.

In the autumn of 1890, when the Ghost Dance excitement was at its height and collisions between the Sioux and the troops had already taken place, Lieutenant Casey's troop of Cheyennes was called out and marched to the scene of the trouble. Here a little later Casey was shot from behind by a young Sioux Indian named Plenty of Horses after he had talked pleasantly with the young man, had shaken hands with him, and turned his horse to ride away. His body was recovered by the scouts, who were devoted to him.

This was the last fighting done by the Cheyenne Indians. On two or three occasions during the last twenty-five years men moved by one motive or another have killed white men on the Tongue River Indian Reservation, and a few years ago the local newspapers at times printed reports of outbreaks by the Cheyennes which never took place. Considering the conditions of reservation life and the number of the people, there is, perhaps, less crime among the Cheyennes than in any community of the same size in the United States.

The fighting days of the Cheyennes have passed. They are now learning the difficult lesson of civilization and work, but the lesson of thrift they have as yet hardly begun to learn. This we may hope will come later.

If the Indian Bureau should adopt a broad and definitely settled policy—one sufficiently elastic to be adaptable to the needs of each of the different Indian reservations—the progress of the race toward civilization would be hastened; but such a policy cannot be thought out and set on foot without preparation. Before it could be outlined, the Bureau would require a vast amount of information as to conditions on most reservations, which it now absolutely lacks and which it would take a long time to get together.   Even if such a policy were adopted, it seems quite likely that at the end of four years it would be changed again, and the new officials—as their predecessors have so often done—would begin to tear down what the previous administration had built up, and a new Indian Commissioner would try out his theories on these helpless people.   There is little hope of any rapid advance of the Indians under present conditions. Yet, unconsciously, they are changing, and will continue to change, and the time is coming, perhaps sooner than we think, when the Indians will be a component and useful part of the population of the country.

INDEX

[The tribal name Cheyenne, which appears on almost every page, is not indexed.]

A

Abert, Lieutenant J. W., 74, 118.
Adobe walls, 71, 308.
Alcohol, effect of, 94.
Algonquian family, 1.
Alights on the Cloud, 71; death of, 75, 77.
Allison, 156.
Alma, Kansas, 218.
American Anthropologist, 67, 120.
American Horse (Cheyenne), 340.
American Horse (Sioux), 346.
American Museum of Natural History, New York, 411.
Ammunition of Indians, 340.
Anadakos, 71.
Anadarko, 122, 310.
Anderson, Major, 218.
Andrus, Colonel E. P., vi.
Angry, 10.
Ankle (Big Ankle), 379.
Antelope Hills, 71, 290.
Antelope Pit River, 33, 194.
Antelope skin, 133.
Anthony, Major Scott, 146, 155, 159, 162.
Aorta men, 58.
Apaches, 4, 14, 35, 43, 45, 55, 58, 59, 60, 61, 62, 64, 69, 259, 260, 265.
Apaches, Mountain, 309.
Apaches, Prairie, 34, 98, 116.
Appointment of Joint Committee of Congress, 170.
Appropriation to carry out treaty, 287.
Arapahoes, 3, 5, 14, 18, 19, 29, 30, 31, 34, 35, 40, 43, 45, 48, 49, 51, 52, 55, 56, 57, 59, 61, 80, 82, 83, 93, 98, 100, 119, 120, 123, 124, 129, 141, 142, 143, 160, 166, 174, 195, 224, 236, 259, 272, 288, 308, 335, 346.
Arapahoes, Southern, 42, 45, 57.
Arickaree Fork (of Republican), 72, 126.
Arikara, 5, 8, 22, 33.
Arkansas River, 13, 18 *et seq.*
Armor, 71.
Arms in Custer fight, 339.
Arrow keeper, 58, 67; lodge, 67.
Arrows, medicine, 67, 296.
Arrows, sacred, of Pĭtă hău ĭ' răt, 77, 79.
Asbury, Captain, 237.
Ash Creek, 138.
Ash Hollow, 100, 105, 107.
Assiniboines, 4.
Atsenas, 29.

Attack on Julesburg, 175; official notices of, 179.
Attack on mail driver, 108.
Augur, General, 259.

B

Bad Face, 97.
Bad Face—band of Ogallala, 225.
Bad Heart, 273, 303.
Bad Man, 290.
Baker Fight, 105.
Bald Faced Bull, 75, 365.
Ball, Captain, 379.
Bancroft, *History of Colorado*, 93, 119, 163.
Bannocks, 351.
Barnit, Captain, 251.
Battle of Summit Springs, 299.
Battle of the Washita, 105, 287.
Battle on Wolf Creek, 42.
Bayard, Samuel J., 116.
Bayard, Second Lieutenant George Dashiell, 116.
Bear Above, 43.
Bear Butte, 196.
Bear Feathers (=Feathered Bear), 278.
Bear Making Trouble, 253.
Bear Man, 136, 167.
Bear Shield, 290.
Bear That Scatters, 102.
Beard, 60.
Beaver Claws, 320.
Beaver Creek, 15, 50, 57, 77, 134, 244, 368, 413.
Beaver Dam, 349, 363.
Beaver River, 59.
Beckwith, Jim, 163.
Beckwourth, James, 163.
Beecher Island, 268.
Beecher Island Fight, 267.
Beecher, Lieutenant Fred, 267.
Before Sand Creek, 143.
Bell, Captain, 413.
Bennett, Captain, 314.
Bennett, Honorable H. P., 143.
Benson, Thomas, 331.
Bent, Agent, 118.
Bent, Charlie, 167.
Bent, George, vi, 27, 41, 99, 115, 119, 133, 152, 170, 174, 198, 199, 261, 308; account of Sand Creek Massacre, 170; death reported, 157, 241.

Bent, Joe, 199.
Bent, Robert, 163.
Bent, Colonel William W., 35, 111, 116, 153, 199, 236, 308.
Benteen, Captain, 333.
Bent's Fort, 2, 18, 32, 45, 48, 58, 59, 61, 104, 115, 118, 308.
Bent's New Fort, 13, 116.
Bent's Old Fort, 308.
Berdash, 228.
Beyond the Mississippi, 119.
Bienville, 35.
Big Ankle, 378.
Big Beaver, 394, 401.
Big Bend of the Rosebud, 331, 349.
Big Breast, 49, 55.
Big Crow (Cheyenne), 176, 366.
Big Crow (Sioux) = Two Face, 181.
Big Footed Bull, 413.
Big Goose Creek, 231.
Big Hawk, 75.
Big Head, 88, 110, 253, 283, 367.
Big Horn expedition, 348.
Big Horn Mountains, 196, 210, 349, 355, 367.
Big Horn River, 199, 316, 356.
Big Horse, 209.
Big Nose, 229.
Big Old Man, 36.
Big Piney Creek, 222.
Big Prisoner, 29.
Big Sand Creek, 10, 132.
Big South Bend (of Sand Creek), 164.
Big Springs, 226.
Big Timbers (of Republican River), 180.
Big Treaty, 69, 96.
Big Wolf, 299.
Bijou Basin, 132.
Bijou Creek, 36.
Bird, 404.
Bird Bear, 366.
Bird Bow, 121.
Bird, Private, 133, 138.
Birdwood Creek, 69.
Bitter Water, 260.
Black Bear, 115, 200, 370, 400, 406.
Black Butte Creek, 14.
Black Coyote, 321.
Black Deer, 259.
Black Eagle, 260, 294.
Blackfeet, 5, 32.
Blackfoot (Sioux), 181.
Black Hairy Dog, 110, 355, 359, 361.
Black Hawk, 369.
Black Hills, 4, 33, 108, 117, 195, 205, 221, 316.
Black Kettle, 88, 127, 140, 153, 161, 170, 236, 244, 260, 288, 298.
Black Lake, 36.
Black Leg, 225.
Black Moccasin (or Iron), 1, 225, 369.
Black Moon, 278.
Black Shield, 225.
Black Shin, 40.
Blacksmith, 410.
Black Sun, 278, 304.
Black Whetstone, 205.

Black White Man (negro), 213.
Black Wolf, 76.
Blind Wolf, 213.
Bloody Knife, 343.
Blue River, 104.
Blunt, Major-General, 154 *et seq.*
Blunt's Fight, plan of, 156.
Bobtail Horse, 338.
Bobtailed Porcupine, 283.
Boggs's Manuscripts, 104.
Boone, 120.
Boone, A. G., 120.
Boone, Daniel, 120.
Booneville, 120, 162.
Bordeaux, James, 103, 104, 126.
Bordeaux's Trading Post, 100, 103.
Bourke, Captain John, 316, 355, 368.
Bow String Soldiers, 14, 42, 60, 85, 94, 209.
Box Elder Creek, 144, 368.
Bozeman road, 222, 232.
Bozeman trail, 202, 221.
Brackett's *History of the U. S. Cavalry*, 114.
Bradley, Lieutenant J. H., 26.
Braided Locks, 365, 367.
Brainard, Colonel D. L., vi, 379, 381.
Brave Bear, 362.
Brave Eagle, 378.
Brave Wolf, 134, 337, 373, 374, 382, 396.
Breaks the Arrow, 283.
Brown, Captain Fred H., 223, 235.
Brulé Sioux, 70, 215, 252.
Brulés, 102, 123, 215.
Bruyere, 370, 376.
Buffalo Calf Road Woman, 324.
Buffalo cap, 67; in war, 68.
Buffalo destruction by whites, 125, 129.
Buffalo hat, 53.
Buffalo Wallow Woman, 366.
Buffalo Woman, 292.
Build the Fire in the South, 42.
Bull, 59, 70, 98.
Bull Bear, 128, 199, 208, 241.
Bull Head, 369.
Bull Hump (Comanche), 35, 36, 39, 62; (Cheyenne), 229, 352, 353, 362, 365, 401.
Bullet Proof, 282.
Bunch of Timber River, 108, 174.
Bunker Hill, 249.
Bureau of Ethnology, Annual Reports, 24, 44, 97, 225.
Burns Red (in the Sun), 352.
Burnt All Over, 245, 248.
Burnt Thigh (Sioux), 80.
Burton, Lieutenant, 139.

C

Cabin Creek, 413, 416.
Cache la Poudre River, 20, 125, 151.
Caddos, 71, 122.
Calf, 338.
Calhoun, Lieutenant, 345.
California trail, 116.

Camp Alert, 116.
Camp Connor, 196, 204, 222.
Camp Creek, 187.
Camp Dodge, 211.
Camp Mitchell, 187, 216.
Camp Robinson, 348.
Camp Sanborn, 137.
Camp Supply, 289.
Camp Weld, 132.
Camp Wichita, 289.
Canadian River, 56, 71, 388.
Canadian River, North, 59.
Canadian River, South, 56, 308.
Cantonment, Oklahoma, 209, (Tongue
    River) 379. '
Capture of Dull Knife's village, 346.
Capture of Julesburg Station, 178.
Carpenter, Colonel L. H., 280.
Carpenter Fight, 282.
Carr, General E. A., 285, 299.
Carries the Otter, 115.
Carrington, General H. B., 206, 222, 235.
Carrying the Shield in Front, 79.
Carson, Kit, 71, 132, 236, 308.
Carver, 34.
Casey, Lieutenant E. W., 379, 382, 416.
Casper, Natrona County, 211.
Century Magazine, 334.
Ceremonial march, 85.
Chadron Creek, 347, 400.
Charcoal Butte, 395.
Charge on Forsyth, the, 273.
Charlot, Major, 154.
Cheans, 35.
Cherokees, 122.
Cherry Brush Creek, 16.
Cherry Creek, 18, 299.
Cheyenne Bottom, 156.
Cheyenne Culture Hero, 3.
Cheyenne name for Crook fight, 324.
Cheyenne Pass, 29, 121, 134.
Cheyenne River, 33.
Cheyenne, Wyoming, 29.
Cheyennes, not indexed.
Chief Comes in Sight, 297, 320, 338.
Chief Joseph, 383.
Chief Soldiers, 209.
Chisholm, Jesse, 263.
Chivington, Colonel J. M., 131, 135, 144,
    154.
Chivington's report on Sand Creek, 168.
Chouteau's Island, 48.
Chubby Roan Horse, 47.
Cimarron Crossing, 245, 249.
Cimarron River, 49, 390.
Civil War, 122, 196.
Clark, Ben, 3, 289.
Clark, Lieutenant W. P., 347, 351, 395,
    397.
Clear Creek, 217, 224, 368, 369.
Cloud Chief, 274.
Cloud Peak, 196.
Coal Bear, 355.
Coal Creek, 144.
Cody, William F., 301.
Cold Face, 259.
Cold Feet, 259.

Cole, Colonel N., 195.
Colley, S. G., U. S. Indian Agent, 124,
    125, 128, 146, 152, 159, 169.
Collins, Colonel, 187.
Collins, Lieutenant Caspar, 198, 214,
    219.
Colmar, Mrs., 332.
Colorado, 18, 119, 120, 123.
Colorado State Historical Association,
    104.
Columbus, Nebraska, 123, 195.
Colyer, special agent, 289.
Comanches, 4, 10, 32, 43, 50, 59, 69, 71,
    98, 121, 308.
Commissioner of Indian Affairs, 120, 143.
Confederate plot rumored, 144.
Confederates, 121.
Connor, General P. E., 161, 195, 217, 236.
Contraries, 43, 232.
Contrary Belly, 323, 338.
Cooke, General P. St. G., 104, 235.
Cooley, 376.
Cooley House, 381.
Cosgrove, Tom, 349, 351.
Cottonwood Fork, 109.
Cottonwood Springs, Nebraska, 145, 250.
Coues, Elliot, 35, 94.
Council at Denver, 153.
Court House Rock, 45, 300.
Coutant, History of Wyoming, 214.
Coyote, 107, 313.
Coyote Ear, 45, 115.
Cramer, Lieutenant, 164.
Crane, 19.
Crawford, Governor, 237, 249, 250, 260,
    288.
Crawling, 366.
Crazy Dogs, 209.
Crazy Head, 370.
Crazy Horse, 316, 349, 355, 368, 369,
    370, 383.
Crazy Lodge, 259.
Crazy Mule, 225, 312, 370.
Crazy Woman's Fork, 196, 349.
Crittenden, Lieutenant, 345.
Crook, General, 316, 385, 412.
Crooked Creek, 49.
Crooked Hand, 77.
Crooked Lance Society, 53, 209, 360.
Crooked Lance Soldiers, 22, 85.
Crooked Neck, 49, 53, 57.
Crooked Nose, 318.
Crook's Fight on the Rosebud, 316.
Crow (name), 358, 387, 403.
Crow Battle, A, 22.
Crow Chief, 136.
Crow Creek, 29, 31.
Crow Indian, 80.
Crow Neck, 290.
Crow Necklace, 356, 361.
Crow Split Nose, 360.
Crow Standing Creek, 23, 368.
Crow Standing Off Creek, 23, 228.
Crows, 4, 22, 33, 34, 40, 69, 80, 98, 134,
    355.
Culver, 269.
Curly, 352.

Curly Hair, 297.
Culture Hero, 67.
Curtis, General S. R., 131, 138, 144, 146, 155, 169, 197.
Custard, Sergeant Amos J., 198, 219.
Custer Battle, The, 333.
Custer, Captain Thomas, 341.
Custer, General G. A., 207, 235, 240, 254, 289, 316, 353, 369.
Custer, Mrs. E. B., 243.

D

Dakotas, 2, 34.
Dark, 112.
Darlington, Oklahoma, 314.
Davis, President Jefferson, 121.
Davis, J. L., 332.
Davis, T. R., 242.
Davis, Captain Wirt, 352.
Dead Man's Fork, 217.
Deaf Man, 55.
Death of Mouse's Road, 10.
Death song of White Antelope, 171.
Deep Holes Creek, 187.
Deer Creek, 211, 218.
Delaney, Lieutenant Hayden, 347, 351.
Delawares, 73, 87, 116, 122, 155.
Denver, 40, 119, 149, 221, 247, 249.
Depredations, list of (January–February, 1865), 184.
De Rudio, Lieutenant, 342.
De Smet, Reverend P. J., 71, 96.
Diary of Scout Whitney, 269.
Dirt on the Nose, 82.
"Dixie," 122.
Dixon, Billy, 311.
Dodge City, 310, 390.
Dodge, Colonel Henry, 94.
Dodge, Colonel R. I., 346.
Dodge, General G. M., 195, 197, 199, 205, 215, 217, 236.
Dog Soldiers, 2, 14, 27, 45, 46, 60, 61, 80, 85, 120, 209, 211, 236, 239, 243, 245, 249, 410.
Dole, Commissioner Indian Affairs, 154.
Doolittle, Honorable J. B., 170, 236.
Douglas, Arizona, 72.
Douglas, Major, 237, 260.
Downing, Major, 135.
Drew, Lieutenant W. Y., 218.
Dripp's Trading Post, 111.
Driven Creek, 394.
Dry Throat, 273.
Dull Knife (= Morning Star), 199, 225, 351, 353, 355, 383, 384, 388, 392, 394, 399, 401, 411, 412.
Dull Knife outbreak, 107.
Dunn, J. P., Jr., 105.
Dunn, Lieutenant, 134.
Dusty Chief, 78.
Dutisne, 35.

E

Eagle Chief, 77.
Eagle Feather, 62.
Eagle Head, 20, 21, 289.
Eagle's Nest, 245, 248, 249.
Eagle Tail, 14, 15, 18.
Early travels and adventures, 255.
Ear Ring, 76.
East, J. H., 72.
Eastern Indian trappers, 72.
Eastman, C. A., 344.
Eayre, Lieutenant G., 132, et seq.
Ēhyōph′stă, 297, 366.
Eight Horns, 277.
Eighteenth Infantry, 223.
Eighth Kansas Cavalry, 124.
Eleventh Kansas Cavalry, 211, 219, 220.
Eleventh Kansas Regiment at Platte Bridge, 218.
Elk Horn Scrapers, 14, 18.
Elk Mountain Creek, 356.
Elk River, 352.
Elliot, Major, 289.
Ellsworth, Lieutenant, 187.
Elston, 215.
Ermine Bear, 274.
Eubanks, Mrs., 148, 181.
Evans, Governor, 120, et seq.
Ewers, Captain, 372.
Executive Document 41, 30th Congress, 1st Session, 118.

F

Fairchild, S. H., 218.
Fall Leaf, 116.
Farley, George, 395.
Feathered Bear (= Bear Feathers), 97, 283.
Feathered Sun, 326.
Fetterman, Captain W. J., 221, 223, 235.
Fetterman Massacre, 235.
Fifth Cavalry, 352.
Fifth Infantry, 379, 381.
Fight at Adobe Walls, 308.
Fight with the Sac and Fox, 97.
Finerty, John F., 317.
First Cavalry, 109, 112, 114, 115.
First Dakota Cavalry, 198.
Fisher, 223; of Bent's Fort, 308.
Fitzpatrick, Thomas, 95, 96.
Fitzpatrick treaty, 28, 69, 72, 96.
Five Years a Dragoon, etc., Lowe, 115.
Flat War Club, 48, 49.
Fleming, Lieutenant, 100.
Florida, prisoners sent to, 315.
Flying, 382.
Food scarcity in Denver, 150.
Ford, Captain, 71.
Ford, Colonel, 236.
Forsyth, Colonel George A., 267.
Fort Adobe, 45.
Fort Atkinson, 110, 116.
Fort Cobb, 122, 288, 294.
Fort Collins, 126.
Fort Connor, 203, 204, 205.
Fort Cottonwood, 147, 250.
Fort Dodge, 237, 249, 310, 393.
Fort Ellis, Montana, 379.
Fort Ellsworth, 237.

Fort Fetterman, 196, 316, 348.
Fort Harker, 238, 249, 250.
Fort Hays, 249, 250, 267.
Fort Kearny, 95, 108, 117, 123, 147, 215, 222, 250.
Fort Keogh, 370, 373, 395, 397, 411, 416, 417.
Fort Laramie, 27, 95, 100, 101, 103, 115, 117, 121, 124, 145, 187, 195, 196, 204, 215, 222, 348, 355.
Fort Laramie treaty, 96.
Fort Larned, 116, 121, 126, 138, 140, 145, 238, 243.
Fort Leavenworth, 104, 106, 112, 115, 220, 249.
Fort Lyon, 36, 119, 125, 141, 143, 145, 160, 169.
Fort McPherson, 250, 307.
Fort Phil Kearny, 206, 221 et seq.
Fort Phil Kearny Fight, 200.
Fort Pierre, 8, 106.
Fort Rankin, 176.
Fort Reno, 196, 222, 349, 384, 385.
Fort Riley, 140, 238.
Fort Robinson, v, 347, 384, 385, 394, 400, 401, 403, 411.
Fort Robinson Outbreak (1879), 399.
Fort Sedgwick, 176, 251.
Fort C. F. Smith, 222.
Fort Soddy, 116.
Fort Sodom, 116.
Fort Wallace, 251.
Fort Washaki, 385.
Fort Wise, 121, 124.
Fort Wise treaty, 125.
Fort Zarah, 237, 239.
Fossil Station, 244.
Four Spirits, 352.
Fourth Cavalry, 112, 124, 349, 352, 385.
Fouts, Captain, 197, 215.
Fowler, Jacob, 35.
Fox Soldiers (see Kit Fox Soldiers).
Fox Tail, 237.
Frapp Battle, 93.
Fremont, General J. C., 74.
Fremont, Nebraska, 77.
Fremont's Memoirs, 93.
Frémont's Orchard, 134.
French Canadians, 116.
French trader, 222.
French trappers and traders, 4.
Frenchman's Fork (of the Republican), 180, 394.
Frog Lying on the Hillside, 54.
Fry, General James B., 281.
Furey, Major, 349.

G

Ganier, 108, 111.
Gantt, 94.
Gay, 250.
Geier, George, 235.
Genoa, Nebraska, 123.
Gens de l'arc, 4.
Gens du serpent, 4.
Gentle Horse, 49, 54, 208, 355.

George-Flying-By, 382.
Germaine family, 313.
Gerry, Elbridge, 127, 150.
Gerry's ranch, 151.
Getty, Lt., 416.
Ghost dance, 417.
Ghost Man, 389.
Gilpin, Lieutenant Colonel, 93.
Girard, F., 342.
"Giving presents to one another across the river," 59.
Glendive, Montana, 413.
Godfrey, General E. S., vi, 260, 334.
Gold in Colorado (1858–63), 118.
Good Bear, 15, 110, 252, 275.
Goose Creek, 316.
Goose Feather, 329.
Gordon, Major, 347.
Gourd (Pumpkin) Butte, 199.
Governor's Island, New York, 353.
Grand Island, Nebraska, 95, 108.
Grant, General, 204, 238.
Grattan, Lieutenant, 100 et seq.
Grattan and Ash Hollow (1854–5), 100.
Gray Beard, 310.
Gray Hair, 55.
Gray (Painted) Thunder, 42, 55, 58.
Greeley, Colorado, 29.
Greenwood, Commissioner, 120.
Greer, Captain, 219.
Grey Eyes, 289.
Grierson, General, 289.
Griffenstein, William, 261.
Grimm, Corporal Henry, 218.
Grove of Timber River, 108, 174.
Grover, scout, 285.
Grummond, Lieutenant, 223.
Guerrier, Edmond, 152, 159, 164, 174, 241, 388.
Gypsum, 363.

H

Hackberry Creek, 153.
Hail, 356, 357, 359.
Hair Rope people, 40.
Hairy Hand, 367.
Halleck, General, 161, 169.
Hamilton, 380.
Hamilton, Captain L., 251, 289, 352.
Hancock at Fort Dodge, May, 1867, 237.
Hancock Campaign, 236.
Hancock, General, 237 et seq.
Hanging Woman Creek, 369, 370.
Hankammer, Sergeant, 219.
Harney, General William S., 100, 104, 105, 106, 107, 236, 259, 287.
Harney-Sanborn treaty, 221.
Harper's Magazine, 242.
Harper's Weekly, 343.
Harrington, Lieutenant, 341.
Harrying the Indians, 131.
Hat Creek, 217.
Hawk, 149.
Hawk's visit, 352.
Haynes Creek, 120.
Haywood, Lieutenant W., 216.

Hazen, General, 287, 294.
He Who Mounts the Clouds, 71.
Heath, 110.
Heavy Furred Wolf, 304.
Henderson, Honorable John B., 259.
Henning, Major, 160.
Henry, Captain Guy V., 317.
Herendeen, George, 342.
Hewitt, J. N. B., 99.
Hidatsa, 2, 5.
High Backed Wolf, 60, 61, 62, 63, 64, 65, 212, 213, 218.
High Bear, 353.
High Wolf, 356, 359.
Hines, Doctor, 224.
History of Colorado, 93, 119, 163.
History of the U. S. Cavalry, 114.
History of Western Missions and Missionaries, 96.
History of Wyoming, 214.
Hoffman, Major, 100.
Ho hĕ, 5, 6, 7, 8.
Hole in the Back, 47.
Hollow Hip, 43.
Horse Black, 213.
Horse Butte, 45.
Horse Chief, 313.
Horse Creek, 27, 96, 216.
Horse Creek treaty, 69, 96, 98.
Horse for war, preparing, 325.
Horse Shoe Station, 218.
Hostility, racial, 96.
House Executive Document, No. 63, 33d Congress, 2d Session, 102.
House Ridge, 356.
Howling Wolf, 55, 253, 323, 413.
How Six Feathers was named, 18.
Hudson Bay guns, 39, 48.
Huerfano River, 35.
Hump (Cheyenne), 370, 376, 381, 396.
Hump (Sioux), 382.
Hunter, John, 131.
Hutchinson County, Texas, 308
Hyde, G. E., vi.

I

Ice, 112, 205, 276.
Idaho, 221.
Ietans, 35.
Immigrant Indians, 97.
Indian Bureau, 384, 386, 417.
Indian Department, 238.
Indian Land Cessions in the United States, 97.
Indian service, 5.
Indian Territory, 70, 383, 384, 385, 386.
Indian War of 1864, 136, 145, 177.
Indian wars, cause for, 170.
Indians of To-day, 3.
Interior Department, 236.
Iron, 213.
Iron Jacket, 71.
Iron Shirt (Apache), 296, 370.
Iron Shirt (Cheyenne), 71, 75.
Iron Star, 380.
Irwin, Jackman & Co., 131.

Ĭ să tai', 312.
Island, 297.
Island Woman, 256.
Ĭs' si wŭn, 68, 88.
Iyott, Sefray, 126.

J

Jackson, Bob, 376, 378, 380, 381.
Jackson, William, 342.
Janisse, Antoine, 126.
Janisse, Nicholas, 126.
Jarrott, 126.
Jerome, Lieutenant L. H., 380.
Jicarilla Apaches, 309.
Jim Pockmark, 71.
Johnson, Captain Edward, 101.
Johnson, Captain J. B., 399.
Jones, 237.
Journal of Jacob Fowler, 4, 35.
Journals of A. Henry and D. Thompson, 94.
Julesburg, 145, 195, 250.
Julesburg, attack on, 175; official notices of, 179.
Jumper, Lieutenant-Colonel, 122.

K

Kansas, 106, 237, 249.
Kansas City landing, 14.
Kansas expedition, 238.
Kansas Historical Collections, 109, 122, 269.
Kansas in the Sixties, 249, 288.
Kansas Pacific Railroad, 237, 247, 249.
Kansas River, 98, 114.
Kansas State Historical Collections, 115.
Kaw, 78.
Kearny, Colonel S. W., 95.
Kearny, Fort, 95, 108, 117, 123, 147, 215, 222, 250.
Keeper of medicine arrows, 27, 28, 29, 42.
Kennedy, Lieutenant, 182.
Ketcham, H. T., 129.
Kichai, 122.
Kickapoos, 122.
Kidder, Lieutenant, 251.
Killed by a Bull, 280.
Kills in the Night, 341.
Kiowa Apaches, 4, 35.
Kiowa chief (Little Mountain), 31.
Kiowa Comanches, 4.
Kiowa Creek, 40.
Kiowa Padduce, 35.
Kiowa Woman, 40, 75.
Kiowas, 4, 10, 32, 39, 43, 49, 50, 75, 80, 89, 93, 97, 115, 118, 129, 131, 141, 147, 152, 236, 249, 259, 262, 292, 308.
Kĭ'rä rū tāh, 90.
Kit Foxes, 14, 81, 82, 85, 209, 350, 355, 360.
Kite Indians, 3.
Kit'kă hāh kĭ, 77, 80, 99.
Kō'kä'kă, 77.

L

La Bonté, Col., 126.
La Bonté Crossing, Wyoming, 196.
Lǎ'hǐ kǎ, 77.
La Junta, Col., 59.
La Salle, 72.
Lake De Smet, 368.
Lame Deer (man), 376 *et seq.*
Lame Deer (place), 376.
Lame Deer Fight, The, 373.
Lame Deer River, 374, 375, 376, 379, 382.
Lame Medicine Man, 58.
Lame Shawnee, 52, 74.
Laramie, 100, 104, 106, 117, 215, 217.
Laramie Plains, 95.
Laramie River, 95.
Larocque, 24.
Larocque's Journal, 24.
Larpenteur, 94.
Last Bull, 355, 359, 360.
Latham, 150, 151.
Lawton, General, 349, 385.
Leading Bear, 62.
Lean Bear, 121, 139.
Lean Man, 297.
Leavenworth and Pike's Peak Express
   Company, 119.
Leavenworth, Colonel J. H., 121, 123,
   124, 236, 238, 260.
Leavenworth, Kansas, 116, 119.
Left Hand, 141, 161, 166, 215.
Left Handed Shooter, 369.
Left Handed Wolf, 363.
Lē sǎ tǎ lǐt'ka, 78.
Letter from chiefs, 152.
Lewis and Clark, 3, 22.
Liberty Farm, 148.
Life and Adventures of Billy Dixon, 314.
Life of George Dashiell Bayard, 116.
Light Hair, 14.
Lightning Woman, 58.
Limber Lance, 369.
List of depredations (January–February,
   1865), 184.
List of distances from Leavenworth to
   Big Timbers, 247.
Little Arkansas, 120, 236.
Little Big Horn River, 207, 319, 331,
   333.
Little Blue River, 148.
Little Chief (Arapaho), 292.
Little Chief (Cheyenne), 71, 370, 386.
Little Creek, 46, 94, 370.
Little Goose Creek, 231.
Little Hawk, 272, 283, 301, 316, 355, 361.
Little Heart, 126.
Little Horse, 200, 201, 202, 232, 233,
   235, 365, 396.
Little Man, 275.
Little Medicine Lodge River, 389.
Little Missouri River, 1, 33, 195, 221,
   396, 415.
Little Mountain, 31, 62, 118, 309.
Little Old Man, 53, 60, 61.
Little Powder River, 205, 209, 210.
Little Raven, 59, 98, 120, 161.

Little Robe, 80, 289.
Little Rock, 291.
Little Sheep River, 369.
Little Shield, 318, 405, 406, 410.
Little Thunder, 104, 105.
Little Wolf, 11, 36, 38, 39, 46, 54, 55, 82,
   107, 184, 229; (Old) 235, 362, 365,
   383, 386, 387, 388, 389, 390, 391,
   392, 393, 394, 395, 396, 397, 398,
   399, 411.
Little Wolf and Dull Knife (1878–9), 383.
Lodge-pole Creek, 145, 217, 368.
Lodge Trail Ridge, 223, 224.
Lone Bear, 167, 303.
Lone Wolf, 12, 13.
Long, 35.
Long Chin, 15, 16, 17, 18, 27, 88; (Sioux)
   106, 150.
Long Chin's Strategy, 13.
Long Hat, 260.
Long Jaw, 364, 365, 366.
Loree (Laree, Lorry, Lovee), agent, 125.
Lost Leg, 323.
Loup Fork River, 70, 123.
Loup River, South, 69.
Lowe, Percival G., 115.

M

MacDonald, Sergeant, 192.
Mackenzie, General R. S., 313, 346, 348,
   351, 369, 384.
McDougall, Captain, 334.
McKenny, Major T. I., 139, 141.
McKinney, Lieutenant, 352, 365.
Mad Wolf, 81, 136, 338.
Mail, coats of, 71.
Man Above, 41.
Man Afraid of His Horses, 103; (Old) 207;
   (Young) 210, 259; proper interpre-
   tation of name, 103, 210.
Man Shot by the Ree, 150.
Man that Walks Under the Ground, 259.
Mandans, 1, 2, 5, 8, 34.
Margry, 35, 72.
Marias River, 105.
Marshall, F. J., 121.
Martinez, Andreas, 71.
Marysville, Kansas, 121.
*Massacre of Confederates by Osage Indians
   in 1863*, 122.
Massacres of the Mountains, 93, 105, 162.
Maximilian, 5.
Maxwell, L., 308.
Medicine Arrow, 296.
Medicine arrow keeper, 27, 28, 29, 42.
Medicine arrows, 14, 22, 24, 42, 53, 58,
   67, 69, 355.
Medicine arrows, capture of, 69.
Medicine arrows in war, 68.
Medicine arrows, moves of, 69.
Medicine Bear, 55, 366.
Medicine lodge, 42, 43, 81.
Medicine Lodge Creek, 146, 261.
Medicine lodge dance, 42.
Medicine Lodge treaty (1867), 254.

Medicine Lodge treaty, commissioners for, 259.
Medicine Lodge treaty, council at, 264.
Medicine man, 13.
Medicine Snake, 56.
Medicine Standing Up, 76.
Medicine war club, 48.
Medicine Water, 53, 54, 55, 72, 73.
Medicine Woman, 280.
Merrill, Reverend Moses, 94.
Mexican, 12, 44, 64, 199, 200, 237.
Mexicans, 35, 116, 308.
Mexico, 32.
Miksch, L. C., 168.
Miles, Agent John D., 314, 389.
Miles, General N. A., 369, 397, 398, 412, 416.
Military Division of the Missouri, 238.
Military posts on Platte River, 147.
Miller, Agent Robert C., 114, 115, 118.
Minneconjou, 102, 103.
Minneconjou Sioux, 100.
Minnesota, 1, 122.
Minnesota Sioux, 123.
Mississippi River, 72.
Missouri, Department of the, 195.
Missouri Intelligencer, 169.
Missouri River, 1, 5, 8, 32, 34, 100, 198, 221, 316.
Mitchell, D. D., 96.
Mitchell, General Robert B., 131, 144, 145, 149, 180.
Montana, v, 32, 221, 316, 383, 386.
Montana Hist. Cont., 26.
Mooers, Doctor J. H., 267.
Mooney, James, 34, 44, 45.
Moonlight, Colonel Thomas, 169, 197, 215, 216, 217.
Moore, Doctor R. C., 255.
Morgan, Tom, 79.
Mormon, 102, 109, 115.
Morning Star, 70.
Morning Star (Dull Knife), 410.
Morrow's ranch, Jack, 250.
Mountain, 62, 63, 64, 118.
Mouse's Road, 11, 12, 13.
Moving Whirlwind, 99.
Mud Springs, 186.
Muddy Creek, 225, 379.
Murie, Captain James, 256.
Murray, 308.
Museum of the Military Service Institution, 353.
Mussey, Captain, 150.
My Life on the Plains, 240, 242, 250, 254.

N

Nadouessi of the plains, 34.
Neal, Colonel, 314.
Nebraska, 69, 123, 215, 217, 221, 394.
Nebraska Historical Society Publications, 94, 95, 196.
Negro (Black White Man), 213.
New Mexican troops, 308.
New Orleans molasses, 64.
Nez Percés, 383.

Nineteenth Kansas Cavalry, 250.
Niobrara River, 193, 198.
No Arm's Creek, 156.
Noisy Walking, 410.
North, Captain L. H., vi, 200, 300, 347, 351, 352, 353, 354.
North Dakota, 316, 383.
North, Major Frank, 195, 197, 198, 200, 202, 203, 204, 205, 256, 301, 347, 351, 352, 353, 354, 368.
North Platte, 249.
North, Robert, 128.
Norwood, 380.
Number of Indians in Custer fight, 343.

O

O'Brien, Captain N. J., 176.
Official Records of Union and Confederate Armies, 121, 140, 148, 150, 151, 184, 195, 204, 236.
Ogallala, 95, 103, 221, 225.
Ogallala Sioux, 207.
Ogallala (town), 394.
Ojibwa, 6.
Oklahoma, v, 385, 388.
Old Bark, 97.
Old Bear, 341, 353.
Old Bull Bear, 208.
Old Little Wolf, 235.
Old Man Afraid of His Horses, 207.
Old Whirlwind, 16, 17, 97, 99, 100.
Olney, Lieutenant, 168.
Omaha scouts, 195.
O mis'sis, 45, 46.
O'Neal, T., 342.
On the Border with Crook, 317.
One Bear, 245, 248, 249.
One Eye, 167.
One Eyed Antelope, 23.
Orchard, 134.
Oregon, 94, 95, 221.
Osages, 57, 78, 98, 99, 122.
Otis, General Superintendent, 150.
Otter Creek, 368.
Overland Stage Line, 197.
Overland Stage Road, 207.
Overland Stage to California, 119, 150.

P

Packer, 291.
Page, Major, 237.
Pa hŭk', 77.
Painted Rocks, 374, 375.
Painted Thunder, 225.
Pai'yo hē, Powder River, 23, 24, 33, 107, 193, 196, 197, 198, 199, 202, 203, 204, 205, 207, 210, 217, 221, 222, 223, 225, 235, 236, 251, 316, 349.
Palladay, Leon, 126.
Palmer, Captain H. E., 196, 198, 200, 202.
Panhandle of Texas, 45.
Panther, 201, 202.
Parkman, Francis, 104.
Parmeter, Captain, 141, 146.
Pawnee Fork, 98, 118, 240, 242, 243, 249.

Pawnee Hero Stories and Folk Tales, 198.
Pawnee Killer, 149, 175, 250, 251, 259, 271.
Pawnee Loups, 71.
Pawnee Man, 245, 248.
Pawnee scouts, 195, 196, 346.
Pawnees, 4, 14, 15, 16, 17, 18, 35, 39, 42, 69, 75, 76, 80, 93.
Pawnees moved South, 70.
Peace with the Kiowas, 59.
Peck, R. M., 115.
Penetethka band, 35.
People of the Bow, 4.
Perry, J. D., 249.
Pettér, Reverend R., 2.
Picket, 17.
Pike, General Albert, C. S. A., 122.
Pile of Bones, 303.
Piles of Driftwood, 61.
Pine Ridge, 403, 404, 409, 411.
Pine Ridge Agency, 347, 402, 409, 410, 411.
Pipe sent to allies, 174.
Pipes, 10.
Pĭtă hău ĭ'răt, 77.
Placido, 71.
Plan of Cheyenne camp, Sand Creek, 165.
Platte Bridge, 198, 210, 211, 215, 217, 218.
Platte Bridge Fight (1865), 207.
Platte Road, 249.
Platte River, 29, 32, 45, 69, 94, 95, 100, 104, 108, 109, 111, 117, 119, 121, 124, 125, 196, 211, 217, 221, 236, 249, 250, 251, 399.
Platte River, North, 27, 33, 104, 210, 211, 216, 218, 348, 394.
Platte River, South, 10, 20, 29, 35, 36, 46, 80, 112, 115, 116, 210, 394.
Plenty Camps, 225, 226.
Plenty of Bull Meat, 302.
Plenty of Horses, 245, 248; (Sioux), 417.
Plenty of Old Camps, 98, 99.
Pliley, A. J., 269.
Plover, 72.
Plumb, Colonel, 211.
Plunder in the camps, 183.
Point of Rocks, 141, 151.
Pole Creek, 369.
Ponca, 36.
Ponca Woman, 49.
Poor (Lean) Bear, 121.
Pope, General, 236.
Porcupine, 56, 254.
Porcupine Bear, 45, 46, 52, 53, 56, 74, 94.
Porcupine Bull, 280.
Potawatomi, 90, 99.
Powder River (pai'yo hē), 23, 24, 33, 107, 193, 195, 196, 197, 198, 199, 202, 203, 204, 205, 207, 210, 217, 221, 222, 223, 225, 235, 236, 251, 316, 349.
Powder River Expedition, 195.
Powder River Valley, 357.
Powell, Captain, 223.
Prairie Apaches, 98, 116.

Prairie Bear, 275.
Prairie Dog Creek, 23, 228, 368.
Pratt, Captain, 315.
Present State of Hudson's Bay, The, 35.
Price, M. T., 332.
Prisoners given up, 153.
Pueblo, Colorado, 120.
Pumpkin Buttes, 196, 199.
Pumpkinseed Creek, 186.
Punished Woman's Fork, 394.
Pushing Ahead, 10, 11, 49.

R

Raccoon, 134.
Racial hostility, 96.
Raiding along Platte, 174.
Raids on emigrant road, 148.
Ranches raided on Platte, 181.
Randall, Major, 355.
Randall, Todd, 348.
Rattlesnake Butte, 413.
Rattlesnake Creek, 263.
Record of Engagements, 289, 317, 334, 348.
Red Bead, 251.
Red Bird, 76, 410, 411.
Red Cherries, 304.
Red Cloud, 199, 223, 225, 346, 348.
Red Cloud Agency, 349, 399, 401.
Red Hair, 294.
Red Leaf (Sioux), 106.
Red Moon, 289.
Red Paint River, 194.
Red Plume (Sioux), 106.
Red River of North, 1.
Red River of Texas, 10, 45.
Red Shields, 14, 47, 53, 55, 90, 209, 210.
Red Skin, 71.
Red Tracks, 45.
Red War Bonnet, 326, 395.
Red Winged Woodpecker, 362.
Rees, 1, 2, 33.
Reno Creek, 318.
Reno, Major M. A., 333.
Report Commissioner of Indian Affairs, 108, 111, 114, 123, 125, 127, 238.
Report Committee Conduct of War, 161, 162.
Report Joint Special Committee, 132, 137, 159, 168.
Report Secretary of Interior, 120, 148, 150, 151, 152, 153, 155, 238, 240, 242, 244, 288, 289.
Republican River, 60, 77, 87, 98, 119, 120, 125, 127, 236, 237, 250, 251, 394.
Reynolds, Charles B., vi.
Reynolds, General J. J., 334.
Richardson, A. D., 119.
Richmond, Lieutenant, 168.
Ridge men band, 58.
Rio Grande, 35.
Rising Sun, 55.
Roan Bear, 338.
Rock Forehead, 58, 88, 237, 296.
Rocky Mountain Life, 94.

Rocky Mountains, 221.
Rolling Bull, 225, 226.
Roman Nose, 204, 215, 240, 241, 268, 275.
Roman Nose Thunder, 293.
Root, Lieutenant-Governor, 260.
Root, *The Overland Stage to California*, 119, 150.
Roper, Miss, 148.
Rosebud River, 316, 349, 369, 373, 374, 381, 411.
Ross, Captain, 71.
Ross, Senator, 260.
Rotten Grass Creek, 370.
Rowland, James, 403, 409, 410.
Rowland, William, 101, 109, 347, 351, 385, 410, 417.
Rowland, William, Jr., 320.
Rowland, Willis, 413, 417.
Royal, Colonel, 300.
Running Water, 394, 399.
Rush Creek, 187.

S

Sac and Fox, 90, 97, 98, 99, 100.
Sacred arrows, 79.
Sacred hat, 88, 355.
Sage, R. B., 94.
Saint Labre's Mission, 369.
St. Mary's River, 32.
St. Peter's River, 34.
St. Vrain, Colonel, 104, 308.
Salina, Kansas, 125, 140, 146.
Saline Fork, 125, 307.
Salt Lake City, 204.
Salt Plain, 146.
Salt Spring, 146.
Sanborn, General, 135, 236, 259.
Sand Creek, 36, 71, 105, 161, 207, 240, 242.
Sand Creek Massacre, v, 159.
Sand Creek Massacre, Indian account of, 170.
Sand Hills, 395.
Santa Fé Road, 98, 240.
Sa tank', 44, 62.
Satanta, 141.
Săvănē', 73, 89.
Săv ăn i'yō'hē, 72.
Sawyer, Colonel, 198, 202.
Scabby, 352.
Scabby Eyelid, 322.
Scalp, 274.
Scalping of Thompson, 255.
Scene of Fort Phil Kearny Fight, 231.
Schoolcraft's *Indian Tribes*, 35.
Schuyler, General W. S., vi, 347, 351, 352.
Scott Creek, 45.
Scott, General W. S., 105, 106.
Scout Creek, 40, 41.
Scouting for the soldiers, 412.
Scouts of Powder River expedition, 346.
Second California Cavalry, 195.
Second Cavalry, 223, 251, 379.
Second Infantry, 124.

Second U. S. Cavalry, 379.
Sedgwick, Major, 115, 116.
Seminole, 122.
Senate, 383.
Senate Document, 34th Congress, 1st and 2d Sessions, 102.
Senate Report No. 708, 46th Congress, 2d Session, 383, 386.
Seven Bulls, 59, 60.
Seventh Cavalry, 250, 251, 289, 333, 353.
Seventh Iowa Cavalry, 195, 216.
Shadler brothers, 311.
Shadow That Comes in Sight, 369.
Shā hī'ē la, 2.
Sha hī'e na, 2.
Sharp, John B., 350.
Sharp, Sergeant, 378.
Shavehead, 62.
Shawnee Creek, 60, 72.
Shawnees, 72, 73, 87, 122.
She Bear, 115.
Shell, 413.
Sheridan, General P. H., 3, 249, 251, 267.
Sheridan, Wyoming, 231.
Sherman, General W. T., 238, 249, 250, 287.
Shi shi'ni i'yo he, 193.
Shoshoni, 4, 32, 69, 213, 225, 349, 358, 385.
Shoshoni, Mountain, 32.
Simla, Nebraska, 186.
Single Coyote, 293.
Sioux, 2, 4, 23, 24, 26, 33, 34, 45, 72.
Sioux, Teton, 34.
Sioux winter-counts, 34.
Sits in the Night, 359, 360, 363.
Sitting Bear, 14, 62.
Sitting Bull, 334, 346, 363, 395.
Sitting Man, 407.
Six Feathers, 19, 20, 21.
Sixteenth Kansas Cavalry, 195, 196.
Sixth Cavalry, 124.
Sixth Infantry, 100.
Skidi, 69, 70, 77.
Sky Chief, 190.
Sleeping Bear, 55.
Sleeping Rabbit, 370.
Slim Buttes, 346.
Slim Face, 297.
Small Man, 30, 31.
Smallpox, 129.
Smith, Adam, 123.
Smith, Jack, 167.
Smith, John, 164, 261, 308.
Smoky Hill River, 14, 18, 108, 114, 125, 127, 236, 244, 249.
Smoky Hill Road, 247.
Smoky Hill Stage Line, 247.
Smoky Lodge, 45.
Snake Creek, 193.
Snake Men, 4.
Snake People, 32.
Snake Woman, 40, 41.
Snakes, 4, 32, 35, 218.
Snakes, Mountain, 32.
Solomon River, 18, 108, 112, 117.
Solomon's Fork of the Kansas, 114.

South Cheyenne River, 217.
Spaniards, 4, 71.
Split Eye, 362.
Spots on the Feathers, 313.
Spotted Bear, 259.
Spotted Crow, 167.
Spotted Elk (Sioux), 106.
Spotted Hawk, 341.
Spotted Tail (Sioux), 106, 149, 175, 259.
Spotted Wolf, 25, 27, 192, 254, 278, 324.
Stä ĭ tăn', 1.
Standing Elk, 259, 385.
Standing Rock Agency, 382.
Standing Water, 167.
Stanley, H. M., 237, 238, 239, 240, 241, 242, 244, 245, 249, 260, 261.
Stansbury's Exploration, 93.
Stanton, Secretary of War, 236.
Star, 140, 278.
Starving Bear, 139.
Starving Elk, 82, 272.
Stations along Platte River, 191.
Stewart, Captain G. H., 109.
Stillwell, Jack, 274.
Stone Calf, 313.
Stone Forehead, 10.
Stone Teeth, 313.
Storm, 98.
Striped Stick Creek, 356.
Strong Left Hand, 401, 403.
Stuart, Lieutenant J. E. B., 114.
Stump, 362.
Sturgis, Captain, 116.
Sŭh'tāĭ, 1, 2, 6, 40, 68.
Sullivant Hills, 222, 223.
Sully, General Alfred, 195.
Summer on the Plains, A, 242.
Sumner, Colonel E. V., 111.
Sumner Campaign (1857), 107.
Sun Maker, 57, 126.
Surprise River, 193.
Surrender of Two Moon's band, 369.
Sŭs'son ĭ, 4, 32.
Sweet Water, 218, 260.
Sweet Water Bridge, 218.
Sweet Water River, 221.
Swift Bear, 348.
Sylvestro, 260.

T

Taboos of war bonnet, 276.
Tall Bull, 15, 16, 82, 243, 271, 300, 352.
Tall Sioux, 304.
Tall Woman, 72.
Tangle Hair, 275, 389, 394, 401, 402, 410.
Tappan, Colonel, 259.
Tappan, trader, 237.
Ta wĭ ta da hĭ'la sa, 79.
Taylor, Commissioner N. G., 259.
Taylor, Joseph H., 128.
Ten Bears, 260.
Ten Eyck, Captain, 224.
Tenth Infantry, 124.
Tenth U. S. Cavalry, 250.

Tenting on the Plains, 243.
Tenure of Land Among the Indians, 120.
Terry, General A. H., 316.
Tesson, 104.
Texans, 121, 122.
Texas, 32, 34, 35, 45, 237, 240.
Texas, Comprehensive History of, 71.
Texas, Oldham County, 72.
Texas Rangers, 71.
Thickwood, 181.
Third Cavalry, 399.
Thompson, William, 254.
Three Bears, 354.
Timber Creek, 181.
Tobacco (Arapaho), 293.
Tobacco (Cheyenne), 252.
To'hau sĕn (Little Mountain), 62, 118.
Tongue River, 33, 193, 200, 201, 202, 210, 223, 226, 229, 316, 368, 369, 370, 372, 373, 379.
Tongue River Canyon, 225.
Tongue River Indian Reservation, Montana, 411, 417.
Tonkawas, 71.
Touching Cloud, 71.
Train wreck at Plum Creek, 255.
Train wreck, Porcupine's account of, 256.
Transactions of Kansas State Historical Society, 218.
Travel up the Platte River, 147.
Treaty of 1851, 96.
"Treaty Grounds," 59.
Troops at Sand Creek, 163.
Troops killed at Fort Rankin, 177.
Trudeau, 280.
Tsau i', 77.
Tsĭs tsĭs'tăs, 1, 2, 67.
Turkey Creek, 108.
Turkey Leg, 254, 259.
Turtle's Road, 367.
Twenty-second Infantry, 379, 382.
Twenty-seventh Infantry, 222.
Twiss, Agent Thomas S., 111.
Two Bulls, 352, 362, 365.
Two Butte Creek, 61.
Two Buttes, 167.
Two Crows, 56, 274, 301.
Two Face (=Big Crow), 181.
Two Moon, Young, 115, 297, 335, 355, 358, 359, 367, 369, 370, 371, 372, 373, 396.
Two Moon's band, 346.
Two Tails, 107.
Two Thighs, 81, 167, 184.
Tyler, Captain, 380.
Tyler, William, 311.

U

Ugly Face, 97.
Umfreville, 35.
Union Pacific Railroad, 249.
Upper Arkansas Agency, 125.
Upper Missouri, 124.
Upper Platte, 111.
Upper Platte Agency, 96, 111, 125.

Upper Platte Bridge, 107.
Utes, 4, 5, 18, 71, 119, 124, 125.

V

Van Wirmer, 129, 144.
Verendrye, 34.
Verendrye Journal, 4.
Verendryes, 4.
Village Indians of the Missouri, 2, 5, 33.
Visiting Creek, 356.

W

Wacos, 71, 122.
Walker, Colonel, 195, 196, 202, 203, 204, 205.
Walking Calf, 352.
Walking Coyote, 11, 36, 37, 38, 39, 53, 54, 55.
Walking on the ground, 313.
Walking Rabbit, 225.
Walking Whirlwind, 352.
Walking White Man, 225, 370.
Walks Last, 326, 367.
Walks on Crutches, 369.
Wallen, Major H. D., 141.
Walnut Creek, 115.
Wandering Buffalo Bull, 233.
War Bonnet, 82, 167.
War Bonnet Ridge, 356.
War Department, 104, 316, 384.
War of the Rebellion, 196.
Ware, Lieutenant Eugene F., 111, 136, 145, 177.
Warpath and Bivouac, 317.
Wars with the Kiowas and Comanches, 32.
Wars with the Pawnees, 67.
Washington, D. C., 125, 388.
Washita River, 11, 43, 288, 312.
Ways of warriors, 9.
Wearing Horns, 77.
Weasel Bear, 274.
Weeks, Ralph, 351.
Weichel, Mrs., 307.
Weightman, Colonel, 121.
Wessels, Captain, 403, 408, 409.
West Point (Military Academy), 111.
Western Colorado, 4.
Western Kansas in 1867, 246, 247.
Wheatley, 223.
Wheelan, 380.
Wheeler, Colonel Homer W., vi, 353, 354, 355, 417.
When the Potawatomi helped the Kit ka hah ki, 80.
Where they stood off the Crows, 23.
Whetstone Agency, 126.
Whirlwind, Old, 16, 17, 97, 99, 100.
Whistler, 259.
Whistling Elk, 24, 25, 26, 27.
White Antelope, 53, 60, 61, 71, 127, 166, 167, 298, 366, 406.
White Antelope, death-song of, 171.
White, A. S. H., 260.

White Bear, 274.
White Bird, 318.
White Bull, 26, 112, 213, 276, 334, 363, 369.
White Butte, 299.
White Butte Creek, 180, 299.
White Clay Creek, 394.
White Contrary, 276.
White Cow Woman, 40.
White Elk, 225, 233, 323, 368.
White Frog, 365.
White Hat, 397.
White Hawk, 379.
White Horse, 75, 76, 214, 243, 271, 314, 365, 396.
White, John Jay, 353.
White Leaf, 155, 184.
White Man's Fork, 180, 394.
White Man's Ladder, 283.
White Powder, 88.
White River, 399.
White Shield, 322, 352, 364, 366.
White Thunder, 274, 370.
White Weasel Bear, 274.
White Whiskers, 369.
Whitfield, Agent J. W., 98.
Whitney, Chauncey B., 269.
Whitney, Chauncey B., diary of, 269.
Wichitas, 70, 122.
Widower, 72.
Wilcox, Captain, 216.
Wild Hog, 225, 355, 387, 389, 401, 403, 404.
Williford, Captain, 198, 199.
Wilson, William, 269.
Wind Woman, 192.
Winnebago scouts, 195.
Winter-counts, 24.
Wŏkaihē′yūniŏ′hē, Antelope Pit River, 33.
Wolf Chief, 139.
Wolf Coming Out, 136.
Wolf Creek, 49, 50, 51, 52, 54, 57, 289.
Wolf Fire, 108, 111, 117.
Wolf Friend, 283.
Wolf in the Middle, 245, 248.
Wolf Left Hand, 229.
Wolf Lying Down, 55, 225.
Wolf Mountains, 320.
Wolf Road, 50.
Wolf Robe, 156.
Wolf Satchel, 358.
Wolf Sleeve, 260.
Wolf Voice, 396.
Wood, 81.
Wooden Leg, 88, 369.
Wool Woman, 369, 370, 372.
Wynkoop, Major, 139, 152, 159, 170, 237, 238, 239, 240, 241, 242, 244, 288.
Wynkoop, Major, Criticism of, 160.
Wyoming, 316.

Y

Yanktons, 123.
Yellow Bear, 82.
Yellow Boy, 62.

Yellow Eagle, 318, 352, 361, 365, 367.
Yellow Hair, 62.
Yellow Horse, 260.
Yellow Nose, 80, 189, 299, 338, 362, 364, 366.
Yellow Shield, 167.
Yellow Shirt, 55, 56, 115.
Yellow Wolf, 35, 36, 37, 38, 39, 40, 49, 53, 73, 167, 298.
Yellow Wolf (Yellow Coyote), 118.

Yellowstone River, 32, 33, 195, 221, 316, 379, 397.
Young, A. L., 332.
Young Blackbird, 323.
Young, Charles, 332.
Young Man Afraid of His Horses, 210.
Young Spotted Wolf, 396.
Young Two Moon, 320, 349, 355, 356, 360, 361, 362, 363, 364, 367.
Younger Bear, 297.